PENGUIN BO

GERTRUDE J

Sally Festing lives with her husband and a large fluffy cat. She has always been fascinated by the links between man, art and landscape. At present, she is working on a biography of Barbara Hepworth.

SALLY FESTING

GERTRUDE JEKYLL

PENGUIN BOOKS

PENGUIN BOOKS

Published by the Penguin Group
Penguin Books Ltd, 27 Wrights Lane, London W8 5TZ, England
Penguin Books USA Inc., 375 Hudson Street, New York, New York 10014, USA
Penguin Books Australia Ltd, Ringwood, Victoria, Australia
Penguin Books Canada Ltd, 10 Alcorn Avenue, Toronto, Ontario, Canada M4V 3B2
Penguin Books (NZ) Ltd, 182–190 Wairau Road, Auckland 10, New Zealand
Penguin Books Ltd, Registered Offices: Harmondsworth, Middlesex, England

First published by Viking 1991
Published in Penguin Books 1993
3

Printed in Great Britain by Clays Ltd, St Ives plc

For Alice, Simon and Harriet

CONTENTS

ILLUSTRATIONS

* Photographs taken by Gertrude Jekyll

BLACK AND WHITE PHOTOGRAPHS

DRAWINGS IN THE TEXT

ILLUSTRATION ACKNOWLEDGEMENTS

The author and publishers are grateful to the following for permission to reproduce photographs and drawings:

Berkeley Documents Collection, drawing no. 1, photographs nos. 1, 3, 4, 5, 14, 15, 16, 17, 19, 21, 26, 27, 28, 31, 32, 38, 42, 45, 46; Dr Jane Ridley and the RIBA, drawings nos. 5, 6, 7, 8, 9, 10, 11; Sir Andrew Duff Gordon, 6, 7; National Portrait Gallery, 9; Lady Juliet Townsend, 10; Maladeen Ltd and His Majesty the Sultan of Oman, 11, 12; Michael Festing, 20, 43, 44; Sebastian Nohl, 22; Mary Lutyens, 24, 33, 34; author, 25, 29; Godalming Museum, drawing no. 2, photographs nos. 33, 34, 87; Eileen Barber, drawing no. 2, photograph no. 39; Mander & Mitchenson Photograph Agency, 40; John Berkeley and Sotheby's, 41.

M unstead Wood is still difficult to find. The bridleway that makes a long hypotenuse with the Godalming–Hascombe and the Bramley–Hascombe roads has resisted twentieth-century modernization. Heath Lane, staggered with oak, beech and sweet chestnuts in furious autumn shades, tells a woodland story Gertrude Jekyll was anxious to foster before one arrived at her home. There is a faint smell of woodsmoke, and groups of rubbery toadstools, tawny in the centre fading pale at the edges, grow around lopped tree boles. A group of magpies startle the air.

Half-way down the lane, set back from it on the south, you glimpse the substantial dull gold sandstone building with stocky chimneys, its first-floor windows, like eyebrows, close under a low head of tiled roof, its entrance mysteriously concealed behind a small archway in an extended wall. It is not in the least 'oldy-worldy', nor does it look new, but as Gertrude Jekyll intended; as if it belonged. More than 100 years have passed since she first possessed fifteen unkempt acres, and the garden that was once her joy, inspiration and greatest work of art sleeps peacefully. The framework is there – trees and shrubs, stonework, pergola and walls. An elusive spell remains. This is where she painted a garden with living things, and someone versed in her works can clothe it with the pictures that drew plant-lovers from far and wide.

By the time Miss Jekyll died, she was much respected. Thirty-four years later, when Betty Massingham's biography appeared, her apotheosis was complete. But another quarter-century's exposure unsupported by significant biographical research has produced a popular impression that is considerably distorted. The first over-simplification is that she was a great artist that might have been, her talent as a painter fatally compromised by poor sight; thereby the life neatly divided, half as an artist, half as a gardener, with Edwin Lutyens auspiciously aiding the change. Granted she believed herself from youth to be an artist, that it was as a composite artist/gardener she was to become known, but she was a persuasive self-publicist. Even the most enduring image we have of her, smoothly bunned, intact, unassailable, in William Nicholson's 'Queen Victoria' portrait, is in many ways an artefact. The clothes she wore at the time were usually frumpish; the assumed quiescence comes from a woman who well understood how to manipulate a tricky world. She was always a little larger than life and far more complicated, abrasive, autocratic, impatient, fun-loving and lovable than she is made out to be.

The other cliché finds her a talented plantswoman, doyenne of herbaceous borders, woodlands and dry stone walls, playing a subordinate role to various architects; the horticulturist of limited vision for whom Lutyens 'became her eyes'.[1] Concentration on her partnership with Lutyens has done much to augment the myth. Since his fame exceeded hers, the collaborations have made most impact though they number few more than a quarter of roughly 400 garden commissions she completed. Some, admittedly, were for single planting schemes, others, like Millmead and Bewdley's Sandbourne, were entire landscapes in which she designed buildings and all the hard landscape besides growing and supplying most of the plants.

Gertrude Jekyll was unusual because she excelled at practical and theoretical aspects of gardening as well as being able, lucidly, to express herself. Over 2,000 articles and fifteen full-length works was a mammoth _œuvre_. She exhorted those who would learn her message to read her books, and they have seldom been out of print. Through them her ideas have been incorporated into the history of the English garden. H. Avray Tipping thought that 'Gardens, not singly or by the dozen, but by the hundred and even the thousand, have profited by her assistance and advice given here in deed, there by writing, and again orally.'[2] In 1962 Russell Page could scarcely think of an English garden in the previous fifty years which did not bear the 'mark of her teaching'.[3] Lord Riddell's personal appeal to King Edward VII to honour her during her lifetime was not answered,[4] and a recent book on women in the Arts and Crafts Movement does not so much as list her in the index,[5] but she will at last be in the _Dictionary of National Biography Supplement_.

She was a woman with a mission that filled almost nine tireless decades, an artist, craftswoman, garden-designer, photographer, businesswoman and writer of enlightening prose; simultaneously _grande_ *dame*, county lady and blue-stocking; instinctive traditionalist and a rebel; a plain woman with a talent for manipulating the eminent; an obsessive, latterly reclusive, worker who inspired a clamorous following. She has also survived as a phenomenon, a single woman who overcame entrenched social and professional hurdles. To those who suggest that she could indulge her perfectionism only because she did not need to earn a living, one can answer that plenty are given the opportunity, but few exploit it. Technical knowledge and artistic ability made her what Roderick Gradidge aptly called a 'one woman Arts and Crafts Movement';[6] the spiritual experience she drew from the landscape and re-endowed make her a garden designer of excellence. Today we would call her a landscape architect. For me to cover all the gardens she designed would be impossible. I have taken some of those best known in chronological sequence primarily to illustrate her development.

Common sense tells us that art is an expression of emotion generated by experience; to greater or lesser extent an artist's life is his or her raw material and from the Romantic Movement onwards the link grows stronger. Gertrude Jekyll consciously strove to consolidate life and art. Knowing more about her may not increase our enjoyment but it can give her work an extra dimension. It has been easier to assess her work than to tease out the contradictions between the person and her public front. It is amazing that someone with positive relish for verbal hassle could get away with the righteous sentiment, 'To listen and learn is more to my liking than to engage in any form of argument,'[7] that someone whose patience in gardening did not extend to people could airily profess, 'I always try to avoid the spirit of intolerance in anything.'[8] Evident bossiness went hand in hand with religious humility. It was, moreover, the realization of deep needs in her own disciplined and highly pressurized nature that helped her understand man's great desire for a sanctuary. Although the early years with their abiding family ties are the greatest guide to her future, the Arts and Crafts Movement provided a template and Ruskin kindled a burgeoning imagination: his call for truth threw her back to the rhythms of nature, his gospel made her look as an artist does at the West Surrey countryside. Family life, a strong sense of family commitment and a profound debt to Ruskin are the areas I especially wanted to explore.

I believe that her real contribution is underrated. Architectural historian Christopher Hussey called her 'perhaps the greatest *artist* in horticulture and garden-planting that England has produced – whose influence on garden design has been as widespread as Capability Brown's in the eighteenth century,'[9] and the late Earl of Morton said, 'Gertrude Jekyll was one of the greatest garden designers that has ever lived, in my view ranking with Brown and Repton.'[10] More recently, Dr Michael Tooley's scholarly research has done much to promote her true contribution, but so far it has failed to penetrate the public consciousness. I would like to acknowledge his generous help. He not only read the manuscript but provided leads from his own research and his bibliography of Jekyll's writings has been invaluable. My second debt is to the late Francis Jekyll who wrote a memoir of his aunt that is strong on facts. Since Gertrude Jekyll's engagement book is lost, the *Memoir* has been a constant guide. My third is to Miss Mary Lee's editorial assistance.

Not all of Gertrude Jekyll's family wanted me to write a biography. There remains material at Munstead House to which neither I nor anyone else has been given access, nevertheless I am indebted to her greatnephew, David McKenna, and his daughter Primrose Arnander for their assistance.

Sir Andrew Duff Gordon allowed me to drive home from Hereford with a boot full of family diaries that do much to elucidate the first part of my book. The late Lord Hamilton of Dalzell showed me Gertrude Jekyll's Bramley haunts and checked through two early chapters, just as Sue Griffiths introduced me to a hitherto unappreciated part of my subject's life at Wargrave and then read the relevant script. Mary Lutyens was spontaneously helpful with queries about her family; Pierre and Elizabeth Nafilyan entertained me at the Chalet above Lake Geneva which once belonged to the Blumenthals; Eileen Barber – Hercules Brabazon's great-great-niece – let me look at and select from his scrapbooks; Thomas L. Twidell supplied details of a fascinating relationship with his grandfather, George Leslie; and Simon Houfe helped me to track down the hitherto little-known Jekyll brother, Edward.

Memories from the few who met Miss Jekyll have been precious; besides David McKenna they include Isobel Durrant, Mary Lutyens, Harriet Mills and Lady Peel. I must also thank, for various contributions, Jeremy Archer, Jane Brown, Audrey Cade, Sir Robert and Lady Clark, June V. Cockell, Michael and Karen Collins, John Crabbe, Sir Victor Fitzgeorge Balfour, John Berkeley, Austin Frazer, Noel Gibbs,

Harrow School archivist A. D. K. Hawkyard, Katharine Heron, Valerie Kenward, Audrey le Lievre, Imre von Maltzahn, John Nicholls, Sebastian Nohl, Rev. Partington, Gerd Perkins, Sir John Quinton, Ellen Richter, Judith B. Tankard, Marian Thompson, Russell Towns, Lady Juliet Townsend, John and Rosamund Wallinger, Catherine Weguelin, Joan Charman and staff at Godalming Museum, Matthew Alexander of Guildford Museum, who checked the chapter on Old West Surrey, Brent Elliott and the RHS Lindley Library, John and Rosemary Nicholson of the Tradescant Trust, staff at the British Museum, the Documents Collection at Berkeley, California, the London Library, Maladean Ltd, the National Record Office in Fortress House, the Royal Institute of British Architects and Surrey County Library in Guildford. Small parts of the text have appeared in *The Garden* and *Hortus*. Lastly I thank Eleo Gordon and Annie Lee for their support.

Dividing the text into five sections gives a rough guide to the chief areas of Gertrude Jekyll's life, but she worked at the art of living as thoroughly and perseveringly as she worked at everything else; she was always more or less artist, writer, home-maker and gardener, so the sections cannot be taken too literally. My liberty in referring to her by her first name is something I should never have presumed in life. If 'Gertrude' suggests a degree of intimacy she would not have condoned, I have done it because it helped me to understand the way she saw herself.

November 1990

PART ONE

BEGINNINGS

CHAPTER ONE

1843–8

A sturdy little girl stands in Green Park clutching a mop-headed dandelion. In the mid-nineteenth century, the park looked much as it does today, with the Broad Walk from its northern, Piccadilly perimeter sweeping through turf lined with huge-limbed trees. But Gertrude was short-sighted, making the things she came close to what most appealed. Dandelions were not appreciated by her nurse, who said they were 'Nasty Things'[1] and forbade her to carry them home. This vivid childhood memory sprang from the time when she thought there were two kinds of people in the world – children and grown-ups. Because she still felt like a child in many ways, a note of defiance tempers its humour. For she had been adamant; Nurse would thwart her enthusiasm. Even the rank smell of dandelions was good, she thought, as she considered them longingly. Dandelion was always for her a London smell.

Gertrude Jekyll was born just north of Piccadilly on 29 November 1843. Number 2 Grafton Street was a fashionable North London address; 3 to 6 are still standing, a broad, Georgian terrace with massive stone-pillared doorways and wide-spaced windows, but the first two houses were demolished before the end of the century to make way for a dull Edwardian building. The Countess of Pembroke lived at number 1, Viscount Dungannon at number 3; well over half the private residences in the short street were owned by titled people. A sense of place was always very strong in Gertrude but, without a pictorial record, the large Mayfair villa must be imagined – a symbol of something she coveted all her life, the good world of culture and beauty.

To a home full of books, music, painting, classical sculpture and visitors, Caroline, or 'Carry', had arrived in 1837, followed by two boys, Edward, known as Teddy, in 1839 and Arthur in 1841. Next came Gertrude, then Herbert in 1846 and Walter in 1849. The theory that as a child first is, so in essence he or she remains, is plausible. A timid infant will be a retiring adult, a curious child continues to be inquisitive. Gertrude showed early signs of being, and remained, curious, clever and strong-willed. If the mature Miss Jekyll beguiled her public with a quaint old lady of patient ways and mellifluous prose who taught us that to 'soothe', 'refine', and 'lift up the heart'[2] are the garden's chief functions, it is largely because this is the way she chose to present herself.

An excerpt from a book she wrote in middle age dwells lovingly on the impressions of her youngest days, four and half years that became a bedrock of future strength. Berkeley Square was even closer to Grafton Street than Green Park, and access was confined to local residents, the key being retained at Gunter's, the newly opened tea parlour in the square. When she collected it, a gentleman treated her to sugared almonds, 'one of those oblong ones with pink or white sugar outside'.[3] Later, her first allegiance was transferred to 'less refined'[4] peppermint bull's-eyes. It was forty years before mowing machines were invented. London's parks and squares were cut in the early morning, when the grass stood sprightly against the blade of a scythe, and another smell she linked with her first home was the sweet heaviness of newly cropped turf. When daisies reappeared she practised the fine art of piercing their stems to make them into chains. 'How difficult it was at first; when I had transfixed the stalk with the pin, the pin got restive and dragged the slit out instead of stopping short of the free end of the stalk to leave the loop large enough to pass the stalk of the next Daisy through, but not large enough to let the head go through too.'[5]

Nurse, nursery maid, footman, butler and Carry's French governess peopled a quintessentially early Victorian household. Besides the servants she mentions there would have been cooks and cleaners. Gertrude never found a structured routine stifling: boisterous children tend to feel secure in a regime that is clearly defined. Sometimes she was allowed to peer through the front door at Lord and Lady Grantley's visiting carriage, huge, yellow and high sprung. Carriages had been 'grand things, well worth looking at',[6] with the coachman in silk stockings and powdered wig. The vignette is of a child treated as a rational being; though it set her apart from others, it preserved her capacity for delight and a freshness of response.

Adult Gertrude was reserved about her ancestors. 'I know little of the records and traditions of the Jekyll family,' complained her friend the philologist, Logan Pearsall Smith, 'nor did Miss Jekyll or her brother, Sir Herbert, ever mention them to me.'[7] It was not for lack of interest. Herbert religiously compiled the family archives and his sister was deeply mindful of social status which, she did not mind admitting, was 'armigerous', 'just', her nephew mused, 'as a cat might call itself a cat'.[8] The Jekyll shield sported three brown deer, two above and one beneath a wide brown line; their motto was, appropriately, 'Avancez'. By the end of the century the upper middle class was not readily distinguishable in its way of life and outlook from the gentry, though the latter was snobbish to a degree. 'Landed gentry' covered a range of society from the untitled owners of comparatively small estates to the great ducal families, Devonshires and Bedfords, whose properties included thousands of acres of land. Because the whole system depended on estates passed down from father to eldest son, there was a genuine community of interest and of outlook. The Jekylls, with their titled friends and small stately home in Berkshire, bridged the fine distinction between the two. If they were not fabulously rich, they were very comfortably off. Gertrude was the product of a time when most of the best things in life, wealth, property and social position, belonged to those who were born to them; she was courteous and diplomatic to people of every class and culture, but basically she espoused the system.

Pearsall Smith guessed that the Jekylls were 'a fine old succession of county people, "quality folk" as they are called',[9] and he was right. Herbert traced his ancestors to the beginning of the sixteenth century, when varieties of the name occurred as Jeakull, Jekiell or Jeaquell besides the form we know. They came from Lincoln, and were probably of Swedish origin, clergymen, bankers, merchants, soldiers, sailors and servants of the Crown. Two men interrupted the robust but unexceptional pattern, the first of whom was knighted by William III. Sir Joseph (1662–1738) rose through a number of judicial appointments to the position of Privy Councillor and Master of the Rolls under George I. His passion was building houses, of which he erected or restored thirty-nine including Reigate Priory in Surrey, where he lived for a number of years. Kneller's painting of him shows a long pale face with a pinched aquiline nose. There is no hint of the fleshy features or strong crease between cheeks and lips that characterized Gertrude's generation.

A bewildering proliferation of Josephs and Edwards make the

family confusing to study. To complicate matters further, Edwards took Joseph as a second name and vice versa. The second celebrity was, as it happens, another Joseph. Gertrude's paternal grandfather (1754–1837) died six years before she was born, though his memory remained a potent presence in the Jekyll household. Neither his political nor his legal career was significant. As MP for the pocket borough of Calne, he was 'a frequent speaker, but positively without weight';[10] as a barrister his circuit was meagre. Joseph's strength was his social circle. Friends included Sir Joshua Reynolds, David Garrick, Edmund Burke, George IV, and he dined with His Majesty in rotation at Windsor's Royal Lodge, the fantasy Chinese fishing temple and a Turkish Tent. A favourite of the Prince of Wales, he was created a Master in Chancery. Once again there were detractors, despite which he became a founder member of the Athenaeum, a Fellow of the Royal Society and of the Society of Arts. His letters in the national press make him sound a bit of a bore but friends and family loved him.

Marrying Maria, daughter of Colonel Hans Sloane – not connected with the horticulturist of the same name – Joseph brought wealth to his family. Maria bore him two ebullient sons, the elder, Joseph junior, dark-haired with blue eyes, strikingly handsome as an adult and so beautiful as a child that he was continually being sought as a model for romantic portrait paintings. Uncle Joseph became a chemist, married Anna Louisa Flint, only daughter of the Secretary of the Irish Office, lived in the family home at Wargrave and was an early advocate of homeopathy. Unfortunately, fringe medicine did not save him from dying in his fortieth year. His brother, Gertrude's father, was not tough either; a photograph of him aged, one would say, approaching fifty, shows a fine-boned, oval, slightly foxy face above a Norfolk jacket, thin, fair hair, a fair moustache and friendly, inward-looking eyes. To look at he was frail and not obviously Gertrude's father. In other ways he was a more unusual man than has yet been acknowledged.

Edward was born in 1804, served in the Grenadier Guards and retired fairly early, a Captain. Officers' expenses were apt to exceed their pay, so the Sloane fortune must have sufficed. At the age of thirty-two he married Julia, daughter of a banker, Charles Hammersley, and of Emily Paulette Thomson. The pair had moved in the same circles; Edward was on the management committee of an amateur musical society with two male Hammersleys and played the flute in the orchestra for another twenty years, but any musical talent he possessed was far outshone by that of his wife. Twelve years after the marriage, they moved south of Guildford in Surrey to provide five children with rural freedoms. This is the skeleton of a life filled out for us principally by Caroline, Lady Duff Gordon, a friend subsequently related by marriage, and by Edward's doting second daughter.

The Jekylls took it for granted that one knew and respected the masters in music and art. When Lady Duff Gordon commented on the 'Gods & Goddesses'[11] in their dining-room, she was referring to the Captain's life-sized casts of the Venus de Milo and Venus of the Capitol, from his large collection of antiquities. He also had Etruscan vases, bequeathed in his will to his wife, 'upon the express condition that she shall at her own cost keep the same in good repair',[12] and must have possessed a certain visual imagination since he illustrated letters about the Crimean War with elaborate military diagrams. But his artistic side was chiefly appreciative, and what struck Lady Duff Gordon most was his involvement in all he did. Essentially he was an entrepreneur, bent on imparting his enthusiasms to family and friends, as natural a teacher as his daughter in turn became. Gertrude intuitively understood her father's respect for his ceramics, vowing that they instilled in her a lifelong reverence for classical art. Like him she became a collector.

Some of the Captain's happiest moments were spent at the helm of a thirty-ton cutter, *Ariel*, on trips recorded from his honeymoon tour in 1836 until the move to Surrey. Latterly the boat accommodated various members of his growing family. It was berthed at Chichester, a coastal area so full of childhood memories that Gertrude often returned to them in later life. In Surrey the young Jekylls made summer expeditions to float model steamers, and during the winter the Captain laboured happily in his workshop. There, with the aid of a young resident engineer, he produced a model theatre, and made electrical generators, magic lanterns and fireworks. When he lectured on his hobbies in neighbouring villages, his own children, accompanying him, noted his ease and sense of humour. Guests might find him in boyish enthusiasm 'entirely devoted to his small locomotive and steam engine'.[13] Playing with water and experimenting with electricity had been such abiding passions that Gertrude could never decide which he preferred.

She never underestimated her father's influence. She inherited some of the things he took pride in – skill with his hands, thoroughness and conscientiousness, writing in her second book, 'And as I think . . . a shred of my father's mantle may have fallen upon his daughter.'[14] She may not as an adult have made engines, fireworks or scientific apparatus, but the Captain's 'busy mind' and 'mechanical genius'[15] were indelibly impressed and she was quick to appreciate that the principles she had learnt in engineering applied to the working methods of other crafts. Familiarity with the names, parts and uses of engines held her in good stead, and despite the fact that she was naturally left-handed, coerced into using her right, she was adept at handling tools. If manual dexterity was one of the workshop's lessons, another was the sense of fulfilment in devising one's own pleasures. From Gertrude's account of her father's model theatre, an exact copy of old Drury Lane, one feels a vicarious thrill for her child's imagination. The stage was six feet deep and precisely to scale, complete with mechanical arrangements above and below. So impressed was she by dramas such as Franklin's expedition to the Arctic that she could never bear to part with the scenery. So her first workshop became engraved in her mind as a 'kind of heaven',[16] a prototype for a rich and satisfying succession.

Today it is thought that encouraging fathers often produce achieving daughters. Captain Jekyll's paternal influence was considerable without being dominating or overpowering, for it was not his desire to impose ideas. But no less remarkable than his ingenuity was his broad-minded acceptance of his daughter. At a time when girls were brought up like the standard Victorian heroine, to accept that their sole function was courtship and marriage, he had few stereotyped images of what women ought to be. His refusal to treat her differently from his sons had obvious repercussions. When Gertrude died, the *Times* obituary acknowledged, 'there was little her skilful fingers could not bring to perfection, from a piece of finely-wrought decorative silver down to the making of her gardening boots. She could toss an omelette and brew Turkish coffee or elderberry wine, compose a liqueur or manufacture her own incomparable pot-pourri.'[17] Thanks to her parents, she was exposed to social interaction, persuaded to experiment with her hands and oblivious of absurd distinctions between 'male' (unseemly) and 'female' (seemly) occupations. Where her interest roamed, doggedly she pursued.

Although Gertrude lived with her mother until the old lady died, she left no record about her. This does not mean that her mother's talents or her contribution to the life of her children were less significant than her father's. Mrs Jekyll produced a weighty portfolio of art, studies of buildings, trees and boats which, in her nephew Francis Jekyll's opinion, proved her talents. Music was her forte. Mendelssohn, a family friend, had once given her piano lessons and all her children inherited some degree of musicianship. Herbert was discovered, while still an infant, beating time to the fugues of the composer J. S. Bach; Walter and Gertrude took singing lessons seriously and both enjoyed taking part in the vocal duets that formed the repertoire of every musical family.

In 1886 Gertrude took a portrait photograph of 'Mrs Baring'. The elaborately dressed old lady with a fine aristocratic face and a Roman nose is her mother's youngest sister, Elizabeth Hammersley. One wishes only that Gertrude had done the same for her mother. Lady Duff Gordon, who was discerning about people, thought very highly of Mrs Jekyll's calm sense of proportion. Surrounded by her young family in the early months of 1854, she was 'kind and good humoured comme toujours'.[18] Twenty years later the elder woman wrote, 'I have the greatest respect and love for Mrs Jekyll & know no one so entirely . . . unselfish';[19] her letters 'and self'[20] were 'patterns of every Christian virtue & temper & patience & cheerfulness'.[21] Mr Jekyll was intermittently unwell. Sometimes he was cheerful, talkative and 'in all respect more like other people',[22] but on various occasions he felt ill all day, 'suffering much from neuralgia',[23] 'white', 'bloodless', 'very suffering',[24] and 'a sick person'.[25] Lady Duff Gordon's comments and the Captain's increasingly rambling letters suggest an unspecified degenerative disease. He also sounds more highly strung than his wife. If Gertrude's determined independence occasionally caused her parents unease, her father had implicit faith in his wife's ability to manage. Practical, elegant and charming, the Captain had discovered in Mrs Jekyll a perfect companion. It was their father's unqualified approval of his wife's tact and grace that reinforced his daughters' desire to be in some ways like their mother.

Prominent family characteristics were intelligence, musicality and an active interest in public matters. The Jekylls had never achieved anything creative in the sphere of art, but the year Gertrude was born three events took place which had a bearing upon her life. John Claudius Loudon, the great nineteenth-century gardener, died and his wife, Jane, published the second part of *The Ladies Flower Garden*.

Though pioneers in their time, the Loudons were ineluctably part of the Victorian gardening scene, and fifteen years later, when Jane died, Gertrude was, as Geoffrey Taylor remarked, 'almost of an age to catch the trowel as it fell . . . from [her] hand'.[26] The second event was E. H. Wilson's sighting of the shores of China after four months' travel from England. Wilson abetted a spate of plant introductions with which Gertrude was deeply involved. The third was the publication by John Ruskin, art and social critic, of the first volume of *Modern Painters*. Ruskin was a visionary whose writings affected every aspect of her future.

Like the society she was born to, Gertrude was industrious and bound to self-education. All her works suggest that happiness and individual well-being depend upon diligent self-culture and self-discipline. To Ruskin, home was 'the place of peace . . . shelter . . . from all terror, doubt and division',[27] a proverbially Victorian sentiment she readily espoused. She became an inveterate home-maker and a powerful arbiter of taste. Her home, Munstead Wood, was essentially a refuge, a concentration of effort designed to benefit the human being it contained. Every domestic process interested her, from plumbing to making jellies, but her home was not, like other nineteenth-century homes, insular, nor was it materialistic. It was an expression of an exceptional woman whose life was spent roughly half in the nineteenth and half in the twentieth century. In some ways she was a modern woman – her own lifestyle in particular was advanced – but she had experienced the harmony and self-confidence of a charmed world based on a strong sense of history and tradition, a world where things fit, and her aesthetic remained a subtle balance of progressive and reactionary.

Something else happened in the long easy days when Gertrude was sampling dandelions from London's green grounds. A baby brother has been mentioned, yet Herbert was not merely a brother but a soulmate. Even in a largely united family, relationships are more complex than they appear on the surface. From the beginning, the Captain adored his third son. Such was the tie that when Herbert, then in his thirties, was called up to fight in the Ashanti War, his father wrote to him every single day. Bonds as close as these with one of six children might easily – but apparently failed to – cause jealousy. In Gertrude's case the reason was clear: if Herbert was the main object of his father's affections, she, too, favoured and indulged her younger brother. Her whole life was intimately bound up with her family and within affectionate but looser ties there throve a special circle of intense love and understanding.

CHAPTER TWO

1848–60

Gertrude was approaching five when the family left Mayfair, Carry was eleven, Teddy nine, Arthur seven, and Herbert not yet one. In Town there was talk of a strange, talented group of artists forming a semi-secret society whose aim was to regenerate art: because they identified with the age before Raphael, they called themselves the Pre-Raphaelite Brotherhood. The Jekylls would miss art galleries, theatre, concerts, the proximity of many friends and the new British Museum building, opened the previous year and displaying among its treasures the Elgin Marbles. Transport was slower than today's and the country-side less built up, making West Surrey a great deal more rural. Gertrude wrote in middle age that the upheaval was made selflessly by her parents for their children's sake.

Captain Jekyll's maternal grandmother had lived at Farnham, which may have drawn him to a hamlet of steeply roofed, tile-hung cottages four miles south of Guildford. Bramley is cradled in the green Tilling-bourne valley below the chalk line of the North Downs. The Victoria County History describes the parish as well-wooded and agricultural, its lack of large commons compensated by extensive roadside wastes. Two streams meet there before entering the River Wey below Godalming. The first rises near Cranleigh, an old centre of the iron industry, and meanders west then north-west, sidling through the Greensand between Bramley and Wonersh. Level with the centre of Bramley, the Wey and Aron Canal once left the river to carry coal to the village. The second stream flows north-east from Hascombe, through what is now Wink-worth Arboretum, under Bramley High Street and so into the Cranleigh Water. Between the Arboretum and the High Street it opens into a series of marshes and ponds, two of which lay in the grounds of Bramley House, known later as Bramley Park. This was Gertrude's new home. A stream issuing from the largest pond turned a cornmill and the 'soothing sound of the working water-mill'[1] was part of its magic.

Until the advent of the railways, local evidence suggests, the parishes of central Surrey were not very different from many others of the English lowlands. Village economic life revolved around agriculture, and social life followed. Today Bramley has 3,000 inhabitants, its workers commute to London or Guildford and the big houses that remain belong to institutions. In Gertrude's time the population was merely 1,000, the village was largely self-sufficient and its big houses were all in private hands. Transport has been the chief invader. First the railway usurped the canal: though the latter was under-used when the railway opened in 1865, barely passable for a small boat in 1872 and dry in 1911. In the last decade of the twentieth century, cars push endlessly through the narrow village High Street on the Horsham to Guildford road. But behind the traffic, old red cottages blink through small windows and round the village there still flows undulating countryside of streams and hollow lanes. Gertrude lived until she was twenty-four in a landscape that was etched permanently in her mind.

Within walking distance of Bramley House there were sandstone hills that enclose the valley, low boggy areas, copses of hazel and chestnut and, higher up, plantations of birch and Scots pine. Plants always feature in Gertrude's memories; there was a great swampy hollow where the royal fern sprouted in tussocks high above her head – 'I remember leaning back against one of these and looking up and seeing how bright the sunlit rusty heads of flower looked against the late summer sky.'[2] Her spontaneous capacity for visual enjoyment was never lost. She loved to wander in the woods and along the track between Hascombe and Bramley, sunk in places thirty feet below ground. Where its eroded banks left giant beech, oak and holly trees suspended, she was amazed by the ingenuity of their contorted roots. The unexpected revelation to the Jekyll reader is that this same track, at its summit, offers rare views of woodland and sun-striped fields dipping into the valley. Gertrude ignored the larger panorama and the explanation can only be that to her myopic sight, woods and lanes, which she could inspect quite closely, were real; views, simply a blur.

It was during her second year in Bramley, she reckoned later, that the sight of a primrose copse brought her an unforgettable mystical experience. Looking at the yellow flowers with their green spread of leaves, it seemed suddenly as if they were part of the earth, as if we too are part of a hidden pattern, and both are parts of a work of art. Her ecstasy implicated a profound presentiment of the presence of 'dear

God who made it, and who made the child's mind to open wide and receive the enduring happiness of the gracious gift. So as by direct divine teaching, the impression of the simple sweetness of the Primrose wood sank deep into the childish heart, and laid, as it were, a foundation stone of immutable belief, that a Father in Heaven who could make all this, could make even better if He would, when the time should come that His children should be gathered about Him.'[3] There was genuine humbleness in Gertrude's deference to her Maker. In later life, an Italian picture of two praying nuns hung in her sitting-room.

Bramley House, an eighteenth-century or older building, was acquired by Captain George Francis Wyndham in 1825. He was interested in the engineering aspect of the canal then in the process of construction and wanted a half-way house between Petworth and London. With James Knowles as architect, he rebuilt in 1837 'a noble erection of Brick and Slate . . . of commanding elevation, and on either side . . . a long Colonnade'.[4] Knowles used enormous dipped girders adapted to the ornamental stucco ceilings in the construction, and laid both hallways with coloured tiles, some of them in a stylized floral pattern made by Minton. The whole project was something of an experiment since he was trying out a new patent cement intended to simulate stone. Presumably the result was satisfactory because Bramley House became the model for a string of ambitious commissions.

By a strange freak of inheritance, Wyndham was destined to be fourth Lord Egremont. His uncle, the third Earl, had not married until after his sons were born; they could inherit the great Sussex home but only his nephew could take the title. Unfortunately, the fourth Earl of Egremont was not to enjoy his title or his home for long. In 1845 he died, passing them to the Petworth Wyndhams, so it was they from whom the Jekylls took out a lease.

Like Gertrude's birth-place, Bramley House has gone, but her capacity to hoard and exploit impressions from childhood make it worth examining what is known about the place in which she spent most of her youth. The house is sometimes described as 'sprawling',[5] which it certainly became later, but during the Jekyll era it was still relatively compact, with Ionic columns on the ground storey and Doric pilasters above bestowing Italianate grace. Inside, the main rooms were lined on either side of a sixty-foot tiled entrance hall in what an architectural historian has called 'rather elementary symmetry'.[6] A ground plan of 1868 shows five lavatories, generosity due no doubt to Knowles having begun his career as a plumber and glazier. The upper floor had ten family bedrooms and seven more for servants. A plan Gertrude drew and labelled shows the position of her bed in 'my first bedroom',[7] which was set inside her sitting-room next to Carry's bedroom on the south-east house front. Later she moved into what had been the Governess's room, a smaller, more isolated enclave between her father's and the spare room, with windows looking north-east on to the park.

Renting large properties was not uncommon in the nineteenth century. During the twenty-year Jekyll tenure, the house was bought by Lord Leconsfield, though he never lived there, and sold to Alexander Clark at the end of the tenancy. Clark added four more bays to the existing five along the upper storey, a *porte cochère* on the entrance front, a billiard room and a strange-looking flat-topped water tower on the south-west, a conservatory on the north. After five years he sold to a stockbroker, Percy Ricardo. Aggrandizement had not improved the appearance or convenience of Bramley House. But the real problem, if less pertinent to its youthful inhabitants, was that the building lay between two ponds and its main south-easterly aspect trapped the sun's slant light behind the columns for half the day. The late Lord Hamilton of Dalzell, Ricardo's great-grandson, lived until after his marriage in what he remembered as a chilly home. It had no central heating or electric light and needed an army of servants: in 1951 he pulled it down. The palimpsest is pricked out in cracking tiles, black, buff, orange and white, beneath a sprinkling of sycamores in the Hamilton estate. A sunken laundry yard where maids pegged out clean linen may date from the Jekyll days, and Clark's billiard room is used as a garage. Part of the Jekyll kitchen garden wall has been incorporated in a tiny new estate of which the High Street gateway was the front, carriage entrance to Gertrude's Bramley House. Some of the trees could also be from her time.

Gertrude's adult writings portray her first big garden as an endlessly happy hunting ground. She 'spent hours and hours in it'[8] befriending trees, shrubs and flowers, and even as a child she was tuned to the subtleties of its mass and space. Around the house there were open, sun-filled lawns intersected with clipped gravel paths and scattered with specimen trees. She was mesmerized by groups of cypress making bold exclamations, the pretty grey streaked bark and clean pinnate

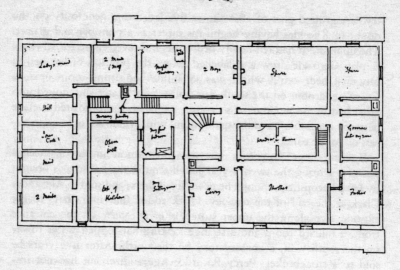

First-floor plan of Bramley House.

leaves of ailanthus (Tree of Heaven), great walnut-like hickories and
the graceful cut-leaved beech. Formality, 'in the regular way of the
time',[9] was restricted to a wire trelliswork rosary and three 'decorative
efforts'[10] – two parterres planted first with spring bulbs, then with
summer bedding, and one of scarlet geraniums centred with a variegated aloe. The only photograph of the house taken during the Jekyll
residence shows a number of circular flower beds encompassed by a
wall of roses. The content is difficult to identify but it could be
summer bedding at the end of the season. In any case it was the partly
shaded, overgrown shrubberies traversed by broad turf paths that she
preferred. In a deep soil, part peat, part sand and always cool, curtains
of native *Rhododendron ponticum* made a foil for acid-loving shrubs.
Gertrude was profoundly loyal to the plants she could recognize long
before she knew their names. One must imagine her returning to them
time and again, rolling the leaves in her fingers and burying her nose
in the flowers. Magnolias wafted outlandish perfume, kalmia hung
exquisite architectural, porcelain-like bells beside sleek-leaved leucothoe
(she called leucothoe 'Andromeda'), tall yellow azalea, spiraea and
pieris (which she called the snowball-tree). There were lilacs, philadel-
phus, homely double kerria (buttercup bush), and *Leycesteria formosa*

threw up pliant soft-wooded branches tasselled with red bracts. In the edge of the shrubbery, reserved for roses, Damask, Provence and moss nodded huge fragrant heads, while the clear pink, perfectly formed native sweetbriar, *Rosa rubiginosa*, wound arching, scented wands among its neighbours. Her sense of smell was phenomenal; each scent was quite distinct, how well she knew them all! The double 'cinnamon rose' was sweet but light, the moss rose a combination of sweetness with a strong sticky mossiness. Some scents were delicate and evocative, others frankly unpleasant; there is something distinctly Jekyllian about her willingness to seek both good and bad. She wanted to allow her senses to experience everything. The common barberry, for instance, could be so objectionable that coming across it unexpectedly she would flee in a 'kind of terror'.[11] It was not, she confirmed, as bad every year; sometimes it was merely sickly.

The craze for grandeur and ostentation, ribbon borders, raised beds and floral pyramids that characterized gardens of the 1850s was totally alien to an instinct developing in natural woodland and subtly inter-woven shrubberies. Gertrude appreciated that what she sometimes referred to as 'shrub wildernesses'[12] made her garden a fine educational resource, though little can the Captain and Mrs Jekyll have realized how important a part in the life of their daughter the country home would play. Her mysticism was inspired by wildings, her reverence for nature deeply implanted by the Surrey countryside. The roots of her career lay in this sensitivity to experience, a shrewd eye for quality and an instinct for organization.

Captain Jekyll had a military fondness for heated glasshouses where red passiflora (passion flower) twined festive heads among deep glossy leaves, strelitzias stalked upwards like giant birds and cereus, the 'torch thistle' cactus, opened its strange night flowers amid a traditional display of Victorian conservatory plants. There were few herbaceous plants in the pleasure garden; Gertrude could only positively recall a large blue cornflower and a broad-leaved saxifrage. But the kitchen garden, with its mixed border of purple tradescantia, day lilies, sweet-scented lilac, phlox and 'shocking' michaelmas daisies, was better endowed. Stocks, China asters and superfluous summer bedding grew with what she loved best of all – divinely scented sweet peas in mauve, pink and white, grey and white and occasional rosy red, a 'wonderful' novelty.[13] Another planting she recalled, lavender growing beside gooseberry bushes, was a subtle association to catch the eye of a child.

They were days of endless discovery. Three small streams and two ponds watered the garden. Questing, urgent and blessed, as young people sometimes are, with a powerful ability to record what she saw, Gertrude watched the crafty ways of water as it tumbled over a cascade and raced into the big mill-pond. 'Bramley Mill Pond The place for gudgeons', she wrote beneath a photograph she chose to illustrate an autobiographical article shortly before the First World War. The print is her own, the focus not very sharp; one sees a grassy lakeside path curving through boskage, a willow low on the lake, reflected light gleaming among its shadows. Moorhens annually nurtured broods of black velvet chicks, and the children caught gudgeon with rods or nets and ate them fried for tea. Before Captain Jekyll purchased a boat, his children used a wooden five-foot beer-cooler to punt their way illicitly to one of three islands. A boisterous trio, Gertrude with Teddy, Arthur and later, beloved Herbert, squatting perilously on a shallow wooden tray, disturbing the water's gentle patina as they steered unsteadily towards the enchanted land. It was foolhardy and probably dangerous, she reflected. Great poplars thrust up from a tangle of alders and small underwood, and magnificent lady ferns grew on the island fringes with a curious green orchid called twayblade. Bright-faced water forget-me-nots edged the mouth of a slower stream, and marsh marigolds studded a damp meadow above the lake where, later in the year, ragged robin, meadowsweet and marsh orchis ran riot. The small pond on the south-east side of the house has been filled in, but the large one remains beside a public footpath. There is one island; no poplars, just a turbulence of shrub, undergrowth, and a somewhat reduced flora. Trout, fished there until 1988, have been replaced with local species.

From long walks Gertrude and her brothers returned laden with fruits and flowers. Partly because she grew up in the middle of four males, but also because she was by nature adventuring, her pastimes tended to be boyish. Carry, seven years older, was happy being domesticated, but Gertrude climbed trees, played cricket and destroyed wasps' nests, joined in their father's model boat trials, made gunpowder, danced round bonfires – feeding their flames – and sat in the workshop on winter afternoons, pasting zig-zags of tinfoil to sheets of glass – the 'humbler appliances'[14] of her father's electrical experiments. When her brothers went away to school, she sat astride an old pony, exploring in ever widening circles with Crim the dog. For half a day, she wrote nostalgically, they might roam in the forest without meeting a soul or seeing habitation 'among the thorns and junipers, tangled with wild rose and honeysuckle and garlanded with bryony; past tall dark hollies; or in woodland of mighty beeches'.[15]

Gertrude was nine when an enterprising governess presented her with the Rev. C. A. Johns's *Flowers of the Field*. The book was one of three lifelong favourites, and became so dog-eared that it was replaced by two other copies, a working one and a spare, the first of which had to be rebound. Initially, she would leaf through until she found a picture of the plant she wanted to name. It was more difficult to identify by genus and family, but the trouble involved, she confirmed doggedly, helped to fix the words in her mind. Gradually she learnt to name wild flowers and began to understand their botanical relationships. Garden flowers were a natural corollary.

The year she died Gertrude wrote six articles for Bramley Church magazine. Up and down the village streets and lanes, from quiet recesses of her mind, she called up the dwellings and their inhabitants. Every prominent tree, building, bank of grass, dip, rise or bend in the road is mentioned, constructional materials, significant garden contents and the villagers' idiosyncrasies commented upon. Most of her life Gertrude had lived in West Surrey, early impressions were constantly being reinforced, yet it is clear that these pictures were stamped during childhood. Relationships would have been fairly controlled, though the old working people responded generously to the vigorous and forthright youngster in their midst. The Bowbricks, for instance, lived in a house on the west side of the High Street, ten feet square, with one room up and one down separated by a primitive ladder. So intrigued was she by the primitive plan that she later took a photograph of the cottage, commenting, 'probably the only one in existence in the country'.[16] It is still there, now used as a store. But how could Gertrude have known, unless she had scaled the ladder, that the old folk slept on a large bag of chaff on the floor? Mr Bowbrick's impeccable kitchen was characteristic of a figure who came to church in meticulously blackened boots, gaiters and a well-brushed coat, his head tied in a clean blue handkerchief to cover the eye he had lost fighting for his country. The portrait radiates warmth and admiration for the gallant veteran. Gertrude understood that little is more extraordinary than life itself.

The occupants of Bramley House were constantly drawn into the village. Kind Mr Snelling, with two middle-aged daughters, plied the children with apples from his tree, Mrs Smith had a little shop where they bought pear drops, and in a small foundry annexed to the smithy, Mr Richard Smith, her brother-in-law, forged and cast the parts for Captain Jekyll's model boats. Such was the connection with their father that 'to us children this seemed to be the most important thing in Bramley'.[17] 'Often some of us would go and watch the tapping of the molten metal, and well do I remember the feeling of mixed fear and delight when the white-hot stream came rushing out into the two-handled cauldron, that was quickly carried away by two men, who poured the terrible fluid into the black sand moulds. This was for the heavier castings wanted in the smith's business; those for my father were of course very small, and mostly of brass and gun-metal.'[18]

Meates, the limping, flame-haired carrier, brought parcels from Guildford in a dog-cart. Gertrude marvelled at the agility, inside his vehicle, of a man reduced to crutches on the ground. Stanton, the wharfinger, taught her to cast a fish net in the old canal. It was circular, with small leads round the perimeter, and under his supervision she had leaned one edge on her shoulder, gathered the remainder of the net in her right hand and flipped dexterously, springing it, with luck, into a perfect circle on the water. Buttons, she remembered humorously, were a beginner's liability. In theory if the mesh should land on one and the button were not tight, the thrower might follow the net into the water. Already her interest in the country crafts was whetted. Intrigued, she watched as Withall, the carpenter's foreman, planed long deal floorboards. Some craftsmen could still be identified by their clothes, and Withall wore a traditional short jacket of thick white baize, bound with grey webbing. Ringlets of golden shavings shot on to the floor and the pine-wood air screeched with the noise of his plane.

Around Bramley there was charcoal-burning, brewing, tanning and brickmaking, while the village itself sported the usual trades, each one, Gertrude's elderly self noted, with its own trappings. Parsons, the saddler's shop, was hung with red and yellow ribbons, brass face-pieces and rosettes that had once festooned the carter's team on market days. It smelled of leather and Stockholm tar, used for dressing the ropes in a long corridor or 'rope-walk' at the back of his premises. The child's readiness for practical experiment was invariably reciprocated with friendly tutelage. She learned thatching, fencing and walling, later on she could shoe a horse and sometimes at harvest time she was allowed a day's reaping. No one, she vowed, would know without actually doing it, how dirty the work was. Already one feels her perseverance in the spirit of Ruskin's 'stern habit of doing the thing with my own hands till I know all its difficulties'.[19] At other times she would contribute to the more traditional role of the big houses, gathering firewood for the cottages on wash days while Carry minded babies.

CHAPTER THREE

1848–60

On Sunday morning voices mingled, schoolmaster, craftsman, Lord and Lady, young and old, in praise that flooded Bramley's Holy Trinity Church, echoing high in the nave, spilling out into the High Street. Matins was an accepted part of the weekly programme and a symbol of village unity, conserving beauty, acknowledging ritual, affording comfort, while rigidly maintaining differences in status. In 1850 a north aisle was added by a local benefactress. Miss Sutherland's aisle, a plaque on the wall informs, was expressly for 'the poor of the parish'. One doubts whether philanthropic Miss Sutherland had an inkling that her parish might be for the poor an inescapable cage. Inside there was security, beyond at best toleration. Perhaps, too, it was a little ironical that four pews running across the northern transept at the top of this aisle were reserved for the big houses. Locally, Lord Hamilton recalled, they were known as 'Hyde Park Corner'.

The Jekylls' standing in the village was implicit in its public duties. Carry laid the foundation stone for the schoolmaster's cottage, another of Miss Sutherland's benefactions, while Mrs Jekyll laid a stone and planted a magnolia tree outside the new vicarage. Beside the church entrance, Gertrude remembered, there were (and still are) several gravestones set flat in the grass, inscribed with old Surrey names like 'Shurlocks'. From the Bramley House pew she had a prime view of Bowbrick on an isolated seat opposite her, and a side view of the door into the vestry where the vicar changed his surplice for a long black gown and bands. Music flowed from a gallery above the main entrance, where a bass viol was bowed with eccentric disregard for the composer's cadence until Mrs Jekyll took charge on a harmonium.

Each summer Bramley House opened its doors to an influx of visitors, among whom the Duff Gordons figured prominently. The two families were related through the Hammersleys. Caroline Cornewall had married Sir William in 1810; thirteen years later he died, leaving her with four active, sociable and intelligent children – Alexander, born in 1811, Cosmo 1812, Georgy 1817 and Alice 1822. Lady Duff Gordon was a strong and engaging character, generous, outspoken and plucky, whose vast circle of eminent friends and relations ranged from politicians to the fringes of artistic bourgeois society. The Millais and the Gladstones turned up at her gatherings, though no one could fill the gap left by her husband. The diaries she resumed twenty years after his death, and kept almost daily for another thirty-two years, tell how desperately she missed him. It was not a family for whom life moved smoothly; she was permanently on edge about one or other of her children and sometimes several simultaneously. But the Duff Gordons were colourful; art and music were part of their mental furniture and the Captain had in Lady Duff Gordon an informed correspondent on current affairs. In fact they were so close to the Jekylls that barely a month passed from the 1840s until the end of the century without some form of interaction at the Jekylls' home or the Duff Gordons' at 34 Hertford Street.

The diaries provide invaluable pictures of Bramley House. Lady Duff Gordon was present at events such as Carry's first communion, and what she was not there to witness, she learned through the Hammersley/Jekyll/Duff Gordon grapevine. They tell of picnics among wild flowers, and visits to shows and bazaars accompanied by Georgy, Alice and Carry, military parades at Aldershot, flower shows, shooting, horse riding, croquet parties, archery and musical afternoons. One tends to forget that Gertrude was as horsey a young lady as any landowning family produced. The year after her death her maid gave to one of her gardeners a cruciform brass key ring she had obviously made. On one side she had engraved the letters GJ, on the other, a horse's head. Lady Duff Gordon generally wintered in Italy, educating her daughters on a relentless social and cultural trail. A spring visit to Bramley was always a pleasure after three months abroad: 'The flower gardens looked beautiful – and the new little fountain was playing away gallantly.'[1] The pace was easy, the adults took drives or visited friends, 'walked & dawdled & sat outside a great deal'.[2]

In 1846, dining with 'all the World and its merry Wives',[3] Lady Duff Gordon had met the budding artist George Watts at Lord Holland's Italian villa and hired him as a drawing tutor for Georgy and Alice. Watts drew them both, Alice the classical beauty, with hair 'like the tendrils of a vine',[4] and Georgy, with whom he fell in love – 'very clever . . . very sincere . . . very decided and active', worldly, outspoken and 'with the most perfect figure in the world'.[5] Georgy was fascinated by the eligible and charming young man who wooed her in a Florentine orangery, but at the crucial moment her mother removed her elder daughter to join Alice in perpetual spinsterhood. A few years later Lady Duff Gordon sat to Watts, 'a terrible task to have to paint my false hair, fat age and unshapely female'.[6]

Alice was the quieter, more dutiful girl, her mother's 'good slave'.[7] Impetuous Georgy rebelled against the tediousness of her existence in constant bouts of unspecified sickness. She had brains and personality but no training, an all too familiar situation at the time. Leisure, a sign of status, was pursued with vehement unproductiveness in fashionable society. But Lady Duff Gordon, too bright to be deceived, copied into her diary a passage from a novel she was reading, 'solitude and want of occupation are two of the banes of women's life', reinforcing the message with her own words, 'melancholy & true'.[8] Georgy, however, was full of initiative, and of the four, she had rather a special relationship with the Jekylls. When Alice joined horseback expeditions, eccentric Georgy 'donkeyed',[9] fell off and rolled in the dust. To Gertrude she and Alice were companionable aunts.

The Duff Gordon sons played a less prominent part in Bramley life. In 1855, after twenty-six years in the Treasury, Alexander became Private Secretary to his uncle, George Lewis, then Chancellor of the Exchequer. Later he was a Commissioner to the Inland Revenue. Alexander was good-looking, sensitive and gentle to a fault; his mother once remarked of him that she wished he could scold. He married Lucie Austin, an intelligent classical scholar, author of *Letters from Egypt*, of whom he was inordinately proud. She bore him two children, but was consumptive and was never really accepted by her mother-in-law. Cosmo, who was far more easy-going, sent the Jekylls some Spanish cocks and hens in January 1854. Three years later, at forty-five, he sold his name in the wine trade to become a 'Gentleman at large and apparently a very happy one'.[10] At forty-seven he surprised everyone by marrying Amerey Antrobus, from Amesbury Abbey in Wiltshire, a cousin and highly approved of. The present heir, Sir Andrew Duff Gordon, aptly remarked that the strength in his family lay in its women, the men were 'merely charming'.[11]

At Bramley on one occasion, Lady Duff Gordon informed her diary, 'Music as usual prevailed all the evening.'[12] Music was a significant part of the Jekyll programme and part of all social encounters with the Duff Gordons. Georgy frequently joined informal sing-songs, while the younger generation's full-blown music parties drew 'such singing and a playing of pianos and concertinerinas as was never before heard in Bramley'.[13] Neighbours fiddled, children sang, Mrs Jekyll played the piano, and perhaps Captain Jekyll was moved to look out his flute. For the younger members of the family there were lasting repercussions. Walter sang and studied music all his life, Gertrude took singing lessons for some years and always enjoyed classical music, and Herbert sang with the Bach choir, their first performance in England of the B minor Mass. He also played the organ until, for pressure of other activities, he presented it to the Royal College of Music.

At other social occasions the Captain organized hopping and sack races, and played conjuror with hydrogen balloons. Snippets of home life animate letters to brother officers. In 1853 the Crimean War broke out between Russian forces and the allied armies of England, France, Turkey and Sardinia. It was the war of the Charge of the Light Brigade and Florence Nightingale, false heroics, maladministration, terrible battles and terrible suffering. Too old for active service, he was nevertheless intensely involved. Lady Duff Gordon received long letters 'full of military prose'.[14] Their clarity, she remarked, 'makes even my utter obtuseness on military matters understand'.[15] It was a family where instruction was almost second nature, The Captain lectured on warfare to audiences at Eton, Oxford and the Royal Institution.

The Jekylls were great sharers. Benjamin Kidd, amateur astronomer, left more impression upon Teddy than his sisters, but in January there were visits to occupy the Burdett-Coutts' box at Drury Lane for the 'Harlequin farce'. Angela Burdett-Coutts of Holly Lane, a wealthy businesswoman said to have enjoyed 'a fame through the country second only to Queen Victoria', was created a Baroness in 1871 for her philanthropic works. Hers is one of the names threading the first half of Gertrude's life without making a prominent entry. Other diversions were provided by Lord and Lady Grantley, both of whom left an enduring impression upon Gertrude, almost as caricatures, but immensely alive. Her Ladyship's party piece was feeding the deer in Wonersh Park with apples from her hand and even her mouth. His Lordship drove through Bramley in a phaeton with a pair of greys, wearing a shining top hat and a scarlet geum buttonhole; the yellow carriage Gertrude remembered from her Mayfair days being now only unshackled to take Carry to balls. Lord Grantley owned the Guildford Theatre and when repertory companies performed there, the Jekylls were allowed to use his private box. The style of these evenings remained radiant in Gertrude's mind. First one of the Grantley carriages would collect them; when they arrived, they were presented with a programme written on white satin. Sitting in state, wearing bouquets made by the gardener, she confessed she had felt extremely grand. Another Grantley treat was escorting the children to the old Guildford race course on the Merrow side of the Downs. On such occasions, Italian Lady Grantley was turned out 'like an oldfashioned beauty'[16] despite her seventy years.

From her parents Gertrude learned to attract people who enriched her own experience, but the pleasures of social intercourse were offset by riding, gardening and passionately involved communings with nature. Fifty years later, she wrote about the first gardens she and Carry had tended, long horizontal strips carved from the back of one of the shrubberies, their short, adjacent sides separated by white shrub roses and a wall of sweet peas. There were borders of box edging and an arbour trailing the 'Blush Boursault' rose, 'the clearest pink and pinkish-white . . . of any Rose I know'.[17] It was vital in her estimation that they had not been inflicted with a problem patch, that every consideration was taken to ensure success. Behind the gardens was a damp ditch and behind that, a bank crowned with a hazel hedge. Beyond the hedge there was a 'wide field that sloped upwards until it met the foot of a steep wooded hill, where we used to go primrosing'.[18] It was her way to describe places as if she were directing someone with the utmost care. The benefit is that reading her, 140 years later, Lord Hamilton knew precisely where the gardens had lain. 'It was still an open strip when I was young, with a small fenced-in piece at the right-hand which had been my mother's & her sister's garden . . . My cousin & I used to be taken there in our prams by our nannies.'[19] The only view which remains virtually unchanged is the wide field where Gertrude went primrosing.

Gertrude described her old garden to inspire future initiates; the flowers she grew, how she adjusted the plant calendar to accommodate the summer holiday and how she set about tidying up when she returned. Later on, her patch was augmented with a piece of adjoining woodland which she used as a 'general messing place'.[20] Between a ditch of black peaty mud, hazels, oaks and old laurels full of blackbirds' nests, she managed to produce a few vegetables and in the space of about nine feet, she began her first building. It was not sophisticated. She had hoped to create a wattle and clay construction she had read about, but it ended up merely an arbour of branches, its sole furniture a wobbly wooden seat she balanced by sitting down very carefully. If only she had understood more about construction, she lamented with the hindsight of someone who never failed to stress the labour and disappointments of her achievement. There was a kind of obstinacy in her nature that refused to be beaten.

Home life was varied with long summer holidays. Until Gertrude was twelve, the family generally went either to Bembridge, the most easterly projection of the Isle of Wight, or to Seaview, a little further round the north coast. Here she built moated fortifications with wooden spades. Her only complaint was being obliged to wear shoes and stockings – not to paddle was an understandable privation. Modern children who dashed barefoot into the waves scarcely realized their good fortune, she wrote in retrospect. But it took someone as close to her as Lutyens to realize just how permanent a record the seaside made. 'Bumps envies the family paddling & says there is nothing so delicious as making holes & waiting for the incoming tide to fill them & dashing the castles.'[21] Three days later, he re-emphasized, 'I told you that Bumps the gardener glorified in the idea of the children being in the sands & would give up all her garden for paddling!!'[22]

From Bembridge Gertrude could climb Culver Cliff for a high view of broad, solitary sands making a long crescent all the way back. Beyond Bembridge on a wooded peninsula, Brading Harbour tucks inland to the estuary of the River Yare. Its present outline was not defined until 1878 when a sea-wall was built on the inland side. In Gertrude's young days every high tide flooded its banks. Seaview was a dreamy place of boats and Continental atmosphere that lured back visitors year after year. As an adult Gertrude herself was lured.

In childhood she would have heard about smuggling on the Isle of Wight. Whole rows of houses in Bembridge were built on its rewards, and there were tales of rafts made from brandy tubs towed at night by a naked swimmer with a rope around his waist. By coincidence, smuggling also took place in Bramley. Most of the south coast trade passed through mid Sussex, but throughout the eighteenth century and well into the nineteenth, goods landed at Shoreham Water would arrive in the Hurtwood, passing through wastes of gorse, holly, juniper, stunted oak and Scots pine quite close to the Jekylls' home, in Highdown and Munstead Heath. The country was littered with old hiding places like the Windmill Inn on Ewhurst Hill and the altar-tomb in Cranleigh churchyard. Rumours of contraband never ceased to excite the child in Gertrude, who explored the woods for pack-horse tracks, listened to tales from people involved in their youth, and collated every scrap of evidence. Not far from Bramley she discovered caves with roomy galleries eight feet high and wide, connected by a maze of bays and passages. The old lair was burrowed in sandy soil just south of the chalk ridge, 'evidently . . . by human hands'.[23]

In 1855 the holiday pattern was broken when Mrs Jekyll decided on a two-month cure 'to imbibe iron'.[24] Gertrude and Carry would accompany her to Bavaria. It was Gertrude's first trip abroad and from the evidence of a letter her father wrote to Lady Duff Gordon, she revelled in the whole experience. Fifty years later she wrote to a gardening friend of *Smilacina bifolium* (false Solomon's seal), 'I never shall forget my delight when, as a child of eleven, I first saw it in woods in Bavaria.'[25] Silver streams, fir-clad mountains and chestnut avenues around Brückenau made a striking background to social encounters, and a friendly, zither-playing monk, admiring her extrovert intelligence, regaled the family with beer and coffee at the monastery of which he was superior. Two weeks later, prattling like a native, Gertrude forsook her mother's party for a large German family whom she entertained with translations of a popular song of the period, 'Villikins and his Dinah', and 'Pop Goes the Weasel'. They thought 'my oddity Gertrude'[26] clever and idiosyncratic, 'a great pet', her father added, though a 'queer fish'.[27] He was not worried about the behaviour of his incorrigible second daughter. Mrs Jekyll was far too 'prudent and discreet'[28] to allow her to adopt errant ways.

So many interests pressed urgently upon her that Gertrude had only to choose among them. Like most children of wealthy parents she learnt to draw in pencil and paint in watercolour, but to tuition she was less amenable. Her only mention of formal tuition is of 'the fixed restraints'[29] of schoolroom hours, and a succession of French and German governesses were said to leave 'no more than a resentful impression on her independent mind and character'.[30] The sisters must have seemed very different; the elder following a prescribed pattern towards womanhood, the younger already chafing at the restrictions of educational and domestic routine.

One morning Gertrude arrived at breakfast without boots. To have flung them from her bedroom window was not an irrational response to nightingales. If she sometimes challenged her parents' concepts of acceptable behaviour and from time to time her dress and deportment were considered to have overstepped permissible limits, one doubts whether on this occasion she was seriously admonished. But an equally telling part of the story is a sensitivity to uncongenial sounds that became almost a phobia. Francis Jekyll concedes, 'her nervous reaction to noise, though she seemed at times to exaggerate it, was really beyond her control'.[31] It was perfectly understood by various children who came within her orbit that neither Aunt Gertrude nor her brother could tolerate loud voices, let alone shouts and screams. The search for peace or 'the sensation of repose'[32] imbues her writings as surely as freedom from 'accompanying and unavoidable vexatious noises of rumbling roar of mowing machine, clicking of shears and clanking grind of iron roller'.[33] To judge from visitors' comments, the natural state of her domain was, apart from bird-song, an almost ghostly hush. The fact that brother and sister shared a deep-seated sensibility points to a childhood source that could be explained by the Captain's recurring illness. He too was irritated by certain noises; cautioned and concerned, his children in turn became oversensitized.

Francis Jekyll hints that the headstrong behaviour manifesting itself resolutely by Gertrude's twelfth year was apt, on occasion, to upset the even tenor of the household. When her brothers went to school she was much alone. She did not mind amusing herself, the trouble was that her pastimes hardly satisfied a demanding and bookish intellect. So, at least, may her parents have reasoned before deciding that she might benefit from a more structured academic education. Cheltenham Ladies' College opened in 1853 among a number of girls' boarding schools, few of which survive. It is hard to prove where she went or precisely what happened, but her parents shortly withdrew her and the episode was not referred to, allowing it to become gently eclipsed. One is left with a strong suspicion that the 'brief and unsuccessful incursion'[34] mentioned only in her obituary notice may have been traumatic. A ready sense of humour might have made her an ideal candidate, but there was a reservedness which precluded intimacy. Was she teased by other girls? Was she just homesick? Did the protective armoury she wore for most of her adult life owe something to the experience?

The childhood idyll Gertrude writes about with such warmth tends to reflect her earliest years. Reticence about adolescence combined with occasional references to a 'deepened ... sense of aloofness'[35] suggests that, like many others, she found growing up difficult. Sometimes she was bursting with life, but she was on her own a great deal, and the isolation tended to make her feel different from other children. In the garden shed, in anarchic silence, hugging privacy to herself, she painted, read, studied and wrote; as she admitted, 'a rather solitary child'.[36] Her sanctuary was firmly maintained; stories tell of her laying the path with cinders because she discovered that her father could not bear the crunch and squeak when he walked on them. Already she was a victim of the need to control minutely her physical environment. The fact that she elected to remember only the good times obviously leaves one doubting her strong self-representation. She was beginning to study the art of concealment often to keep people at a distance.

CHAPTER FOUR

1861–2

Like her father, Gertrude was incapable of doing nothing; instinctively she filled her time, not just with human energy but with purposefulness. By the time she was seventeen she knew what she wanted to do. An artistic heritage, rapport with classical art, love of visual beauty and, not least, the important matter of independence, persuaded her to enrol as a student at South Kensington or the Central School of Art. For the next two years she alternately studied in London and took up the old vigorous out-of-doors Bramley life, riding, walking and contemplating the rich world about her. To some extent the two complemented each other. 'No man,' wrote John Ruskin, 'ever painted, or ever will paint, well, anything but what he has early and long seen, early and long felt, and early and long loved.'[1]

It is reasonable to assume that all Ruskin's major works were purchased for Bramley House as they appeared. Everyone in cultured circles read Ruskin, and for the Jekylls the impact was augmented by personal connections. The Captain's Etruscan collection brought him in regular contact with the Department of Greek and Roman Antiquities at the British Museum, where Charles Newton was Keeper. Newton had shared Ruskin's company from time to time since Oxford days together, and he and Ruskin were both good friends of the Duff Gordons. Since the publication of *Seven Lamps of Architecture* and *Stones of Venice*, Ruskin had become the leading protagonist of Gothic Revival. Both works Gertrude read and annotated.

Ruskin espoused artistic causes with Messianic zeal, one being that architecture was the foundation and proof of a great nation. He thought the Pre-Raphaelites were in the great painting tradition because nature was their model and truth their banner, and both Turner and the Pre-Raphaelite painters owed their influence in no small measure to his championship. The first volumes of *Modern Painters* had begun to appear. Powerful and controversial, they were less of a treatise on art than a prolonged meditation on the relationship between man, God and the natural world, leading, the author acknowledged, 'into fields of infinite enquiry'.[2] On Gertrude, her nephew conceded, Ruskin's impression 'would be difficult to exaggerate'.[3] From his earliest years Ruskin had experienced periods of ecstatic communion with nature. There were parallels, and she must have recognized them, in her exaltation of trees and plants. In one man she had discovered rare intellectual scope, penetrating analysis, subtlety, depth of emotions and a relentless morality. By 1861, with the fifth epic volume in circulation, Ruskin's opinions on art were treated almost as Gospel.

If Ruskin was the prophet of Arts and Crafts, it was William Morris, painter, designer, printer, weaver, dyer, wood engraver, author and poet, who transformed his ideas to practical reality. The other substantial event of the year was Morris's founding of the firm of Morris, Marshall Faulkner & Co. with Dante Gabriel Rossetti, Ford Madox Brown, Philip Webb and Edward Burne-Jones – a strong Pre-Raphaelite element – among its partners. Morris had visited the Great Exhibition when he was seventeen and been appalled. Harnessing steam power and applying it to manufacture had produced more and more mechanical control of the environment; each new factory process was applied to products irrespective of aesthetics or artistic discipline. In the furniture section, everything made of wood had been passed through machines until not the smallest area of its surface remained flat or natural. The aim of the exhibition, to improve the application of art and design in industry, was made a mockery. A sympathy for Classical form that had lasted for over 100 years had been destroyed. Monstrosities illustrating the catalogue showed that it was a period of 'unexampled hideousness'.[4] The South Kensington Exhibition of 1862 was a testing-ground for Morris's claim that the artist was superior to the machine. The firm's success, according to Professor Pevsner, marked 'the beginning of a new era in Western art'.[5]

The design schools had set a worthy precedent in women's education. Nineteen years before, the Female School of Design at Somerset House began training girls for 'honourable and profitable employment'.[6] From the start there was a long waiting list, classes were crammed and the standard was higher than that in the male school. Six hundred and ninety pupils had passed through since 1852, and courses for working and artisan class were besieged by gentlewomen. It was time for the art schools to follow suit. Six years earlier Maria Theresa Villiers, grand-daughter of Lady Ravensworth and niece to two distinguished politicians, Lord Clarendon and Charles Pelham Villiers, had joined the Central. Theresa declined a court appointment as one of the Queen's Maids of Honour because she felt that her father would not have approved of something so frivolous. She was related to the Duff Gordons, and later on Gertrude was to know her well. For the moment there could scarcely have been a better precedent. Rich students were welcomed because they paid full fees. It was the first year the Royal Academy opened its doors to women but, despite pioneers, art college for women was by no means universally accepted. It was enlightened of the Jekyll family to support their daughter's plans and brave of Gertrude to enlist. She was discovering in herself a strength of character which never would be overpowered by circumstance.

Ten years before Gertrude's decisive plunge into higher education, Prince Albert had had a dream to unite the arts in a giant cultural complex – museum, art school and botanic garden. Five years later, the first students at South Kensington had moved into an eighteenth-century building on twelve acres adjoining Brompton Oratory, the site of the present Victoria and Albert Museum. Linked to the north of Brompton Park House, a series of temporary wooden classrooms known as the Brompton Broilers led to the architect James Pennethorne's circular towered lecture theatre.

The nucleus of the arts centre was to be a garden. As president of the (now Royal) Horticultural Society, the Prince was endeavouring to boost its dwindling fortunes by creating a leading example of the architectural garden style he had promoted at Osborne. The year Gertrude began her studies, trees were being felled, a maze grouted, a vast multicoloured French fountain acquired and statues commissioned from contemporary sculptors. William Nesfield was called in to design a plan for the plot between the art school's new and old buildings – a grand amalgam of French, Italian and English influence, to combine architectural contours and horticultural sophistication. Geometry pricked out with clipped evergreens, bold floral patterns and sculpture dominated; within a year there were complaints about brash bedding and general openness. The English climate, some sectors of the public felt, demands shelter. But the influence of the Society's garden was undoubted; Nesfield and his sons rose to a peak of popularity. Five days a week Gertrude passed the site, before and after study. For ladies, always taught separately, sessions lasted from 1 to 3 p.m. and from 7 to 9 p.m.

Education is no less subject to fashionable fluctuation than the art of gardening, the dominant characteristics in 1861 being rigidness and bureaucracy. Henry Cole, at the Department of Science and Art (recently transferred from trade to the education umbrella), and Richard Redgrave, his Superintendent, were the instigators and virtual dictators of a system that affected art schools throughout the country, and South Kensington was the model. What was it like for a student, a virtual nobody except by virtue of his or her personality? Maria Theresa Villiers became 'more and more convinced of the importance to a girl of having an interest in life over and above her affections and trifling domestic duties'.[7] Art school, she allowed, was preferable to the fashionable drawing-master who taught his pupils to make poor copies of his own sketches and touched them up for parental approval. But she knew from experience that the 'dryness', and the 'drudgery'[8] imposed during the early stages of her course, the endless copying from models rather than drawing freehand or from nature, had annoyed professional and discouraged amateur students. Gertrude never publicly criticized Redgrave's formidable syllabus, developed through twenty-three stages from 'Linear Drawing by aid of Instruments',[9] to 'Technical Studies',[10] but she was adept at absorbing what she needed from what was prescribed, and a student so highly motivated cannot fail to have benefited.

Underlying Redgrave's pragmatism was the assumption that 'design' could be taught like language, first grammar, then syntax, until finally a student could be freed to explore the whole medium. To the orderly mind of Henry Cole, the system possessed admirable advantages; everyone was taught the same thing in the same way. Students simply proceeded from one level to the next as soon as their competence was proven. Asked to defend the fact that they were taking over a year to complete a single drawing, Redgrave replied, 'I should think, if they do they are improving themselves . . . if a student sees the shades of difference, then he becomes a man of taste.'[11] Plenty of Victorian educationists admired the character-training potential of a well-drilled South Kensington teacher, though John Ruskin credited Henry Cole's professorship with corrupting 'the system of art-teaching all over England into a state of abortion and falsehood from which it will take twenty years to recover'.[12] In practice Ruskin's views had little influence. Those who agreed with him included some of the professors obliged to teach the course and some of its students. The first of Redgrave's General Principles was that 'The decorative arts arise from, and should properly be attendant upon architecture'.[13] Mrs Oliphant satirized the effect upon a victim of the Cole regime, young Rose Lake in *Miss Marjoribanks*, who 'instead of allowing herself in vague garlands of impossible flowers, clung with the tenacity of first love to the thistle leaf, which had been the foundation of her early triumphs. Her mind was full of it . . . whether to treat it in a national point of view, bringing in the rose and shamrock, which was a perfectly allowable proceeding, though perhaps not original – or whether . . . she should handle the subject in a boldly naturalistic way. and use her spikes with freedom.'[14]

In view of Gertrude's future, it is relevant that the Superintendent used the garden-designing profession to promote his scheme. 'How many are there to whom a power of geometrical imitation is far more valuable than that of perspective imitation! For instance in working drawings, patterns [and] . . . the plans used by the gardener.'[15] Botany was inextricably woven into the syllabus. There was no need of books, or prints, or museums, said Redgrave, 'only go abroad into the fields and hedgerows'.[16] Considering the type of art-work he promoted, his words are a little ironic. But Gertrude may have been attracted by his landscapes of Surrey, and many years before she joined the school he had lectured on the importance of botany to the ornamentist. Plants provided decorative material and by adapting to their surroundings, taught the illustrator 'fitness of purpose'.[17] John Lindley, Professor of Botany at University College, had once taught there and Christopher Dresser, who attended the college as a pupil, was the current botany Professor. Besides being a progressive and exciting designer, Dresser was more clear-headed than Redgrave and a real force in the school, 'the only member of the South Kensington Circle who practised the simplicity they all preached'.[18] His reductions of plant forms have been called 'true precursors of the symbolic and sign-like ornaments of Art Nouveau'.[19] Perceptiveness and simplicity, two of Ruskin's tenets, would be bound to have impressed Dresser's new pupil.

Ladies did not attend life classes, a point on which Ruskin's 'Truth to Nature' received a mixed reception. In 1859 a censure from the Lord Provost of Glasgow had sparked a heated argument in the press, and Lord Elcho MP gave his public opinion that drawing the living naked female was disgraceful. But overtures about the art schools concealing what went on were squashed in the House of Commons by Palmerston. Ruskin himself preferred to evade the issue and Redgrave did not believe painting from the nude was important to art training, though Cole, who was no prude, had taken Queen Victoria to see some of William Mulready's nude studies against the advice of the President of the Board of Trade. The truth was that Cole approved of any class provided it brought in fee-payers. Drawing the nude male was vindicated in the seventies, yet female models had been forbidden in almost all public art schools in 1850 'and later',[20] a state of affairs Pevsner called hardly believable. Not until the eighties did the female become respectable. Lady art students were not supposed to know about their own nakedness.

Scanty evidence on this period suggests that Gertrude was particularly influenced by lectures on anatomy from Professor John Marshall. She possessed the capacity for minute observation, and now she was learning to delve beneath the surface of everything for significance. Twelve anatomy lectures were arranged each session, the spring course being open only to women. Something about the quality of Gertrude's work drew Marshall's attention, because after collecting his students' notebooks at the end of the first class, he selected hers for reference and later borrowed it to help prepare his lectures for publication. *Anatomy for Artists* is the best known of a number of books he produced for teachers to use in schools; none of them, however, acknowledges his former pupil.

The study of colour was acquiring a body of literature. Gertrude could learn, for instance, from Redgrave's *Elementary Manual of Colour* (1853), to compare the theories of the celebrated Michel-Eugène Chevreul with a number of earlier works, one of which was by a Central School lecturer, a scholar of Moorish, Italian and Chinese ornament named Owen Jones. It was Chevreul who left most impression. As a result of a commission to improve the use of dyes for the Gobelin Tapestry Works, he had published *The Principles of Harmony and Contrast of Colours*. In 1854 his book was translated into English with a preface noting that French manufacturers were indebted to the author for the superior colour sensitivity of French goods displayed at the Great Exhibition. Henceforth it was regarded as an authority. The first, fairly obvious, point in Chevreul's long and abstruse work is that all colours are modified when placed beside each other. Indeed Chevreul was doing no more than confirm Ruskin's thesis that 'a colour, in association with other colours, is different from the same colour seen by itself'.[21] Chevreul suggests that either related colours or contrasted (complementary) colours can be harmonious: 'the complement of red being green; of orange, blue; of yellow-green, violet; of indigo, orange-yellow'.[22] A sub-section of his book is concerned with applications to horticulture, but it would be quite wrong to assume that Gertrude accepted him wholesale, she merely selected among a plethora of facts and hypotheses those she would use.

Gertrude was personally influenced by men like Christopher Dresser and Owen Jones, and, never one to waste opportunity, she browsed in the new Museum befriending the staff. But Ruskin, for the moment travelling through Italy in a private carriage with the overawed Burne-Joneses, continued to be her chief guide. In a famous passage from the end of the first volume of *Modern Painters*, he calls for 'simple bona fide imitation of nature',[23] as the best training for young artists. Gertrude was being offered not only two very different doctrines but two very different vocabularies, and she must have been aware of the contradiction between Ruskin and Redgrave's teachings. Twenty years after leaving South Kensington she announced that gardening was 'painting a picture'; colours should be placed 'with careful forethought and deliberation, as a painter employs them on his picture, and not dropped down in lifeless dabs, as he has them on the palette'.[24]

Gertrude felt that an artistic trained perception sought extra sophistication, and her refined colour sense arose from academic study. Frequently in her writings she refers to her advantage. It must be said that the rank and file of the Arts and Crafts Movement had an entirely different creed. Contemptuous of art schools, favouring the idea of student apprenticeship adopted in medieval times, they thought that so far from the artist's being a superior person, every man was, as Eric Gill was to say, 'a special kind of artist'.[25] By comparison, Gertrude's highflown presumptions about fine art and art-school learning were really very pretentious. Quite an irony, since pretentiousness was something she was quick to nose out and declaim in everyone else. Ruskin, however, she had discovered for herself. It is said that his pupils were able to look at art better than any generation in history, and they looked for the roots of beauty in the patterns of nature. Gertrude was perfectly equipped to follow trends set in motion by Ruskin and Morris.

CHAPTER FIVE

1863

When Lady Duff Gordon stayed at Bramley in August 1863 the Jekylls had been mourning for four months. Lieutenant Arthur Jekyll had drowned from a ship called the *Orpheus* off Manukau Harbour in New Zealand. He had been in the Navy for ten years, otherwise little is known about him. Shortly after, when Mrs Jekyll's father, old Mr Hammersley, died, Lady Duff Gordon accorded him a flattering epitaph, 'There are very few better or kinder Pere de famille!' [1] In such a united family these deaths would have been a severe blow, but emotion was seldom overtly stressed. Gertrude had a new workshop converted from a laundry building near the stables, to which Lady Duff Gordon sallied forth in a donkey chair. The flowers were 'lovely', the country 'beautiful' and she was impressed by Gertrude's 'wonderful power of drawing all and anything'. 'She has a Bookfull of Aldershott Soldiers in all forms and shapes, exceedingly clever, and shows her facility in Drawing figures'. [2]

Within months of collecting her certificate from the Central School of Art, Gertrude had accepted an invitation to tour the Aegean Islands, a prospect doubly enhanced by the thought of travelling with Charles and Mary Newton. Mary was the daughter of Joseph Severn, a painter friend of Keats. Even before she was married she had sometimes accompanied Gertrude to the British Museum. Newton had hit the headlines with his excavations at Halicarnassus on the coast of Turkey. They were an immensely high-powered, intelligent and talented couple. For Gertrude there were few greater virtues than intelligence. Scarcely could she imagine more favourable companions.

The Newtons' marriage had caused quite a stir. Effie Ruskin called Charles 'a great genius' [3] and 'a Greek living in our day with his whole mind devoted to its art'. [4] He was said to look 'like a Greek god', [5] and boasted that 'all the pretty women in London' [6] attended his lectures, but he was shy, which made him seem arrogant and intimidating.

Though he dined out a great deal, he did not make friends easily and found it difficult to relax with girls. In Mary, he had found someone who satisfied his moral and intellectual standards; 'the most talented child in a talented family'[7] was also a woman of great charm. After studying in Paris she had been commissioned to make portraits of the Royal Family, on three occasions she had exhibited at the Royal Academy, and already she was earning more than her father. But they were not obviously compatible and Mary, who was romantic, creative and essentially giving, had serious doubts about marriage before submitting to Newton's grand passion. Mary was younger than her husband but eleven years older than Gertrude, in whom she found 'a good creature and so willing'.[8] Her seniority was a good recommendation. In Gertrude's youth all her closest friends had known her parents first, re-enacting parental patterns with instruction and approval on one side, deference and shared interests on the other. Mary's brother, Arthur, was a life-long friend of Ruskin. Charles too knew the man who had for some years animated Gertrude's sense of direction; subtly, she was moving into Ruskin's intimate circle. But what cemented the relationship between the two women was a shared sense of humour. Three months was a sound test. Gertrude had tremendous respect for Charles and confessed that she had never loved and admired a woman friend more than Mary.

The first motive for the trip was Charles Newton's desire to visit a site of Hellenic remains being dug at Rhodes and consult authorities in the Library of the Seraglio at Constantinople before completing a book called *Travels and Discoveries in the Levant*. Overland to Trieste and then by steamer, the party would make its way through the Ionian and Aegean Islands, stopping off at Smyrna (now Izmir) on the Turkish mainland, Constantinople (Istanbul), Athens and Rhodes. Throughout the journey, Gertrude and Mary drew and painted industriously – portraits, landscape, townscape and Hellenic remains. Gertrude's only regret, she admitted in an introduction to an illustrated travelogue added many years later, lay in not having made the expedition when she was older and might have benefited more from its educational and cultural content. 'For I was very young for my age.'[9] She is severe on her young self; the travelogue is a model of informative precision and by no means a discredit to its author. A protected, privileged girlhood had left her emotionally immature, but with a strong sense of identity and wonderfully open to experience. It is evident that the mature

Gertrude was very strong inside the twenty-year-old who would one day counsel, 'Eye and brain must be alert to receive the impression and studious to store it to add to the hoard of experience'.[10]

It was her first prolonged absence from home and everything was novel and exciting. One of Mary's telling sketches shows her friend in a wide skirt and coat, with a paint board slung over one shoulder, purse and paint pot tied to her waist, a stool in one hand and a bag in the other. Round spectacles, a hat set at a determined angle and earrings swinging like golf balls convey the spirit evoked in Ruskin's celebrated maxim, 'nothing but Art is moral: Life without Industry is sin, and Industry without Art, brutality'.[11] What Mary referred to as 'heavy marching order'[12] portrayed a preparedness her friend was to maintain. Lutyens mentioned much later how Gertrude would travel equipped for action. Already she was putting all her energy into everything she did, the woman who once admitted, 'pure idleness seems to me to be akin to folly, or even worse . . . in some form or other I must obey the Divine commands: "Work while ye have the light".'[13]

On 13 October 1863 the party left England with huge trunks of clothing, medicines, books, stools and painting equipment. As the night train crawled up the Alps towards the Semmering Pass, Gertrude, wide awake, caught moonlit glimpses of flickering streams deep in their mountain gullies. At the end of a week, with a large contingent of English passengers, she and the Newtons boarded an Austrian Lloyd boat at Trieste. Quickly she introduced herself to the Captain before settling down beneath hot sun to sketch the coloured sails of becalmed Venetian fishing boats from the top of the deck-house. Before long she was attempting the likeness of the Triestine First Officer. Unable to write, he spelled out his name to caption the portrait.

The day the passengers disembarked at Corfu, Gertrude had risen, bristling with energy, to see the sun scale the Albanian mountains. It was beautiful high country terraced with grapes, olives and citrus fruit, but politically unstable. No sooner had she disembarked than it was obvious something was amiss. Life had taught her that facts were by themselves of supreme importance, constantly she sought explanations, 'And it does not do to give [it] up because the first person asked cannot put one in the way of finding out. One must ask everybody . . .'[14] When Napoleon was defeated, the Congress of Vienna had given Britain control of the Ionian Islands. Union with Greece was popular yet obviously not a unanimous option, since the inhabitants she met were complaining vociferously about the withdrawal of English troops. Gertrude and her friends, however, received courteous hospitality. A soldier showed them the Citadel and Lady Wolfe drove them to some ruins outside the town. Archaeological sites were a priority, though there was much else to see, draw and question.

The trio left the island in a different boat. Henceforth there was only a handful of Europeans in spacious first-class accommodation, where, as might be expected, the élite received attentive service. Long, mild-flavoured melons were served cut in a zig-zag fashion, Gertrude observed with approval. Once again she established relations with the ship's senior crew. Time, on board, might slip the unwary, but she felt that every minute was accountable. When there was nothing to admire at sea, she and Mary arranged to draw their more flamboyant fellow passengers, and catching the Captain by himself, she took the opportunity of explaining to him Admiral Fitzroy's theory of circular storms. One of Mary's sketches shows her crouched on a stool, with a drawing pad on her knees, sketching a group of children and turbanned adults. Behind her, silhouetted against the rigging, more conventional passengers gaze in indolent admiration.

After nosing among rugged Greek islands, the boat halted at Syra to pick up some decrepit Jews and a party of Cretan Turks wearing turquoises and silver rings. Once again Gertrude wanted reasons for everything. The Jews were on their way to die in Jerusalem; the Turkish women were interned in a wooden pen with awning and canvas sides because they were considered too dirty for the cabins. The feather coverings they carried, she was assured, kept them comfortable.

Gertrude was easy with strangers regardless of their station, and intrigued by their crafts and commitments. That is not to say that she was indiscriminating or patient with bores. Quite early in the voyage she met a kind but tedious German doctor, whom she subsequently dubbed Magenschmerz because it was the word he used to describe a patient and 'somehow the name seemed to fit'.[15] The doctor spoke no English and Gertrude remembered only schoolroom German. With much perseverance on his part, however, they managed to communicate. Poor Magenschmerz, attracted by her vitality, pursued her vigorously. Alas, he was a pedant. She found his ingenious appearances a nuisance, and without being discourteous, took pains to avoid him. The truth was that she sought the quick wits, originality and lively companionship she herself possessed.

Before the end of October the party had steamed up the Gulf of Smyrna, a long arm of the sea faced with bold mountain scree, and caught a train to the site of the medieval city at Ephesus. Where tides once raced in and out at the foot of the city, the land was plugged with evil-smelling marsh. But it was fine country for game birds, wild boar and panthers, albeit infested with brigands. Gertrude's sense of adventure was inspired by lawless 'Zebeks' who swaggered, fearless, about the streets. One obliged by sitting for a drawing with his sword gripped between his teeth.

Rhodes was definitely a highlight, 'so beautiful', 'so crammed full of interest',[16] and the natives made splendid subjects for portraits. Women arrived like peacocks, in assorted scarves, turbans and huge silver brooches; only in removing their veils did they have to be cajoled. Men were bolder and happy to be paid for sitting. One delighted Gertrude by inquiring whether she was for sale. Gertrude was trying to view everything from a painterly point of view. 'Mary and I went to the town to do some drawing at the Amboise Gate,'[17] the travel diary discloses. It was the chief gate leading into the old town, the headquarters of the Knights Templar during their 200-year domicile on the island. After sketching in a confined thoroughfare, the friends moved into the Street of the Knights. Alas, its fine Gothic doorways were spoiled by Turkish wooden bays, their latticed windows supported by 'flimsy-looking'[18] struts. In Gertrude's dogmatic opinion, architecture should be substantial.

Sitting sideways on pack saddles covered with carpet, the pair rode mules along the island's dusty tracks, mounting, when no suitable wall was present, from a block made by the muleteer's back. Where narrow tracks overhung a precipice, Gertrude's horsemanship held her in good stead. The mules wore, she explained, an iron band over their noses in lieu of a bit. Sometimes the band rubbed them sore. Mule-bound they came upon rock crevices sprouting myriads of wild cyclamen, narcissus, crocus and iris, aromatic herbs mingled with prickly bushes and, wherever the rocks overhung and made cool places, verdant maidenhair ferns. Gertrude noted a terebinth (*Pistacia terebinthus*), palms, half-wild orange trees and a pleasing combination of plant and architecture where plane trees and olives sheltered the remains of an ancient stone aqueduct. It was in Rhodes that she plucked a white-flowered iris from the Turkish cemetery and took it home, identifying it as *I. albicans*. Her sole grumble was dearth of greenery; only the maidenhair fern was 'really green and fresh'.[19]

One day there was a mild earthquake. The heat was intense, a strong wind blew and the house in which the friends lodged was discovered to have cracked. They had been advised to stand beneath the lintel for protection if there were insufficient time to escape, and Gertrude dismissed the incident with equanimity. But proof of the hazards attending travellers in the eighteen-sixties was reinforced with tidings that the boat which conveyed them so confidently to the island had been wrecked on the Cyprus coast the following day. Fortunately, no lives were lost. Departure from the island coincided with the beginning of winter rains. The *Imperatore* drew out of harbour in continuous lightning, as veils of rain hid the disappearing contours of Rhodes. From the deck Gertrude watched nostalgically until she was forced inside.

Each port of call had its wonders explored, culinary delicacies sampled, social customs and exotic clothing remarked upon. At Ephesus, Gertrude noticed, 'the soil had a curious shiny, almost greasy, appearance';[20] Syrian sheep had large horns and flattened tails. These might be reports from any observant tourist. More characteristic is her comment on a frail old Turk from Rhodes who, disdaining a spoon, ate bread and honey in his fingers with exquisite delicacy. A mark of quality or a job well done was certain to arouse her admiration; artisans' treasures were praised as much as the rubbish they often accompanied would be berated. Gertrude either approved or disapproved, her opinions could be categorical and vehement. What worried her especially was Turkish women's idleness. Beyond eating and chatting, dressing, undressing and painting their faces, they had little to do. How she pitied them! In notes that are constantly humorous, she recalled a drive home from the Turkish cemetery in Constantinople, called to a halt when a rotten shaft of the carriage broke. Prepared with an assortment of cord and strap, the driver proceeded to mend it while several Turks stood by without offering to help. 'They only looked on and said: "God is great!"'[21] On the fifth of November, she cleared the yard and lit a bonfire, informing the doubtful guide that her activity marked a British patriotic-religious observance. Thereafter he watched with much respect.

The next stop was at Tenedos to take on more passengers. With nearly 400 up, the boat chugged through the Dardanelles, affording views of scattered inland hills behind low land on the east and a precipitous peninsula on the west. Gertrude was amused by a Turkish woman trying to empty a pail of urine to windward 'with very ill success'.[22] By 23 November the boat had steamed through the Sea of Marmora in broad sunlight to reach the furthest point of the expedition.

Constantinople was another treasured opportunity. During two weeks there, the English friends made long excursions by foot and open carriage from a Greek hotel. Accompanied by a guide or 'dragoman',[23] they shambled through rough narrow streets, over bridges, past St Sophia and other magnificent mosques. The coat of the Sultan's huge Afghan mount called forth a paean of praise in the travelogue. No one, Gertrude reckoned, could imagine the effect of a well-bred, well-groomed Eastern horse without actually seeing its 'warm, cream colour' and 'pearly' coat; 'Like polished metal . . . reflected in a looking-glass.'[24] Her description minds one of Ruskin's stricture, 'We are constantly supposing that we see what experience only has shown us . . . constantly missing the sight of what we do not know beforehand to be visible.'[25]

Only one disappointment received a diary entry. Doubtless, summer was the best time to appreciate the cool gardens along the shore of the Bosphorus, and probably her expectations had been pitched too high. Gertrude hastened to accept responsibility for what might sound like ungratefulness. A caique ('very cranky boats, but they go a great pace')[26] took the party to an old Byzantine fortress on the Asiatic coast with a grand view of the Black Sea, 'looking really black with a heavy rainstorm passing over'.[27] Surrounding hills were clad with bay, some prickly bushes and a good many trees bearing fruit the size of cherries, like a long green plum or a Muscat grape. The local name was 'Trebizond date'; the taste, initially sweet, became astringent. Gertrude kept a stone to plant. Too late to join the returning steamer, she and the Newtons ate 'the common stiff' caviar,[28] dried figs, coffee and unleavened bread, flabby as pancakes, before returning. Two men rowed, each with two oars, Gertrude described with tidy economy. A wooden bob inside the boat bore most of the weight and a well-greased thong of raw hide passed round the oar and 'tholepin',[29] a pin in the gunwale of a boat used as a fulcrum for the oar. The boatmen wore splendid straw-coloured crêpe shirts, their wide sleeves falling in luxurious folds.

The Library of the Seraglio was a holy of holies, and abandoning galoshes outside, the party was shown a book with paper made partly

from gold. Mary made drawings of a Greek figure from the Mauso-
leum of Halicarnassus for her husband's forthcoming book, and
Gertrude, ever responsive to purposeful industriousness, set to work
copying fifteenth-century Latin manuscripts. While tame ostriches
sauntered in the gardens, the three drank coffee from cups studded
with diamonds.

Gertrude was never to pay marked attention to calendar celebrations.
A twentieth birthday came and went with scant comment a few days
before she visited St Sophia, a 'great and wonderful place'.[30] After
surveying its interiors the travellers took a Turkish carriage at Scutari,
where she purchased green glazed pottery and inspected the inside of
an old Christian church. With a grand roof mosaic of prophets, saints
and martyrs fresh in their minds, they packed to leave.

The twelfth of December found the party in Athens, wandering
among the ruins of the Parthenon. If Gertrude bent so as to look along
the upper step, a small rise could be ascertained in the middle. 'What
luck to be there with Mr Newton! He showed me that curious thing
only recently observed – the trajectory of the Parthenon.'[31] In the
palace garden, with wide views of the Acropolis, she identified orange
trees, acacia, peppers, aloes, pines, arundo and a few palms. Before
leaving she plucked a seed-pod from a plant with sharply cut leaves to
add to her selection of souvenirs. It was like a solanum; she would
grow it in Bramley to remind her of beautiful Athens.

Even in the last months of the year, the Mediterranean flora were a
constant delight. What looked from a distance like bare rocky outcrops
harboured, in nooks and crannies, a number of sweet-scented, thyme-
like herbs. Elsewhere there were cypress, myrtles and sweet bay. Over
and again in later life, Gertrude drew on the flora of the Greek
archipelago, with its scattered growth of low, aromatic bushes and
herbs. 'As you move ... every plant seems full of sweet sap or
aromatic gum.'[32] But soon she was bound for Marseilles, rising early
to spy out the Straits of Messina. On Christmas Day she was in Paris,
on 26 December at Bramley, tired and thankful. Home was always
back in some measure to the meaningful happiness of childhood.

PART TWO

ARTIST

CHAPTER SIX

1864–7

Twenty-one-year-old Gertrude wore her dark hair scraped behind her head in an austere single knot; her chin was beginning to recede and her eyes were a little high in her face, too piercing, too intrepid for comfort behind the round, steel-framed spectacles with heavy lenses that helped to correct her myopia. To her credit, her posture was upright, she wore clothes well and moved with poise. A hunting sketch by J. J. Carter shows her sitting a horse side-saddle, bowler-hatted, straight as a pin and tightly reined. No one called her pretty, of which she could scarcely fail to be aware, and there are indications that she never entirely accepted her physical self. Certainly she came into contact with young men at county and military balls, though it is difficult to imagine quite what a youth of her age would have made of the largish, slightly eccentric, dauntingly quick-witted girl and there is no indication that she had thoughts of a marriage partner at this time. With her wide interests, artistic talent, and intelligence she did not lack confidence; on the contrary, it was the energy of her mind and body that drew first comment.

Because Gertrude was capable of being excellent company, one might imagine her gregarious. This, however, would be a mistake. As her father had owned, she was a queer fish, and intermittently she had a real need to be alone. Emotional restraint may have been expected from middle-class women, but her reticence was not entirely a question of the times. She had been for much of her youth like an only child; demanding and rebellious. If there were moments when she resented her parents' sensible guardianship, they had really behaved in an exemplary manner towards their maverick daughter. Wandering about Bramley, she had had what seems like an ideal childhood and she was learning the stoicism that makes intimacy difficult. Besides, reticence was a family trait; she was not even intimate in her writing, though from this time until her final illness, she maintained a diary cum record of her engagements. Typically, it was almost entirely factual. Throughout her public life she erected a mask behind which she learned to manoeuvre the different faces of a complex personality.

Lady Duff Gordon felt that the drawings Gertrude made in Constantinople and Athens were 'very clever the countenances of the individuals and characters very cleverly expressed'.[1] After her long trip abroad, Gertrude was stimulated to a fever of activity. If William Morris's firm could produce furniture, wallpaper, chintz, tapestry, carpets, tiles and stained glass, she too would try everything: painting, carving, gilding and inlay. Occasionally, her nephew suggests, the family felt the scope of her experiments was detrimental to expertise in any one, but she was an infinitely painstaking and exhaustive worker, determined to find the best expression for her creative talent. From the workshop there issued a stream of production. Gardening was another calling among the activities that smudge the distinction between art and craft: the Mediterranean spoils were planted, among them a white iris from Rhodes, seeds of the cut-leaved solanum-like plant from the palace at Athens, and the 'Trebizond date', otherwise *Eleagnus angustifolia*, a deciduous shrub or small tree covered, when young, with silvery scales. Between indulging her own interests, she was lapped into the flow of country house life with its riding, ladies' cricket and croquet parties. As many as forty attended one such event lasting well into the night. For illumination she had constructed a large transparent owl.

Lady Duff Gordon was growing deaf. At Bramley she complained, 'I sadly miss my Ears in this kind talkative house.'[2] Georgy's visits were frequent as ever, and in London she often accompanied Gertrude to picture galleries. To be forty-three and unmarried was a predicament that called for annual lament, usually on her birthday. Much as Lady Duff Gordon would miss them, she would dearly like to have seen both daughters settled in homes of their own 'before that moment comes!!!!! that inevitable day that . . . can not be very far distant'.[3] As she added later, 'then comes the untying the bundle of faggots!!'[4] Country house living might have lacked stimulation for a married woman but marriage gave women a form, their only acceptable one, of social power. For a spinster, life was generally worse. In London Georgy took to her bed at regular intervals, smouldering with vexation from repressed sexuality and idleness; at the Jekylls she was invariably restored to 'great talk & good spirits'.[5] The young artist George du Maurier's picture of her, 'an imperious old maid',[6] sounds a little harsh. Like her mother, Georgy was opinionated, but she had also inherited her mother's sense of fun, a refreshing preference for 'intellectual life, without any bores or social plagues'.[7] The Jekylls were extremely fond of her.

In 1865, Carry was twenty-eight. A photograph shows her in a pale dress with a wide brocade front, its crinoline draped round an overstuffed chair. Her hair is coiled in two rosettes above each ear. Probably it is the softening hairstyle and the eyes, demurely lowered into a book, which make her appear less severe than her sister, though the fact that she was 'more petite and more feminine' is verified by someone who knew them both.[8] At all events, Carry had a wooer in Frederick Eden, Commissioner of Fisheries. 'She has never liked but him,' Lady Duff Gordon marvelled, '& at last Mr Jekyll has given in kindly.'[9] Since Julia Hammersley's brother, Hugh, had married one of Frederick's sisters, it was the second match between the families. Early in the New Year Frederick took the hand of his bride in Bramley parish church. 'No tears were shed.'[10] The day was fine, the villagers made wreaths and arches, the children threw down snowdrops at the feet of the new couple and 'all seemed happiness and comfort'.[11]

For all of the Jekylls, the marriage had repercussions. Carry had gained a husband but her parents had lost the daughter of the house, and without an elder sister at home, pressure on Gertrude to take up the role could not be ignored. The Captain and Mrs Jekyll were growing older, their younger daughter would be left with independent means and her future as an artist was not necessarily something they took seriously. The Captain's extensive discourse on the possibility of her marrying and producing children, in a will he wrote the following year, suggests that he was by no means reconciled to her singleness. So naturally did the role of carer fall on Gertrude that it was difficult to avoid without conflict. She valued and was grateful to her parents but she had different if yet unformulated plans for her future. To someone of her ambitions, one thing clear was the importance of freeing herself from domestic duties. Opposition was not simply a family matter, she was up against the conventions of society. In the circumstances, it must have been heartening to learn that her portrait of her brother, Teddy's, Indian dog was to be hung in the Academy Summer Exhibition. It was titled, *Cheeky, a native of Cawnpore, 64th Regiment.*

Gertrude had a strong inner determination to go her own way, and there are signs over the next few years that she was doing all she could to avoid being at home. London with its various circles of family and friends was the obvious escape, and there the Weguelins were 'eager to welcome her'.[12] Thomas Weguelin, director of the Bank of England, had married first Charlotte Poulett Thomson then, when she died, her cousin Julia Jekyll's sister, Catherine Hammersley. Of thirteen children, Christopher, five years Gertrude's senior and a talented amateur dramatist, would shortly take up his father's professional position. Two other London houses in which Gertrude was assured hospitality were those of longstanding mutual friends, the Newtons and the Duff Gordons. At 34 Hertford Street Georgy and Alice were sharing, it was said, a single egg for breakfast;[13] Alice began with the white and Georgy, the enthusiastic one, gobbled the yolk. Gossip gives an atypical view of the sisters. When Alice was not looking after her mother, she often worked at the Samaritan Hospital, while Georgy invariably sought adventure. They prayed at different churches and 'walked their different ways'.[14]

Before the first month of the new year was out, Gertrude and Herbert were joining Georgy, Alice and 'Little Lord Brooke'[15] in the Duke of Bedford's box at Covent Garden. Gertrude loved music and the Duff Gordons; besides, London was the place to make artistic contacts. Talent, energy and the conviction that she had something to offer were not enough: to create a future she needed to meet the right people. Lady Duff Gordon was adept at making introductions.

The Newtons were also good people to know, though currently they had problems of their own. It is doubtful whether Mary would have confided in her young companion. Outside the Severn family, few were aware of the stress she found in marriage. Charles had always driven himself hard; the trouble was that he expected her to follow his taxing routine. *Travels in the Levant* was published in 1865 with a number of his wife's pencil drawings as illustrations. In addition to her painting, Mary was endeavouring to keep household accounts, a perpetual headache, and to make all the drawings for her husband's lectures. If the slightest detail was wrong, they had to be done again. The same sort of difficulty infused their private life. When the pair returned home from a day at the museum, Charles liked to dine with friends or entertain. Mary longed to relax but, uncomplaining, did as he wished. Before the trip to Rhodes she had been thin, and the family thought the holiday had done her little good. Though she appeared composed in public, she was sleeping badly, she told her sister.

Suddenly she would wake from a dream, believing she had been drawing all night. In the circumstances she may have found it comforting to visit exhibitions – Holman Hunt, Frederic Leighton and Myles Birket Foster – with a faithful friend.

'Holy Hunt', as he was called, was the most conservative of the Pre-Raphaelites – he alone clung to what he believed were the true principles of the movement; and nearly everyone in art circles knew Sir Frederic Leighton, the 'deuce of a swell',[16] including both Newtons and the Duff Gordons. During Gertrude's trip to the Greek Islands, Charles Newton had acquired some flower-patterned earthenware plates from Rhodes on his behalf. Leighton's grandfather had been court physician to the Tsar of Russia, and the young man had disappointed a line of medics by straying into the field of art. But at his first Royal Academy exhibition he sold a picture to Queen Victoria for £600, launching himself on a long and successful career. By the time he became Lord Leighton, Baron of Stretton, a painter was of equal status to any in the House of Lords. He was not a Ruskinian. Pernickety Ruskin complained that Leighton had misrepresented the number of eyes in a peacock's tail. Still, his 'pretty girls' were 'very nearly beautiful'.[17] Today the miniature palace that was a mecca for his Pre-Raphaelite friends is a public museum in West London's Holland Park Road. Leighton's 'House Beautiful', one of the most dynamic expressions of the Aesthetic Movement, was conceived by George Aitchison, although the most exotic part of all, the Arab Hall with its ancient eastern tiles and plopping fountain, was added later.

Birket Foster might not have been a pillar of the Victorian art establishment, but he shared Gertrude's interests and the proximity of their homes makes it highly probable that she knew him. The previous year he had moved to Witley, near Guildford, where he painted delicate watercolours of farm girls driving their ducks and geese, with 'meticulous finish and with astounding technical skill'.[18]

Of course meeting artists and looking at pictures were secondary to the business of painting. In her converted workshop Gertrude produced *Jehu Driving Furiously*, a canvas considered by Ruskin 'very wonderful and interesting'.[19] Two years later it was shown at an exhibition of the Society of Female Artists, a group founded in 1855 to encourage women painters and sculptors. Like the other nine watercolours she exhibited between 1865 and 1870, it has been lost or withdrawn from public circulation, so Ruskin's verdict must suffice. An event the picture may have prompted is marked by a brief engagement entry on 17 November 1865, 'To see Mr Ruskin'.[20] The invitation to call must have seemed to bring her to the approaches of the world she longed to enter. It was the first of many similar engagements.

One can only guess what the twenty-two-year-old artist and the forty-four-year-old critic said to one another. Gertrude was well informed and gave the immediate impression of being someone to be taken seriously. In no way did she resemble the psychotic, undernourished beauties who captured Ruskin's imagination as Rose La Touche had done, but human companionship of the right sort, 'Carlyle, some ladies, and a few favourite children',[21] still maintained the power to cheer him. There were points of contact in Turner, art, the countryside and shared friends, though Ruskin was presently consumed by socialism and politics. It was three years since the publication of *Unto This Last*, of which the first three instalments had been presented to an immense readership in Thackeray's new monthly magazine, the *Cornhill*. Ruskin wanted government intervention to provide social justice for the worker, and gradually it became clear that he was questioning the whole basis of capitalist, industrial progress. Periodically, he announced that he was tired of trying to do good, but he could never resist 'just one more howl'.[22] Gertrude had little patience with the downtrodden, and never espoused Ruskin's passion for social reform. But one can see her asking questions, trying to draw him into conversation as a grown-up daughter would. Time and again she would tame a new friend or admirer.

While Gertrude was gaining ground, Mary Newton was losing it. The Severn family watched, powerless, as she succumbed to one malaise after another. Obsessed by the suspicion that she might never be able to bear a child, she was sublimating her fears in work. At a crucial time she caught measles from a boy whose portrait she was painting. Lying in bed at her home in Gower Street, she saw a maidservant fall from the top window of the opposite house; her scream was haunting. All day Mary was unconscious and the following day, 2 January 1866, she died. Lady Duff Gordon was horrified. Charles had dined there recently and given no hint of his wife's real condition. To Gertrude, who had known them both, his behaviour was characteristic, though the stark finality of Mary's death was difficult to accept. Like Charles, however, she felt it her duty to conceal her pain. Matter-of-factness was always her strategy against grief: feeling her loss keenly, she spun into new exploits.

The first days of 1867 brought such a severe freeze that a man 'skated'[23] up and down St James's Street, Piccadilly. Then spring bloomed softly in London. Music might play second string to art in Gertrude's life, but it was her chief social pastime, and encouraged by the Duff Gordons she began taking private singing lessons with Georgy's friend and teacher, Fiori, at Lady Lindsay's home in Grosvenor Square. Together with Georgy she sang away many an evening, and attended morning concerts. On her own or sometimes with Herbert, she spent day after day copying Turner's paintings at the National Gallery. Ruskin was constantly trying to make the Turner collections more accessible to students. First he had catalogued the oils at Marlborough House and arranged them in chronological order; later he turned his attention to the sketches and drawings at the National. Because they were so valuable, curators were reluctant to put the best ones on view. At the Louvre a few were shown beneath glass tables, but this was only satisfactory where the light was good. At the National, he refined the service by mounting 100 of Turner's most characteristic sketches, illustrating a tour up the Rhine, through Switzerland, to Venice and back. Visitors were allowed five or ten protected in glass frames, to move, copy, contemplate and compare as they wished. 'I can hardly use terms strong enough to express the importance I should myself attach to this exhibition of Turner's sketches, as a means of artistical education,' Ruskin wrote in his introductory remarks.[24] 'Every touch in them represents something complete and definite.'[25]

To judge from Gertrude' and Herbert's Turner paintings in circulation, they were both extremely proficient copyists. Two of Herbert's are in the prints and drawings department of the British Museum, and a family story recounts that one day towards the end of his life he was visiting Christie's for a preview of a Turner sale when he noticed a watercolour that looked familiar. An assistant assured him that it was genuine, but Herbert knew better because he had painted it himself. Gertrude's *Clapham Common*, now in the Duff Gordon family collection, was given by her to Sir Gilbert Frankland Lewis, a relation of Lady Duff Gordon's with a London house in Gertrude's old road, 11 Grafton Street. His brother, Sir George Cornewall Lewis, Home Secretary and a scholar, lived at Harpton Court in Radnor, in a wide green valley surrounded by clean, slate hills. It was a Duff Gordon summer refuge to which Gertrude and her parents were no strangers;

entertained by Lady Lewis, Gertrude became acquainted with the hub of Lady Duff Gordon's Herford-based, paternal family and their vast circle of political and professional friends.

No more of Gertrude's own canvases were hung at the Royal Academy, although the Society of Female Artists showed two at exhibitions in 1867, when *Toby in Snow* was sold privately. Three were sold the following year and three more in 1870: most were paintings of animals. Since Mary's death, Gertrude was also making herself useful to Charles Newton by drawing his lecture illustrations. Seeing Newton as an idealist rather than a callous man, she did not blame him, as the Severn family did, for Mary's death.

Georgy still took regular sojourns in Italy and France. From consultations with a doctor in Paris she returned refreshed, as much, one would imagine, from the change of surroundings as the benefits of medicine. In a new role as Gertrude's chaperone, she set out again for Paris. This time Paris meant the Louvre, where Gertrude set up her easel to copy old masters. Perhaps Georgy's youthful earnestness about art was wearing a bit thin: according to Lady Duff Gordon was 'tired with the Louvre & Gertrude charmed'.[26] Not that commitment to arts and crafts prevented Gertrude from wanting to exploit every potential she might possess. Speculative singing lessons with the celebrated Galvani proved that her tuneful voice was not equal to the rigours of serious training. This did not stop her continuing her lessons with Fiori.

Of all the Jekylls' acquaintances, none were more aware of Gertrude's talent, generous in praise, or assiduous in assistance than the Duff Gordons, and it was they who introduced her to George Watts of Little Holland House on 16 June 1867. Recently elected a Royal Academician, and building a new studio for his sculpture in the grounds of Holland Park, Watts was very much part of the establishment. Frederic Leighton claimed forty unbroken years of friendship with 'England's Michelangelo', and Ruskin concurred, 'a great fellow, or I am much mistaken'.[27] Watts's marriage to the lovely actress Ellen Terry had foundered, because, as she admitted, 'I was so ignorant and young, and he was so impatient.'[28] After temporary deflation Ellen was back on the stage and Watts returned to his old position among adoring women and miscellaneous lame ducks, a rambling community of artists known as the 'Passionate Bromptonians' of Little Holland House,[29] a place, incidentally, where Virginia Woolf's mother, Julia Jackson, spent a great deal of time as a child, pouring out tea and handing round strawberries to distinguished men.

Gertrude's request to copy Watts's *White Oxen* formed the beginning of a long acquaintance. After their first meeting she felt she had been 'in paradise',[30] and Lady Duff Gordon, loyal to her protégée, thought the oxen 'wonderfully well done'.[31] Watts eventually married Mary Fraser-Tytler and moved to Compton, not far from Bramley on the chalk downs. Gertrude visited him nine times before 1893.

In July Georgy had to leave Bramley because the house was full; in August she accompanied her mother there. It was a good time for exchanges. Teddy, who had followed his father in the Grenadier Guards, was wheeling Lady Duff Gordon round the garden in a chair; Gertrude was there and so was Herbert, a Lieutenant at the Royal Military Academy. 'Plenty of music passed the day.'[32] Painting remained for Gertrude the supreme art but she was being driven by the urge to develop all of herself.

At twenty-five Gertrude was as ebullient as ever and fully mature. There remained the important question of marriage. She was a person of strong instincts, and there is no reason why she should not have been susceptible to masculine beauty in life as well as in paintings. But men seldom treated women as responsible companions and women were expected to repress any part of their personality that might disrupt household harmony, facts that must have influenced at a subconscious level someone driven to assert her own future. At the same time, she had all the respect for matrimony one would expect from the child of a happy union. So far as is known she never had any love life, but this does not mean she was not a romantic and it would be wrong to assume that spinsterhood was altogether what she wanted. She may have remained single because a suitable man did not ask her to be his wife. She would not have settled for less.

One of the luxuries that was open to her was travel. Gertrude went abroad a dozen times in her life, apart from one long stay in North Africa, always to Europe. But because she knew precisely what she wanted to see, assimilated information for twelve hours a day and retained a large proportion of it, the impact of these trips was out of all proportion to the time she spent away. Early in 1868 she and a fellow art student, Susan Muir Mackenzie, headed for Rome via the Riviera and Genoa on what was her first visit to Italy. 'In what other country of the world can one receive such impressions of poetry and mystery?'[1]

Susan was the daughter of a baronet from Perthshire, whose brothers rose to an eminence denied their unmarried sister. All Gertrude's women friends were lively and, no exception, Susan sang dramatically, played the piano with verve, admired French art and sat to John Millais in a yellow cloak. In Rome there was time for riding in magnificent woods of cork oaks and Gertrude naturally made copious sketches. Francis Jekyll mentions museums and churches, though she must also have visited two of the greatest Renaissance water gardens, the villa of Hadrian and the Villa d'Este, where ingenious water trickery, thrusting curtains, cascading falls and plumelike jets contrast with great, rectangular, reflective pools. The Villa d'Este, 'with its superb avenue of ancient cypresses, its terraces and noble stairway and its varied play of many waters',[2] left an impression on her never to be forgotten of a living link between the present and Classical periods.

Installed in the artists' quarter, Gertrude patronized a private art school known as Gigi's Academy, and spent many full days in the workshop of an Italian carver and gilder named Placide. Some thirty years later she was to claim, 'I have never missed an opportunity of learning from good workmen,'[3] paying her respects to 'the kindly padrone' who 'put me through a piece of work from beginning to end'.[4] First she carved a frame, then painted it with size, delicately manipulating the hardened coats with special steel tools. Two more coats of transparent size were applied before gold leaf could be floated on. Water-gilding was a far more elaborate technique than oil-gilding, she explained with a perfectionist's obsession for tools and techniques. None, in her estimation, compared with the Italian decorators, closely bound with Ruskin's 'noble painters of the school of Venice'.[5] The episode seems to have made a profound impression. More than once Gertrude returns to it. But if the prime benefit of Italian tutelage was its thoroughness – the idea of precision as a kind of end-all – the natives' willingness to impart their knowledge was an important ingredient. In her experience, English workmen were reluctant to share their secrets for fear of competition from amateurs. The lady amateur, 'perpetually tingling to sell her work before she half knows how to make it',[6] being a specially vulnerable target. Financial support from her family meant she could afford to undercut the skilled workman, earning thereby his distrust, but if she needed to take up work on a professional basis, her competence was suspect. On every side women's confidence was assailed.

Leaving Surrey was a possibility Gertrude had no reason to contemplate until her return from Rome. It was then she learnt that the family home on the banks of the Thames was vacant. For twenty years she had lived in Surrey. Wherever she travelled, however frequent her London sojourns, nothing diminished the impact of its bracken-covered heaths scattered with stripling birches, sunken leafy lanes and tangled woods. From leaf, branch, trunk and root she imbibed the seasonal rhythms of nature, through the small-scale landscape of valleys and tree-clad slopes she rode and walked. Cottages hewn from local materials harboured men and women whose crafts linked them with the land. Everything fitted, and all, she saw with highly-coloured, short-sighted poignancy, was part of a greater unity. Quite suddenly it seemed as if she was in danger of losing everything she most cherished and relied upon. Herbert and Walter objected almost as strongly, and Lady Duff Gordon, staying there the last summer, was 'very sorry to think we shall never see Bramley again'.[7] But parental influence prevailed. Two months later, on 8 June 1868, Gertrude sorrowed in her diary: 'to my great grief left Bramley for Wargrave'.[8]

The grey-brown bend of the Thames can scarcely fail to dominate the village rising above its eastern bank, where comely, red brick houses with riverside lawns overlook fields framed by tree-clad hills. Many of Wargrave's larger houses were built during the late Victorian period, when commercial traffic on the Thames declined and it became a fashionable riverside summer resort. By the 1860s the population was about 1,800; growth continued steadily, and in 1868 there were two bakers, a grocer, a butcher, a chemist, several carpenters' shops, four blacksmiths, a plumber, a wheelwright, a coal merchant, a laundry and a basket-maker. Other tradesmen worked from private premises.

George Leslie, an artist of the St John's Wood set, frequently spent part of the summer exploring by punt and row-boat the wide arc of river that leads downstream towards Henley and upstream into the Loddon river at Shiplake Weir. Writing in *Our River* of morning mists that gave way gradually to sun, gleaming willow foliage and evening banks filled with glow-worms, he called Wargrave 'a sweet, quiet little' place.[9] To the water traveller moving downstream from west to east, the village begins with the tower of St Mary's Church, and passes a substantial building set back, high, and glimmering palely through its trees. This is Wargrave Manor, the new Jekyll home, built in the 1780s by Joseph Hill, uncle to the poet William Cowper and then called, one imagines for its situation as well as the family names, Wargrave Hill. Joseph Hill was a great-nephew of Sir Joseph Jekyll, who left the property to him as far back as 1810. When Hill's widow died, it had become a second home for young Edward – Gertrude's father – and his brother, her Uncle Joseph. As was usual, it passed to the elder: Uncle Joseph had lived there until he died. Afterwards it was occupied by various tenants until the death of the last of them left it free.

Superficially, Wargrave Hill had much in common with Bramley House. It was white and imposing, with neo-classical columns supporting a substantial portico along its south, it had its river, and even an island sporting 'summer snowflakes like gigantic snowdrops'.[10] Both were essentially rural, agriculture and its supporting crafts being the chief occupations. Here the resemblance ends, because Wargrave is terraced into the side of a hill with stupendous views over the river, far more silhouette and more sky. Today the building is substantially restored and has a small new wing. But long arched galleries on the ground and first floors still have their nineteenth-century radiator covers, and oak panelling in hall and library are probably original, as are several ceilings.

Gertrude had not wanted to move to Berkshire and the fact was bound to colour her receptivity. Writing to Leslie, she explained that while she was 'quite sensible'[11] to Wargrave's beauties, she admired but had 'no sympathy'[12] for the scale. She was unable to adapt because the countryside that had nurtured her creative impulse was intimately woven into her personality. Her assertive nature tended to polarize, things were bad or good, black or white; and what she really missed was Surrey's tangledness. But she was resigned to making the best of things and persistent at forging her future. In only slightly truculent resignation, she flung herself into a new life.

Redecorating the house called for positive enterprise and, happy to encourage their daughter's creative talent, the Captain and Mrs Jekyll gave her a free rein. Francis Jekyll writes of the 'thoroughness which she brought to all her tasks, whether congenial or otherwise'.[13] Chinese screens, pearwood frames, open-work silver pins, and 'Rhodian' earthenware pots were among the projects that occupied her for the remainder of the year. Every wall, door and mantelpiece, her nephew avers, offered scope for some decorative enterprise. Old photographs of the house show five shiny, glazed earthenware pots, presumably similar to ones she had seen in Rhodes, standing about three feet high, four between the columns and one on the terrace below. Another one, planted with yucca and ivy, made a focal point in a garden corner. So well did they suit the bold elevations of the house that they were left standing by successive occupiers until at least the second decade of the twentieth century, long after the Jekylls had left Wargrave.

As in Bramley, the new inhabitants consorted with their more active neighbours. The versatile Hannen family, whose third generation nurtured Nicholas, the talented Shakespearian actor, were summer visitors at Wargrave House. The Hannens joined in amateur theatre to which Gertrude contributed 'cat's head masks' and 'surinam toads' for the drama wardrobe.[14] There were interludes with the Higford Burrs at Aldermaston Court in Reading and visits to Cambridge, where Walter was an undergraduate at Trinity College.

Two years earlier Lady Duff Gordon had found Walter 'one of the nicest Boys I ever saw, so intelligent & well informed & so childlike & full of Boy's sports!'[15] Like Teddy, he was sent to Harrow, but their scholastic record was quite different. While Teddy, in his two years, was placed consistently below the middle of his class, Walter, over four years, came always near the top. In class he was regularly commended and 'copy'[16] was sent to the Head Master. Leaving fairly promptly, he maintained Lady Duff Gordon's faith unimpaired, 'He is *too clever* for his age & can bear no more there!'[17] Walter had been a distinctly unusual and original kind of boy, and not one who would easily be forced into standard moulds. Extraordinary childhood sensitivity can be inferred from a short autobiographical passage he wrote when he was fifty-five concerning 'an awful Sunday book of my childhood which haunts me now'.[18] *The Burning Island* was a hellfire and brimstone tale about a hedonistic race who suffered for their sins on the Day of Judgement, and its moral was rammed home with bluntness that made a lasting impression upon its reader. 'I always identified myself with the lost. How could I hope to escape damnation – for I understood the parable but too well – when it was only the few that were saved? . . . I was the rich man – did I not belong to that well-to-do class of which it was said, How hardly shall a rich man enter into the kingdom of heaven. And children suffer in silence. They never complain. They shut up their agony in their little hearts, accepting it as inevitable.'[19]

Walter was too much of a maverick to be institutionalized, something brother and sister had in common. The difference was that Gertrude never took refuge in the guise of an outsider, whereas school was the beginning of Walter's plight in fitting the pattern prescribed by his family. For the moment, however, the five Jekylls were close; Walter being, for Gertrude, second only to Herbert. At Cambridge she took lodgings on her own, which was unusual for a girl in 1869. A buoyant sense of liberation set a precedent for spontaneous solitary sorties she made for the rest of her life. She and Walter may have punted on the Cam, though Gertrude was averse to 'long awkward river skiffs'.[20] More to her taste was the tub of a row-boat she was lent in Wargrave, which reminded her of the one they had had in Bramley. During her first year in Berkshire, neighbours might often have spied a well-built, astonishingly efficient, bespectacled figure, in expensive, unobtrusive clothes and sensible shoes, tugging at oars with the expertise she fastened on all she undertook, skimming the banks of the Thames in search of wild flowers. Four decades later she wrote, 'Every one who has known the Thames from the intimate point of view of the leisured nature-lover in boat or canoe, must have been struck by the eminent beauty of the native water-side plants.'[21] Another of her books recalls a spongy green weed she encountered when fishing for mussels. 'Of course I wanted to examine it, so I scooped some up on the blade of my oar and got hold of it, and turned it over to see it in all positions, and smelt it.'[22] The 'horrible'[23] smell gave her, at twenty-four, the same sort of horror she had received from barberry as a child.

For ten years Lady Duff Gordon had complained of poor hearing; she was growing older, deafer, and increasingly confined to her room. This did not prevent her being a centre of communication. Sometimes she crept downstairs, otherwise she sat in bed with a trumpet in her 'one (good) ear',[24] conscientiously filling her diary with reports on her faithful children and a stream of visitors. At the end of a bitter January, Alexander accompanied Gertrude and Mrs Jekyll to Miss Burdett-Coutts's box at Drury Lane to see the Christmas pantomime, *Puss in Boots*. In February, Georgy went to Wargrave. In March, Gertrude made another decisive step in her vocation.

Gertrude and Henry James both met William Morris for the first time that March. Gertrude's visit to Bloomsbury's Queen Square elicited only a meagre engagement entry 'to see Mr Morris';[25] James was more explicit. Morris's unconventional exterior, 'short, burly, corpulent, very careless and unfinished in his dress' and his 'very loud voice' belied, James felt, a good commercial instinct, and 'clear good sense'.[26] But behind the bluff exterior, he discerned a nervous and excitable temperament. He was probably right: what is more, behind the Pre-Raphaelite dream of purity and madonna lilies lay endless complications. Beautiful Mary Zambaco had attempted to commit suicide in a histrionic bid for Edward Burne-Jones's attentions and Morris had prepared to rush off to the Continent with his friend.

Morris's own wife, Janey, was pulling away from him on a pretext of ill health while he was drawn increasingly to Georgiana Burne-Jones. To distract himself from a chaotic love life and the worries in the firm, Morris was writing his mammoth Medievalistic saga, *Earthly Paradise*.

The obvious link between William Morris and Gertrude Jekyll was Ruskin. Morris described *The Stones of Venice* as 'one of the very few necessary and inevitable utterances of the century',[27] and the eulogy it contained for medieval crafts and guilds was central to the ethos of the firm: 'In each several profession, no master should be too proud to do its hardest work.'[28] They were in some ways much alike. Morris worked obsessively, his only respite from one activity being another sort of work. Henry James called poetry 'his sub-trade', everything he manufactured 'quaint, archaic, Pre-Raphaelite', 'exquisite' and 'of the very last luxury'.[29] He designed, moreover, 'with his own head and hands all the figures and patterns used in his glass and tapestry, that is, embroidery, and furthermore works the latter, stitch by stitch, with his own fingers'.[30]

There is no evidence that Morris had anything but respect for the female sex. From the start women were actively involved in his firm, most of them family or friends. Morris's daughters, wife, and her sister; Charles Faulkner's sisters and Georgiana Burne-Jones were in the forefront of the movement. The odd thing is that even May Morris, the daughter who supervised the embroidery section (a traditional 'feminine' branch of the crafts) does not seem to have been paid for her work. The only women who received wages were countless employees producing the bulk of the firm's embroideries. Thus there was a fairly strong form of discrimination in an establishment with radical social aims. Morris was not likely to have warmed to Gertrude's femininity. Neither her mind nor her appearance fitted the Pre-Raphaelite ideals – clouds of hair, preferably red, large grey eyes, a swan-like neck and pallid complexion. There is no doubt about her interest in Morris's work; many years later she wrote of the 'enormous influence he has had in the education of public taste'.[31] Did Morris, though, recognize in her someone with talents and abilities similar to his own? What made Gertrude conspicuously odd man out in the Arts and Crafts was her aloofness from the emphasis on the innate ability of the working man, the wider intimacies of family and brotherhood, the conviviality that was such an important part of the movement in Britain.

There is a parallel in William Morris' and Gertrude Jekyll's failures

to produce significant work as painters. Both had laboured conscientiously; George Leslie felt that but for her eyesight, painting would
have been Gertrude's greatest talent and Ruskin made his tantalizing,
albeit inconclusive, remark about a single canvas, yet like Morris she
was unable to depict figures. Both she and Herbert were adept at
copying Old Masters and she herself attributed giving up painting to
the deterioration in her eyesight. On the other hand, even Lady Duff
Gordon, who thought highly of her ability to copy and record, hoped
'she will range into a higher line'[32] and the idea that poor eyesight
caused Gertrude to renounce painting for crafts and gardening has to
be set against her mother's aside to Herbert in 1874, that between the
attractions of music, metal work and nature, she was giving rather less
time to painting than her parents could wish. The last three paintings
Gertrude exhibited sound, from their titles, more like humorous
illustrations than serious art: *Froggy Would a Wooing Go, Mr Punch's
Dog Toby* and *Portrait of Thomas, a Favourite Cat in the Character of
Puss-in-Boots*. The very fact that she turned to craft, moreover, suggests
that her commitment to painting was less than total. Crafts were
allowed to absorb an increasing proportion of her time. One cannot
help suspecting that this is because she was a better designer and
craftswoman than painter.

Leslie, fellow river-dabbler and artist, was completely stunned by
Wargrave's new inhabitant. His mother had moved to Henley in the
summer of 1869, shortly before his brother-in-law, William Smith,
bought an attractive cottage ornée in Wargrave from the novelist
Henry Kingsley. Henley became the artist's river headquarters, but
deep water and a muddy bottom precluded good punting. At Wargrave the punting was superb; therein lay the initial lure. But Wargrave
itself soon tempted him. Through William Smith he met Gertrude,
and here, he felt immediately, was a unique, irreplaceable being.
'Clever', 'witty', 'active', 'energetic' and 'singular', she 'would at all
times have shone conspicuously bright amongst other ladies'.[33] Not
only was her artistic talent, in his opinion, remarkable, but the crafts
she had mastered included carving, modelling, house-painting, carpentry, smith's work, repoussé work, gilding, wood-inlaying, embroidery
and gardening. Before long she could add sign-painting to her accom-
plishments. Several of her signs, hung in the neighbourhood, inspired
Leslie to try his own hand, and when he repainted Wargrave's *George
and Dragon*, she lent him a large pot of white lead. Since Leslie was also

a writer, the combination of integrity and drive which he saw in his new acquaintance has been chronicled.

Later in the year, Georgy and Alice sat to the fashionable sculptor J. B. Phillip, better known for carving eighty-seven figures on the podium of the Albert Memorial.[34] Gertrude enjoyed their more purposeful encounters but did far less ritual socializing. Creating a routine imbued with real and important purpose required continual discipline, and instinctively she recoiled from frittering time. Her scale of priorities remained adamant.

In London, Gertrude was pursuing her studies and extending social contacts; 'something of a phenomenon'[1] – a single or 'bachelor girl'.[2] Idleness thrust upon women by the Industrial Revolution was augmented by society's unwritten sentiments. Few professions were open to them, all but marriage regarded as unwomanly and ungenteel. But either way, there was a trap. In marriage, Sir William Blackstone had written in 1865, 'the very being or legal existence of a woman is suspended, or at least it is incorporated and consolidated into that of the husband under whose wing, protection and cover she performs everything'.[3]

The problem was being challenged. Nine years earlier, John Stuart Mill had written on women's exclusion from the electoral role, 'I have taken no account of difference of sex. I consider it to be as entirely irrelevant to political rights, as difference in height, or in the colour of the hair.'[4] Yet there was no concession to the fact that women in Great Britain outnumbered men by nearly a million. Goodness knows how impecunious spinsters were expected to survive. Society continued to imply that it was right and proper to come and go with a man, to be looked after and protected, to be two. Shy of courting physical attention, Gertrude must have hated being conspicuous. In no way does such speculation affect her achievement, but it does explain the struggle in herself for artistic integrity when so much was forbidden by contemporary culture. Even when women worked, their calling was supposed to reflect their limited feminine capabilities.

Carry Eden was finding a niche without breaking conventions. Frederick had had a childhood accident and did not enjoy good health. Lady Duff Gordon had remarked earlier on her 'always sick Husband',[5] now he was 'much the same'.[6] Before the end of the year the couple had moved to Palazzo Barbarigo in the glamorous setting of Venice's Grand Canal. 'No noise, no flies, no dust,'[7] Frederick remarked prosaically. Carry was, like her mother, a tireless hostess and the wonderful setting gave her an opportunity for exercising her Jekyll capability. Soon tired of idling, her husband bought and began to cultivate a six-acre garden on the Guidecca that formed the great work of their lives.

There was more news from the family. Teddy was a keen sportsman. On one of his hunting expeditions in the Black Forest he had met, and now he married, Baroness Theresa, daughter of Baron von Biel of Zierow, Mecklenburg-Schwerin. It is not known what pulled him from the Surrey base to the village of Tingrith south of Ampthill in Bedfordshire, but there were German connections among his neighbours, one of whom, his greatest friend, Sir Anthony Wingfield of Ampthill House, had a number of German aristocrats staying with him from time to time.

Herbert too was making changes. When he was twenty his aunt had predicted, 'He will be a very remarkable Person some day – he is so clear headed, hardworking and so right-hearted and full of consideration for his Father.'[8] There were many paths Herbert might have taken and for some reason he abandoned hopes of becoming an architect. All his education was at the Royal Military Academy in Woolwich, so perhaps it was easier to move into the army. For the past two and a half years he had been a lieutenant sapper on submarine explosives. But he shared his father's fascination for the mechanical world and was 'immensely employed in studying engineering in all its branches'.[9] Lady Duff Gordon reckoned this 'shining extra intelligence'[10] had been rewarded. News had just come through of his promotion as an officer in the Telegraph Company of the Royal Engineers. Never before had so coveted a position been offered to anyone so young and inexperienced.

London found Gertrude in the National Gallery, copying Dutch and Italian masterpieces and Turner's great Venetian scenes. 'An artist's time and power of mind are lost chiefly in deciding what to do,' Ruskin noted adroitly, 'and in effacing what he has done: it is anxiety that fatigues him, not difficulty.'[11] It was wisdom on which she resolutely styled her life. At Wargrave her workshop was a model of discipline and method, the tools all arranged in order and scrupulously kept. There, she cut and measured, testing the 'lovable quality'[12] of implements that enabled 'the hand to obey the brain',[13] taking 'much pleasure in working and seeing things grow under my hand'.[14] There was a steady output of bellows and fans, 'much drawing, carving and gilding'.[15] At some point she had mastered the art of using a blow pipe for soldering gold and silver, a technique that involved maintaining a stream of air in the pipe while inhaling. Not even her instructor could manage it, but with perseverance she caught the trick. 'What a joy it is, after much trying, to catch the trick of a tool!'[16] Her parents understood this desire to create, waiting and watching the busy workmanlike preoccupations of their independent, self-motivated and single-minded daughter.

Provided her freedom and solitude were acknowledged, Gertrude was game to take part in family and village life. On 22 April and the following day, two concerts took place at Wargrave Hill to raise funds for repairs to the organ at St Mary's. The full programme was written up and thanks duly accorded in the parish magazine. 'It would be an impertinence to offer any remarks upon the music and the admirable manner in which these Concerts were prepared. Suffice it to say that the Parishioners are very grateful to Mr and Mrs Jekyll and their family for the kind trouble they have Taken.'[17] Twenty-one pounds gathered amply covered church debts. One must add here that the church was burned to the ground by suffragettes in 1914 and afterwards rebuilt.

Old country and village traditions lent meaning, variety and local colour, intriguing Gertrude almost as much as did old crafts. It was customary throughout April for the children of Wargrave to canvass the occupants of wealthier houses for second-hand clothes to wear during May Day celebrations. But the previous year – a particularly cold one – several youngsters recovering from measles had been out all day in skimpy muslin dresses. The whole event had become something of a trial to the adult population. There was obviously scope for improvement, which Gertrude, who was excellent at organizing, undertook to establish. No more raggle-taggle children in 'scraps of dirty finery';[18] henceforth, donations would be restricted to ribbons for tying nosegays. Participants would rally at a central spot carrying hoops of flowers hung round white willow sticks, twelve schoolgirls would bear a trophy and the procession would visit each house in turn. Preparedness was the key to success. Garlands and trophies would be made in advance, the money-box for collections safely locked and the school band would provide accompaniment.

As the palest silvery green leaves patterned the willow trees beside the river, Gertrude fashioned the 'May-day trophy'. Many years later, she was to describe in a gardening book for children, how the 'dear girls at the vicarage'[19] assisted her in making the centrepiece from willow and wild flowers. An illustration shows a gaudy affair of leaves and flowery bunting, constructed and raised on a frame of light poles. Moss was bound around bare wood, and laurel twigs twisted into heavy swags before the flowers – cowslips, primroses, daffodils, snowflakes, bluebells and flowering currant – were threaded into multicoloured ropes for a regal-looking canopy. 'But the glory of the trophy was the great Cowslip ball that hung in the middle.'[20] The ball took three days to assemble and a vast amount of work.

Photographs of little girls that sprinkle the pages of one of Gertrude's books belie the fact that children were always deeply in awe of her. For Gertrude expected high standards, both from others and herself. Without apparent effort, through the force of her definite, spectacled and powerful presence, she governed proceedings. The village children earned 'quantities of pennies'[21] and three years afterwards the parish magazine reckoned that the new arrangements had been an 'entire success'.[22] Georgy Duff Gordon, who was sitting at the window of her room at Wargrave Hill, 'answer[ing]'[23] the nightingales, was delighted that 'the old time of keeping May Day continues',[24] with children 'singing', 'flowering'[25] and dancing round a hop pole. Her mother had no idea that 'such good rustic amusements continued'.[26] Gertrude's May Day arrangements became one of her most enduring personal contributions to the village. In the last decade of the twentieth century, crowning a May Queen and maypole dancing take place each year at Wargrave Piggott Junior School.

Another local project she was involved with was building a small roofed enclosure over a public spring. Rebecca's Well, known then as Phillimore's Spring, stands close to the high or main road leading from Wargrave through a tiny hamlet called Crazies Hill. A muddy bridle path climbs steeply into the woods behind the village, and some 100 yards in, a strange decorated building of brick, tile and pebble-dash looms between the trees. Only a shallow basin protected the spring head prior to 1870, and in the summer, despite frequent cleaning, a mass of green algae coated the water. 'To obviate this, the spring has been sheltered from the sun, by an erection, that it is hoped, will satisfy at once the "taste" of the cottagers immediately interested in its purity, and of the critics – harder to please – who will expect also something like beauty and propriety.'[27] The spring was named after the former curate of the parish, the Rev. Greville Phillimore, who built the foundation with its cross, biblical text, and Chaucerian verse. Phillimore's work was untouched, the parish magazine informed; Miss Jekyll's was merely superimposed, at the cost of £15. 'The design and whole trouble of . . . the present work'[28] were entirely hers.

A note of progress made four years later gives the previous rector combined credit for the spring's 'restoration', yet the parish magazine makes it sound as if Gertrude constructed walls and roof unaided. The Rev. Phillimore's inscriptions on the dome-like back of the brickwork must have been part of the early work but the date below the painting in the brick gable is 1870, and the fresco, *Rebara and the Servants of Abraham at the Well of Mahor*, though three times repainted, was originally by Gertrude. Planting round the spring engaged her throughout the winter months and into the following year. Several times she returned to embellish the site with naturalistic broom and furze.

Mrs Jekyll brought flowers from the country to Lady Duff Gordon, who would soon be eighty-one and felt 'My days must be numbered!'[29] Lamenting the loss of friends but still keeping the diary that is vibrant with personality, she recorded Charles Dickens had died and Georgy was at Wargrave Hill. War had been declared between France and Prussia. One by one, German states joined in until the whole of France and Germany were involved. Gertrude found herself an active member of work parties, collecting and tearing up old linen for French hospitals.

Since her visit to the Morris workshop the previous year she had been concentrating on textiles and embroideries. Needlework was an obvious outlet for her talent. At South Kensington Art School she was exposed to the influence of plant-inspired fabric designs by Christopher Dresser and Owen Jones, but from the evidence of photographs, patterns and embroideries still around, her designs were more fluid and more united than those of her teachers, closer in fact to those of William Morris. It was at an exhibition with the London International Exhibition Society in New Bond Street that Fred Leighton, home from a year's journeyings by steamer up the Nile, saw a sample of her work and was immediately struck by its 'remarkable merit in point of colour and arrangement'.[30] One design with scrolls of fishes was 'so good as decorative invention'[31] that he hesitated to attribute it to an amateur, he told Georgy Duff Gordon, to whom he wrote in hopes of obtaining something similar for himself. Uneasy about approaching Gertrude directly because she was 'a lady of independent means',[32] he was using his old friend as an intermediary. Did Miss Jekyll embroider 'solely for her delight'[33] or was her work for sale? If so, what would be the price? Encouraged by the reply, Leighton wrote again, with specific suggestions. A table-cloth for his dining room should be of 'some good design and rich tone'[34] executed in 'serge and wool, or wool and silk, about six and a half feet or seven square'.[35] Tact was required, he impressed, for it was 'a very delicate matter to ask such a question of a lady'.[36] A happy outcome was confirmed by Gertrude's note in the winter of 1870, 'Began Mr Leighton's table-cloth.'[37] According to the inventories at Leighton House, the cloth or table-throw incorporated pomegranates in its design. It is no longer at the museum, though two small panels also listed in the inventory have been discovered beneath a later cover of a seat on the staircase. The design is a rhythmic undulation of flowers and leaves in autumnal shades of brown, ochre, rust and lavender, very faded, but recognizable in blending colours, with vigorous long and short stitches, changing direction to catch the light and enhance the three-dimensional quality. 'When I pointed out that the delicate embroidery in colour silks was not suited for bearing the usual treatment of a chair-seat,' Gertrude wrote, 'he [Lord Leighton] gave me the comforting answer: "Never mind, nothing but my eye will ever sit upon those chairs."'[38]

Before mid-November she had made a weathercock for a house at High Wycombe and painted some elm bowls with 'peg-top legs'.[39] In London she called on two artists, Albert Moore and Frederick Walker, and visited galleries with Mrs Poynter. Moore was a decorative figure painter, Walker a talented thirty-year-old illustrator who belonged, with George Leslie, to the St John's Wood clique. He had begun to paint poetic pastoral watercolours; Ruskin disapproved of his 'galvanized-Elgin' figures, but romantic scenes, similar to those of Birket Foster, were already popular. Agnes Poynter was the sister of Georgiana Burne-Jones, and Alice the future mother of Rudyard Kipling. 'The good-looking one of the family'[40] married Edward Poynter, 'that grave and industrious man'.[41] Poynter rose from Slade Professor to Director of the National Gallery, eventually following Leighton as President of the Royal Academy. He was successful and self-important.

Gertrude was making such a point of extending contacts and keeping up with family friends that one knows she positively enjoyed people. The feeling, moreover, seems to have been mutual. London appointments interrupting two months of intensive craftwork at the end of the year were with Leslie, Newton, Seymour Haden and Godfrey Webb. Like the Jekylls, the Webbs moved in 'county' circles and Gertrude's parents must have known Robert, 'the typical English squire' [42] of Milford House near Godalming, whose wife, Barbara, was to play an important part in young Lutyens's life. Godfrey, the unmarried brother, was the sort of man who makes excellent company for a single girl: a good shot, easy wit and superb entertainer, a favourite with the younger set in quasi-artistic country houses. He was idle, though an expert Shakespearian and an expert ornithologist. Haden was a newcomer, a prestigious surgeon who had spent his evenings at art schools while studying medicine at the Sorbonne. In mid-life he took up etching seriously, married Whistler's half-sister and founded the Society of Painter Etchers. Eventually he was knighted for his services to art.

Stimulated by her artistic communications, Gertrude turned out gilt bowls, Venetian ironwork links, plated iron and brass, more bellows, rush-seated chairs, a large tobacco jar, a table with legs of cotton reels and several pieces of embroidery. Needlework probably offered most scope for her talent of all her craft-related skills. In 1870 she completed a set of cushion-covers with designs of dandelion, mistletoe, pomegranate and strawberry. Unfortunately they no longer exist, but the periwinkle and iris she worked next were used to illustrate a *Handbook of Embroidery* published ten years later by the Royal School of Art-Needlework. The School was founded in 1872 with twin aims of employing women for useful occupation and raising the standard of ornamental embroidery. The manual was compiled by L. Higgin, edited by Lady Marian Alford, chairman of the Council, and since it included a section of patterns, served simultaneously as text-book and catalogue. There are designs for bedspreads, table-covers, curtains and wall-hangings; prospective purchasers could either buy material traced with a stencil or the finished article made up by an experienced 'Gentlewoman' embroiderer. The cost of materials for a cushion-cover made to Gertrude's design was between 7s 6d and a guinea; embroidered they sold for between two and five guineas. Illustrations of her designs accompany those of artists like Edward Burne-Jones, Walter Crane, George Aitchison, William Morris and Fairfax Wade, and with any they compare favourably. Her naturalism is closely observed, her line fluid and pleasing, her use of space unforced.

Since the Victorians thought it vulgar for women to work, only working-class women did so. Three-quarters of the way through the nineteenth century, leisure was a sign of success, anything more than pin-money demeaning to a girl of gentle birth and humiliating to the males whose role was to provide. What motive for earning could she possibly have? That someone should countenance trying to support herself as a matter of achieving self-respect was barely conceivable. It was a situation that weighed heavily against Gertrude, one she chose to meet by calling herself an amateur. Amateur status was used as an argument against paying women properly, but this did not worry her. Ambition was, after all, a little difficult to acknowledge. Gertrude was worldly and money-conscious. What she received for commissions was of the utmost importance to her, but being the daughter of a wealthy man, she did not need to earn a living, and never asked as much as she might have. Acknowledgement and prestige were what counted. In every other sense she was a consummate professional and, like so many successful artists, she seems to have had natural business sense. It is clear, for instance, that she was constantly trying to find outlets for her work. Her network of friends was a start; exhibitions were also important.

A commission might require several visits to establish its precise nature, and the early months of 1871 find her visiting Frank Buckland, inspector of salmon fisheries, at the South Kensington Museum, an extraordinary naturalist who served his guests with mice on toast and stewed rhinoceros. It is doubtful whether Buckland's insatiable and unconventional pursuit of natural history would have appealed to Frederick Eden, but he may have been known to Gertrude's brother-in-law. For Gertrude, however, versatility was a high recommendation and she always cherished the acquaintance of people who knew about things. Starting out as a surgeon, Buckland had been drawn to the great eighteenth-century anatomist John Hunter and, like him, the younger man had studied abnormal zoology. Later in life he became a prolific writer. When Gertrude met him, Buckland was establishing a huge collection of fish-hatching apparatus, models and fishing implements. It was to be the first collection of pisciculture, expanded two years later into the International Fisheries Exhibition, and she contributed painted casts of fish.

The previous month Gertrude had met Simeon Solomon, a brilliant and precocious artist, only thirty-one but already well past the height of his talent. Solomon illustrated books for Swinburne, and as Joan Edwards suggests in Tooley's collected essays, Gertrude may have been considering illustration herself. It is difficult to guess what else she and Solomon might have had in common. While Gertrude was drawn towards fellow eccentrics, they tended to be assertive and successful. She might dip privately into her own problems but she faced life without self-pity and never had much time for lame ducks. Solomon was arrested for homosexual offences some months later. Deserted by his friends, he became a complete social outcast.

An April week in Hertford Street is a good guide to Gertrude's pace and energy. The first day, after dining with Caroline Hammersley, she went to the opera; the following evening, after a full day with Georgy at the British Museum, she saw a French play. To *The Magic Flute*, another French play, and back again to *The Magic Flute*; thus she continued for seven days, with engagements all day and every night. In June, at Wargrave Hill, she interrupted the familiar workload – iron-stands, brass plating, chairs and bellows – to set up an easel in the garden and paint her borders. Plants and gardens had been instilled in her youth, and played a prominent part in her designs. Throughout her most intensive years of studio craftwork, Gertrude had continued to love, look at and grow plants. It was her fourth summer in Berkshire and she had made a garden worth painting.

A book had recently been published by a young professional horticulturist with whose Ruskinian thesis she entirely concurred. In *The Wild Garden*, William Robinson decried the insensitive, flashy and expensive bedding system responsible for the demise of hardy plants, advocating instead the naturalization of native and exotic plants from the temperate regions in fields, woods and copses and neglected places as well as in almost every kind of park and garden. Wild flowers were being idealized by the Pre-Raphaelite painters and studied by botanizing ladies, while others had extolled the benefits of hardy plants. But Robinson channelled the romance into gardening. The climate was perfect for such a book. With its sympathy for 'half-wild places'[43] and 'a pretty plant in the wild state',[44] the new book created a tremendous stir.

George Leslie wrote of Gertrude's expertise in 'all manner of herb and flower knowledge and culture'.[45] But it is an entry in her engagement book that expresses her absorption most clearly. 'Much interested in garden plants – always collecting.'[46] Gertrude Jekyll did not, as legend suggests, somewhere in mid-life exchange her paintbrush for a spade. At twenty-seven she was perusing cottage gardens, returning home laden with seeds and cuttings. This is when she began to cultivate, compare and assess plants. If gardening shared her time with beating out silver spoons and painting murals, it does not in any way denigrate the quality of the former.

Muddled and eclectic styles revealed at the 1851 International Exhibition had provoked various attempts to introduce a new, 'modern' spirit in design. Gertrude's interest in interior decoration seems to have been aroused by 1867, when she went to Dorchester House with Georgina Duff Gordon to copy illustrations from relevant books, and within five years she was busy in the homes of a widening circle of clients.

Almost any social activity might open up opportunities, and one of the chief events of her previous year had been an introduction to Jacques and Leonie Blumenthal of 43 Hyde Park Gate. 'Monsieur', a composer whose song collections were popular in the nineteenth century, had been a teacher and court pianist to Queen Victoria; 'Madame' was a well-known London hostess, 'unusually gifted in all manner of minor arts'.[1] The Blumenthals obviously felt that Gertrude was legitimate. Their circle, including a fair proportion of single men and women, was establishment without being stuffy – Lutyens once said that Madame 'Blumie', as he called her, was 'apt to disappear in the attics to cut her toenails and doesn't hear the bell'[2] – pioneering, but not trendy; and their home overlooking Kensington Gardens became somewhere to meet artists and musicians. Most important to Gertrude, they were people among whom she felt at ease. All her life she set great store by friendship, in particular the friendship of people whose minds struck her as being original. Much has been made of her reclusiveness by those who knew her late life and this was genuine, but it is important to stress that her drive evoked much admiration, she was a good and humorous conversationalist, always what Lutyens called 'worldly', and provided people were not intimidated, they found her stimulating. At Hyde Park Gate the pleasure was mutual. It was not long before she was invited to the retreat for Monsieur and Madame's most carefully selected friends and protégés, a Swiss chalet near Montreux.

It is surprising how many of Gertrude's new acquaintances were willing to accept her services: HRH Princess Louise, daughter of Queen Victoria, the Duke of Westminster, the Blumenthals themselves and Hercules Brabazon. 'Braby' was almost old enough to be her father, wealthy, talented though self-deprecatory; eminently engaging; alternately gregarious and self-contained: an odd mixture of artist, intellectual and boy scout. John Singer Sargent's portrait of him shows a finely structured head, cerebral forehead, heavy eyebrows, moustache, side whiskers and clean-shaven chin. He was tall and thin, bird-like, eager, mischievous and adventurous. Eileen Barber, Brabazon's great-great-niece, who often heard her grandmother speak of him, said, 'Gertrude adored him.'[3] Indeed, credit must go to Gertrude and to Herbert for recognizing Brabazon's gifts when he was still virtually unknown. Perhaps Brabazon too deserves credit, for asking Gertrude to paint a bay window in his music room with green and gold pomegranates.

At public school Brabazon had been very unhappy, though he went on to graduate from Cambridge with an honours degree in mathematics. Studying art in Rome cost him his father's favour and with it a sizeable allowance. But singlemindedness was rewarded, for at this juncture he inherited the fortune which assured him independence. There was no need for him to sell his work; painting was a challenge to his skill and an outlet for his imagination; that was enough. When he felt like it, he painted, in watercolour, without commissions, easel or studio. From time to time he set off for long treks with a compact paintbox, sketch pads and a small bag of clothes, visiting art museums all over the Continent, painting whatever attracted him on the way. He could not say his 'r's' properly, an idiosyncrasy he drew attention to by decrying 'scweaming pwimawy colou(r)s'.[4]

For Gertrude, Brabazon's music was another attraction. He was sufficiently proficient as a pianist to give recitals in his rooms at 5 Pall Mall. At Oaklands in Sedlescombe, not far from the East Sussex coast, his style of entertainment was more relaxed. 'Eight hands on two pianos would be going for hours, the floor of the room would be littered with scores of operas.'[5] Gertrude caricatured her host's enthusiastic attitude as he edged his concert partner towards the end of the piano. But like much of her work, the drawing has disappeared since Francis Jekyll described it. Not until he was seventy-one was Brabazon persuaded to hold an exhibition, and his reception was euphoric.

Gertrude, then deeply immersed in flower gardens, wrote to congratulate him from Munstead. He replied, 'Now that I have made a name in the Art World I shall always think of and shall never forget that I received my first encouragement and my first praises from you and dear Madame Bodichon.'⁶ Gertrude was, as she often acknowledged, equally indebted to him.

At Hertford Street there was a crisis and the Jekylls rallied round, doing what they could. Gentle Alexander Duff Gordon had returned from New York feeling desperately unwell. In October 1872, after a protracted and painful illness, he died, aged sixty-one, from cancer of tongue and throat. His mother's diaries chronicle a death no less shattering for being expected. To distract her, the Captain forwarded letters from Walter and Gertrude, passing through Milan to stay with the Edens in Venice. It was almost twenty years since Ruskin had written his seminal and provocative work on the city, and in no small part was *Stones of Venice* responsible for the flood of visiting English. Gertrude possessed his works, which must have coloured this first visit to his beloved city. Herbert, being in London, dropped round several times at Number 34 to help Alice sort out Alexander's pictures and Gertrude paid her respects the minute she returned. Lady Duff Gordon thought her latest batch of old masters' copies 'Wonderfully good as to drawing – to colouring and exactness of countenances etc.'⁷

Interchange between the families recommenced the following spring, when Gertrude and Walter slept for five nights in Alice's spare bedroom and Gertrude 'tired herself'⁸ visiting galleries – a rare event. She and Georgy saw the horticultural garden, then Gertrude met Thomas Armstrong, a painter who produced several decorative schemes for interiors, and William de Morgan, master of tiles. De Morgan had been inspired by Morris to manufacture stained glass, pottery, and ceramics with all the idealistic devotion of a genuine Pre-Raphaelite. It was the year he established his first factory at Chelsea, where he was principal designer and a brilliant kiln technician. Working independently, he supplied the Morris firm.

It was through Brabazon that Gertrude met Barbara Bodichon, although she was also a cousin of William Smith from Wargrave. D. G. Rossetti had described Barbara bluntly as a young lady 'blessed with large rations of tin, fat, enthusiasm, and golden hair'.⁹ Presently forty-five to Gertrude's twenty-nine, she was probably the strongest and most effective of all her women friends. Barbara's family, the

Leigh Smiths, were wealthy, with a strong pioneering inheritance, Florence Nightingale and Hilary Bonham-Carter being first cousins, and her brother an Arctic explorer. Unlike Gertrude, who paid lip-service to convention, Barbara remained impervious to outsiders' opinions. But the two had much in common. Barbara had a close and formative relationship with her father, Liberal MP for Norwich with advanced views on education and women's rights.

Childhood had been boisterous, much of it spent out of doors, and her artistic aptitude was encouraged by being taken to meet Turner in his studio. She studied with William Hunt the elder and later took herself to art school. From this time, Barbara's biggest dilemma was the sheer number of her interests and abilities. Art was always important: she studied with Corot, painted with Daubigny and exhibited nearly 300 watercolours, mostly landscapes, over thirty years. But art, philanthropy and politics competed for her time: it was a problem she never really managed to solve. Gertrude must have admired Barbara's painting, because six framed watercolours and an oil by her fellow artist were hung at Munstead Wood. There are more of them on the walls of Girton, yet it is for her contribution to the Women's Movement that Barbara is remembered first.

By the time the two met, Barbara had helped to establish a mixed community school, played a substantial role in the inauguration of the Women's Movement and built Scalands, in a Sussex pine-wood near Robertsbridge, in the style of a local cottage. Finally she married a farouche Frenchman, a surgeon who had settled in Algeria. Her marriage to Eugène Bodichon perplexed her friends. After all, she had once described wedlock as a state by which a woman passed 'from freedom into the condition of a slave'.[10] They were no conventional couple. Dr Bodichon turned up to London parties accompanied by a bevy of sheiks in full native regalia, and in Sussex he sat on pine needles wearing Arab dress, explaining in broken English to his wife's puzzled relations, 'My ancestors lived in woods, and I like to live in a wood.'[11]

Each year the Bodichons spent the winter in Algiers, the summer in England, where Barbara, a generous if demanding friend, entertained, among a great many others, the novelist George Eliot, the early Pre-Raphaelite painter, D. G. Rossetti, his wife, and the poet William Allingham. In Algiers she got out her paintbox, but she could never for long resist the lure of new radical ventures. Eighteen fifty-seven found her watching slaves being sold from a market in New Orleans. In 1872 she was drawing up plans to build, on two acres of land outside Cambridge, the first women's college to award degrees. Without sharing her opinions, it would have been impossible to spend much time with her. Gertrude did not, like her friend, visit the world's trouble spots, but there is no more overt sign of her sympathy with women's rights than two huge banners she designed and embroidered for the Godalming and Guildford branches of the National Association of Women's Suffragette Societies.

London was a positive way of varying the routine, but prompted by her new friends, Gertrude prepared for a much bigger adventure. In mid-September, shortly before her thirtieth birthday, she set out for what was to be the longest excursion of her life: five and a half months, stopping at the Blumenthals' chalet overlooking Lake Geneva, then travelling by train through Turin, Genoa and the Riviera down to Marseilles. From there it was but a short trip across the sea to join the Bodichons on the outskirts of Algiers.

The eastern shores of Lake Geneva were a playground for rich English during the last decades of the nineteenth century. It was an exodus that may well have been encouraged by Ruskin's rhapsodies on mountain scenery in the fourth volume of *Modern Painters*. Jacques Blumenthal must have known the dramatic site beside the road that climbs steeply from Montreux to Les Avants, and between 1868 and 1888 he purchased five pieces of land. Chalet de Sonzier, or Chalet Blumenthal as it was known locally, was built in 1869 on a platform carved from deciduous woods on the south side of a hill. South and west, views overlook the lake; south-east, the valley of Sonzier; and eastwards, September mists lift to reveal the magnificent, rugged, snow-capped peaks of Rocher de Naye. The dwelling is a somewhat anglicized version of a Swiss chalet, deceptive from the outside as to size and elegance. Balconies run along north and south elevations, above which there remain a few samples of the green and white ceramic tiles that covered the top third of the building. It is not impossible to imagine now, what was actually a formal bourgeois residence. The semi-basement storey was entirely kitchen quarters, the ground floor still has an enormous sitting-room, its original parquet floor inlaid with ebony and satinwood, and a finely carved wooden stairway rises two floors through ten large bedrooms with a bathroom apiece. Stables and servants' quarters have been rebuilt into a separate dwelling. The Blumenthals' glasshouse, woodshed and hayloft have gone and various stoneworks have been erected in front of the house, but the magic of the place with its lake, trees and mountains is untouchable.

Gertrude's introduction to the Chalet was in the company of Hercules Brabazon, Princess Louise, with an accompanying maid, travelling under the name of Lady Sundridge, Mrs Blumenthal's aunt, Mrs O'Connell, and someone called Miss Hervey. There was Mr de Walkoff, a Russian 'of journey fame',[12] Lionel Benson, a gifted amateur madrigal singer, and Walter Jekyll, recently graduated, and considering entering the church. Despite uncertain weather, they sketched, gardened and walked in flowery meadows before settling to evenings of improvised music and drama. Gertrude's occupations on a typical day were 'Drawing in garden, embroidery, Mr B. teaching me harmony'.[13] She was, she wrote home to her parents, quite bewildered by all there was to do and see.

It was two years since Princess Louise had married the Marquis of Lorne, and soon after, her uncle, the Duke of Westminster, had introduced her to the Blumenthals. The Marquis assured the Queen that his wife's 'dignity of manner, which is great, will always protect her from snobbish familiarity'.[14] In fact, she was a talented artist with interests in women's education and spent much of the time trying to avoid Royal protocol. Numbers at the Chalet had been limited so that she could relax and enjoy 'games and surprises'.[15] 'There is no formality of any sort, so we are all a most pleasant party,'[16] Brabazon wrote to his sister, with a low-key allusion to their Royal visitor. Using nicknames increased familiarity. Princess Louise was known as 'Hoheit' and Gertrude, 'Stiegel', from her host's pronunciation of 'Jekyll'. The atmosphere was relaxed, high-spirited, articulate and curiously innocent. Brabazon, a friend opined, 'loves young men and fathers them'.[17] The number of unmarried males from the decorative arts suggests that homosexuality, like eccentricity, was tacitly tolerated, but overt sexual behaviour was not even considered. It is this that gives surviving vignettes a certain prep-school jollity.

References to Gertrude invariably invoke horticultural exploits. One example is a verse by her brother.

> I know a house of great delight
> Perch'd upon Sonziers firclad height

Where jokes are rife from morn till night
                        The Chalet.

To great and good is also there,
To mend – and write bills of fare,
Mount hills and fetch the maidenhair,
                        The Stiegel.

Another is by Lionel Benson:

Miss Jekyll
Went up a hill
To fetch a flower she sought there.
The price in town is half a crown
For each like root she bought there.[18]

Sometimes sketching was serious, but not always. A couple of drawings that ended up among Brabazon's papers include caricatures by Lionel Benson of Gertrude, squat, booted and round-shouldered, carrying a vast pick-axe, dragging a collecting trolley up a mountain. In its sequel she lies prostrate over the summit, plucking an alpine flower.

After the high, convivial tone of the Chalet, some aspects of Algeria may have appeared unsavoury. But if social conditions produced effects on Gertrude 'not altogether salutary',[19] she was excited by the local flora and by Algerian art. It is not so surprising that a cultured Englishwoman should find herself in North Africa during the winter of 1873: the climate compares favourably with London, the scenery is arresting and Arab culture was enticingly bizarre. 'It is really one of the most intoxicating places under the sun,'[20] Barbara Leigh Smith had decided on her first visit seventeen years before. Algeria has always been a country of contrasts: colour and warmth offset by squalor and lack of hygiene, winds, rain, dust and desert sand. Once it became fashionable, boatloads of consumptives were sent out on the advice of the European medical profession, and patients who failed to die of malaria or cholera were inspirited by the rag-bag of colour and glamour, Koran chanting and wavering prayer calls.

Carthaginians, Romans, Vandals, Arabs, Turks and French had successively plundered; the Algerian heritage was bloody but rich in art. Gertrude was familiar with Oriental design. Owen Jones, Professor of Ornamental Art at South Kensington, had been famous for his researches on Moorish ornament, de Morgan was inspired by historic

Lionel Benson's sketches of Gertrude Jekyll, from Brabazon's scrapbook.

Islamic sources, and her Aegean trip with the Newtons had already exposed her to the genre. Ever one to exploit an opportunity, she employed Mr George Cayley, an artist and teacher, to give her an intensive course on Arab decoration. Much of the time she spent sketching and copying designs from dresses, embroidery and tiles; some of the tiles, she noticed, were of Dutch origin, brought to Algiers in vessels captured by Barbary pirates.

In botany the expert was M. Durando, professor from the University of Algiers, who circulated detailed itineraries of prospective walks: 'Le rendezvous est à 6 heures 1/2 du matin ... on récoltera les plantes suivantes ...' The place was 'a paradise for flower-rambles, among giant Fennels and tiny orange marigolds'.[21] Rambles took place along silver shores of the Mediterranean and among hills wooded with olive and cork oak trees. Anyone who has read in *Wood and Garden* Gertrude's eulogy on the blue *Iris stylosa* (*unguicularis*) will recollect the relevant passage: 'What a delight it was to see it for the first time in its home in the hilly wastes, a mile or two inland from the town of Algiers!' She had found it, apparently, riding in the desert before breakfast. There were 'immense bulbs of *Scilla maritima* standing almost out of the ground', 'many lovely bee-orchises', 'fairy-like *Narcissus serotinus*', and what she particularly remarked on, the associations: groves of prickly pear wreathed and festooned with graceful tufts of the 'bell-shaped flower and polished leaves of Clematis cir- rhosa!'[22] Among the few British residents in Algiers was the Rev. Edwyn Arkwright, who discovered a white-flowered sport of *Iris stylosa*. Gertrude applauded his diligence in digging up and distributing the plant among his friends.

In Algeria, striking architectural foliage plants abound. The yuccas that are a prominent part of Gertrude's later gardening theme may well owe their inspiration to opuntias, cultivated in tiny domestic allotments with figs and apricots, gigantic agaves that line the roadsides or palms and banana trees which stand like monuments in public squares. Country gardens, she noted, were ignored or poorly kept, but some city gardens were well worth investigating. She was analysing gardens in detail, and one that she subsequently wrote about was built in terraces decorated with solid, subterranean cisterns supported by rude marble columns. A 'bower' thickly roofed with roses and honey- suckle provided a marvellous view of the hillside town and sea. There were seats of painted tiles, a fountain, slate steps, 'the perpendicular part being sculptured in low relief',[23] and cemented irrigation channels running the width of each terrace. In order to save water, vegetables were grown in shallow trenches at right angles to them. This first full description of a garden layout is remarkable in that long before meeting Lutyens, Gertrude was struck by some of the architectural features that are associated with his designs. At Orchards, there is a pretty water basin set in old Dutch tiles. The majority of their joint gardens possess pergolas and slate steps with inset verticals, while The Deanery and Hestercombe among others contain long water channels.

Six years after her Algerian adventure, an editorial in *The Garden* commented on some of Gertrude's paintings. One was of an immense belt of prickly pear, such as 'only porcupine and the delicate pale yellow clematis could penetrate',[24] another of brilliant flame-like poinsettias, twelve feet high, cropped each year to the old wood. Her sketchbook caught the starkness of Berber mud houses against vivid blue skies, courtyards hung with crimson bougainvillaea, twisted carob trees and ruined Roman cities 'guarded by asphodels'.[25] Ochre-coloured mountains were silhouetted against cloth-of-gold sunsets and mosques against palms. Man-made structures softened and enhanced by planting were soon to become important Jekyll features.

Gertrude spent January's bleakest days with the Cayleys, 'working at chain, silver, and pottery', 'inlaying iron', 'melting silver for buttons',[26] and scouring the bazaars that lined narrow streets with working jewellers, potters, weavers and cobblers. Donkeys with panniers squeezed through almost impenetrable crowds of gesticulating men and women, and children with eyes like olives played in the dust. On either side hung bloody carcasses, goat-skins, knotted carpets, jewelled

Gertrude Jekyll's drawing of a donkey, from her Algiers sketchbook.

daggers, silks, ceramics and ancient tiles. While still in Algiers, she met Fredrick Walker, consumptive, homesick and depressed. Neither he nor his travelling companion, Mr North, spoke French, and it amused Gertrude that the old woman who cooked for them took orders from drawings of duck and green peas, sketched on a white-washed wall. But Walker was not well and Gertrude was the sort of woman who responded to an emergency. Tales of the moral support she provided were gratefully communicated by Walker to their mutual friend, George Leslie. In *Our River* Leslie tells how she supervised Walker's luggage, 'assisted him in every way, and brought him home almost like a poor stray kitten under her arm'.[27] Walker had insisted that if he could again sit in a hansom cab in London he would be happy. At Charing Cross, his escort delivered her charge, saying, 'There, Mr Walker, this is Charing Cross, and there is a hansom cab.'[28] One is grateful for the brief respite her brisk concern offered. Walker died, tragically young, the following year, to be buried where he painted many of his pictures, at Cookham-on-Thames.

For a month or more three Jekyll children had been out of the country. No doubt the parents were resigned to their daughters' absence, but the Captain's delight at Herbert's promotion in the Royal Engineers had been quite spoiled when he heard that the unit was to serve in West Africa. Terrified at the risk to human life in the 'horrible Ashantee country',[1] he had advised his son to leave the army. Notwithstanding, Herbert had dutifully left for the Gold Coast, comforting his father, who sent long daily letters, with vigorous and informative replies. Some of Herbert's correspondence was forwarded to Lady Duff Gordon, who warmly approved, it was 'so honestly descriptive, no humbug, no complaints',[2] ... 'and he hurrying on with his engineers to get the wires fixed'[3] to ensure communications between the ships and the interior. There were curious fishes in the sea, and one cold night Herbert was resting in a thicket when a cobra dropped from a tree. In the first months of 1874, however, after less than a year, he succumbed to jungle fever. To the Captain's enormous relief, his favourite son was ordered home.

Welcomed at Hertford Street with 'much singing',[4] Herbert was looking 'wonderfully well'[5] considering his ordeal. At twenty-eight he was slim and athletic, fine-boned like his father, and neatly moustached. If he did not physically resemble Gertrude at this stage, he had her intellect and creative instincts. They were, moreover, as close as they had ever been. Withdrawn from active service, Herbert was claimed by the War Office and Gertrude found him a flat in Morpeth Terrace, a quiet street on the east of Victoria Station where Hercules Brabazon already had a town dwelling. It was only a brisk walk or a hansom-cab journey to and from Whitehall. Furnishing and decorating the new quarters was a task that gave Gertrude much pleasure, for she too now had a permanent London address. It is evident that the arrangement provided an ideal balance of support and independence. Herbert married in 1881 and his profession won him a knighthood, but neither marriage nor career was to interfere with the understanding between brother and sister.

With four venues in town, Gertrude was well set up to receive commissions. At Hertford Street there were the hospitable Duff Gordons, at Blandford Square Barbara Bodichon's far-flung humanist concerns drew a bizarre mixture of bohemian, artist, altruist and social misfit. At the Blumenthals' culturally more homogeneous milieu in Hyde Park Gate, she was assisting with decorations. At Morpeth Terrace she helped to entertain, among others, the visitor who was to become her most prized patron. Princess Louise's uncle, the Duke of Westminster, was 'one of Britain's noblest gentlemen', 'grave . . . kind and courteous'.[6] He won the Derby five times but, characteristically, refused to bet on his horses.

The Duke had inherited Eaton Hall in Cheshire and spent £600,000 on its transformation. Nothing but the best would do. The chimneypiece in the dining room came from a palace in Genoa, the dinner service was Minton's showpiece from the 1851 Exhibition, material for upholstery in the state apartments was specially woven at Spitalfields.

Alfred Waterhouse, architect of South Kensington's Natural History Museum, rebuilt and extended what Nikolaus Pevsner refers to as 'the most ambitious instance of Gothic Revival domestic architecture anywhere in the country'.[7] Frederick Shields worked stained glass and mosaics in a sumptuous private chapel, Stacy Marks decorated the walls of the drawing room with paintings of the Canterbury Pilgrims and in another room, he painted birds for a setting Gertrude had designed. Besides assisting in the overall arrangement of certain apartments, she received orders for curtains, panels of silk embroidery and other fittings. It was all a tremendous boost. As Lady Duff Gordon reported, 'Ld. and Ly. Westminster were very civil, kind and pleased. She (Gertrude) slept at Chester as the House of Eaton is all in confusion and repair. It is a work of great interest to her and occupation and very flattering.'[8]

Herbert's settling in London had cheered his father to new health. Lady Duff Gordon was amazed to see the Captain 'toddle on his two sticks'[9] up her stairs and Mrs Jekyll was her 'excellent, good, bright, cheerful'[10] self. All the Jekylls were in London; the two families met up and moved on like partners in a country dance. Georgy went to see Watts at Little Holland House, where she met Gertrude, then on to

Holland House where Lady Holland was entertaining Herbert. Georgina might not have possessed Gertrude's single-mindedness but at
fifty-seven, she refused to resign herself to middle age. Watching the
newly invented skating for ladies 'on little Rollers [instead of skates]
on a smoothed surface in a Court . . . Georgy who is an awful skater,
thinks of subscribing & entering the Field'.[11] A month later she
plucked up courage to try, fell and sprained an arm. 'Most unlucky . . .
as she never had a fall on real Ice.'[12]

Gertrude had sterner obligations. A letter from Emily Davies,
Mistress of Girton, to Barbara Bodichon refers to the fact that Gertrude
Jekyll had been consulted about decorations there. But Eaton Hall was
the chief venture during the autumn and much of the following year,
when embroidered panels she referred to as 'Turret Doors' were
worked by the Royal School of Embroidery 'under my [Gertrude's]
occasional supervision'.[13] A tribute to their quality was paid unconsciously by a team of French decorators, one of whom was heard to
remark, 'dessin de Paris, fabrique de Lyon!'[14] The Duke of Westminster was amassing magnificent trappings, the problem was that nobody
could agree how best to display them and all the suppliers quarrelled.
As the official opening drew near, he appealed to the unflappable Miss
Jekyll: 'I wonder if you could accept the position of umpire-in-chief as
to the furnishing generally at Eaton? I don't see how without your
advice it can ever be satisfactorily accomplished.'[15] He was quick to
realize that Gertrude's calm sense of order and leadership could provide
the artistic supervision which the Morris Company claimed could
alone bring about harmony between the various parts of a successful
work. With her shrewdness and good sense, she had an extraordinarily
ordered mind.

Waterhouse's 'Wagnerian palace'[16] was largely demolished in 1961,
leaving no physical record of Gertrude's contribution. At Hyde Park
Gate, however, photographs she herself took in later years supplement
other documentary evidence. In 1875 the grateful Blumenthals held a
party to celebrate the completion of her work. Princess Louise, the
Duke and Lady Westmorland, Lady Shrewsbury and Mr Percy Wyndham were among those invited to admire in the drawing-room a wall
painted with gold peacocks and orange trees, a carved chimneypiece,
an ornamental hanging display cabinet, a door inlaid with floral
designs in mother-of-pearl and sweeping quilted curtains worked in
huge circles of symbolic, petal-like motifs. Gertrude designed and

partially sewed the Blumenthals' curtains. Recent information[17] on the inlaid door suggests that she and her hostess worked together.

The party was a complete success; commissions multiplied. 'Job, Kensington Palace'; 'Job, Lord Ducie's', 16 Portman Square; (Lord) 'Stratford job, many days'.[18] Gertrude's absences from home were frequent and prolonged. Neither an autumn break at the Chalet nor further studies with Mr Cayley were allowed to slow down the production of silver repoussé work, blotting-paper covers, experiments 'in niello'[19] – a black composition used for filling engraved lines in ornamental metalwork – and embroidered 'quilts'. Quilts requested by Frederic Leighton and Edward Burne-Jones were presumably like the curtains she made for Hyde Park Gate.

Parallels between needlework and painting were pertinent to James McNeill Whistler, to whose first one-man exhibition Gertrude repaired on 6 June. To a fellow painter, he had written, 'It seems to me that colour ought to . . . appear in the picture continually here and there, in the same way that a thread appears in an embroidery.'[20] When the Academy of 1874 rejected his pictures, Whistler organized his own show in Pall Mall: thirteen paintings and fifty etchings set off by palms and flowers, blue pots and bronzes. The exhibition shocked London. It was partly the decorations and partly the paintings, but mostly the paintings' names! Borrowing musical terminology, Whistler called them Arrangements and Nocturnes. It is interesting that Gertrude profoundly respected the work of a more challenging artist than the Royal Academy set with whom she generally consorted. Whistler was a good friend of Princess Louise and he decorated houses, first his own, then those of friends. His reputation was growing. Before long he was in demand for prestigious places like the South Kensington (Victoria and Albert) Museum and the Grosvenor Gallery – headquarters of the new aesthetic movement. Like Hercules Brabazon, Whistler was inspired by music, but he was ostentatious and Ruskin did not approve of his art. A few years later, Ruskin caused a rumpus by describing Whistler's pictures as 'flinging a pot of paint in the public's face'.[21] It was not a wise remark and provoked a famous court case. The great supporter of avant-garde was succumbing to a rigidity he had once deplored. Despite obvious mutual sympathies, Gertrude was wary of making personal overtures. 'I wonder why his signature is always called a butterfly,' she mused dryly to William Nicholson, nearly fifty years later. 'It is a mixture of a pansy & a little capering devil. The pansy stands for his wonderful sense of colour; the little devil for some of the rest of him, & he is careful to remind you that he has a sting in his tail.'[22]

Ruskin was Gertrude's guiding spirit in all things; indeed she accepted his lessons in restraint more fully than he himself. It was the year Rose La Touche, his ethereal child lover, died, and the great reformer was half out of his wits from worry and overwork. Gertrude eschewed the dramatic tenor of her fellow artist's emotional entanglements: she did not like excesses of any sort.

Tuned to the Arts and Crafts Movement, she was seeing all her activities as an extension of life. She thought that an artist should develop a visual memory, and looking, more than anything else, helped to refine her taste. Everywhere she went, she looked at houses and gardens. As a child she had been in and out of the cottages in Bramley. Now her interest in them was more defined. The idealized gardens of Victorian paintings were the fruits of centuries of development. They had survived periods of formality and the landscape movement which virtually banished flowers from the park, becoming rich depositories for rare and selected plants. By the turn of the century, when Gertrude was writing about primroses, she was able to look back twenty-five years to the time she first crossed a strain called 'Golden Plover' with a white nameless one from a cottage garden. Throughout her writings she acknowledges her respect for and debt to 'the little cottage gardens that help to make our English waysides the prettiest in the temperate world. One can hardly go into the smallest cottage garden without learning or observing something new. It may be some two plants growing beautifully together by some happy chance, or a pretty mixed tangle of creepers, or something that one has always thought must have a south wall doing better on an east one.'[23] Her debt to the cottage has been acknowledged: what the popular estimation of Gertrude Jekyll fails to realize is that since her arrival in Wargrave, she had been gaining a reputation among those who knew her as a superior plantswoman.

It is not known precisely how Gertrude's planning instincts were put into practice at Wargrave Manor. Photographs of the garden in the early twentieth century show a place of trim lawns and bedding, a thatched and trellised boathouse by the landing stage at the edge of the river with a thickly wooded driveway. A pergola and a small planting of Scots pine were probably hers. But Leslie describes it in her time as 'a perfect wilderness of sweets, and old-fashioned flowers'.[24] There were huge lavender hedges, and long would he remember 'the generous way, she with a lavender sickle of her own construction, reaped me an armful'.[25] Near the house waved forty acres of lavender. The proprietor, Zachary Allnutt, lived and distilled on the premises. One doubts, however, whether Gertrude needed encouragement to grow a plant that had been a favourite since she discovered it in the walled garden at Bramley.

Another gardening enterprise that had intrigued Leslie had been Gertrude's attempt to improve the prospect outside Herbert's earlier North London rooms. With a long rod, scooped into a ladle at its end, she conveyed a dressing of rich soil to the top of a wall, and various seeds were dropped on the surface in the hopes of their germinating. For some reason, rain, smoke, cats or sparrows, the plan went awry. This was not the only town garden she had devised. Much later she explains in one of her books how she was moved to answer a mill employee's advertisement for information on cultivating a window-box. Advice was duly sent, with stones to create hills, little plants of mossy and silver saxifrage and a few small bulbs. A flowering snowdrop and an early blue squill drew letters from the grateful recipient to which Gertrude added a note of indulgent charity, 'And I thought with pleasure how he would watch them in spare minutes ... and think of them as he went back to work,' how 'the beauty of the full-blown flower would make him glad ... while minding his "mule" in the busy restless mill'.[26]

It always was Gertrude's habit to seek advice from the expert. Who better could instruct a burgeoning love of plants than William Robinson, author of *The Wild Garden*? In the first month of 1875 they met at his Covent Garden office. Robinson was thirty-five, a manic worker and a shrewd self-publicist. Within four years, since he had launched *The Garden*, it had attracted contributions from well-known horticulturists such as Canon Ellacombe, Dean Hole and James Britten. Even before the appearance of his fourpenny weekly, Robinson had written eight books and travelled widely, gathering plants and exploring gardens on the Continent and in North America. *Alpine Flowers for English Gardens* was the first detailed British book on the subject, and like *The Wild Garden*, *Hardy Flowers* and *The Subtropical Garden*, made a significant contribution to garden literature. True, Robinson was apt to stress his own novelty and quick to exploit an opening where others had quietly laid the groundwork, but he saw the scope for popularizing current themes. By and large, formality had ruled since John C. Loudon had written *The Suburban Gardener* in 1839. Many books and many editions later, Loudon's message was taken up by the most Victorian of nineteenth-century garden writers, Shirley Hibberd, in *The Amateur's Flower Garden*. 'Geometric gardens may be designed on paper by . . . placing a few bits of coloured paper in the debuscope [a kaleidoscope] and then copying the multiple scheme so produced.'[27] Only after five chapters on the attractions of the parterre and bedding system does Hibberd turn to the hardy herbaceous border. Patterns came first, plants after: how Robinson must have cringed.

Ruskin's writings about mountains and mountain flora had first drawn Robinson to alpine country. The two men corresponded, *The Garden* borrowed a fitting Shakespearian quotation for its motto –

> This is an art
> Which does mend nature: change it rather: but
> The art itself is Nature[28]

– and Ruskin became one of its early contributors. Setting himself up as the high priest of 'nature and naturalness', Robinson could be as pugnacious as he liked about ribbon borders and 'twisting masses'[29] of carpet bedding.

Herbert was the first Jekyll to appear in the magazine, albeit anonymously: a début resulting from private correspondence with the Rev. Reynolds Hole, author of *A Book about Roses*. The clergyman had expressed anxiety about a proposal to raise a line of telegraph poles along the road in front of his house, and Herbert, then busy erecting poles in West Africa, had commiserated engagingly: 'Knowing you to be pre-eminent as a horticulturist, I beg to bring to your notice a magnificent species of the Aloe tribe (Agave telegraphica). This highly ornamental plant flourishes best by the side of roads and on railway embankments, and I can strongly recommend it to your notice, feeling it would succeed admirably at the edge of the high-road at the foot of your lawn, where it would be seen to great advantage from your drawing-room windows.'[30]

Herbert's letter and sketch of the 'new species'[31] were published on the letter page of *The Garden*'s second issue, December 1871, together with the Dean's reply. If the beautiful plant were 'pegged down and layered',[32] the telegraph wires would be out of sight, underground.

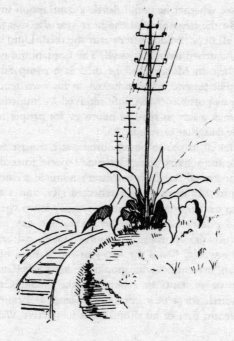

'Agave telegraphica' from William Robinson's *The Garden*.

When Gertrude visited William Robinson's Covent Garden offices, she could not possibly have guessed that clients whose houses she was embellishing in the seventies would be paying her, ten years later, to plan their gardens; or that she would become the editor of his magazine. But Robinson would have been on the alert for new writers, and something must have suggested to her that a personal visit was most likely to be fruitful. Her boldness paid off. Six years were to pass before her first article appeared in *The Garden* but she had a friend for life. Not everyone could manage Robinson's querulousness even if they appreciated his ability, but Gertrude was good at managing people. Besides, she did not feel vulnerable and unattractive to bachelors like Brabazon and Robinson, who met her on an intellectual level.

Lady Duff Gordon was eighty-four. In the spring of 1874 she wrote,

'I should have been dead long ago!!'[33] Six months later, Herbert was consulted to see whether he could devise a contraption to help her get out of bed. By the beginning of the next year she was feeling 'like a rotten Apple all over'.[34] Soon afterwards she died. Until the end Lady Duff Gordon watched over Mr Jekyll. The Captain did not, however, long outlive her. In March 1876 he died at a comparably youngish seventy-two. His funeral was conducted, at his own request, 'with as much privacy as possible'.[35] His wife received an immediate legacy of £1,000 and 'such a sum as may be necessary for proper mourning for herself and my daughter Gertrude'.[36]

It was the Jekyll nature to be humorous, affectionate and stable but not emotional; and activity being Gertrude's special formula for distress, she escaped for several weeks to her sister's home in Venice. There was plenty to inspire her in this water-reflected city, and a family friend was amused to see her emerging from a sacristy laden with lace ripped 'hot from the priest's back'.[37] In the Piazza one day in September, tripping between the effortlessly beautiful Doge's palace, 'the central building of the world',[38] and the 800-year-old Basilica of San Marco, 'a treasure-heap, it seems',[39] who should she meet but Ruskin, installed with a group of assistants in a hotel on the Grand Canal. He was gathering material for a new edition of *Stones of Venice*, and for St George's Museum, part of his utopian but ineffective Working Men's Guild.

The Captain left Wargrave Hill to his eldest son, raising the crucial question, for a family now reduced to Mrs Jekyll and three unmarried children, of where they should live. Herbert was a lieutenant in the Royal Engineers and Walter had been ordained; both were virtually independent. Gertrude was thirty-two – a year in which she acquired a godson in Harold Falkner of Farnham – but showed not the slightest sign of getting married. Having vindicated at least partial independence, she was willing to live with her mother, so the question involved her considerably. If the eight years she had lived in Berkshire felt like exile, 'a perpetual homesickness and inability to be acclimatized',[40] it was hunger for what she had lost rather than lack of appreciation for what she had gained. 'You see, I only hated Berkshire because it was not Surrey, and chalk because it was not sand,'[41] she wrote to George Leslie, 'just as poor Walker, when he grew ill and wretched, hated Algiers because it was not Bayswater.'[42] The magnificent view from her windows was by no means lost on her; even the gaunt perpendiculars of Huntley & Palmer's biscuit factory chimneys at Reading had their good points. What annoyed her was that every visitor should identify them. Perhaps Mrs Jekyll, too, never became entirely reconciled to Wargrave. All the evidence suggests that the decision to return to Surrey was unanimous.

PART THREE

HOME-MAKER

CHAPTER ELEVEN

1877–81

Bramley House was no longer available, nor would Mrs Jekyll have wanted to return there. The Captain had left his widow the bulk of his wealth; at sixty-four, with £140,000 at her disposal, there was no reason why she should not at last build a home to suit herself. In hindsight it is easy to assume that the move to Munstead was inevitable. This would be a mistake. Of two sites she and Gertrude seriously considered, one was beyond Liphook, the Hampshire side of the Surrey border, overlooking the Sussex Weald. The country was glorious, it was only fifty miles from their old home, but remote from communications and further from London than was convenient. The other possibility was twenty acres midway between Bramley and the market town of Godalming, 400 feet high on Greensand bedrock, in an area of open hills. Visually, it was another pastoral retreat; there was not even a biscuit factory to gauge the effects of the Industrial Revolution on rural life. Neither Mrs Jekyll nor Gertrude could possibly have foreseen what Munstead would have in store. The decision, however, was made in its favour, temporary residence was found at Summerpool House in Bramley, John J. Stevenson was selected as architect, and within a year of Captain Jekyll's death building had begun.

Gone is the empty heath where the first grey stones for Munstead House were trundled from the quarry by donkey. Apart from the Godalming–Horsham road there were only sandy bridle paths; in country now thickly wooded, scattered Scots pines were the only trees. Gipsies frequented the area, smugglers were not unknown, and Mrs Jekyll's friends worried that she would be afraid to live in so lonely a spot. Even by the turn of the century, Gertrude was complaining that it was 'rather thickly populated'.[1] Ferns plentiful in her youth had been torn out, and some of the roads had been tarred.

It was Falkner, Gertrude's architect godson, who mentioned how

high she rated – he thought overrated – architects. But she was
nurtured on Ruskin's principle that the qualities of a nation can be
discovered in its architecture. Add an obsession for thoroughness and
what Robert Lutyens referred to as her 'tireless interest in the architecture, crafts and traditions of "Old West Surrey" ',[2] and it is plain that
she was going to be more than a passive spectator in the construction
of Munstead House. Mr Stevenson, no doubt meticulously chosen, was
the first architect to win commissions for work on an ocean liner. He
had designed saloons for the SS *Orient*, elementary schools for the
London School Board and some large houses, mostly in Scotland. At
Munstead he chose a 'kind of Scots vernacular'[3] for a three-storey
building with a wing for Gertrude containing her bedroom and a large
workroom connected by winding stairs. Every detail of Munstead
House was required to pass her scrutiny. Water could be found only at
great depth, yet she was with difficulty restrained from descending the
well because the workmen dreaded the thought of having to raise her
to the surface. Her personal contribution was designing and carving
two fireplaces, a 'Jacobean' one in her workroom and another in the
hall. Herbert's was an 'impressive'[4] panelling after Grinling Gibbons in
the dining room. The chimneys and third floor of Munstead House
have gone, the drawing room was remodelled by Lutyens and a new
orangery was built to his design. The orangery has subsequently been
rebuilt, but Gertrude's and her brother's work remain.

'I can never satisfactorily imagine a house without knowing the
particular site,'[5] she wrote to William Robinson. 'A house must grow
up between the ground on one side & its master on the other & must
marry both. A house planned in air would be as soulless as an
Aldershot hut.'[6] It is a token of the importance to her of integration
that her mother's house and its surroundings developed simultaneously.
'Moving plants to Munstead' and 'Waggon of fruit trees from Wargrave'[7] are indications that by the autumn of 1877 the new garden was
well under way.

Gertrude's own painting continued to yield to craftwork, though
the summer of 1877 found her sketching at the Slade. Mr Cayley had
died and his widow chose to commission a tombstone from his
favourite pupil. It is a moving instance of the warmth and loyalty that
so often developed between Gertrude and her teachers. Other contacts
continued to bring in work. A spate of silver repoussé drew demands
for ornamental dishes and other decorative objects from Lord Gros-

venor and Lord Carnarvon, to whom Herbert was Private Secretary, while Leonie Blumenthal's aunt ordered a hanging cupboard called a 'richezza'. There were decorations for new neighbours and more commissions for the Duke of Westminster. Sometimes she was joined by Barbara Bodichon, who wrote to her niece, Amy, about this time, 'Working very hard at my drawings for exhibition in Miss Jekyll's studio.' 'With Miss Jekyll in Surrey, private,'[8] was confided in another sisterly note. Barbara's hitherto gallant energy was about to be shadowed by ill health. She had seemed well enough, but disliking the cold, she was staying at Zennor in Cornwall to catch the first warm days of spring. 'Here we have blue bells and windflowers everywhere.'[9] It was in May, while she was sketching the wild scenery of the Atlantic coast, that she had the first of a series of strokes that were to leave her debilitated during her last fourteen years.

Generations of artists have gathered round St Ives on the south-west limb of England, a coast as craggy as the tail of a giant sea-horse. Sheer cliffs plunge into a surging sea, waves slap rhythmically against the rocks, gulls wheel and great outcrops of granite rise up from the soil like the surfacings of the earth's skeleton. Lured by its sombre rock grey, sage green, and the brown of winter bracken, Barbara bought a granite cottage with square windows and a slate roof in the last years of the 1870s. The Poor House and what it meant to her is one of the episodes Gertrude chose not to enlarge upon. In her first book she mentions bringing a wall pennywort from Cornwall, 'where it is so plentiful in the chinks of the granite stone-fences'.[10] She must have visited several times, maybe many times. She must, moreover, have loved its exposed wildness for Barbara to have left the cottage to her when she died. It was a private pact between two women, a place that brought them together through the things that meant most to them, painting and landscape and, probably, gardening. Gertrude owned it between 1891 and 1896, when she sold it to a painter, Alice Westlake, who owned Eagle's Nest next door. But Katharine Heron, who presently owns the Poor House, recognized immediately that the granite walls enclosing what once were gardens on two sides of the cottage were unlike the vernacular Cornish walls. Instead of incorporating lumps of moor stones, they are deliberately cut and regularly coursed, leaving ledges and plant pockets. Nothing is documented but it seems more than likely that plants were introduced in the protecting walls.

Gertrude was also helping Barbara Bodichon at Scalands. The cottage was enlarged after Madame Bodichon's death, and partly destroyed by fire in the mid 1950s when the Leigh Smith family had left. Rebuilt on the same site, it remains an enduring and endearing Jekyll landscape in a setting of woodland and the valley of the Glottenham stream. Today, brick paths pass unobtrusively through pine trees from the road to a wide herringbone-patterned terrace, a shaded sunken garden on the west is tangled with old rhododendrons and the channel of light that sweeps up the valley on the garden side bears a huge specimen tulip tree. As with interior decoration, Gertrude's main emphasis was in relating different parts of the surroundings. But like all her gardens, Scalands was not just to look at but to live in. As she was to say, and as was re-emphasized by the fact of Barbara's semi-invalidism, 'the first purpose of a garden is to be a place of quiet beauty such as will give delight to the eye and repose and refreshment to the mind'.[11] Among the photographs she was later to take there is one of an existing dry stone wall seat. Madame Bodichon's garden fervour is manifest in one of her books at Girton, a *Hooper's Gardening Guide*, dated January 1878, annotated with plant lists. The same month a letter she wrote to her niece's husband, medical scientist, polymath and eventually Sir Norman Moore, reported, 'Bricks ordered for Scalands and work began for digging out the earth.'[12]

'To Munstead for good.'[13] Gertrude's September diary entry does far more than record; it implies finality. At thirty-five her allegiance was total. Excepting working assignments and infrequent holidays, she would spend the next fifty-four years within a short radius of the new home.

So closely is she associated with the garden at Munstead Wood, it is seldom appreciated that its forerunner, the first she laid on virgin soil, incorporated virtually all its characteristic features. They were used not only in her final garden but over and again in her commissions. Munstead House had a pergola, a parterre and a hardy flower border, a long grass walk flanked by cypresses in concession to the Italian landscape, alpine and rock gardens imitating mountain scenery at Montreux, and a nut walk inspired by Surrey's woodlands. It was not simply the features but their cohesiveness that inspired William Goldring to note that the garden had been laid out 'in quite an unconventional way'.[14] Like Munstead Wood, of course, it was situated on the poor sandy soil that becomes such a refrain in Gertrude's garden writings. But as Tooley has argued in his essay on Jekyll landscapes, the basic and seminal innovation that set her garden at Munstead House apart from others of the period was its heathland setting. Natural vegetation was cleared only in the vicinity of house and outbuildings. Elsewhere the heath and scrub with its cover of Scots pine, chestnuts, birch, holly, juniper, heathers, gorse, grasses and ferns was 'made to mingle with [the garden] in a charming manner and trodden tracks only instead of sharply defined walks traverse the heath in various directions leading from the lawn and the garden'.[15]

For more than half a century, gardeners had forgotten to 'consult the Genius of the place'. Gertrude had already spent twenty years and would spend a great many more patiently investigating the wild neighbourhood of her pioneering gardens. In *Wood and Garden* she was to write, 'No artificial planting can ever equal that of nature but one may learn from it the great lesson of moderation and reserve, of simplicity of intention, and directness of purpose, and the inestimable value of the quality called "breadth" in painting.'[16] Ideas she learned from the Surrey countryside were transposed into the garden, and eventually communicated to the architects with whom she collaborated.

She was cultivating a steadiness of purpose. There was no sudden change from one branch of her activities to another, not even – because she treated gardening like any other craft – a real change of direction. Yet the new garden absorbed her increasingly. It is only by perusing contemporary plans and reading visitors' comments that it is possible to appreciate the scale of her accomplishment during the first couple of years at Munstead. By the summer of 1880 she reckoned that the results merited the attention of two of the most celebrated gardeners in England, William Robinson, with whom she had maintained close contact since their London meeting, and his old friend the Vicar of Caunton, the Rev. Reynolds Hole.

It was almost a decade since Herbert had first written to Hole, and anyone with gardening interests knew by reputation the author of *A Book about Roses*, 'Alike in the palace or the bothy, the same genial smile, the same ready wit.'[17] Hole had the many-sidedness that crops up in so many of Gertrude's friends – he was a theologian, sportsman, hymnologist and gardener. Above all he was a rosarian, founder of the National Rose Society, whose cheerful, if somewhat arch enthusiasm is reflected in his classic work. Gertrude had seen his garden near Newark in Nottingham clotted with blooms. Hole was closely involved with *The Garden* during its early years. Long after success was established, he remembered sitting 'with my friend William Robinson under a tree in Regent's Park . . . suggesting *The Garden* as a title for the newspaper which . . . has been so powerful in its advocacy of pure horticulture.'[18]

On New Year's Day 1881 the snowdrops at Munstead House were showing white tips. An exceptionally mild period was followed by severe late frost towards the end of February, but fortunately snow protected the bulbs. Much of Gertrude's minutely trained faculty for observation could usefully be employed. Hitherto she had written only a couple of anonymous pieces in the 'Justicia' column of *The Garden*. In the following twelve months she submitted nineteen signed articles varying in length from a couple of lines to an average 1,000 words. One was for Robinson's slightly more technical paper, *Gardening Illustrated*. Old friends continued loyal: M. Durando, her tutor from Algiers, had sent an assignment of hardy and half-hardy plants, and *Garden* readers were to hear of a *Cyclamen africanum* tuber measuring $22\frac{1}{4}$ in and weighing 3 lb 5 oz, as well as one of *Scilla maritima* $22\frac{1}{2}$ inches, weighing 5 lb 13 oz with its leaves.

Her visits to nurseries also increased, an occasion which stood out in 'imperishable memory'[19] being a meeting at Mr Barr's Tooting nursery with Mrs Bennett-Poe, wife of a plantsman, and Sir Michael Foster, eminent Professor of Physiology at Cambridge and Secretary of the Royal Society. Since the beginning of the 1860s Barr had proven his Robinsonian allegiance by offering seed packets of mixed annuals to scatter in waste places and woodland walks. Gertrude had already sought his advice on narcissus; this time the study was hellebores. But what particularly struck her about Foster was his retentive memory, perhaps because memory was a quality she cultivated in herself.

In June she was judging at the Horticultural Society show, precursor to Chelsea, in Regent's Park. To have been asked was a sure sign of her standing, and brought her in touch with other principal figures in gardening. Among them was George F. Wilson, munificent spirit behind the Society's gardens at Wisley. The son of a candlemaker and a man of great versatility, he was jointly responsible for a patent that enabled inferior fats to be used in candle manufacture. Commercial success bought him the Wisley estate near his Weybridge home, where he again began to experiment. Seeing its poor acid soil as an ideal habitat for lilies, iris and rhododendrons, he carved out pools and planted lavishly. When someone told him it was fascinating but not a garden, he replied, 'I think of it as a place where plants from all over the world grow wild.'[20] Already Wilson was taking prizes at RHS shows; eventually he won the Victorian Medal of Honour and became Vice President of the Society. Gertrude was to vote his garden 'about the most instructive it is possible to see'.[21]

Midsummer allowed her a break with the Blumenthals on a breathless eighteen-day sailing tour down the coast of Brittany, stopping at Quimper just long enough to visit the local pottery. Home again, Gertrude was playing pupil to her new friend at Weybridge; Mr Wilson was 'kind enough to let me come and do actual spade work with him'.[22] Goldring was impressed by the construction of the rock garden at Munstead House, where stones were subservient to plants 'which surround and overspread them with good effect, and in a most natural manner'.[23] At Weybridge, she and Wilson produced a 'flat Alpine garden'[24] with slightly raised beds of rock divided by sunken brick paths, forming a series of island beds 'to keep the eye of the visitor on a level with the plants'.[25] It does not sound as if the experiment was geologically stratified like the rock garden constructed at Kew the following year in imitation of a Pyrenean stream-bed. In both, however, excavation was more prominent than construction.

Alpine gardens were much in vogue. As Ruskin had realized in 1856, 'the influx of foreigners into Switzerland must necessarily be greater every year'.[26] He was chiding the itinerant who wanted home comforts in the valley of Chamouni, but travel inspired as well as exposing shortcomings, and there were those who, seeing alpine outcrops and alpine flora, coveted them at home. During the 1860s and 70s rocky landscapes proliferated in English gardens. Where natural rockwork was not available, James Pulham and Co. might manufacture artificial outcrops complete with geological faults, strata and suitable plant 'pockets'. Some, thinking picturesque boulders the imperative feature, planted awesome specimens with native ivies and cotoneasters, but interest in alpine cultivation was growing and others were, like Gertrude, using stonework as a naturalistic setting for plants.

At Munstead House she made a large self-contained alpine garden surrounded by shrubs, as well as a 'rockery' against the west side of the kitchen garden wall. No sooner was the mission accomplished than she was tackling another alpine garden in a quarry at Chalet Sonzier. It was her fourth Chalet visit. There was time for horse treks through wooded hills and playing charades, but gardens were much on her mind. Photographs of the place some seven or eight years on show it half lost behind festoons of jasmine and wisteria. She is probably responsible for the fine specimen trees – Oriental plane, Cedar of Lebanon, and behind them, beech, *Picea abies*, tulip tree and two striking droopy firs, possibly *Abies* × *vilmoriniana*. There is an irregular sunken garden surrounded by nut trees of distinctively Jekyllian flavour. Pergolas stood, until recently, on either side of the building and a summerhouse, undoubtedly hers, at the edge of the steep southern slope. Even now it is possible to trace a path from the site of the summerhouse through the edge of the woods into the quarry garden.

Travelling home from Montreux, Gertrude broke the journey to visit Froebel at Zürich. Francis Jekyll interprets her engagement book entry to mean a Froebel Institute kindergarten. Far more likely is Tooley's suggestion that Gertrude met Otto Froebel, nurseryman raiser of choice waterlilies, begonias and antirrhinums. Once home, she was swept into a whirl of gardening and garden writing. A brief suggestion to *Garden* readers, to combine pink China roses with a bough of flowering ivy, initiated some sixty articles on 'Flowers and plants in the house'. She wrote only about what she had done, and from the beginning with more than a hint of authority. The topic stretched her painter's eye for combinations, and discovered a keen readership. Although they are written in the first person plural, her pieces were signed simply 'G. J. Surrey'.

Before the year was out, the second edition of William Robinson's *The Wild Garden* had been released. It is not perhaps insignificant that where the first spoke of the 'charming results'[27] of 'a combination of hardy exotics and native flowers in half-wild' locations, the revised introductory chapter refers essentially in Jekyllian terms, to 'beautiful pictures'.[28]

Mr Jekyll's death had repercussions throughout the family. After retiring from the army as a Captain, Teddy had become Adjutant of the Bedfordshire Volunteers and a father to two girls, Millicent, born in 1872, and Grace two years later. Simon Houfe, art historian and Ampthill resident, had a grandfather, the Rev. A. E. Houfe, who was Vicar of Pulloxhill and knew his parishioner well – a hunting, shooting and fishing man, a stickler for neatness and the introducer of rubber carriage tyres to the neighbourhood. Surviving letters find him a kind man, 'very well known and much respected throughout the Ampthill district',[29] perhaps something of a pedant. With Jekyll administrative flair if not the artistic vision, Teddy became JP and Deputy Lieutenant of the county. For many years Bedfordshire had been his base; he was attached to it and Tingrith Cottage had served him well, but now he was nominally head of the clan he could afford something smarter. On a gently shelving piece of agricultural land south of Pulloxhill, he used his father's legacy to build what Simon Houfe remembers as 'a gothic inspired pile with tall chimneys and a wooden porch at the side'.[30] Higham Bury, with its slightly gauche exterior, was pulled down in 1960 to be replaced with a smooth Georgian-style building. Most of the garden went with it, though a three-sided block of stables and utility buildings has been converted into an indoor swimming pool and the wall along one side of the kitchen garden plus a charming summerhouse remain. Needless to say Gertrude planned the garden on her not infrequent visits to her brother, and judging from the wheelbarrow photographs taken at Higham Bury, she made a physical contribution as well.

Old ordnance survey maps give the outline of a large kitchen garden, an orchard beyond it, and an entrance drive lined with double lime avenues. The formal gardens north-east of the house were not allowed to interfere with spectacular views glimpsed through a veil of trees to west and south. 'Situation lovely',[31] an unnamed valuer was moved to write in the margin of his manuscript book in 1925. 'Miles away from anywhere.'[32] This was five years after Teddy left, but the comment applies today. Miss Marion Shepherd, who lived in Teddy's house for four years from 1929, remembers its double hedge along the east side of the kitchen garden and, inside, a long herbaceous border. Within, the plot was divided into four by crossing paths, each section of which was lined with box. There was a medlar trained like an umbrella and a mulberry in the orchard, but most memorable of all were bulbs in the woodland, 'masses of snakes' head fritillaries, stitchwort, *Anemone blanda* and crocus, and later the daffodils'.[33] In front of the house was a big bed of bamboo, and more bamboo grew among willows that landscaped the ponds made by excavating clay for building. Miss Shepherd has always assumed that the photograph on page 10 of Gertrude's *Colour in the Flower Garden* portrays daffodils at Higham Bury.

Changes about to occur in Herbert's life were as momentous as those in Teddy's. Without the benefit of his sister's art training, Herbert was a skilled carver, and perceptive about architecture; he bought pictures, visited exhibitions and knew a great many noted men of arts. Among them was Burne-Jones's greatest patron, God-fearing William Graham, Liberal MP for Glasgow and a discriminating collector of Italian primitives. Agnes was the Grahams' eighth child, their sixth and most high-spirited daughter. By the time she was a young woman, her parents' religious rigour had softened to the point where her mother was persuaded to hold a dance at Grosvenor Place, and there she met and fell in love with Captain Herbert Jekyll.

Graham is said to have viewed the prospective match with misgivings until Herbert diplomatically fortified his suit with an 'Old Master' he had bought in Italy. After that, events followed a natural course. Both families were close, and it was to be a very happy marriage. The older Herbert got, the more like Gertrude he became – even physically, since both developed the Jekyll crease on either side of the mouth. David McKenna, one of his grandchildren, remarked how 'they [Gertrude and Herbert] were very much of a pair'[34] and when Herbert died, his sister-in-law, Frances, Lady Horner, described him with words that might easily have alluded to Gertrude, 'rare gifts . . . an excellent gardener, a very remarkable artist, wood carver, and designer; he helped to adorn every home with which he came in contact, and never withheld his help and sympathy from anyone who claimed them'.[35] Herbert had social triumphs but social climbing was not his nature. 'Aggie', with her attractive mixture of warmth and seriousness, maintained a perfect buffer between her husband and the demands of society. Years later Mary Lutyens called her a 'very cultivated woman'.[36]

Gertrude may not have needed a man to validate her, but the family with its reciprocal obligations had continued to play an essential role. She was extremely put out at the prospect of another woman coming between herself and the brother she idolized. The situation was potentially disturbing and it says a lot for Agnes's diplomacy that she managed to allow a possessive sister-in-law to share her husband. As a start the couple chose Guildford, within a short distance of Munstead, to set up home.

Carry Eden had chosen her lifestyle before the Captain's death, Walter was almost immune to material change, and Herbert's marriage may not have been affected by it. For Teddy, Gertrude and Mrs Jekyll however, the impetus provided new direction. Gertrude had what she wanted before all else, a home in Surrey. From the inviolable and 'jealously guarded'[37] sanctuary of her new quarters, a rootedness in the countryside that was also a return to the raptures of her young days led her steadily into the main stream of her life's work.

CHAPTER TWELVE

1882–5

If William Morris, Edward Burne-Jones, Philip Webb and Ford Madox Brown were the giants of the Arts and Crafts Movement, Gertrude had a fair number of their abilities and all their concerns. She abjured the cheap and shoddy, sought tirelessly to improve the quality of design, and insisted upon seeing each creative process through from beginning to end. The movement had involved her at every stage. Ruskin and Carlyle sparked off the reform by speaking out against the exploitation of human labour, and the first Schools of Design espoused the campaign. Even Henry Cole had played a part by insisting on good design. The foundation of the Royal School of Art-Needlework was another milestone, and a number of Arts and Crafts organizations were set up including the Art Workers' Guild. What is surprising about the Guild is that a key body in a radical movement excluded women from its ranks. The chief reason why Gertrude's Arts and Crafts role is insufficiently acknowledged is her aloofness from the Movement's social ethos, but a more feminist climate would have given her more prominence.

The next years were ones of intensive trial and consolidation. Gertrude had met Ruskin and Morris, the two great crusaders against Victorian materialism. Ruskin remained a great mentor, and Morris an inspiration, but her professional ally was undoubtedly William Robinson. When he was in London he often drove out to Munstead House. He had been in Egypt, however, and pithy epistolary exchanges took place instead. In his absence Robinson had entrusted Gertrude with the task of obtaining new gardening boots; on 12 February they were forwarded with the shoe he had lent her cobbler as a pattern, and a box of grease. Nothing was too much bother for her to get right. The parcel was identified on the outside 'for fear your people in your possible absence might think they were Flowers Perishable and put them in water'.[1] Robinson was not to worry about their pale colour, a few greasings and wettings would cure it. The heels, she noted critically, were a good eighth of an inch higher than he had ordered.

Gertrude wrote fifty-eight pieces for Robinson within the year. 'Flowers and Plants in the House' continued to be a prominent feature, usually at the head of a column marked 'Seasonable Work'; there were short entries on individual plants of particular merit, and longer, editorial pieces on special themes. Work and life were one, and Gertrude's writing was essentially empirical; sometimes the prose is so immediate that one can imagine her, deftly arranging a bowl of flowers, standing back to assess the effect, pen in hand, before she begins, 'In a large blue china jar is . . .'[2]

Whether she was setting a bowl of roses or planning an estate, Gertrude was governed by what she called 'simplicity of intention'.[3] Ruskin had said, 'Out of necessity of Unity, arises that of Variety',[4] and almost instinctively she knew that diversity must be subservient to the whole. Utmost sophistication might be employed in achieving an effect but unifying Nature would guide. The garden at Munstead House was essentially a movement from formal parterre – a minute square of scarlet pelargoniums and succulent begonias she laid out immediately behind her wing of Munstead House, through flowery incident and clipped lawns from which paths disappeared like the wings of a stage, drifting imperceptibly into shrubby heathland, to leave views 'free and quiet'.[5]

Artistic perception was her other chief guide. 'Should it not be remembered that in setting a garden we are painting a picture,' she wrote in *The Garden*, 'only it is a picture of hundreds of feet or yards instead of so many inches?'[6] In nature, variables were infinite; art and unity should be supported by intimate knowledge of a considerable range of plant material. Not without tireless labour did Gertrude bring gardening into the realm of Arts and Crafts. As a perfect poem uses the best possible words in the best possible order, she sought, 'the best use of the best flowers'.[7]

It was while Gertrude was making her first hardy flower border that she largely developed her famous colour theories. The border lay south of the kitchen garden, bisected by a path leading to a gate in the wall. Like its famous successor at Munstead Wood, it was 160 by 14 feet. She regarded it as one of her most innovative features, and William Goldring felt by August 1882 that both colour and form were unique. 'The brilliancy of the border . . . was beyond anything we had hitherto seen in the way of hardy flowers — as different from the ordinary mixed border as night from day.'[8] Drifts were broadly massed, each one large enough to have 'a certain dignity'.[9] Colour juxtapositions relying on harmony and contrast were planned for spring, summer and autumn to ensure successional interest. Part of the border assigned to red might therefore contain Oriental poppies to flower in May and June, red hot pokers for mid-season and scarlet gladioli for autumn. From the start Gertrude liked silver plants for edging, warm colours in sunny places, and more delicate, 'cool' ones for shady borders.

A correspondent who dared to criticize her about colour prompted a sturdy defence. 'I do not advance remarks on colour arrangement as general and vague . . . but as the practical result of what I have worked out with my own hands.'[10] The principles of harmonious colour were the very reverse of bedding with its rigid blocks and colour patterns, Gertrude explained in *The Garden*. She had 'no sympathy with the system',[11] was 'happy to perceive its decline' and 'wished only for its extinction'.[12] Sometimes she took it upon herself to throw out opinions like some commanding empress. Taken out of context, her words suggest as die-hard a stance as Robinson's. Her attitude can be a little confusing. At Munstead House she had actually planned a small parterre, and the majority of gardens she designed used bedding plants. What she objected to was the exclusive and insensitive use of offending styles. Whether the pattern was formal or informal, moreover, her advice was to study 'Nature'. From long experience she had allowed nature to dissolve into her imagination; from it she took her best images and intensified them.

Six years from its conception, and publicized by her journalism, Gertrude's garden continued to attract horticultural enthusiasts: Sir Joseph Hooker, erudite botanist, plant collector and Director of Kew, James and Harry Mangles, pioneer rhododendron-growers from Farnham, and the Rev. C. Wolley Dod, a retired Eton master whom she described as a 'scholar, botanist and great English gentleman; an enthusiast for plant life, an experienced gardener and the kindest of instructors'.[13] Among them was a notable woman, known at least by hearsay to the Jekylls. Theresa Earle was seven years her senior and from the start her career had followed a similar pattern — South Kensington School of Art, interior decoration and now gardening. Gradually the lives of these two women were edging together.

Edward Woodall sounds a little too high-bred to have numbered among garden visitors referred to in the Jekyll family as 'Gertrude's funnies'.[14] He had met her through Canon Hole, stayed at Munstead House, which implies a fair degree of acceptance, and shared her love for 'those fine plants called Yuccas'[15] which he grew in two gardens, at Scarborough and Nice. Others making the pilgrimage included Dr Alfred Russel Wallace, a zoologist, botanist and Far Eastern traveller renowned for his Darwinian evolutionary theory; John Bennett-Poe of Tipperary, who gave his name to a now forgotten daffodil; and W. E. Gumbleton, celebrated for generic collections in his garden at Belgrove. There was botanical painter Henry Moon, who had joined the staff of *The Garden* as artist, and Marianne North, a traveller in the New World, commemorated with a gallery at Kew Gardens full of bold paintings of tropical flowers. Apart from Robinson, all belonged to 'that wonderful company of amateurs and others who did so much for better gardening in the last half of the nineteenth century'.[16] Perhaps the only guests who received a lukewarm welcome were Herbert and Aggie. Their weekend visits were 'greatly welcomed by Granny Jekyll', Agnes wrote, 'and more tepidly by Gertrude, to whom we were a sad interruption'.[17]

Gertrude's links with Algiers remained fruitful. On 3 February 1883 she was burying white Algerian hoop-petticoat narcissus, just arrived from M. Durando, in a warm bank of turf. In June both vines in her small vinery looked sickly after fourteen perfectly healthy years. What could have caused the malaise, she queried in the pages of *The Garden*. In July she was sending to Sir Joseph Hooker at Kew some *Mertensia maritima* and 'in case it is of any interest or value'[18] a species of adiantum, a fern brought from Brazil in 1872 by the late T. W. Hinchliff. In return she begged *Sedum cyaneum*, obtainable neither from friends nor from nurseries, but it was not in the Kew collection either. Traffic in plants was two-way, and the stream she sent to Kew and Glasnevin was answered by twenty-one herbaceous plants and three packets of seeds, according to the Outwards Books at Kew, in 1883 alone. She was selecting intensively, producing varieties such as *Aquilegia* 'Munstead White'. Herbert, at the War Office, was by chance simultaneously sounding Sir Joseph about the preservation of tropical forest, portraying a marvellously modern, environmentalist attitude. 'There has been, I know, a good deal of controversy upon this matter in Ceylon, and I have no doubt it is becoming an important question in other Colonies.'[19]

On 9 November, the first bloom on Gertrude's *Iris stylosa*, her coveted Algerian introduction, beat all previous records. It was harbinger to a momentous development. The problem about horticultural enthusiasts at Munstead House was inflicting them upon Mrs Jekyll. Gertrude herself was approaching her fortieth year, and the need for mother and daughter to possess wholly independent homes was evident to both. The outcome was purchasing a roughly fifteen-acre triangle of land adjoining Munstead on the north. For Gertrude the magic of possession was immediate. One imagines her opening the inconspicuous gate in the hedge on the far side of the road, making her definite, unhurried way along a dividing path through gorse and heather dotted by holly, birch, pine and chestnut. The entire plot sloped gently away from her, the southern, broad corner of the flattened isosceles triangle being occupied by ten acres of old plantation, birch and pine, cut to the ground in 1877, full of stumps and roots and self-sown with seedlings 'so thick that it was impossible to get between them'.[20] In this corner the leached sandy soil was thinnest of all. Ahead of her stood a grove of chestnuts; beyond it, moving west, she came to an arable strip, then a tiny corner of garden ground. At last she had a place entirely to herself! Each day she must have trodden paths into the new site, familiarizing herself with its trees, sensing its strengths and weaknesses, building very gradually in her mind a picture of the right and beautiful home that would one day melt into its setting of trees, shrubs and flowers. From this time forth, her main energies were transferred to laying out and planting what she referred to as 'OS', an abbreviation for the 'other side' of the road.

The end of the month saw, with the publication of William Robinson's *The English Flower Garden*, one of the great gardening landmarks of the century. About ninety people are credited with contributions to its second part, five of them women, among them Gertrude who had written a chapter on colour that is one of the book's outstanding features. It was a comprehensive manual of design and horticulture, embracing all the hardy and half-hardy flora, written in rhetoric more appropriate to politics, but calculated to sell. 'At present the rule is no art, no good grouping, no garden pictures, no variety,' little but ugly, repetitious patterns and 'the choke-muddle shrubbery'.[21] But even the smallest garden could be 'a pretty one'.[22] It was clear immediately that *The English Flower Garden* would be a bestseller.

Only winter released Gertrude from her new garden. Lord Grantley, her old friend and neighbour from Wonersh Park, had died in 1875 but his wife survived him. What could be more refreshing than a week or two with her on the Isle of Capri? When Gertrude was not sketching or fishing, she was plant-hunting with Max Leichtlin, a well-known nurseryman from Baden-Baden. A short article she wrote about a treasured plant-collecting pick-axe explained how she scaled the heights and prized out seedlings, impaling the ground while clinging to vegetation with one hand. *Lithospermum rosmarifolium* caught her eye, hugging the limestone cliffs, frequently in combination with a prostrate form of rosemary. To both William Robinson and Joseph Hooker, new director of Kew, she sent specimens because 'the colour of its flowers is brighter than that of any blue flower I know'.[23] At Naples she was joined by the Blumenthals, who accompanied her to Rome, Florence, Alassio and Genoa before leaving her to find her way home through France, via the great cathedrals at Sens and Amiens. Ruskin, her spiritual guide, always harked back to the Medieval with its Gothic and its faith.

Gertrude's articles on flower-arranging had made her aware of the dearth of good containers. If she felt the need for something, she buckled down and made it; the result in this case being a range of simple, inexpensive shapes designed for production by Messrs James Green and Nephew of Queen Victoria Street. Robinson vigorously promoted the Munstead flower vase. Market forces were flooding the British shops with Victorian knick-knacks, and there was too much of what *The Garden* called 'decorative rubbish'[24] about – flashy, patterned and coloured glass 'bad in design, ugly in colour, and in all ways unfitted for [its] purpose'.[25]

Each piece of work Gertrude did increased her reputation, eliciting further requests for assistance. Maybe it was at Cadogan Square that she had first met Jane Henrietta Adeane, granddaughter of the first Lord Stanley of Alderley, who now consulted her about a garden. Miss Adeane was, according to Violet Martineau, 'a great friend'.[26] She had lived in the Stanley home, Penrhos in Holyhead, until her brother died, at which juncture she bought a grey house banked with tall pink geraniums called Llanfawr. Here her immediate thought was to contact her old friend for advice. 'On Monday Miss Jekyll comes,'[27] sister Constance was informed, 'I hope it will still be bright so that the views will be as beautiful as they are now.'[28] On 3 July 1884, Gertrude arrived in Holyhead.

Miss Adeane settled at Llanfawr for the remainder of her life, enriching the island community by her good works. To provide evening occupation for local lads she set up a unit under the aegis of the Home Art Movement, importing, at her own expense, a master carver. She was a generous supporter of Bangor University, with nationalist sympathies for Welsh customs and legends, Welsh dress and the language, which she spoke fluently. Kind-hearted, open-handed and hospitable, Miss Adeane was not without quirks, secrecy and abhorrence for the terms 'spinster' and 'old maid' being the most prominent. It was a penalty for an unmarried daughter to suffer a grief so sore she could not cover it over. A golden rule among nearly forty fond nephews and nieces was never to use the offending words. On Miss Martineau's testimony her aunt 'made her little garden at Llanfawr very pretty under advice of Miss Gertrude Jekyll'.[29] The following month Gertrude drew a garden plan for Mr Okell of Manchester. Her career in landscape gardening had begun.

Gertrude read extensively and she asked questions from those she considered best equipped to know, 'constantly', as a friend remarked later, 'thinking, contriving, giving or storing information'.[30] Part of her mind was occupied with thoughts of the house that would fit her wooded setting, and Ruskin, consulted on the choice of materials, recommended black and grey limestones from Derbyshire, with 'Good whitewashed timber and tapestry'[31] interiors. Oak beams and white-wash met the entire approval of his correspondent; the vision of a house beautiful equipped to perfect service grew in her mind as she prepared to visit old friends in the Severn district. In Exeter she was again judging, this time at a fruit fair. At home she was searching for cottage rarities and writing for *The Garden*. In mid-November, she was delighted to find eighty plants in flower in her garden. Correspond-ents might die down in the winter, she wrote early in 1885,[32] but, like 'true perennials',[33] they tended to reappear in the spring. One who reappeared only to contradict her praise for *Iris tuberosa* reckoned it was 'a dull-coloured' (underlined) 'ugly curiosity' (twice underlined). The miscreant was promptly referred to Ruskin. 'The finer the eye for colour, the less it will require to gratify it intensely.'[34]

Robinson waved Ruskin's flag almost as bravely as Gertrude; it was obvious that communications would be fruitful between the mutually respecting proselytes, especially now they were both considering new homes. Journalism had brought Robinson a sizeable income, and when

The English Flower Garden emerged he was richer still. The same year
he had engaged an architect to draw up plans for a house. It need not
be grand, he told Gertrude, but should be well built and original.
Immediately she was involved: 'Your architect has fine vigorous
wholesome notions – I should like to talk to him. It will interest me
extremely to see your house plans – I always think no house, however
small, should have a mean or pokey place to come into – My ideal
house, after an enclosed porch would have a good size habitable hall or
room. If space or means could not allow it as an extra sitting room it
would be the place to dine in & the stairs would rise from it.'[35]
Nothing came of Robinson's building – presumably he had decided to
opt for an older house – and suddenly he was sharing new excitement.
An advertisement had appeared in *The Times* for a picturesque Eliza-
bethan mansion in Sussex with two lakes and extensive undulating
parklands. Was it a sound investment? Inspection proved there was
everything conceivably wrong with the place. Yet Gravetye had innate
dignity; Robinson was beguiled and not given to dithering – he
bought it and moved in. Henceforth he and Gertrude would both be
creating the environments that were their greatest personal monuments.

The day after Robinson's momentous purchase, on 18 July 1885, there
was a delicate image in *The Garden* of the fragrant, white-flowered
American *Carpenteria californica*. It was five years since the shrub had
arrived in England, and Gertrude grew it at Munstead House where she
had taken the photograph. Credit for the first blooms she could not accept;
Canon Ellacombe in Gloucester and Mr Ewbank in the Isle of Wight had
beaten her by a year. But her début as a photographer was in itself an
achievement. She does not seem to have needed to reconcile her new
technological enthusiasm with her allegiance to the Arts and Crafts.
Photography had emerged from inventors' workshops to be practised in
studios and then in the open air, outdoing the human eye and hand at
capturing the true resemblance of face and scene. Gertrude acquired a large
plate camera – possibly the Collins with a Dallmeyer lens, left at Munstead
Wood when she died – fitted up sinks and dark-rooms and, tutored by
Herbert, began to process the first of over 2,000 images. 'Bad light', 'Keep
the camera level', 'more pyro – more bromide', are scribbled sternly on the
back of her prints in her brother's more rounded hand, while a note from
her own diary, 'Phot. at 4 a.m.',[36] suggests that having assembled her
formidable abilities, she was as energetic in this pursuit as all her others.

Six chronologically arranged albums have survived extraordinary vicissitudes to document the new hobby. For sixteen years after Gertrude's death they lay at Munstead Wood before being auctioned, among eleven, with the contents of the house. Mrs Agnes Milliken, then director of the Reef Point Gardens Corporation, purchased them for £18 from a bookshop in Guildford in 1949. Beatrix Farrand, leading American landscape architect, Jekyll enthusiast and founder of the Reef Point Collection, had acquired the bulk of Gertrude's garden plans the previous year. Both were kept in her library on Maine's Mount Desert Island before being donated to the University of California at Berkeley in 1955. Judith Tankard and Michael van Valkenburgh have since published a selection in their annotated catalogue, *Gertrude Jekyll: A Vision of Garden and Wood*.

For Gertrude, photography was a new art form, a tool for clarifying mistakes and a visual notebook of ideas for future reference. For years she had fuelled her creative effort by teaching herself to observe; now she could focus the landscape on to ground glass, producing images of effects her eyes could not clearly see. By examining the images she could study in detail the results of her work. Photographs taken intensively over the next years include some of her first abortive attempts, a hilarious uncalculated curiosity – a cat frantically wagging its head over some catmint, reduced by long exposure to a blur, and some images considered good enough to illustrate books and magazines. Like a pictorial diary they interweave her writings, portraying artistic sensibilities, feline tragedies ('My Dear Toosey – dead'),[37] humour, and varied crafts, rural traditions, vernacular architecture, landscape projects, domestic incidents – nieces, pussies, and the largest group of all, material from her gardens at Munstead Wood.

Despite competition from the dark-room, she managed to complete some craft commissions, among them a bay-leaf design by Burne-Jones incorporating the Monogram 'LL' to be made up as a silver panel for Laura, wife of Alfred Lyttelton. Collaboration may have been arranged by Agnes's father, though Burne-Jones, obsessed with the symbolic language of flowers, could well have sought Gertrude himself. The panel was photographed and pasted into the second album, but unfortunately it has since been removed.

In a single year, Gertrude progressed from her first misty images of the rock garden at OS to photographs of intensely convoluted cabbagy bergenias, showing as fine a textural display as the drapery of a small classical figure cast from Greek terracotta that she refers to as 'La Bellatrice'.[38] Others show the perfectly poised simplicity of *Narcissus bulbocodium*. One can see what she was after; the raw material of her inspiration is here, in naturalistic plant groupings, flower arrangements, old buildings – the Malthouse at Bramley – portraits, of Mrs (Reynolds) Hole, a lovely, open, energetic and reflective face, and '3 Irish people & viper'.[39] All three are horticultural: Miss Owen wrote about greenhouses, Frederick Moore was Director of Glasnevin Botanic Garden and Frederick Burbidge was Curator of Trinity College Garden in Dublin. He had collected plants in Borneo for James Veitch and was already the author of seven books on plants. The photo albums show roses snapped with the dew still on them, innumerable arched bridges and tremendous forked tree-boles with their intricate tracery of branches.

Refusal to be satisfied until a process was mastered was basic to the Arts and Crafts. In October one of Gertrude's photographs was acknowledged among four joint winners of a competition run by *The Garden*. It showed cedar-planted lawns at Peper Harow, the Midletons' park which she had loved since childhood.

CHAPTER THIRTEEN

1886—91

To judge from Gertrude's Algerian sketchbook, the odd water-colour, and drawings in possession of the family, she was a mediocre painter, a gifted craftswoman and a unique garden designer; she must have been aware where her talents lay because in whatever she undertook she strove to reach excellence. On one level she was dissociating herself from pure art, on another she was achieving a rare relationship between art and gardening, and all the evidence suggests that it was her own inclinations that led her where her contribution was most original. She never ceased indoor crafts, some of her surviving shell-work dating from shortly before her death, but since she discovered her forte, there had been fewer departures from routine, increasing satisfaction in what Wordsworth called the 'dark inscrutable workmanship that reconciles discordant elements'.[1]

At Wargrave she had begun selecting primrose seedlings and now she had hundreds of strong plants. Every year she harvested the seed and in 1880 a pure yellow had appeared, the first important colour break for over 100 years. Towards the end of the decade she introduced to commerce the first seed strain of the modern polyanthus, her Munstead 'bunch-flowered primroses' in delicate shades of yellow and white. Naturalizing primroses beneath nut trees was being promoted by The Garden;[2] there were, it said, parts of East Anglia where it was rare to find a hazel copse that did not also succour them. At Munstead House Gertrude's colony had been shaded by nuts; at OS the soil was deeply dug and enriched before the final move to a clearing near the northern boundary, half shaded by oak, chestnut and hazel. They were planted not far from the site left for a house, beside gently winding paths, where strong spring sun would filter green through the trees, turning the petals translucent.

Work set a pattern interrupted only by the arrival of visitors to see whatever happened to be in bloom. Photography continued apace.

Late in the spring of 1886 Gertrude took a series of plant portraits marked 'EFG' to provide illustrations for the second, 1889, and subsequent editions of *The English Flower Garden*. Combining close scrutiny of the natural world with a passionate sympathy for its every manifestation, she sought the turbulence behind apparent order that makes a totality of human experience. At the end of December, when a violent storm had played havoc with forest trees, she was out with her camera at Busbridge Lower Lake, photographing the ravages of fine Scots pines thrown down by wind and lightning. Late in the spring of 1887 she was at Gravetye, helping Robinson record his new home, reflecting his obsession with fireplaces. Their mutual friend, the Rev. Hole, she heard with pleasure, had been made Dean of Rochester.

These were the years of most intensive work at OS. In one of the most telling sequences in the genesis of Munstead Wood, Gertrude describes how she handled the groundwork in the piece of native woodland where a pine plantation had been felled, nature being compelled, so to speak, to group the trees. Birch, holly, oak, rowan, chestnut and seedling pines were regenerating naturally. By reducing the species in each area and eliminating what was superfluous, she stamped the identity of different parts. Silver birch and holly were encouraged together for contrast, beech and chestnut maintained in single stands, and a few pine saplings were left around the edges of the wood. Treating each area individually and merging them with under-cover, she achieved a series of uncluttered, simple and harmonious pictures. Among some seventy garments and textiles she eventually deposited at the Victoria and Albert Museum are a couple of finely embroidered nineteenth-century Chinese water scenes, very simple, very reduced. Because the richness and abundance of her gardening inevitably conceals some of its art, it is worth stressing that she was a master minimalist. What was taken out was as important as what remained. In the area she generally refers to as the 'copse', a few old Scots pines were chosen as focal points for grassy walks, radiating out through carefully planted floral glades, and paths were cut 'on the easiest lines',[3] major ones more boldly than subsidiary ones, to serve the future house and formal garden.

Francis Jekyll stresses the quiet, directed labour of his aunt's days. 'Freedom is a positive condition,' said the art critic, Herbert Read, 'freedom to become what one is . . . It is not a state of rest, of least

resistance,' but 'of projection, of self-realization'.[4] Financial independence gave Gertrude the opportunity to seize the freedoms it provided,
yet freedom imposed an obligation; call it, perhaps, justification. In
what must be one of her most keenly self-analytical passages, she
asked, 'And is it a blessing or a disadvantage to be interested in many
matters. That, seeing something that one's hand may do, one cannot
resist doing or attempting it even though time be already overcrowded
. . . and sight steadily failing. Are people happier who are content to
drift comfortably down the stream of life . . . I know not which, as
worldly wisdom, is the wiser.'[5] Drifting was not necessarily comfortable; she was well aware of the frustration of imposed idleness, a
condition she strained every fibre of her being to avoid. But only she
knew the price she paid for her urgencies.

Communications were governed increasingly by work schedules.
The woman who had once fled from a garrulous German admirer on a
Mediterranean cruise still had a horror of being cornered by a bore.
But apart from wasting time, talking to people she did not care about
on subjects which did not interest her required an effort she was
reluctant to make. She was, on the other hand, happy to discourse
with knowledgeable people, and friends, which they often became,
remained in a category of their own. Each year brought its quota of
eminent men: Alfred Russel Wallace's invitation to participate in an
'experiment'[6] may have been a collaboration on hybridizing primroses,
and Sir Francis Galton, one of the founders of genetics, arrived to take
impressions of her hands. Galton thought intelligence had physical
manifestations; to test the theory he distributed small, specially designed
booklets to all the members of a family and to others ranging from
university dons to prison inmates. Each finger had to be rubbed with
carbon chalk before being applied to a page. Doubtless Gertrude's
prints are housed among several thousand gathering dust in the medical
library at London's University College.

The largest group to make the Munstead pilgrimage would always
be gardeners, notable among them the Hon. Mrs E. V. Boyle of
Huntercombe in Buckinghamshire, 'a woman of the sensitive artist-
temperament',[7] Gertrude approved. Making her début as an illustrator,
Mrs Boyle was responsible for 'one of the first beautifully illustrated
colour printed books',[8] a German translation that cost £1,000 to
produce and was already a collectors' item. Mrs Earle tells how the
author had sat next to Millais at a dinner party shortly after its

publication when, without realizing to whom he spoke, he praised the book 'up to the skies'.[9] She had married the younger, clergyman son of the eighth Earl of Cork, but since he had died, two years before, she had moved from the Boyle estate at Marston and become a devoted gardener. E.V.B., as she called herself, had written the first of three garden autobiographies, *Days and Hours in a Garden*. Thomas Hanbury also visited Munstead Wood. He had fallen in love with the country around Ventimiglia in northern Italy, bought a derelict *palazzo* with 200 acres, and proceeded to create La Mortola, one of the greatest gardens of the nineteenth century.

Of rather a special nature were Gertrude's escapades with three Liddells whom she had known since childhood. Victoria and Eleanor were daughters of the 1st Earl of Ravensworth and therefore cousins to Mrs Earle; Charles was another cousin. Gertrude's photograph of Lady Victoria shows a slim, thin-lipped lady in riding dress holding a pekinese; one of Charles, a well-covered young man with large rings on either hand, carefully restoring a piece of pottery. He worked at the British Museum, and all were 'in their several ways responsive to the artist's call'.[10] Lady Victoria had married Captain Edward Fisher-Rowe of Thorncombe, an estate next to the old Jekyll Bramley home, from where it was but a stone's throw to Munstead. In summer, in a spirit of humour and affection, the three would mount the dog-cart Gertrude used, to her friends' amusement, as a method of transport, and go picnicking. The cart was pulled by a stout cob whose reins passed through a ring. The ring appeared to be placed opposite the centre of the seat, but discovering that she took up more room than the majority of her passengers, Gertrude had it shifted several inches away from her. The vehicle appears in one of her photographs, a trim little conveyance bearing her name and address: its equilibrium, however, was uncertain. But fun, for Gertrude, was a concept that would always centre on unelaborate self-made pleasures. Some well-known spot was visited, a fire was lit and water boiled in a specially designed, square, squat-shaped picnic kettle, a 'point of honour'[11] being to do so within five minutes of the first flame. It was a party piece repeated for special friends with a kind of girlish zeal that Gertrude generated well into middle age. Precise details for choosing a site, cutting turf and laying a grid are explained in a book she wrote many years later for children. She was, of course, a perfectionist; George Leslie had remarked upon it and so did Logan Pearsall Smith. Even revels were accomplished with finesse; nothing was exempt.

In March, sharply pointed bottle-green tips had pierced heavily manured soil at the edge of the copse and expanded into leaves. In June, flower stems had shot up eleven-foot spears, and on 17 July 1888, the flowers had opened. It was an epic calendar feature; and the stage was set to photograph, for the second consecutive year, a group of lily-like *Cardiocrinum giganteum*. The third year, partly as a gauge for height but also to dramatize the effect, Gertrude engaged one of her gardeners, P. Brown, swathed in a cowl, to pose beside the plants, meditating and reading a Bible, a crucifix hanging from his neck. She had gone to the trouble of borrowing a cowl from the Franciscan monastery at Crawley and made up an identical garment for her Pre-Raphaelite stunt.

Days drawing into autumn found her writing to Viscountess Wolseley, wife of the first Viscount and Field Marshal, enclosing rough sketch plans for replanting parts of her garden in Farnham. 'No raspberry canes to send, as they have been thinned out . . .'[12] Gertrude regretted; the first indication that she was providing plants for her commissions. In time to come, the Viscountess's sixteen-year-old daughter, Frances, would set up a school for lady gardeners of which Gertrude would become a trustee.

There were lamplit hours for craftwork, brass scutcheons, wooden corner cupboards and silver tigridias – half-hardy, three-petalled flowers from Mexico, much like an iris, whose symmetry lent well to current art nouveau and craft designs. Probably they were chased or engraved. Another project, 'Appliqué worsted parrots',[13] was obviously needlework. The following spring Gertrude was again using silver: a paten engraved with a biblical reference, was, according to Francis Jekyll, commissioned by the Liddells to present to Witley Church. Her meticulous workmanship was also finding purchasers on the open market. An iron tray with a silver border, and a tortoiseshell casket exhibited in the Women's Work section of an Exhibition of Victorian craft at Earl's Court, were snapped up by the Museum of Science and Art.

Between 1885 and 1888 Gertrude had taken 900 of the photographs that make such a potent celebration of time and place; of the garden at OS, the countryside around her, cottage porches smothered in roses, stately homes, near and occasionally further afield. Personal photographs tell of interludes at Scalands with Barbara Bodichon attended by Nurse Hornsby in frilled cap and starched dress, breaks which came to an end when Barbara died, after a long illness, in 1891, leaving to

Gertrude not only the Poor House but all her Spanish pottery. The Chalet provided a poignant scatter of period pieces. There was a house guest, an artist called Theodore Waterhouse, breakfasting on the balcony between screens of exotic trailing plants; Condesa O'Connell, Leonie Blumenthal's aunt, heavily brocaded beneath the pergola; and Gertrude's hosts, Monsieur and Madame Blumenthal, in elegant relaxation with sunshade and newspaper. Huge, trumpet-flowered daturas were symbols of Sonzier's secrets as much as Pear de Tongue, the famous dessert dish, showing every pimple on their sun-shiny skins, and mists dispersing with the sunrise to reveal the Dent du Midi above Lake Geneva.

Day after day, Gertrude's familiar figure, bespectacled, well shod and quietly dressed, frequented woods, farms, mills and outlying villages around Munstead. The photographs show what she selected from the environment that meant most to her, south towards Chiddingfold on to the wooded edge of the Weald, south-west over the heath towards Milford and Witley, and further into Haslemere; westwards along the river at Godalming to Eashing, Peper Harow and Elstead. North-west took her to Compton and the More Molyneux's Loseley, with its great chestnuts and moated garden, a park she had known since childhood; north-east to Shalford and Chilworth below the chalk downs and east, past Great Tangley Manor with its Philip Webb renovations, to the low-lying, Sunday cricket-playing villages of the Wey tributaries, Cranleigh, Ewhurst, and Shamley Green. Tunnels and arches remained constant themes: in Gertrude's tunnels one is tempted to find a symbol for the narrow passageways by which the ego communicates with the world, and she was later to write that a framed view had a 'strange kind of beauty'.[14] Knotted complexities of tree roots cling desperately to life in unpromising circumstances and ivy-festooned trunks portray the struggle between host and invader, potent for one attracted to delve beyond appearances to nature's extremes. There were images of moments that would never again be repeated. The 'happy days'[15] in the spring of 1886 when two garden enthusiasts, Mrs Davidson, author of *The Unheated Greenhouse*, and check-capped Bennett-Poe, 'could hardly pass any plant without . . . an illuminating discussion on its ways and wants'.[16] Few were more aware of the ephemeral nature of their surroundings, how easily things that were wholesome or well designed were spoiled, devalued or replaced. A cottage entrance in Shackleford shows flagstones laid to form a pretty, utilitarian gutter seep; Captain Nelson's towering *Yucca gloriosa* is a study in pride; there are village portraits, each one a poignant mixture of love and care, custom and enterprise. 'Mrs Joy – Selhurst Common & her window plant',[17] Mrs Hunterfield sitting outside the back door, work-worn arms clasped over a torn apron, while flowers and leaves spill on to uneven flags. The cottage life was not easy, but the moment was marked by a stillness the photographer found appropriate.

Monet, Renoir, Pissarro, Cézanne and Degas had produced a fever of excitement across the Channel; now their work could be seen in England. Gertrude profoundly admired the Impressionists whose painting was interacting boldly with photography, and she may have been influenced by the rivalry between younger photographers and the established picturesque or 'academic' set. Dr Peter Henry Emerson, physician turned photographer and author of a delightful album of East Anglian scenes, was one who felt that Nature, not painting, should be the photographers' study. By varying the sharpness of different objects and merging into soft focus at the edges, he reckoned he came closer to truth, and the earnestness of his working people makes Gertrude's old ladies in starched white sun-bonnets look a trifle posed. Frederick Evans was another amateur turned professional, to some extent influenced by Impressionist painting: a master of technical expertise and delicate tones. Evans saw the play of light in the horizontal layering of larch trees and the steps of Wells Cathedral as Gertrude might have done, and both had their photographs accepted by *Country Life*. Gertrude's work has been compared with that of the great French photographer and indefatigable chronicler of Paris, Eugène Atget. But apart from sharing a passion for twisted trees, they are not really comparable. Atget's water-reflective images are more sophisticated, and dramatic. Perhaps the most important point about Gertrude's work is that she had something strong to say and knew how to say it as no other living person could. Drawn like a magnet to archways, gateways, exits and entrances, her vision is essentially secret and English. It was as if she moved into a new field with a vision already matured, intimate, feminine and inward-looking.

Which person out of hundreds met will become part of one's personal orbit? Gertrude shunned the *hoi polloi*, but made old friends, especially if they were plant people, an essential part of her social ritual. Harry Mangles of Thursley, who was both, had invited her to meet a nineteen-year-old architect he had appointed to design a cottage – the young man's first commission. Long after Ned Lutyens became Sir Edwin, he described the rhododendron 'reflecting'[18] conversation, the silver tea kettle and Gertrude, 'quiet and demure',[19] in her 'Go-to-Meeting Frock',[20] her only hint of extravagance a black felt hat with sprightly cock's-tail feathers, its brim turned up behind and down in front. The feathers may have suggested to someone who did not know her that she was not entirely demure. With respect, Lutyens noted her intelligent, beady eyes.

Edwin Lutyens was born in 1869, the son of an army officer turned oil painter; a delicate, impressionable child who spent a great deal of his youth wandering through woods and along lanes, 'imagining'.[21] He did not only imagine, he needed to express his creative intensity, and drawing as naturally as leaves grow on a tree, soon found himself at South Kensington School of Art. Ned, as he preferred to be called, was aesthetic and sensitive, with a wonderful humour; he retained, moreover, an attractive child-like side to his nature. So much of his early experience was like Gertrude's that it has always been difficult to know what each learned from and taught the other. But it was this collaboration with the world of childhood as much as anything that allowed them to side-step the weight of convention. Gertrude was forty-six, attracted by young people's zest but intolerant of stupidity and almost neurotically sensitive to noise. It sounds more like awkwardness than arrogance that prevented her from addressing the palpably interesting young man during the tea-party, for once outside, 'with one foot on the step of her pony-cart and reins in hand',[22] she invited him to tea at Munstead the following Saturday. It was a stage in her life when all sorts of decisions brought momentous consequences.

The second meeting confirmed the first. On 'the tick of four', Ned was received by 'a somewhat different person'.[23] At home, Gertrude's abrasiveness was subdued and modified. He was surprised at the genial transformation. This time she was dressed entirely in blue, a shorter skirt, box-pleated blouse and linen apron with a pocket full of horticultural implements that became a kind of trademark. After a tour of garden and workshop, Lutyens was introduced to Mrs Jekyll. It was the beginning of a friendship with Gertrude that lasted until her death, a relationship during which, Ned acknowledged, his affection and admiration ever grew. In Mary Lutyens's biography of her father, she describes Gertrude as the woman who 'of all others',[24] was to have most influence on his career.

Short sight was something Gertrude had lived with for more than forty years. Among artists the tendency is not unusual. Many Impressionists bore the trait, and so did Tennyson, who won his readers' admiration for truth to nature. Gertrude was aware that her predicament might not be altogether a handicap, 'And I know from my own case that the will and the power to observe does not depend on the possession of keen sight. For I have sight that is both painful and inadequate; short sight of the severest kind . . . and always progressive . . . but the little I have I try to make the most of, and often find that I have observed things that have escaped strong and long-sighted people.'[25] But close work was involved in practically all she did; it was a strain and gave her headaches. Because sight was vital to work, and work was vital to her entire sense of worth, she may have shirked from knowing the truth. Was her sight getting worse, if so, how fast? Was close work actually speeding the process? In the summer of 1891, she travelled to Wiesbaden in order to consult Pagensteter, a leading ophthalmologist.

The news was bad. There was no cure, and only by avoiding close work as far as possible, painting and embroidery in particular, could she hope to arrest deterioration. Francis Jekyll calls it a 'problem',[26] Betty Massingham, theatrically, a 'life sentence',[27] and because Gertrude befriended Ned Lutyens the same year, the events have been connected. The myth has an attractive balance. Fate that forbade painting, compensated with Ned's genius – a beautiful inverse to hers. The trouble with simplifying is that it also distorts. Much has been made of Pagensteter's report as a turning point, but though one concedes that it may have alarmed, it is not obvious that Gertrude altered her life in consequence. She continued to copy paintings, but for the past ten years she had been doing less indoor craft and very little original painting. Already she had become *a priori* a gardener and garden designer. The optician's prognosis seems to have done little more than re-emphasize her choice of path. With a clearer vision of her mission, she forged ahead.

Shortly after his wedding, Herbert had been in France with Ruskin and heard the critic say, 'Brabazon is the only man since Turner at whose feet I can sit and worship and learn about colour.'[1] In what appears to be the first recorded appreciation of Brabazon's painting,[2] Herbert communicated Ruskin's words to their subject. Later, Brabazon's brilliantly tinted, Turneresque landscapes earned Ruskin's personal tribute; 'If you and I could be rolled into one, we should astonish the world of painting'.[3]

To Gertrude, such praise was no surprise. Part of Brabazon longed shyly for recognition and sometimes her service lay in helping people, by the light of her experience, to see what they really meant or felt. She had always maintained a delicate, insistent pressure on him to show his watercolours. Back in 1867, at the same time as Ruskin and Rossetti, Brabazon had been elected to Burlington Fine Arts Club. His talent had been recognized yet he could never quite be persuaded to exhibit his work. More recently, however, he had been championed by a band of young radicals who had set up the New English Art Club in opposition to the more establishment Royal Academy. On being elected a member, Brabazon felt he owed his supporters an exhibition and, receiving good reviews, he sent one to his old friend. No one could have been more delighted. Gertrude returned it, with the comment that to him, more than anyone, she felt she owed her appreciation of colour. Could he lend her a sketch of Velázquez's *Infanta Marguerite* from the Louvre to copy? 'So near to nature does Velázquez come,' she wrote, 'that Ruskin says of his portraiture. "He flings the man himself upon the canvas."'[4]

In 1892 Brabazon had his first one-man show at the Goupil Gallery in New Bond Street. The reception was astounding. All sixty-six watercolours sold immediately. Suddenly the art world reciprocated the Jekylls' sentiments. D. S. MacColl proclaimed Brabazon the 'best water-colour painter we have since Turner'.[5] George Moore wrote, 'The love of a long life is in those watercolours – they are all love . . . Mr Brabazon's eyes were strangely his own.'[6] Another critic reckoned him 'as much an Impressionist as Monet himself'.[7] At seventy he was treated like a newly discovered artist.

While Brabazon was delighting in the glow of unexpected attention, Gertrude's newest friend was adding an altogether fresh dimension to her days. Because Lutyens had had rheumatic fever as a child, he had suffered only two hated years of school. Lack of male company and a close rapport with his mother gave him an instinctive understanding of how to appeal to and benefit from older, more experienced women. He needed strong and self-reliant people upon whose judgement he could rely and in whose affection he could feel secure. Barbara Webb had been the first to take up the oddly shy, gentle, but tensely charged and imaginative boy, sympathizing and nurturing his artistic instincts through adolescence. Gertrude's efforts to draw him out were immediately reciprocated. She was to become the prominent influence throughout his twenties, during which time her influence on his character, development and career, according to Christopher Hussey, was 'magical'.[8] One oddity is irresistibly drawn to another and Gertrude was such by nature, but far from taking refuge in the guise of an outsider, she made it her business to be 'in'. Her worldliness was terribly important to Lutyens's ambition and confidence. Intuitively she divined the young man's brilliance, but only another artist, one, moreover, whom he respected, could have adopted her influential role.

Gertrude expected high standards both from others and from herself, and exhibited a certain imperiousness with fellow mortals who failed to match up to her 'austere moments'.[9] A cousin, Nellie Baring, wanting help with a garden near Lyndhurst in Hampshire, sent a list of fairly elementary questions to help her gardener follow Gertrude's instructions, and replies contained the rejoinders, 'nonsense', 'don't be silly' and 'do use your head and consult my chart'.[10] Some felt a little ill at ease in her company. Lutyens himself wrote of her intimidating influence on 'Lady Maud', whose 'chatter will bore Bumps awful but [I] don't suppose to Bumps that she does chatter!!'[11] Even her friends admitted that she had adversaries; after all, she 'could differ decidedly, promptly and completely, and she was sometimes not in the least disinclined to show it'.[12] But her need to give and receive affection was as pronounced as anyone's. Ned's effortless charm and quick response hit exactly the right note of admiration, and she could rely on him for almost unconditional acceptance. Far from being intimidated, he capitalized on what Christopher Hussey calls his 'little boy's art of amusing, cajoling and winning affections',[13] teasing with nonchalant irreverence, calling her 'Aunt Bumps, Mother of all Bulbs, Mab for short',[14] and Mab is Queen of the fairies.

All the Jekylls shared Gertrude's fondness for the new recruit. Ned found old Mrs Jekyll 'courteous, gently considerate and patient',[15] Herbert, a 'wise counsellor and gifted friend',[16] and Aggie was his model of a perfect hostess. For Ned, with his bohemian family, the Jekylls' searching standard of values, their 'fastidious learning',[17] was a constant inspiration. So genial were his visits that the Munstead week-end became a habit. Side by side in the dog-cart, he and Gertrude must have made an incongruous couple. A long-legged, dark-haired, skinny youth and the elderly, schoolmistressy lady, straw-hatted, ribbons streaming behind. On 'many a voyage of discovery'[18] they drove the length and breadth of Sussex and Surrey, down crumbly roads and narrow, muddy lanes, past woods, heaths and green fields. Every so often they would halt, reining the pony before an old house, farm or cottage, exchanging notes about 'their modest methods of construction ... their inmates and the industries that supported them'.[19] Lutyens, with his passion for Philip Webb's earthy construction, may have contributed technical architectural insight, but Gertrude had a great knowledge of rural tradition, including Surrey vernacular architecture, and as architect Herbert Baker recognized, her 'outstanding possession was the power to see, as a poet, the art and creation of home-making as a whole in relation to Life; the best simple country life of her day, frugal, yet rich in beauty and comfort, its garden uniting the house with surrounding nature'.[20] So it is open to question who pointed out to whom the details in the weavers' cottages around the Godalming area, exquisite decorative brickwork, satisfying geometric patterns or the garretting threaded with tiny ironstone chips from the greensand that Gertrude photographed. Studying intently, they memorized forms, colours, combinations and relationships. Lutyens had a horror of sketching, feeling his visual memory should suffice, but Gertrude certainly took photographs when they were together. West Surrey was full of picturesque buildings made from old English materials admired by Ruskin, the timber frames, mellow bricks and sweeping thatch or tiled roofs currently extolled in the paintings of Birket Foster and

Helen Allingham. In the years after meeting Lutyens, Gertrude took many more architectural photographs than she had done before, including some of his early projects.

Both were individualists, energetic, ambitious, determined, and equally obsessive about their work. Gertrude, moreover, could be almost as puckish as Ned. Where there was such sympathy, clearly each could benefit. It was not long before she was making tentative suggestions for the garden to a small country house called Crooksbury that Lutyens was building on a site near Farnham for a friend of Mrs Webb. Soon after, they collaborated on Gertrude's childhood friend, Susan Muir Mackenzie's, Hermitage near Effingham. Neither woman suffered fools gladly, but Miss Muir Mackenzie had given herself a social role by filling her country house with impoverished artists.

Ned had not been to public school or university, both considered essential prerequisites to making suitable contacts, but the Jekylls, grander than the Lutyens, did their best to provide clients, his task often to deal with the architectural adjuncts to gardens on which Gertrude was consulted. One was Adeline, widow of the 10th Duke of Bedford, who moved to a school for 'young ladies' on the Chenies estate near Rickmansworth after the Duke died. C. E. Kempe was commissioned to extend it and Lutyens did some work on the house, although his major contribution was to design the garden – one of his first important ones for an existing house, and an early commission outside Surrey. Despite several changes of ownership and subdivision, since 1976, into three separate dwellings, the garden remains largely as it was laid out in the summer of 1893, one of a number of Lutyens/Jekyll gardens in which the planting, if not authentic, has been maintained in a way that is sensitive to Jekyllian spirit.

The house nestles into the north side of a steep hill in a picturesque home counties setting of lush farmland, beech trees and bluebells. All its natural assets are exploited in Lutyens's simple axial design, its main north-facing vista cutting through terraces down to the River Chess, uniting in a single sweep house, lawns, flower borders and a plot of land beyond the river, now annexed to a neighbouring property. Bulky yew hedges channel the eye through the vista, giving a sculptured, Italianate impression. Twice the line of vision is arrested: by a stone sundial, and a columned, Jacobean-style stone arbour adrift with roses and clematis. Pictorial evidence from a *Country Life* article of 1901 and a watercolour by Beatrice Parsons, reproduced as the frontispiece in E. T. Cook's *Gardens of England* (1908), suggests that an initial non-Jekyll scheme was succeeded by another, either hers or based on her principles. In 1977, when the house was bought by Mr and Mrs Roland Edwards, the garden was rampant and it was not clear what had been planted since the Duchess's time. Undaunted, Mrs Edwards immersed herself in the Jekyll tradition before clearing and replanting.

It is not known whether Gertrude drew planting plans for Chenies, but when the garden was conceived she was working so closely with Lutyens that her influence is likely to have affected it substantially. Ten years before, she had written to William Robinson about the importance of the 'place to first come into'.[21] Though alluding to a house, she invested each garden entrance with the same, almost sacred significance. It linked more formal areas of the garden and the countryside, but even more importantly, it led to the private sanctuary of a human being, a buffer between the quietness which was home and the hurly-burly of the great fraught world outside. At Chenies Lutyens's elaborate, canopied roadside gateway leads to a path overhung by a vast Atlas cedar. Light falling between its furred grey branches is splintered among informal colonies of bluebells, ferns, lily of the valley and mosaics of cyclamen.

Chenies had an octagonal arbour, Munstead House had a pergola, the Chalet had two, and the pergola at OS, in place by 1890, was one of the earliest features. They were forerunners, moreover, of what was to be a regular feature of the Lutyens/Jekyll garden. It was twenty years since Gertrude had eulogized over bowers of roses and honeysuckle-draped columns in the House of the Bougainvillaea in Algiers. In her beloved Italy, pergolas and tree trunks trained with vines, roses and wisteria were a common sight; transposed, they evoked the tangled, perfumed abundance of hotter climates. She was also interested in the spatial concept of landscape; what could be more intriguing than a combination of plant and architecture, where shadows played endless trickery according to season and time of day, a three-dimensional, airy structure wrapping space around it like some fabulous mobile sculpture, without totally blotting the view. To Gertrude, a pergola had to be both functional and robust; it should lead from one part of a garden to another. Both she and Lutyens had enjoyed fishing as children and been fascinated by the play of water. The Chenies arbour, a focal point at the cross-roads of the design, originally stood over a circular pond, adding water to the elemental imbroglio. Possibly because rose leaves spoiled the effects, the pond was replaced by a fountain and marble basin, and subsequently, just a statue.

Herbaceous borders are probably the most renowned feature of the Jekyll garden, though not, incidentally, something Gertrude invented. Hardy plants were grown in groups in England at least 100 years earlier but mild weather, ample rainfall, cheap labour and the anti-bedding-out faction combined to encourage popularity in the late nineteenth century. Gertrude had laid out a notable border at Munstead House, and her refined plant and colour combinations were to reach an apogee in her most famous borders at Munstead Wood. At Chenies, hedges of lumpen yew enclose parallel herbaceous borders filled with her beloved greys, their textured softness emphasized by the density of deep green walls. The flower colours are soft – *Stachys lanata*, *Artemisia ludoviciana*, knapweed, onopordon, cardoons, lavenders, catmint, sea holly and anaphalis. Bright bedding plants in four octagonal stone-edged beds at each corner of the arbour are actually what the eye meets first. After 'strong rich colouring', Gertrude affirmed, 'the effect [of a grey garden] is surprisingly – quite astonishingly – luminous and refreshing'.[22] A stream flowing from the Chess dives beneath a small wooden bridge into rock and water gardens where informal planting, hellebores, geranium and bergenia, make way for a thick seasonal head of bamboos and *Gunnera manicata*. Here again, the colour is restful and harmonious.

When Gertrude met Lutyens, she had been developing the garden at OS for six years, patiently awaiting the right architect for her house. Four years later, the main axial lines west of the pergola were laid down and the spring garden fully formed. Shrubberies and copse in the eastern half of the garden had been mature for years, leaving just the central parts, between the pergola, the site of the house, on the south-west, to finalize. Would Lutyens, she asked him, draw some plans for two cottages and her permanent home? Little has been made of the first, abortive attempt. If there was one thing Ned sought from Gertrude above all, it was approval; and it was typical of her to have played down the endeavour. But his design for her house was elaborately Spanish-looking, which she knew immediately was not what she wanted. In retrospect, the project was useful as a trial; Munstead Wood was in the process of being realized. First, however, Ned would prove himself with smaller buildings.

Had Gertrude died at fifty, she would have left a mark among her generation of women but she would not have been remembered. Her first incorrigible energy had turned into dogged industriousness; and she was organizing her days to an optimum level of productiveness. If her receptivity to new ideas was tailing off, her work retained a gaiety and assurance that was fed by a well-stocked memory. Collaboration with Lutyens was stimulating. They had worked together on a number of properties; it was clearly a fruitful partnership, and she decided to build the two little cottages he had designed, one for the head gardener, the other, 'The Hut', to be a transitional home for herself.

The Gardener's Cottage was an essay in reinterpreting local vernacular architecture; tiny and half-timbered, with two elevations tile-hung and the back built into the western boundary wall. The previous year Munstead had gained what proved to be an immeasurable asset, Albert Zumbach, a Swiss retainer from the Blumenthals' Chalet. Zumbach had become a fervent disciple during Gertrude's visits, trotting round after her, talking plants; and eventually the stocky, moustached and somewhat taciturn man made what was for him a brave gesture, leaving behind his native mountains to become head gardener at Munstead. A year later he moved into Lutyens's cottage. Zumbach's wife, Margrit, accompanied him and at some point, Gottfried and Molly completed the family. Though Zumbach was subject to periodic fits of homesickness, Gertrude employed a Swiss servant who may have provided him with company, and 'intelligent obedience untainted by ideas at variance with her own'[23] proved a diplomatic formula. For over thirty years Zumbach maintained undisputed leadership over Munstead's garden staff.

The Hut was small, substantially built, and picturesque; so successful in Gertrude's eyes that had she not been encumbered with the trappings of a lifetime, she professed, 'I should scarcely have wished to live elsewhere or in anything larger.'[24] Even when Munstead Wood was built, she had great fondness for the little place glimpsed in her photographs, behind a huge garland rose. In her second book, she allotted a chapter to it. Ruskin was adamant that what one might call the 'real' world, the dirtiness and the ugliness, should be excluded from home; and not with his heartiest huffings could the archetypal wolf villain have blown down the substantial West Surrey cottage, with its brick path to the front door through a tunnel of yew. The way Gertrude stressed the thickness of its walls, the totally unnecessary affirmation that they would not 'let in a drop of wet',[25] emphasized

their protective function. Her respect for spareness, purity, and honesty
was essentially Arts and Crafts; every part was simple, functional and
well made.

All the important functions of Gertrude's life were centred in her
home, and unlike most homes, which simply portrayed what was
fashionable or generally acceptable, each of hers expressed her personality. The large downstairs room of The Hut, with a big east-facing
window, had a handsome inglenook, brick floor, whitewashed walls
and an oak-beamed roof. This was her workshop and sitting room,
'good to paint or work in'.[26] The kitchen and her bedroom were also
on the ground floor, and the housekeeper had one of the two tiny
rooms upstairs. If it sounds ascetic, Gertrude assured, 'When on winter
evenings there is a great log-fire blazing, and hot elderberry wine is
ready for drinking and nuts waiting to be cracked, and good comrades
are sitting, some on the inner fixed benches and some facing the fire's
wide front, singing . . . familiar rounds and catches, it is a very cosy
and cheerful place.'[27] Such an occasion did take place with Ned
Lutyens and Emily Lytton for company.

The cottage model was extended into the garden, where box-edged
beds of China roses, ferns, lavender, peonies and other simple flowers
growing beneath sprays of Gertrude's favourite hybrid musk rose,
'The Garland', emphasized the rural setting. The chimney could be
swept with a bunch of holly with a weight on the end of a rope. All
was neat, manageable and controlled. Achieving the simple life, making
things by hand and improving the world with one's integrity, were
the great dreams of Arts and Crafts. She always retained this image of
the tiny cottage as the ideal for a perfect life.

With gardening schemes at OS that led Henri Correvon, Director
of Le Jardin Alpin d'Acclimatation in Geneva, to claim that Munstead
deserved its 'universal reputation for excellence',[28] Gertrude had reduced her journalism during the first five years of the 1890s, but a long
article she wrote in the *National Review* describes images of home life
she was trying sedulously to reinforce. Inveighing against pretentiousness, lack of simplicity, and the tawdriness of so much made by
machine, she erupts in a crushing vehemence for the 'errors or miscon-
ceptions that disfigure so much of modern work'.[29] Fervent aesthetic
opinions were expressed with phrases of biblical solemnity: 'sincerity
of purpose', 'good to endure', 'simplicity of purpose', 'the best and
rightest thing'.[30] The battle against fashion was one she would wage

until she died. If she could not bring to others the knowledge of principles she was peculiarly equipped to recognize, then people would go on making mistakes.

Five and a half years earlier, she had reckoned that her mother, then aged seventy-six, was 'younger than anybody'.[31] In July 1895, after a week's illness, Mrs Jekyll, a long steady influence in the lives of her children, died. Gertrude suppressed emotion on principle. Herbert and Agnes had three children: Francis, known in the family as Timmy, aged thirteen and exceptionally bright, Barbara, eight, and Pamela, six. Munstead House being left to them, there was every reason for making headway with 'Aunt Gertrude's' permanent home. After the settlement of their mother's estate, Teddy wrote to Herbert from Bedford suggesting that she might benefit from an extra £2,000. She was not really short of money but it was an action that emphasized the mutual good will among Jekyll siblings.

The month her mother died Gertrude was visited by two American women, Mary Cadwalader Jones and her daughter, garden-designer Beatrix Farrand. Surrey was a hotbed of gardening; two days later they went to Mrs Earle, then on to Gravetye. But Beatrix was strongly affected by Gertrude's impressionistic garden colour and use of native plants. Later she was to play a significant role in the history of the Jekyll photographs and garden plans. While the past was drawing to a close, the future was being composed.

Gertrude had possessed OS for thirteen years. The garden was mature and she was passionately involved with the conception of her final home. She had no doubt that she should employ a professional architect. Lutyens was twenty-seven, master of his craft, and already her collaborator on eight gardens and two cottages. If his first plans for a house had failed, she had in him the utmost faith. Lutyens tried again, and this time, almost as if he were extracting a mental image she carried in her head, he 'conceived the place in exactly such a form as I had desired, but could not have described'.[1] There, in genesis, was the goldish building with tiled roofs, tall brick chimneys, gables and oak-framed casement windows, 'an aesthetic based on folk tradition and moral rightness'[2] in the idiom of William Morris and Philip Webb. Munstead Wood had a modest approach 200 yards off the road from a country lane. The woodland journey had already begun.

'No house,' Francis Jekyll maintained, '. . . was ever built which bore more indelibly the impress of its owner's personality.'[3] This was unusual. The Victorians extolled home-making as a practical and moral function, aiming for generalized comfort and good taste. But for the genuineness that Morris was after, individual expression, interests and activities must shape the environment. Gertrude's standards were insistent. Nothing would be 'poky or screwy or ill-lighted',[4] though her rooms are on the dark side because she disliked strong light. This time, too, there would be sufficient room for a person 'of an accumulative proclivity'.[5] She knew what she liked. The house should be 'right' in every part, which meant to someone who lived alone and crammed each minute of her day, efficient. Fittingness to purpose also lent the 'precious feeling of repose'[6] she was always after, with sunlight and silence caressing mind and spirit through profoundly industrious, though amply fulfilling, in many ways triumphant days. Every detail was discussed with her architect, she wrote in the opening chapters of *Home and Garden*, and being his tireless advocate, she felt bound to stress failures that arose from her intervention. Once only, 'one might say that any "fur flew"'.[7] The clash concerned a choice between expense and external appearance, and Gertrude, by nature economical, claimed that she had intimidated Lutyens with a long-worded fusillade. Ned was to admit, 'Bumps rampant is an awful sight.'[8]

She was intoxicated by the entire building process. The Hut was scarcely eighty yards away, and from the summer of 1896 until the completion of Munstead Wood, a year and a few months later, when the Dunsfold builders from the firm of Thomas Underwood were on the site, Gertrude was never very far away. 'How I enjoyed seeing the whole operation of the building from its very beginning! I could watch any clever workman for hours. Even the shovelling and shaping of ground is pleasant to see, but when it comes to a craftsman of long experience using the tool that seems to have become part of himself, the attraction is so great that I can hardly tear myself away.'[9] Precisely what the workmen thought of their obsessively implicated, appreciative but exacting employer can only be imagined. Careful work did not lack encouragement; to the stout, grey-haired lady, the sights and sounds of construction were full of melody. 'The chop and rush of the trowel taking up its load of mortar from the board, the dull slither as the moist mass was laid as a bed for the next brick in the course; the ringing music of the soft-tempered blade cutting a well-burnt brick ... to see the ease of it, the smiling face, the rapid, almost dancing movements, the exuberant though wholly unaffected manifestation of ready activity; the little graceful ornaments of action in half-unconscious flourishes of the trowel, delicate fioriture of consummate dexterity.'[10]

Knowing Gertrude's horror of pretentiousness, it is plain that nothing about Munstead Wood would be 'sham-old': it was not a copy of something older, nor did it use distinctive methods from another region. It was, in short, as she had felt a house should be, 'simple' and 'straightforward', made from local materials in the Surrey style. It was plainer in décor than the houses of the generation, with white walls instead of Morris papers and bare floorboards in the hallway. There were no modern improvements which were to become such anathema to her; she tried to be unaffected and in some ways she was successful, but Munstead Wood was as consciously cultured as a stately home. No short cuts to excellence had been permitted, 'no random choosings from the ironmonger's pattern-book; no clashing of styles, no meretricious ornamentation, no impudence of castiron substitute for honest hand-work, no moral slothfulness in providing all of these lesser finishings'.[11] Seldom had Ruskin been more assiduously conjured: 'Though the work of the London builder is more technically perfect, it has none of the vigorous vitality and individual interest of that of the old countryman.'[12] The fact that Gertrude had known three great oak beams stretching across the ceiling of her sitting-room when they were trees on the outer edge of a pine wood added to the mystique. Functionalism and durability were a natural corollary of good design. In sensuous approval, she notes the strength, perfect dimensions and fine carving of its glossy oak. 'Everything about it, is strong and serviceable, and looks and feels as if it would wear and endure for ever.'[13] Perhaps the greatest credit to the architect, and a perfect measure of what his client called 'rightness', was that the house never seemed stark or new. Harmony with the landscape had been a fundamental precept. It was set in a mature garden with grass walks, borders, birch and chestnut coppice. Even so, it was a triumph that it gave the impression of being a couple of hundred years old, growing 'naturally out of the ground'.[14] It is strange that William Morris should have described very similarly his beloved seventeenth-century Kelmscott Manor: 'grown up out of the soil and the lives of those that lived on it'.[15]

Some years before, Lionel Benson had introduced Robert Lorimer, an Edinburgh architect, to Gertrude. Describing her first, 'a great authority on gardening and arts and crafts, and a great character generally',[16] Lorimer goes on to give a euphoric picture of how she 'laid out a complete place [Munstead Wood] ... paths, gardens, bought a barn that was being demolished and re-erected it, and some other buildings about the garden, and left a hole in the centre of the ground for the house and now it's built'.[17] He too remarked upon what Gertrude called its 'comfortable maturity'.[18] It looked 'so reasonable, so kindly, so perfectly beautiful that you feel that people might have been making love and living and dying there, and dear little children running about for the last — I was going to say, thousand years, anyway six hundred. They've used old tiles which of course helps, but the proportion, the way the thing's built (very long coursed rubble with thick joints and no corners), in fact it has been built by the old people of the old materials in the old "unhurrying" way but at the same time "sweet to all modern uses"'.[19] No part of the house was more individual than the celebrated wooden staircase and the sixty-foot gallery to which it leads. Purely for the pleasure of passing through the gallery, Gertrude chose her bedroom at the furthest end. Writing of 'seasoned calm' absent from Lutyens's previous work and so evident at Munstead Wood, Christopher Hussey infers, 'In fact it is clear that these qualities were due to Miss Jekyll, who, as has been shown, added to the claims of a client the influence of a collaborator.'[20]

So closely did Gertrude identify with Munstead Wood that it reflected all the major aspects of her personality. The colour and beauty that were her vision, the dignity and restraint she strove to live by, the private needs of a complicated person juggling between the demands of work, and human fellowship. Since childhood she had possessed traits that seemed contrary. She was not afraid of accosting strangers and fully appreciated the riches that could be extracted from old people with traditional ways. But she was wary of personal intrusion – even to her dearest friends she was seldom intimate – and she built up relationships on a relatively structured teacher/pupil pattern. In middle age her tendency to withdraw became more pronounced: Lutyens had felt this when he first met her, 'A bunch of cloaked propriety.'[21] No man had found her sufficiently attractive to want to marry. For a Victorian, spinsterhood was likely to be to some extent humiliating, and sensitivity about her shape made Gertrude shy of casual acquaintances. Architect Oliver Hill remarked perceptively that her appearance seemed at odds with her character, the one 'lumpy', the other 'light and witty'.[22] But as Pearsall Smith realized, 'Miss Jekyll had received that luckiest of fairy-gifts; a calling, an industry, something that she loved to do.'[23] She was an artist, moreover, for whom life and work were one. Munstead Wood, the scene of dedicated and unremitting labour, would provide what Gertrude variously described as 'restful(ness) to mind and body',[24] 'repose and serenity of mind',[25] 'that precious feeling of repose',[26] 'serene contentment',[27] or 'a little of the feeling of a convent'.[28]

Lutyens understood Gertrude well. It was he more than anyone who fostered the considerate, amusing, and affectionate private person his correspondence intimates over the next decade. Gertrude's single-minded devotion to him was like that of a mother, soothing, supportive and endlessly reassuring. Not without cause did Lutyens call her the 'best friend a man could ever have found'.[29] She fed him 'most sumptuous'[30] meals, of which he ate 'largely – very largely',[31] labelled his luggage and took him in the dog-cart to Godalming station. Since the springtime, moreover, there had been an extra *frisson* to his confidences, because Edwin Lutyens was in love. He had accompanied Barbara Webb to one of the Blumenthals' fashionable parties at Hyde Park Gate, where he met Emily Lytton, a serious-looking girl with pale gold hair. She was deaf, she owned later, to music, and largely blind to the visual arts; but she was very literate, and when something amused her, her face became illumined. Emily was the daughter of Robert, 1st Earl of Lytton, who had died some years before. In order to finance her younger son's education, Lady Lytton had been obliged to let Knebworth, the turreted Hertfordshire ancestral home, and become a lady-in-waiting to Queen Victoria. The suggestion that Emily might be a maid-of-honour, however, was ill received.

Lutyens's subsequent meetings with Emily confirmed his first inclinations, but coming from so exalted a social circle, she seemed almost unobtainable and it was still a one-sided affair. In his quest, it is apparent, Lutyens appealed to both his substitute mothers. Mrs Webb promised to bring the couple together at Milford House, and 'Saturday we will dine all 3 with Bumps.'[32] At this point the story begins to take on a new vibrancy. Lutyens was courting romantic love on one side, mature love and approval on the other. He was relying on the shared sense of respect and acceptance he had built up with Gertrude, and while the half-built shell of Munstead Wood glowed mellow among its trees, The Hut became the setting for an unlikely entertainment.

Following a conventional morning introduction, Lutyens and Emily reappeared unexpected, at the front door of The Hut, heaped with provisions for a 'surprise dinner'.[33] It was something of a liberty, and in her confusion Emily dropped the eggs, she told her mother and the Rev. Whitwell Elwin. Caught unawares, Gertrude was dressed 'like a man',[34] that is, in rough clothes, but she 'bore the shock splendidly',[35] and the couple 'reeled into the house shrieking with laughter . . .' Gertrude radiated energy, humour and sympathy; Emily felt at once affection for this godmother, and awe of her power to define their lives. 'She is the most enchanting person and lives in the most fascinating cottage you ever saw.'[36] 'Bumps' was a perfect name: she was fat and stumpy with tiny eyes. Spontaneous hospitality prevailed. The three prepared an impromptu meal of chops and tipsy cake followed by hot elderberry wine – good, wholesome, genuine food, with a nice attention to plenty, consumed, as Gertrude describes in one of her books, in the inglenook, before a blazing log fire, to the romps of assorted cats and kittens. For Emily, it was 'altogether the most heavenly evening'.[37]

Emily's father had been Viceroy of India, her paternal grandfather was the novelist Edward Bulwer-Lytton and her mother was one of Mrs Earle's younger twin sisters. Emily had a fine mind and attractive moral seriousness. Gertrude's snobbishness placated, she could only approve. Lady Lytton took time to be coerced, a process in which Emily's sister, Lady Betty Balfour, and Lutyens's two effective champions, Barbara Webb and Gertrude, did all they could to help. Ned was working on Munstead Wood, Bumps was busy scheming his career and he was genuinely devoted to her. With care, she was included at each stage of a prolonged and earnest courtship. In turn, Emily was scrupulously prepared for the varied faces of his fairy godmother: 'D'you know Bumps is also known by these names Oozal Woozal [and] in austere moments Miss Jekyll. If you get there in time come out with Woozal. She will laugh. The "crassness of the Woozal" means when she is more than ordinary gug.'[38] 'Plazzoh' was Munstead Wood. Rather as the Chalet circle had used nicknames, Ned was breaking barriers with private language.

Emily was genuinely delighted by Gertrude. 'We saw Bumps yesterday who was charming to me. I do love her.'[39] She was lovable, Ned agreed, 'only don't let her abuse me. She knows nothing of how much you are to me, and if she did, even Bumps would see that you could make me a man! and give my work the serious touch it wants.'[40] That Ned meant to be 'a big worker & no nonsense'[41] was plain to Gertrude, and Emily's recognition of his genius was all-important. 'I read her your darling lecture on business relations,' wrote Ned. 'She thought you so wise, and was so astonished.'[42] Bumps was right, Emily agreed, she must not be a frivolous influence on his career.

Humour was a vital ingredient in the triangular relationship. Early in February 1897, Ned wrote to Emily enclosing Gertrude's poem. 'Rather good isn't it.'[43]

The Lament of the Neglected

The Architect's wanted galore, galore,
The work's at a standstill for evermore;
The brick layers playing – they've nothing to do;
The carpenters smoking – they're idle too.
The plumbers carousing till all is blue.
   'Oh Plazzoh go hang, old Bumps is a bore
  For Nedi's gone courting galore, galore!'
                Bumps Poet Galoreate.[44]

Lady Lytton was eventually won to Lutyens's cause. With the marriage fixed for the following August, there was much thought of setting up house and Bumps was consulted at every turn. 'I shall buy linen for you to match,' Lutyens wrote to Emily, 'but I shall first consult Woozal.'[45] 'Ask Bumps why blue [table] cloths dont wash out.'[46] 'I shall go to Bumps and tell her all the news.'[47] 'I shall ask Bumps about blue marking.'[48] 'Discussed household matters with Bumps who was delicious & no gugness.'[49] 'I shall tell Bumps to make us lavender bags & sweet smelling pockets.'[50] The vision of The Hut with its lavender and pot-pourri remained with him always as an ideal. Gertrude and Lutyens were far more involved with the material aspect of home-making than Emily would ever be, and Lutyens delighted in sounding 'World-wide Bumps'[51] especially about 'conveniences under bed'.[52] Visits to 'Bumpstead'[53] were *a priori*, to keep an eye on the rising Munstead Wood, but letters suggest a working rapport that extended to joyful appreciation of one another's company. In April, after hunting a marauding cat, armed with a bag of sand, '(most exciting but scored no hits)',[54] Lutyens had dinner with Gertrude and talked 'to Woozle all about Emy & how I loved her & Bumps thinks me so lucky . . . and we just purred & I gave her a good hug (most unbusinesslike) because she loved Emy.'[55] The following day Bumps would discuss their wedding present, meanwhile, she sent best love: 'She is so nice and just creams with affection, nonsense games and comfy all round . . . dear old Bumps is so kind and if she is let into our lives it does warm her dear old soul up and I know she loves us both just as her own special sort of human pussies.'[56]

The most encouraging part of Gertrude's support was the faith she had in Lutyens, but typically she backed it with practicality; the majority of his clients were met directly or indirectly through the

Jekylls. William Robinson was one of her few unfruitful introductions but he was notoriously difficult. Lutyens found him 'exactly like a gibbing horse',[57] and the idea that the 'foozle headed old bore'[58] entertained hopes of marrying Emily's brilliant, unmarried sister, Conny, was 'ludicrous'.[59] Initially, Lutyens was careful to rub 'his waistcoat just the right way',[60] and Robinson was delighted to be invited to the wedding. But he drove Lutyens frantic with impatience and a few years later Lutyens was suggesting an effigy, 'Robinson in yew'.[61] Lutyens simply could not be obsequious and generally got on famously with his patrons. Princess Louise was a status symbol, he was quick to appreciate. First she had commissioned some work on her house in Inveraray, then she wanted additions made to the Ferry Inn on the shores of Gareloch. Gertrude passed on the new commission, though when gossip reached her that the Princess was wasting Lutyens's time, 'Bumps rose in her thousands & gave her [the Princess] such a lecture.'[62] There was something possessive about Gertrude's support that sprang from a need in her own personality. She was, however, constantly on the alert for openings, and lightning-quick when an opportunity arose.

During the first months of 1897, Mr and Mrs (later Sir William and Lady) Chance had bought twenty-six acres of land within a mile of Munstead Wood and commissioned an architect, Halsey Ricardo, to design a house. Alas, they did not like the result. At the crucial juncture, the Chances happened to be walking up the hill from Godalming when they spied a 'portly figure'[63] directing some workmen from the top of a ladder. It was leaning against what Mrs Chance was inspired to feel immediately was 'a wonderful house . . . a revelation of unimagined beauty and charm'.[64] Naturally Gertrude was delighted to enlighten such appreciative guests, and the minute she realized the nature of their interest, she began scheming on Lutyens's behalf. 'Bumps wishes to say Something most amusing & highly flattering to Nedi & rather mysterious . . . The mystery is quite galorious!! What can it mean . . . someone wants to give me an enormous job!'[65] Lutyens was right, though Gertrude refused to divulge her secret until 'we sat cheek by jowl on the cenotaph of Sigismunda'[66] – a wood and masonry garden seat beneath a birch tree, thus named by Charles Liddell.

There was a problem in that the Chances felt committed to Ricardo, who was an old friend. But being diplomatic with rich neighbours was the sort of thing at which Gertrude excelled. 'What could they do?'[67] Ned buffooned, 'O Bumps had such a long story to tell, played so nicely with the Chances, and eventually undertook to overcome my scruples . . . in short – the Chances have chucked Ricardo – I am to do their work.'[68] Julia Chance was a Strachey, a garden sculptor and much in accord with Gertrude's and Lutyens's idea. Notwithstanding, Gertrude's success was a triumph, and Emily's gratitude was immense. 'I feel I must rush off to Bumps and dance with her and hug her it is all so glorious and exciting.'[69]

As the wedding approached, £25 arrived from Gertrude, a toasting fork and £10 from Aggie and Herbert Jekyll and two 'quite dear'[70] silver candlesticks from Madame Blumenthal. Ned had plans to 'lay in Bump's vintages'[71] for their married quarters. Frothing with good will and furiously busy, he delegated to Emily the task of sharing their pleasure with Gertrude. 'Go see dear Bumps & make her happy.'[72] In July, Bumps approved 29 Bloomsbury Square: 'We *must* get it.'[73] Seven days before the wedding Ned had visited. 'Dear old Bumps was just beaming over with love for you darling & how beautiful you were . . . I just hugged her & I suppose because she thought I was too happy – she said I was much luckier than ever I deserved.'[74] On 4 August they were married in Old Knebworth church. Two days later Lutyens wrote to Lady Betty Balfour, Emily's sister: 'However happy you may be now . . . you can never have been one litho as happy as we are . . . Bumps comes here Saturday.' (At this point the text is illustrated with a drawing of Bumps digging a sunflower.) Some months before, Ned had written to Emily, 'We shall mother Bumps – a relationship without precedent.'[75]

For Gertrude, everything had conspired to make 1897 a sublime year. Her final home was building, Lutyens was around a good deal and she enjoyed her two-year sojourn in The Hut. 'Dear Little Hut! how sorry I was to leave it.'[76] The move that was a climax, a perfect end and an auspicious beginning, coincided with a celebration of somewhat different order. To commemorate the sixtieth year of Queen Victoria's reign, it was decided a Victoria Medal of Honour or VMH would be conferred by the Royal Horticultural Society on sixty eminent gardeners. Gertrude was one of two ladies to be honoured; the other being Ellen Willmott. They had known one another since 1873, when Miss Willmott was only fifteen. She was on the Narcissus Committee of the RHS, and was in many ways as unusual as Gertrude.

Lutyens's drawing of Gertrude Jekyll digging a sunflower, 6 August
1897.

But on this occasion, Miss Willmott, who may have been abroad, left
the floor to Miss Jekyll.

The *Gardeners' Chronicle* described the ceremony as 'high festival'.[77]
The *Journal of Horticulture* affirmed, 'Never before had such a crowd
assembled in the hall in St James Street.'[78] Several references were
made during the proceedings to 'the lady' amid 'the gentlemen here
present',[79] and the President, Sir Trevor Lawrence, conceded, 'The
medal being instituted to celebrate the Jubilee of her Gracious Majesty,
nothing could be more becoming than that we should have some
members of her sex as medallists.'[80] But Dean Hole took the prize for
wit by remarking that if they were honouring Her Majesty, the one
lady member present was certainly 'Queen of Spades'.[81] The *Gardener's
Magazine* responded to the occasion with a large pull-out spread of
photographs of all the recipients. Gertrude appears, amid a great many
old friends, in the black hat with waving cockerel's feathers she had
worn when she first met Lutyens. It was 'a great surprise & delight',[82]
Gertrude wrote to her ten-year-old niece, Barbara.

The day before the horticultural function, Munstead Wood became
Gertrude's final home, one that provided the base for her next thirty-
five years and sealed Ned's career. 'Who do you think did this for her?'

Lorimer asked, 'a young chap called Lutyens, twenty-seven he is, and I've heard him described . . . as a "Society" architect. Miss J. has pretty well run him.'[83] Roderick Gradidge may come even nearer the truth in his assessment: 'No young architect, however talented, could have reached such refinement so soon – this is Gertrude Jekyll's work.'[84]

PART FOUR

WRITER

CHAPTER SIXTEEN

1896-7

Like her father, Gertrude was a compulsive teacher. During the early years of her friendship with Lady Chance, the two women saw each other several times a week, either in the workshop or in the garden, and Gertrude's first remark was invariably, 'Any questions?' Lady Chance remembered her neighbour's kindness and unfailing interest, 'and I was never afraid of wearying her by my endless questions'.[1] More than 2,000 notes and articles, fourteen books and an enormous correspondence are proof that the didactic role was always in the forefront of Gertrude's consciousness. Her intellectual gifts, moreover, found their best expression in action; writing encouraged her to absorb facts, clarify opinions, and intensify her searches in the natural world.

Six months before the building of Munstead Wood she had embarked on a new journalistic commission. Daniel Conner Lathbury was a neighbour and editor of the *Guardian Newspaper* (generally referred to as the *'Guardian'* but not to be confused with the present *Guardian*, then prefixed by *'Manchester'*). Lathbury's paper had been founded in 1846 when it absorbed the *Churchwoman*. It was a high church Anglican weekly though not exclusively sectarian, with progressive reviews of the arts and a special appeal to women. One of Lathbury's conspicuous contributions had been a first-rate garden section; so popular had notes by the Gloucestershire gardener, Canon Henry Ellacombe, become that he was persuaded, at the end of the series, to publish them as a book. In casting round for a worthy successor, Lathbury elected Gertrude to write on garden and woodland. Provided her articles were attractive she had a fairly free rein. At least twice a month throughout the year, she took a notebook among the trees, shrubs and plants she knew so well, chose a vantage point and allowed the garden to flood her senses. With infinite care, she might view a long-considered vista, the shapes and colours of flowers, a chance bend of trunk, a straggle of ivy, a textured juxtaposition of fern and bulb.

The first of sixteen articles evoked a day in February when winter's clutch allowed the merest inkling of spring. The precise nature of the intimation was elusive. Perhaps it was scents, mossy and sun-coaxed, that carried the tidings. For how little green there was! Thirty-three years before, on the wintry island of Rhodes, she had made much the same complaint, 'There is nothing really green and fresh but the little maidenhair fern,'[2] lamenting the absence of 'repose' and 'refreshment', as if green were something her nature craved. What had winter done to the bracken? 'That best of all undergrowth'[3] '. . . of all our Ferns the one that is really important in the landscape'.[4] How did the new bramble leaves compare with those of the previous year?

About colour, she briefed readers, asserting her art consciousness, the uninitiated invariably deceive themselves. Art school had taught her to appreciate fine distinctions and the matter was 'simply without end'.[5] Later she compares the different blues of March-blooming scillas and chionodoxas. *Scilla sibirica* has a 'suspicion of green' and a 'curiously penetrating quality',[6] *Scilla bifolia* 'does not attack the eye so smartly',[7] *Chionodoxa sardensis* is a 'full and satisfying colour . . . enhanced by the small space of clear white throat'.[8] *C. lucilia*, on the other hand, varied from pale to dark, from blue to almost lilac. In all things she esteemed clarity and precision. Quaintly meticulous descriptions are interspersed with information on modern varieties; and ever pragmatic, she advises how to gauge the hue of a distant green by tearing a roundish hole in a large, bright leaf such as burdock, by looking through the hole and comparing the shades. Examining plants for winter colour, she selects bergenia, almost a by-word in Jekyllian planting, admiring the red tints, clean outline and vigorous rounded leaves that give it a 'grave and monumental look'.[9]

As if she had looked at the world afresh and found it more various and beautiful than even she had thought, her prose grew more melliflu-ous. Sometimes her journalism is perfunctory; in these *Guardian* pieces, she must have been pleasantly conscious that as a writer she had come into her prime. One can feel the weight of patient revision. It is part of the attractiveness of Gertrude that perfection never came immediately, but as she spoke of making pot-pourri, one wins 'by trying, and feeling one's way, and getting to know'.[10] Occasionally she overloads her informative images, yet she had a wonderful musical ear for cadences and she did not merely write about plants; she wrote, and the plant knowledge is deeply contained, as if it were folklore. So completely grounded was she in experience that plants, on occasion, become the subject of her notes: 'Hardy ferns are grateful', 'cyclamen are happy'.[11] She was, she subsequently admitted, 'on closely intimate and friendly terms with a great many growing things'.[12] The lilt in her phrasing is sometimes hymnal, 'lovely are the flowering bulbs'.[13] Four years later she likened the gardener's enjoyment to a 'constant hymn of praise'.[14] What is surprising about the shrubs she discusses is how many of them grew at Bramley in her childhood home. This was partly because she was still on an acid soil, but it is difficult to avoid the suspicion that the images cast in youth had become the most sacred.

Investigations generally began in the southernmost corner of the copse, from where turf paths made leisurely tours through pine and birch towards the central, at first unoccupied, space for her house. A fine barometer to the weather, Gertrude took stock of the east or north-east wind that mummified the land at the end of March! Flowers were retained 'but as it were under protest',[15] scents were withheld and the soil appeared robbed of fertility. That a west wind wrought, within hours, 'a marvellous change'[16] was one of nature's miracles. Later in the year, when the soil warmed and the sap stirred, she lauded the felling of woodland oak, fungal foray, song of the nightingale and resonant ring of the woodman's axe against Scots pine. Alternately cajoling and beguiling her readers, she allowed herself to be drawn to the primrose garden and to cogitate anew on the carpet of bracken. *Orobus aurantiacus*, 'one of the handsomest of the pea family',[17] was not as popular as it deserved to be, another plant was too rampant.

What will grow beneath Scotch briar? How does one divide the wiry roots of spring bittervetch (*Orobus vernus*)? Moving from copse to formal garden, alpine garden and hardy borders, she paused to question herself, praise a particular plant or air some pet aversion. 'In all things that live,' Ruskin had thundered, 'there are certain irregularities and deficiencies which are not only signs of life, but sources of beauty.'[18] Elsewhere he advised 'the natural combination of flowers',[19] criticizing 'all dahlias, tulips, ranunculi and in general what are called florists' flowers' which 'should be avoided like garlic'.[20] It was in his spirit that Gertrude decried show florists and breeders who ignored the 'grandest' plants,[21] rejecting beautiful colour in their quest for uniformity. She was quick to sniff out sham and affectation; faddish plant breeding inspired her persistent, emphatic odium.

The articles are easy to read though her authority is woven through the prose like a metal thread. In June her readers, as loyal to Gertrude as they had been to Canon Ellacombe, were introduced to her colour spectrum for hardy azaleas – 'never [to] be planted among or even within sight of'[22] a wandering rhododendron. In a plantation straggling over half an acre, she kept whites at the shady end, passing to pale yellow and pale pink. A large central climax in an open clearing throbbed orange, copper, flame and crimson, then colours graduated in reverse, through strong yellow and the pale yellow of wild *Azalea pontica*, before drifting back to quiet woodland hues. As, she claimed, South Kensington had taught her, so she invites her readers to look, learn, and enhance their floral palette. Her principle was never to be garish, never less than pleasing to the eye.

All gardeners love roses, and Gertrude was ultimately to devote a book to them. In the *Guardian* she emphasized relatively little used, old-fashioned groups and species, making a special plea for the native burnet rose (*R. spinosissima*) with its greyish foliage, lemon-white blossoms, glossy black hips and fine bronzed autumn colours, 'between ashy black and dusky red'.[23] Typically, she viewed roses in total context; scent, colour, foliage and habit. For blooms crimped and puckered as a party frock, especially the delicate, apple-blossom pinks, she had a strong personal predilection; and roses which passed her stern criteria, 'Aimée Vibert', 'Dundee Rambler', 'The Garland', 'Blush Rambler', 'Jersey Beauty' and the pink Chinas, she used over and again.

Gertrude wrote about moonlit sorties from The Hut at midsummer to catch the scent and watch the 'strangely weird dignity'[24] of the cardiocrinums, then called *Lilium giganteum*. Snippets of romance, folklore, etymology, botany, plant history, local history and gleanings from old gardening books are all laced into the text without destroying her intrinsic theme. What had happened to 'blew Hulo' (a carnation with flowers of 'purplish murry'),[25] she asked on 26 August? The flower's popularity had never waned; why its good old name, 'gilliflower', had dropped from use she was at a loss to know. In high summer she was drawn to the hardy borders. In shortening days she was collecting leaves, mulching and protecting plants for the months ahead. When winter came, she again contemplated the woodland.

Ravages received in a January snowstorm by the great wild junipers had called her attention to 'the pride of our stretch of healthy waste'.[26] There was in the foliage, she saw, 'very little of positive green; a suspicion of warm colour in the shadowy hollows, and a blue-grey bloom of the tenderest quality imaginable on the outer masses'.[27] Gertrude's nature worship is akin to the pantheism of the Romantics. Her most authentic visional effects arise from intent, exultant, observation.

It is surprising how much of her personality escapes into these writings. When Hussey comments on Munstead Wood being 'like its owner', 'terse and epigrammatic',[28] he is discovering qualities of precision, economy and freedom from cumbrousness that underlie all she did. It is not as if her existence was in any way frugal or self-denying. Her family conceded a pleasurable indulgence in most of life's good things. Yet she was always thrifty, interested in prices, and absurdly pleased to discover ingenious ways of using old materials. She salvaged Lutyens's correspondence to write rough copies of her letters on the back and once wrote stridently, 'Waste is not only wrong but is an unpardonable stupidity, akin to the dull vice of sloth.'[29] Recycling was entirely sympathetic to her way of life. Was economy not a token of production and rightness? How pleasant a way to 'end one's days',[30] she purred, on the subject of old wheel-spokes being used as plant labels. To her mind, being inscribed with soothing words like *Dianthus fragrans* was a salutary experience for a hard-worked piece of equipment.

The sanctity of labour was another of Gertrude's obsessions, her contempt for the clumsy or slapdash being equalled only by her praise for a job well done. The woodman felling and lopping trees, disposing of each cut of timber in the most economical way, inspires a piece of prose as concise and memorable as the actions it describes. An oak trunk, roughly two feet thick and weighing perhaps a ton, lay on the ground. It had to be cleft into four and moved 100 feet to the side of a lane, 'His tools are an axe and one iron wedge.'[31] Step by step, with deliberation born of long practice, he nicked the sawn surface of the trunk and prized in the wedge. Gertrude's phrases catch the long and short rhythms of the axe, the controlled energy. Not a word is surplus to an account so vibrant that the reader almost hears the fibres tear as the 'tremendous rending power of the wedge at last bursts them asunder'.[32]

Naturally enough, these articles generated interest beyond the normal circulation of the *Guardian*. There was a precedent in Canon Ellacombe's *In a Gloucestershire Garden*, released as a book and selling well. Why were Gertrude's pieces not also revised and reissued as part of a longer work, friends and followers asked? Ellacombe's naturalism drew from a common core, but comparison, for breadth of vision, is invariably to Gertrude's advantage. The other publication which must surely have offset any diffidence was the first of Mrs C. W. Earle's *Pot-pourri* trilogy.

Ellen Willmott, Helen Allingham, Barbara Bodichon, Mary Newton, Lady Caroline Duff Gordon and Leonie Blumenthal – Gertrude attracted a sisterhood of strong and successful women among whom Theresa Earle takes a distinguished place. She was a Villiers, and one of her twin sisters had made a glamorous marriage. After falling in love with someone who was not approved of by her family, Theresa acquired another partner they found more acceptable. Charles Earle was to become director of the Original Australasian Telegraph Company, but when they married he was just a young soldier. Mrs Villiers complained of the company her daughter kept, but Theresa refused to be stodgy. Her strength was to love and be loved by an enormous number of friends, artistic neighbours as well as aristocratic ones. She ran a soup kitchen, though she could not believe it did much good, and joined the committee of the Society in Berners Street for promoting women's employment. She possessed Gertrude's tough-grained intelligence and the same reverence for Ruskin, claiming of *Modern Painters*, 'I can honestly say no book so influenced my youth, or tended so much to form my ideals.'[33] A move to two acres in Cobham opened new prospects. It was not long before she had spotted a role for herself as a self-appointed promoter of the art of home-making.

Cobham is twenty miles from Munstead Wood, which Mrs Earle called 'the most lovely Surrey garden I know'.[34] She was strictly an amateur. Until her book appeared, she had not tried to make money from gardening or anything else. She was also the poorer – two acres against fifteen – but the first edition of *Pot-pourri from a Surrey Garden* appeared to an even warmer reception than Ellacombe's book. Buy it! Dean Hole had recommended. Like its companion volumes, *Pot-pourri* ranges over vegetable cultivation, recipes and flower arrangements, herbs and herbals, listing and commenting on gardening books, discussing art exhibitions and poetry, from cooking bottled green gooseberries to Tennyson or when to give your son the front door key, from Ruskin to instructions for making a light spray watering can, from babies to black beetles, modern marriages to belladonna lilies. They are truly pot-pourris. Mrs Earle bubbles and sparkles with sound practical advice, she is chatty, never tedious. Behind her femininity she hides a formidable accomplishment. But the bittiness that is the charm of the *Pot-pourris* becomes a distraction.

The first *Pot-pourri* predates Gertrude's first book, *Wood and Garden*, by a year. But by the time it appeared, Gertrude's journalism went back a further fourteen years and being an avid pupil, Mrs Earle had studied it closely. Patently, there was cross-fertilization between two women making achievements at the same time and in the same field. They have the same abhorrence for creepers that conceal good architecture, the depredations of plant breeders and the bedding-out system. In cases such as *Choisya ternata*, they reserve special praise for the same plant. Both have much to say about flower arrangement, recommend hardy plants and old roses. They shared, of course, a debt to William Robinson, G. F. Wilson and other mutual friends, and on old roses, they represent the views of a clique of Robinsonian writers. Dean Hole, for instance, had mentioned all the old roses that Mrs Earle so warmly recommends, in his popular book of 1869. But Gertrude and Mrs Earle are bound to have discussed them when they walked together in the gardens at Cobham or at Munstead Wood. Like Gertrude, Mrs Earle called for bold groupings, extolled simplicity and felt the cottage garden had much to offer. Unlike Gertrude, she was not a landscapist. Her advice on colour was merely to keep similar hues together, she considered banishing the herbaceous border to the kitchen garden at a time when Gertrude was using it as a major landscape element, and her instructions for dropping a sunken garden in the centre of a lawn, without reference to the larger setting, sound dubious. In the end it is Gertrude's overview, her principle of unity knitting house, garden and landscape as a background to man's body and soul, that put her in a separate category.

It is difficult not to extend personal comparison to two women who moved among each other's friends and neighbours. Differences were fairly marked to Lutyens children, who felt that 'Aunt T' beat 'Aunt Bumps' by a wide margin for broadmindedness. By that time Aunt T had brought up three boys; marriage and motherhood allowed her an outlet for human sympathy, she was less intense and far more accessible to children than Gertrude. Indeed, their attitudes to education are valid clues to their approach to the younger generation. Gertrude, conveniently forgetting her inability to cope with formal education, championed the public school where 'by wholesome friction with his fellows' a youth had 'petty or personal nonsense knocked out of him'.[35] While Aunt T, who recommended French novels as a preparation for young mothers with growing sons (Emily Lutyens thought the novels awful), believed boys fared best at day school. She much regretted that such facilities were not better, and having once chided Henry Quilter, Sir Cuthbert's brother, for straying from Ruskin's principles, she admitted upon reflection, 'I fear now that I fell into the usual fault of the elder to the younger, and scolded him too much.'[36] Edwin Lutyens loved them both, 'argufy[ed] a goodish bit'[37] with Aunt T, found her 'amusing' and 'full of common sense', but was more alive than his children to her 'scorching criticisms' and 'vituperative epithets'.[38]

There may have been a hint of competition on Mrs Earle's side, for she was only human, and Gertrude set standards that few dared to touch upon. Both had a powerful urge to preach, and it was in character for Mrs Earle to speak what she referred to as 'my matter-of-fact mind',[39] but she was a discerning admirer of her friend's wisdom. The first *Pot-pourri* contains a generous tribute to Gertrude's monthly series in the *Guardian*. Miss Jekyll actually grew the plants she wrote about in her 'instructive'[40] garden. Every plant she mentioned was worth procuring from Munstead Wood, where 'surplus plants, all more or less suited to light soils',[41] were sold. Before long the articles would be republished as a book. 'For every word in them deserves attention and consideration.'[42]

CHAPTER SEVENTEEN

1898–1900

Gertrude's first book was released by Messrs Longman in April 1899; roughly two-thirds was an amplification of her articles in the *Guardian*. *Wood and Garden* is a magnificent one-woman creation: she had composed the text and processed sixty-five of her own illustrations, largely of her plantings, flower arrangements or artefacts like the Munstead vases, made up to her design. She wrote about the art of living with great simplicity, in fluent, understated prose. There is no straining after effect, only a concern for scale and comfort. Success was immediate; six issues were out within the year. By its tenth edition, it had sold 13,000 copies.

Dean Hole called the new book 'the most perfect example of practical wisdom in combination with poetical thought ... It is her [Miss Jekyll's] reverent appreciation of beauty which empowers her first to realize for herself, and then to impart to her readers, a sense of the grace and of the glory which surround us.'[1] Hercules Brabazon wrote to Gertrude and she replied, delighted. She had felt 'there was something here and there that might be sympathetic to you, yet I had no idea that it deserved all the good things you say'.[2] That she obtained a certain satisfaction is evident from Lutyens's remark to Lady Emily, 'Bumps says that all the best she has written about flower borders is in [a] chapter called Flower Garden & Pergola in "Wood & Garden".'[3] Compared with her original photographs, the reproductions in her books are very poor. One can only say that the images from copse, garden and high wood, of trees, craftsmen, local cottages and their inhabitants, relate closely to the text. First the 'Garland' rose is depicted in the wild, 'showing natural way of growth';[4] in a later picture, it wreathes the end of a terrace wall with sprays of bewitching abundance. The presiding message, a moral one to which all others are subservient, is for man to learn from the power and beauty of Nature.

Gertrude had much sympathy for the beginner, whom she advised to plump for the crux of a problem, acquiring knowledge with patience and perseverance as she herself had done. 'Never say "I know".'⁵ The encouragement and common sense in *Wood and Garden* seems to readers almost consoling, 'For the love of gardening is a seed that once sown never dies, but always grows and grows to an enduring and ever-increasing source of happiness.'⁶ Sense of proportion would govern all things. Working facilities should be manageable, potting sheds roomy, tools properly eased and oiled, everything well and appropriately designed. Practice which broke one cardinal rule was, in her opinion, liable to offend another. Thus a twenty-acre kitchen garden besides being pretentious was absurdly wasteful, an 'uncomfortable disproportion'⁷ which made her prudent heart sink. Quality before quantity was another rule. There was nothing to beat a well-designed, well-organized country house estate, but there was no reason, through ingenious attention to detail and 'sympathy with the place',⁸ why small should not be beautiful. A cottage garden of old-fashioned flowers, wallflowers and double daisies drifting into white roses, pinks, thrift and 'clustering masses of perennial Peas'⁹ could be an exquisite experience. It was no use taking on more than one could cope with. Better to beautify a woodland than sweat exhausted over acres of cultivation.

Gertrude's school-marmish severity was part of her perfectionism. There were habits and practices that seemed to her unpardonable. She felt very strongly about them, was not prepared to compromise, and writing offered her a platform for protest. Since John Tradescant searched new hemispheres for plants 'strang and rare'¹⁰ there have been some who treasure bizarre forms, but to her there was only one recommendation for anything, and that was beauty. In *Wood and Garden* she enlarges upon the short remonstrance in her *Guardian* notes about selecting and breeding plants 'teased and tortured and fatted and bloated into ugly and useless monstrosities'.¹¹ 'What a silly little dumpy, formless, pincushion of a thing'¹² the new dwarf ageratum was, she scoffed. On occasion a dwarf kind was useful. The snapdragon, if no great beauty, was a harmless 'little floral joke';¹³ love-in-the-mist, on the other hand, was ruined. Nurserymen are admonished for a different sort of failure. One can see how Gertrude's concern for precision was riled by 'Slip-slop'¹⁴ descriptions of flower colour, 'bright golden yellow'¹⁵ for bright yellow, 'gorgeous flame coloured'¹⁶ for bright scarlet and 'snow' as an epithet for white. Snow-white was 'more symbolical than descriptive'[17] and 'very vague'.[18] White was either yellowish or bluish; if a term for warm white was required, why not use 'chalk'? It was respect for accuracy that led her to appeal to nurserymen for realistic descriptions of plant heights, and love of precision in the use of English that prompted her to object to the confusing description of a new zinnia, *'robustus elegans'*. To her godson, Harold Falkner, she explained smartly, 'I should call you *robustus* but I should not call you *elegans.*'[19] Concern for language also led her to regret the loss of 'all that rollicking company ... Bobbing Joan and blooming Sally and bouncing Bet'[20] (wild arum, French willow and soapwort). There were, she recognized, plenty of other plant names that conjured old country romance – travellers' joy, meadowsweet, speedwell, forget-me-not, lads'-love, sweet cicely and love-in-the-mist. Language was unpredictable. 'Perfectly good strong, much-wanted'[21] words like 'sperage' (asparagus) dropped out of use and 'feeble' substitutes were adopted, 'dependable' for 'trustworthy', 'pluck' for 'fortitude' ('school-boy cant').[22] With glee, she unearthed a country appellation for a tiny yellow stonecrop, 'Welcome-home-husband-be-he-ever-so-drunk'.[23]

Since the depredations of bedding-out first earned Gertrude's contempt, the fashion had waned. So strenuously had the proponents of 'good old flowers'[24] championed their cause that the 'great inundating wave ... almost drowning out the beauties of the many little flowery cottage plots'[25] that reigned for nearly a quarter century was no longer in full flood. Now was the time, Gertrude decided, to consider more coolly the merits and demerits of the system. Nothing was wrong with bedding in the right place. A parterre could provide a satisfying nugget of colour in the formal garden. Nor did she dislike the maligned geranium or calceolaria in themselves, but only their 'grevious misuse'.[26] The point is reinforced by photographs of bedded geraniums that she planted with lilies and cannas in her paved, south-facing courtyard. Bedding plants were only passive agents in their own misuse.

Gertrude's conviction that class and education are commensurate with ability colours her attitude towards the working man. Deprived of opportunities for 'enlarging his mind',[27] a gardener could scarcely be expected to make an imaginative contribution, and 'Various degrees of ignorance and narrow-mindedness'[28] had to be expected. *Wood and Garden* closes with a section about people she reckoned duty bound to do as they were told. The servant might 'set up the canvas and grind the colours, and even set the palette, but the master alone can paint the pictures'.[29] She was a strident élitist with a stern contempt for democracy, and the fashionable but limited social code under which she had been brought up remained a permanent obstacle to absorbing fresh ideas about social status. The ferocity of Gertrude's snobbery and prejudice occasionally emerges in her writing, the most blatant account being four years later, on the subject of clothing. In her opinion, so long as labourers wore genuine labouring garments, all was well. When they allowed themselves to be lured by cheap, fashionable Sunday garments and wore them to work, the result was 'sordid, shameful, and degraded'.[30] Fashion, she asserted, was such a draw for working-class women, they could not even be trusted to buy a good-sized handkerchief. If not realizing one's station was a sin, the ultimate decadence occurred when the poor aped the wealthy. Rather as if she were describing a prize pig, Gertrude chastised the bridegroom labourer's 'poor, anxious, excited face that glistened with sweat';[31] unease occasioned by his large buttonhole bouquet and 'white cotton gloves'.[32] Predictably, she approved of the old woman who had walked to church, walked home, and cooked the matrimonial dinner of two chops. Perhaps her patronizing views were a rigid extension of her insistence on everything being in its right and proper place.

Since moving into two of Munstead's prominent houses, Herbert and Gertrude had, like the Jekyll parents, taken on responsibilities of what the villagers called 'the best people'. 'Nothing went on in the Parish without the Jekylls being in on it,'[33] Harriet Mills, then called Harriet Keen, a lifelong resident of the Brighton Road, recalled. Church was still central to village life. The church of St John the Apostle, designed by Gilbert Scott in Bargate stone, had been dedicated and consecrated by the Bishop of Winchester in 1867. What Ian Nairn and Nikolaus Pevsner describe as a 'good example of the masculine style . . . of this rare architect'[34] is situated on rising ground to the south, Busbridge side, of Godalming, linking the town with Munstead and drawing its congregation from both. William Morris contributed a striking altar embroidery of vine leaves and grapes, and late nineteenth-century Arts and Crafts additions were undoubtedly conceived under Jekyll influence. There are stained glass windows, east and west, by Burne-Jones in familiar blues and greens and there is a delicate metal chancel screen made up by Starkie Gardner to Lutyens's designs. Two angels, kneeling face to face, become the roots of a tree-like composition bearing Christ. The screen fills the upper parts of a pointed chancel arch, to be complemented by egg-grey marble slabs set into a small stone screen below. Lutyens's truncated cruciform memorial to the First World War rears up from a prominent corner of the churchyard on the west of the Horsham road, and his strange tomb and monument to the Jekylls make Busbridge church a place of pilgrimage for disciples.

Gertrude was now, as much as any time, creating her reputation. The problem with successful writing was that it created a precedent. No sooner was the first reaction to *Wood and Garden* assessed than friends and publishers were urging her to bring out another book in which the house should play a more prominent role. Her deep involvement in the realization of Munstead Wood made the prospect tempting, although her days were already crowded. Gertrude warmed to and took every possible advantage of increased recognition, but what she found hard to accept were demands on her time and privacy. The writing was not peaceful and she admitted afterwards to the 'very real fatigue' [35] the task had involved. Despite distractions including a long article for the *Journal of the Royal Horticultural Society* and at least fourteen landscape commissions, *Home and Garden* was completed on schedule and released to the public in 1900 with more than fifty of her own illustrations. 'A somewhat larger measure of peace and privacy' [36] for the resident was its accompanying plea. 'Pushers would push their way in, I believe, in the most shameless fashion,' [37] an acquaintance commented. It was the beginning of a precarious relationship with a public she simultaneously needed, served and despised.

Sensitive to every fluctuation in temperament, Lutyens found Gertrude alternately 'The one that wishes to scold and correct (ME)' and Bumps 'engaging a problem or a joke'. [38] There was Bumps being 'very dictatorial' [39] and 'Swoozle – . . . in her most beneficial mood', [40] 'very delicious and glad'. [41] That summer he wrote to Emily on an enormous sheet of paper, 33 cm × 53 cm, illustrating his letter with endearing drawings and the remark, 'Bumps thinks it is rather cruel to make so much of her innocent rotundities.' [42] To those who knew her, it was plain that she sought equanimity in her surroundings, yet entering them in the way she wished required a certain solitude. The public would arrive, enthusiastic but often naïve, uninvited and totally unaware of the demands Gertrude made on herself or that Munstead

Lutyens's drawing of himself with a T-square, Gertrude Jekyll with a
cat, 29 September 1896.

Wood was her most sacred precinct. From time to time, of course, she
needed a change. In September, she spent two weeks at Thornham, on
the wind-blown coast of North Norfolk, while the Lutyens and their
first daughter, year-old 'Barbie', minded the house. Bumps was in
'splendid feather. Younger than ever'[43] as the year drew to a close, but
by the following August she was again, she said, ready for a holiday.

Gertrude's first two books are often considered her most personal
and inspired. *Home and Garden* starts by celebrating her house and
continues with a miscellany of nature walks, advice on taste, horticulture and design, building up, like its predecessor, to the art of living.
Once again, nature communings and the lessons to be learnt from
them take priority. Myopia was causing her discomfort and fatigue but
her mental vision was clear. No country lanes in the temperate world,
she believed, held such rampant garlands of fern and flower, wild rose,
honeysuckle, hop and bryony, no magic was more potent than that of
West Surrey's woodlands. 'An unmade woodland track is the nearest
thing to a road-poem that anything of the kind can show.'[44] She was
alive to the tangle and mystery of splintered light through under-

Lutyens's drawings, 'I make obeysance' and Gertrude Jekyll as an angel,
6 August 1899.

growth, the romance of trees meeting overhead, gentle winds, insect
wings, squirrel, rabbit, red deer. 'What will the next reach disclose?'[45]

The principles she drew from nature were basic to her theories of
landscape. To preserve unity in a naturalistic area, be it rock garden,
valley or woodland, there should be throughout a groundwork of
certain plants. Another lesson was planting in longish drifts, not only
in herbaceous borders but in all free or half-wild garden plantings. She
would study the wild honeysuckle making 'a loose copse-carpet'[46] or,
where it finds support, and 'seems to go up with a rush, and tumbles
out in swags and garlands that in the long summer days are lovely and

fragrant with the wealth of sweetly-scented bloom . . . So they advance up the tree, sometimes leaping away from each other, and then again coming together and twining'[47] – interpreting its trailings and weavings in a way that reminds one of Ruskin's encounter with ivy twisting the stem of a hawthorn tree. Having stopped to draw the composition, he found it aroused in him such a powerful physical reaction that he suddenly re-saw its beauty in terms he had but dimly understood before.

One of the rewarding aspects of being a celebrity was the contact it brought from old friends. When *Home and Garden* was published Mrs Hole, 'one of the best of gardeners',[48] wrote in appreciation. Gertrude was 'so glad of her good words',[49] wished they lived closer and commiserated with her friend for being in Rochester 'away from the good simple things and clean air that we were certainly meant to live with'.[50] In *Home and Garden*, Gertrude wrote, 'How I loved the small and simple ways of living'[51] and 'if it were possible to simplify life to the uttermost, how little one really wants'.[52] Simple life is a recurring theme, the goal that she had come closest to in The Hut, where, unencumbered by all but essential possessions, Gertrude could live with the simplicity and economy she preached but never quite managed to follow because she was searching for an emotional condition that her intellect would not allow. The inventory of a sale of her belongings held in 1948 lists the trappings of a highly cultivated woman, someone, moreover, who loved possessions. What she owned was not necessarily of intrinsic value. In the gallery, deeply set with cupboards, she stored the unconscious pickings of a traveller, delicate pieces of Venetian glass, Florentine and Venetian 'brocades, damasks, embroideries, fringes, braids and great silk tassels'.[53] There were boxes of Algerian ware, peasant handkerchiefs from France and Italy, gifts from friends no longer living, shells, feathers and, in the workshop, Mediterranean pottery. Some objects were kept for their associations, others fed her artistic imagination and she gathered her local horse trappings because they were becoming obsolete – brass face-pieces, harness and rosettes of worsted braid for wagon-teams on market days. Mary Lutyens, who lived at Munstead Wood after 'Aunt Bumps's' death, was impressed by the meticulous organization of a home stuffed with treasures, shells and pieces of coral in the work-room, 'carefully graded as to size and colour'.[54]

One of the photographs in *Wood and Garden* shows some of Gertrude's handicraft, embossed and chased silver-work, inlay and embroidery, all finely executed with broadly swirling plant-inspired designs. In the foreground stands the 'tutelary divinity of the workshop',[55] a small black ugly primitive-looking figure, half absurd, half magic, that she kept as a mascot. 'Pigot' made deliberate appeal to her unconscious responses. 'His eyes, bland, passionless, mildly benevolent, but capable of flashes of scornful indignation when bad work is done or the gluepot boils over, are of mother-o'-pearl; his spotless waistcoat (he has a suit to match) is of ermine. His necklace is of coral beads and little pink cowries; its middle ornament of silver, suggesting the form of a hand. All the joys and sorrows of the workshop are known to him; his mild eyes beam; in glad sympathy with the elation of success, and smile a kindly encouragement to weariness or the dejection of failure.'[56] The little idol was a highly self-reflecting image.

Since childhood Gertrude had felt at home with tools. 'Without [them] brain and hand would be helpless.'[57] In *Home and Garden*, she had written about the amazing co-ordination that develops between a skilful worker and the tools of his craft; and she was gratified to hear that Mr Leslie singled out these parts for praise. Staying with Barbara Bodichon, she had met a builder called Mr Clarence Greenfield who was dying of consumption. For keepsake she had taken a photograph of the man who could not 'bear to go'[58] when he thought of his tools. Many of her own tools she designed herself and had made up by a local blacksmith. Herbert Cowley, later the editor of *Gardening Illustrated*, had a trowel and a wooden mallet made to her design.

Another side of Gertrude known and understood by fellow devotees was the repressed maternal affection she lavished on a large number of what she always referred to as 'pussies' – initially four or five but soon running 'into double figures',[59] for as Lutyens noticed, 'Bumps cats always have kittens.'[60] Their physical attributes were part of the attraction; short-haired tabbies being preferred, ideally with white fronts and paws. Francis Jekyll remembered a time when every seat in the sitting-room would be occupied by the matronly form of a pregnant puss, his aunt's attention being divided between him, the teathings and 'Pinkieboy' or 'Tittlebat'. Gertrude fostered her image as a cat-lover. Travelling in foreign cities, she allocated marks for felines counted on each side of the road with a high score for 'Puss in a window'.[61] A visit to Mr Robinson was enhanced by an inn called the 'Tabby Cat', and nominally for the entertainment of Herbert's children, she indulged in what might seem, to the uninitiated, fairly dotty pussies' tea parties, recorded, with deliberate mock dignity, in the pages of her recent book. Nursing the creatures from 'smallest babyhood',[62] she learnt the minutest tricks and diversities of their natures. Henceforth each animal's mood was registered and responded to, their simulated combat, hunting and variety of appreciative purrs providing an endless source of speculation. To be on 'purring terms'[63] with pussies augured well for one's relationship with their owner. Lady Chance, who constantly sketched her own feline family, felt sure that her appreciation helped to promote a bond of sympathy between herself and Gertrude. Orchards was a mecca for cat-lovers. Drawings of long-haired cats hung on the walls among lions and tigers. The fireplace recess in the study was tiled with pale blue cat designs and the weather-vane was a crouching cat form that ought rightly to have been called, Gertrude insisted, a 'weather-cat'.

The Leslies were all fond of cats, particularly George, Peter (his youngest son) and Kate (his niece). Peter had had polio as a child, was horribly lame and could not go away to school with his brothers. He was destined to be another artist, and an oil he did of his father shows George reclined on a wicker chair with a coral silk scarf round his neck and Peter's cat, Sandy, on his lap. Peter cat-talked with Gertrude, and a photograph she sent him of her deceased 'Tavy' occasioned a wave of correspondence. George's eldest brother, Robert C. Leslie, was Kate's father, a good marine artist and author of *A Waterbiography*. The appearance of *Home and Garden* with its pussy chapters prompted Kate to write to its author, enclosing photographs of her own feline entourage. 'Many thanks,' Gertrude wrote back. 'My Tabby since his picture was done, has grown much bigger and handsomer. Alas! both Pinkieboy & Tittlebat are gone. It is quite heartbreaking & yet one must have the dear things, they are such delightful company every hour of the day.'[64]

Her books had attracted two new fans. Edward Hudson and Ernest, generally referred to as E. T. Cook, sought her soon after the appearance of *Wood and Garden*. Cook was one of the reliable, hard-working figures who sit behind the front lines of any successful public organization, a colleague of Robinson on *The Garden*, and astute enough to guess that Gertrude's works would eventually become classics. Hudson had founded *Country Life* in 1897, a magazine he was fast developing from small beginnings into what William Runciman called 'the keeper of the architectural conscience of the nation'.[65] Gertrude had a knack of getting to know people likely to prove valuable to her.

CHAPTER EIGHTEEN

1900–1901

William Robinson had edited *The Garden* for twenty-seven years. At Gravetye he was enlarging his estate and making huge constructional alterations to the house, his books were constantly coming out in new editions, he had four magazines to look after, and he wanted to make a return visit to America. Something had to go, and by the end of 1899 he had decided to offer editorial duties on his first paper to Gertrude and E. T. Cook. Gertrude had opinions, the right contacts and a reputation, Cook had energy, quiet charm and office experience. Beginning his career as a student in the RHS garden at Chiswick, he had worked under Shirley Hibberd on the *Gardeners' Magazine* before moving to the Robinsonian empire on *Gardening Illustrated*. He was a rose man and gardens' adviser to Hudson at *Country Life*. A visit to Munstead Wood on behalf of the magazine made a logical prelude to collaboration.

Gertrude kept the equivalent of office hours when she was at Munstead Wood, but she arranged her schedule to suit herself. To adapt, in her late fifties, to a job with its own rhythms and deadlines was a tremendous sacrifice. Of course she had been associated with *The Garden* for many years and knew its style, content and all its major contributors. In the circumstances her duties could have been largely organizational. But this was not her way. Having accepted the challenge, she streamed her energies into the venture; in no time the paper began to bear her distinctive voice. Ruskin had died in January and the Vice-President of RIBA gave a resounding tribute to 'the man who probably awakened the English people to a knowledge of what art really meant'.[1] Ruskin had stressed that art is important to everyone and Gertrude felt bound to pass on his message. Perhaps it was in tribute to him that the third editorial of *The Garden* under its new leaders, 'False Ideals',[2] was devoted to one of her periodic digs at the plagiarisms of plant breeding.

The question of doubling and dwarfing flowers had been interpreted as part of a much larger issue brewing for years between 'naturalists' and 'formalists'. It had come to a head in the early 1890s, when architects like John Dando Sedding, Reginald Blomfield and Inigo Thomas, his illustrator, promoted a revival of formal gardens, and every opportunity revived the debate. Sedding, Master of the Art Workers' Guild and a religious man, was the author of *Garden Craft Old and New*. He understood plants and appreciated much that Robinson wrote at the same time as approving 'the general rightness of the old ways',[3] and a garden that 'curtseys to the house'.[4] But his case was made in a gentle, idealistic way that offended no one. Gertrude had given an excellent account of his book in the *Edinburgh Review*; more than once she quotes a writer who says 'the art of gardening has for its root, man's enthusiasm for the woodland world'[5] and 'an English garden is at once stately and homely'.[6]

Blomfield's *The Formal Garden in England* took a more rigid view. Architectural or 'formal' gardens were harmonious with the building and therefore good, while landscape gardens, 'Unless you are content with a mud-hut and cover it with grass',[7] were unequivocally bad. William Kent, Launcelot (Capability) Brown, and the most flamboyant of modern advocates, William Robinson, were roundly condemned for making pictures from sky, trees, water, flowers and grass. The attack would have carried more weight had not much of its argument been fallacious. Blomfield's shortcomings were far too good an opportunity for Robinson to miss, and though Gertrude found *The Formal Garden* 'delightful in itself',[8] Robinson ridiculed its inaccuracies and distortions at every opportunity. 'We live in a time when men write about garden design unmeaning words or absolute nonsense.'[9] The old battle, art versus nature, was being aired, and words taken out of context on either side could lead to false, often extremist views. Robinson swore there were two styles, 'one straight-laced, mechanical . . . with water-squirts, plaster-work, and wasted sculpture; the other natural – and in most cases, once free of the house, accepting the ground lines of the earth herself'.[10] But so much leeway did his qualifying phrase, 'once free of the house', allow that he was forced to admit, 'Formality is often essential to the plan of a garden.'[11] Gertrude was the first to point out that he, king pin of the wild garden, had an architectural terrace at Gravetye.

The long article Gertrude had written for the *Edinburgh Review* shows just how clear-headed she was. 'Both are right, and both are wrong. The formal army are architects to a man; they are undoubtedly right in upholding the simple dignity and sweetness and quiet beauty of the old formal garden, but they parade its limitations as if they were the end of all art; they ignore the immense resources that are the precious possession of modern gardeners.'[12] Gertrude's insight, sound judgement, and the power of grasping quickly the real nature of an argument made her a perfect editor. Cautiously she moved between opposing factions. There was to her no conflict in learning from nature, even, on occasion, letting 'well alone',[13] while championing formal gardens 'of the best kinds'.[14] An undated sketch from the Reef Point Collection[15] shows an extensive Italianate garden of parterres, terraces, fountains and vistas that would not be out of place in the *œuvre* of Blomfield, Mawson, or Nesfield. Moreover, her essay found her acquainted with every formal historic feature, from Jacobean knot garden to the great waterworks of Tivoli.

Regretting the destruction of old avenues and gardens that the landscape style entailed, she never had much sympathy with the Brownian ethos. Brown's successor, Humphry Repton, was 'of much better taste and education',[16] she approved. The anomaly is that she actually espoused the synthesis of art and nature that was the dream of the eighteenth-century landscapist. 'Groups of grand trees'[17] whose spreading branches brushed the lawn, a typically eighteenth-century image, presents, she wrote, a picture 'perfect in its unity and peace, in its harmony of line and fine masses of form'.[18] Conversely she deplored the disparate nineteenth-century scattering of specimen conifers. 'What once was a sanctuary of ordered peace is now a wearisome and irritating exposition of monotonous commonplace. The spiritual and poetical influences ... are gone.'[19] It was a little difficult for her readers to understand Gertrude's refusal to take sides in various ideological factions that split the horticultural world.

Debate, however, was useful to an editor and Gertrude's new position prompted old friends to write in. One who rose to support her provocative leader was George Leslie, the only Royal Academician to be also a fellow of the Royal Horticultural Society. Since Gertrude left Wargrave, Leslie had bought a rambling old house of crooked passages on the banks of his beloved Thames. At Wallingford, amid a growing family, he painted girls weaving garlands of flowers, watched birds and tended his garden of old-fashioned perennials. He had

written three books, *Our River*, which had a preservationist theme, and
two works compiled from correspondence on the pleasures of rural
life. His writings make the author sound genial but Thomas Twidell, a
grandson Leslie raised from the age of seven, said that was the wrong
word. He was a clever conversationalist and someone who 'could be
touchy'.[20] When Leslie complains about careless flower painters, he
sounds exactly like Gertrude. 'Frequent liberties are taken with the
colour of the foliage of laurels and other shrubs . . . introduced in
backgrounds, a cold bluish green is used when it should have been a
deep rich olive, and vice versa.'[21] One wonders how much, during the
Wargrave days, he was influenced by the young woman of whom he
thought so highly; whether, indeed, Leslie's stock of old-fashioned
flowers originated from joint visits to cottage gardens.

Gertrude's association with Hudson and *Country Life* was quick to
pay dividends. Large, plain and laconic, Hudson, a printer's son, was
'indifferently educated but avid of culture'.[22] Biographer Hilary Spurling calls him 'gross, inarticulate, outwardly unprepossessing but profoundly romantic at heart'.[23] Francis Jekyll gives no reaction from his
aunt to a man who, in the words of his obituary, 'needed knowing'.[24]
Naïveté and deep social insecurity made him awkward, but he had
quickly risen above his beginnings. At twenty he had quit law, taken
over the family concern and begun to publish periodicals. Business
acumen and a passion for 'princely mansions and quaint old houses of
long-lineaged householders'[25] would take him a long way. With
almost parental affection he nursed his magazine, gathering round him
a remarkable band of associates and winning their loyal support. Avray
Tipping, Sir Lawrence Weaver, Lord Conway, Arthur Oswald and his
editorial successor, Christopher Hussey, were all part of the team. He
was as anxious to trap Gertrude Jekyll as she was to be caught.

Country Life centred round the home and a traditionally English,
outdoor living – a taste for old furniture and pictures, hunting, fishing,
motoring, shooting, golf and the social side of land ownership. The
scheme to describe and photograph principal houses at home and
abroad had immense appeal to the upper classes, and recording aspects
of endangered English scenery and local craft was attractive to conserva-
tionists. Readers, it seemed, would swallow any amount of glamour
and picturesqueness. At the same time the publication eulogized
country values and set a new standard in journalism, in particular for
the quality of its illustration. Nothing like it had been on the bookstalls

before. After three years the magazine was doing extremely well. To Gertrude, contributing to *Country Life* was an inviting prospect and Hudson had other important connections which might prove advantageous to Lutyens. The Jekylls had continued to negotiate on the young architect's behalf. It was the year of the Paris Exhibition and Herbert, Commissioner for the British Section, had secured for him the plum job of designing the British pavilion. The building was not in itself important, though the prestige was enormous. Then the first illustrated article on Lutyens's work appeared in *Country Life*. He had completed a number of houses in the tradition of Munstead Wood. Some critics feel that apart from his Viceroy's House in New Delhi, they constitute his most important work, and Hudson's recognition of his talent, with his consequent high profile in the magazine, was a tremendous fillip to his reputation. After the exhibition he moved on from the relatively small world of Surrey businessmen to the international scene.

Besides supporting friends, the Jekylls firmly promoted each other's interests. Walter seemed to be drifting away from the family and it was a good opportunity to bring him back, as it were, into the fold. From the start, their élitist upbringing appears to have affected Walter differently from his brothers and sisters. Even as a child he had been worried by moral issues and now, past his fiftieth year, he led an increasingly idiosyncratic bachelor existence. For twenty years he had served the church in various capacities, as a deacon at Rochester and a curate in Heydon, a village south of Cambridge, before being appointed a minor canon at Worcester Cathedral. But in 1879 he had emigrated to Malta and abandoned his religious vocation. A book called *The Bible Untrustworthy* sets out to prove the fallibility of the Bible through its inconsistencies, simultaneously suggesting that he was disenchanted with the church's cramping morality.

He did not lack enterprise. After leaving the church, Walter studied singing with Francesco in Milan, and translated his teacher's *The Art of Singing* into English. Returning to England, he 'gave penny singing lessons to poor people'[26] in Birmingham before moving to Bournemouth and befriending Robert Louis Stevenson. His holidays were spent in remote parts of Norway with Ernest Boyle, Lieutenant Colonel in the Honorary Artillery Company and grandson of General Sir Lorenzo Courteney Boyle, then the legacy from his mother's will allowed him to winter in Jamaica, and before long, a temporary home was to become a permanent one. Seventeen miles from Kingston, 2,000 feet above sea level, he built a tiny bungalow with mountains ranging high above it on three sides. The fourth side allowed a view deep into a valley with a roaring little river. Of the family, Walter was probably closest to Teddy's daughter Millicent. Grace, the younger daughter, had died when she was eleven, but Millicent had married in 1896 Baron Erich von Maltzahn, of an old and distinguished Prussian family. At this juncture the couple went out to visit Walter in Jamaica.

New homes were apt to stimulate the Jekylls' horticultural enthusiasm. Walter first wrote about Jamaican plants, and now that Gertrude was editor of *The Garden* he had a ready outlet. Eleven articles he contributed to her paper tell of a vigorous ascetic life, scratching a living from an acre of coffee and bathing before breakfast beneath thirteen natural waterfalls. Labour was erratic. His principal gardener would toil assiduously for four days before abandoning himself to drink for the rest of the week. But the flora was exciting, every house with its stephanotis on the verandah and twin cotton trees so vast that they dwarfed a sixteen-foot Seville orange to the size of a bush. There was fruit in abundance all the year – grape, mango, orange, bananas, various types of passion fruit, custard apple, pawpaw and yellow melon. In the family tradition, Walter liked pussies, 'not only a pleasure, but expedient',[27] and his reference to garden pictures, grass paths and the meeting point between garden and plantation suggests that he had read and absorbed his sister's teachings.

All the Jekylls were achieving in their various ways, and with Agnes's ready support, Herbert had more than fulfilled Lady Duff Gordon's expectations of him. During more than a year in Paris in charge of the British Section of the 1900 Exhibition, the couple had, 'by their friendly intercourse in many circles of French society',[28] done a great deal to ease relations strained by the South African War. On Herbert's return to England he was offered a knighthood for his services in connection with 'the defence of the Empire'.[29] Starting as Assistant Secretary to the Railway Department in the Board of Trade, he would serve in the Civil Service. At Munstead House Herbert had, with the assistance of W. J. Bean, just begun to develop a garden of Himalayan rhododendrons when the horticultural exploits of Frederick and Carry Eden in Italy were brought to public notice with a four-page tribute in *Country Life*. A little later, Frederick Eden brought out a small, beautifully illustrated leather-bound volume entirely devoted

1. Believed to be Herbert Jekyll, 1846–1932, who was knighted for service to his country. He married Agnes Graham and lived next door to Gertrude in Munstead House. Some of Gertrude's earliest photographs are those she took of her family in 1885. This one of her brother is not fully in focus.

2. Edward Joseph Jekyll, 1839-1921.
Gertrude's eldest brother retired from the
army as a Captain and was a JP for
Bedfordshire.

3. Caroline (Carry) Jekyll, 1837-1928,
married Frederick Eden and lived
on the Grand Canal in Venice.

4. Believed to be Frederick Eden,
younger son of Arthur Eden,
Deputy Controller of the
Exchequer.

5. Walter Jekyll, 1849–1929, the family maverick, left the church to study music and philosophy.

6. Lady Duff Gordon, Scottish school, nineteenth century. She was a family friend and a staunch supporter of Gertrude's talents.

7. Georgina Duff Gordon by Johns, 1829. Friend and chaperone, she enjoyed much music with the Jekylls.

8. Bramley House, the Jekyll home from 1848 to 1868. The only photograph before substantial enlargement took place.

9. Mary Newton, née Severn, self-portrait. A fellow artist and fellow
traveller together with her husband, Charles.

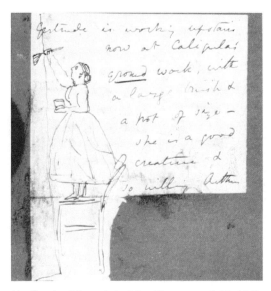

10. Sketch of Gertrude by Mary Newton, probably 1863.

11. Wargrave Manor, September 1912-January 1914. This was after the Jekylls returned to Surrey, but Gertrude's terracotta pots remain in front of the house.

12. Wargrave Manor, with another of Gertrude's pots. She filled the garden with old-fashioned cottage garden flowers.

13. George Leslie, in his punt on the river near Wargrave.

14. La Bellatrice, a classical figure Gertrude photographed in 1885. The fold and texture of material was important to her in the same way as the texture of plant leaves.

15. Primulas, the twelfth photograph in Gertrude's first album.

16. Mrs O'Connell, Leonie Blumenthal's aunt, outside the Chalet de Sonzier on Lake Geneva. Gertrude advised on the planting.

17. Monsieur and Madame Jacques Blumenthal at the Chalet.

18. Hercules Brabazon by John Singer Sargent. From Brabazon Gertrude learned a great deal about colour.
19. Gertrude's lush planting at the Chalet, 1887.

20. Munstead House, where Gertrude lived with her mother between 1877 and 1894 and laid out her first complete garden.

21. The workshop at Munstead House, showing some of Gertrude's oil paintings, her inlaid work and her pottery collection.

22. Family group at Higham Bury, Ampthill, *c.*1877, when Gertrude was helping her eldest brother lay out his garden. From left to right: Captain Edward Jekyll (Teddy), the Rev. Walter Jekyll and Gertrude. Seated is probably Miss von Maltzahn, Millicent Jekyll's sister-in-law.

23. Gertrude Jekyll in about 1880, wearing the hat in which she met Edwin Lutyens.

24. Edwin Lutyens in 1897.

25. Woodside House, Chenies, Buckinghamshire, laid out by Lutyens in 1893 for the widow of the 10th Duke of Bedford soon after he met Gertrude Jekyll.

26. Gertrude's pony and dog-cart.

27. Hyde Park Gate, the Blumenthals' London home. This was the room in which Lutyens met his wife. Gertrude designed the quilted curtain and the inlaid wooden door, helped to make the curtain and probably inlaid the door herself.

28. Mr Bennett-Poe and Mrs Davidson, two horticulturists at Munstead House in 1886.

29. Knebworth House, Hertfordshire, Emily Lutyens's family home. Gertrude Jekyll designed the herb garden in the foreground in 1907.

30. William Robinson, from an etching by Francis Dodd.

31. Cottage entrance in Shackleford. Gertrude was intrigued by the stones laid to form a gutter-seep and used the photograph in *Old West Surrey*.

32. Munstead Wood, 1889.

33. The drawing-room at Munstead Wood, by Mary Lutyens, who stayed there in the latter part of 1933. It was almost a year since Gertrude's death but nothing had been moved from the house.

34. The oak gallery, by Mary Lutyens: part of the house Gertrude especially admired.

35. Viscountess Wolseley, who ran a school for lady gardeners.

36. Maria Theresa, otherwise Mrs C. W. Earle. She and the Viscountess were confirmed feminists.

37. The Manor House, Upton Grey, home of John and Rosamond Wallinger, who have restored the garden to Gertrude Jekyll's 1908 plans.

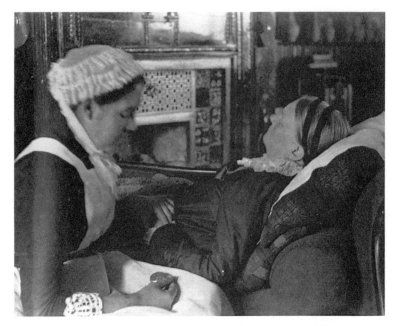

38. Barbara Bodichon, artist and co-founder of Girton College, at Scalands Wood near Robertsbridge in Sussex during her last years.

39. The Bodichons' house on the east side of Algiers, where Gertrude stayed during the winter of 1873. A sketch by Barbara Bodichon.

40. Amy Brandon Thomas, known to Gertrude as Mrs Brand, of Woodhouse Copse, Holmbury St Mary.

41. Ellen Willmott of Warley Place. Both she and Amy Brand were Gertrude's friends until her death.

42. Woodlands were central to Gertrude's perception of a garden. She took many photographs of trees.

43 and 44. Hestercombe, near Taunton, where Lutyens's geometric layout incorporated many of Gertrude's ideas.

45. Mrs Hunterfield sitting outside the back door of her cottage, a picture illustrating the wholeness of life that Gertrude endeavoured to emulate.

46. Bramley Mill Pond, 'the place for Gudgeons'. Gertrude chose this photograph to illustrate an autobiographical sketch she wrote about herself. The pond was in the grounds of her old home, Bramley House.

47. The elderly Gertrude Jekyll at Munstead Wood, photographed by her
friend Mr Cowley, editor of *Gardening Illustrated*.

to his 'Garden of Eden'. Lutyens found Frederick in middle age 'entirely selfish and self absorbed'.[30] Caroline, on the other hand, was 'Not in the least clever or alarming – a nice tame mixture of smiling Colonel and a worldling Bumps ... uglier than either but more knowledge and care for clothes and everyday appearances.'[31] What she lacked in beauty, she seems to have made up for in personality and social grace. Aggie called her 'a well-loved hostess and centre of all that was best and brightest in Venetian society'.[32] The English Hospital in Venice and the Sailors' Home there 'owed much to her influence and support'.[33]

The Edens' garden lay to the south of Venice proper, on the south-east of the Guidecca, from where the romantic approach was to slip, by gondola, across the lagoon. Building on formal lines made by the canals, an abandoned orchard had been crossed with straight walks covered by 600–700 yards of square-topped vine-clad pergola. The paths were bordered with box or old bricks, laid underfoot with crunched shells from the Lido and flanked with borders of flowers. Between the walks there were areas of bedding, rectangular pools of water bordered with potted lemon trees, a cherry orchard, a kitchen garden and a shed housing fourteen cows. Illustrations give inviting glances of slender, shadow-reflecting pergolas marshalled by Madonna (St Anthony) lilies, masses of roses, palms, traditional well-heads and ancient statues. Neighbours are said to have had reservations about the Englishman's six-acre garden voluptuously flowering in their midst. They might have been prompted by envy. Norah Lindsay seems to have been involved with the garden at a later stage, and she was influenced by Gertrude. Since her marriage, moreover, Carry had returned periodically to England. The garden was obviously something she and Gertrude discussed together.

The only landscape commission Gertrude undertook in 1900 was at Hatchlands in Surrey, where she provided plans for Lord Rendel to Admiral Boscawen's simple bow-fronted red brick, eighteenth-century house. 'Fountain as now has a dull and gloomy look with its high parapet covered with ivy – would be much better with two broad steps,'[34] she wrote. Fourteen years later she made for Rendel's grandson, President of the Royal Institute of British Architects, two plans for the south parterre. The first, a sunburst between a grassy bank and a fine Oriental plane tree, was devised in canna, coreopsis, calendula, and calceolaria, and marked 'this proposed arrangement too late as they are away in August'.[35] In 1990 the National Trust began restoring to the more conventional second plan, a June garden of peonies and roses inside herbaceous beds.

It is a measure of the value Gertrude put on her friendship with the Lutyens that she tried to entice them to purchase Warren Lodge, a house Ned had designed at Thursley Common that was up for sale. Nothing came of it, though the thought set Emily 'terribly dreaming'.[36] Young Barbie Lutyens was two years old. 'Bumps says that Barbarawee is the most beautiful & perfect mortal she has ever seen . . .'[37] She had been named after Barbara Webb, a policy which Mary Lutyens recognized might have produced a 'Gertrude' but thankfully failed to. At Munstead Wood, one balmy August afternoon, Emily drove over with her young daughter and finding Bumps writing in the workshop, decided to visit the Chances at Orchards. After 'hesitating between pleasure and duty',[38] Gertrude yielded to amenable diversion. The three mounted a brougham where 'Bumps' was, Emily wrote to her husband, 'most delicious and amusing'.[39] She knew that luring Gertrude from Munstead Wood had been 'a triumph'.[40]

Gertrude was writing extremely long hours and, according to one visitor, 'always . . . a little tired'.[41] Yet she had a capacity for fun. 'Last night I wrote a letter to Bumps purporting to be from an illiterate gardener – asking the Editor for information,' Lutyens congratulated himself; 'it took her in completely to . . . her great joy & merriment!'[42] Other passages from his letters show the Bumps he met in private, a more earthy, unspinsterish and uninhibited Gertrude than anyone else reveals. 'She left the room this morning – for obvious reasons & as she returned quite soon I said "ugh!" it was only a polite vitesse – & she laughed and laughed!! Wasn't it naughty. She also told me to tell you this episode just before lunch I kissed her hand & she said "well now I must wash" wasn't it rude! but she did delight in the saying of it – & we played like little children & her eyes got well & she got a headache from drinking beer & I helped to wash Russian cucumbers & she was the good old Bumps – stern but revelling in every petty naughtiness – she roared too at my latest story but said I was only to tell it to people who had real humour.'[43]

The reason for Gertrude's industry became clear when two full-length books made their appearance: an illustrated monograph, *Lilies for English Gardens* and *Wall and Water Gardens*, were both published in the *Country Life* Library series. A fair portion of the first had, Mrs Earle noted in her *Third Pot-pourri*, already appeared in *The Garden* during Gertrude's first year on the staff. It was a short, specialized guide for amateurs compiled from questionnaires sent out largely at Gertrude's own instigation to some thirty top lily growers. One of the illustrations – long stands of *Lilium candidum* either side of a flimsy, vine-covered pergola – is of Carry's garden in Venice. *Wall and Water Gardens* received a full mention in *The Garden* in an anonymous piece, probably by Cook, and Mrs Earle professed it at least the equal, perhaps even more 'useful, original, and instructive' [44] than Gertrude's first works. The whole idea of laying low, uncemented and earth-filled walls was novel. For new gardeners, the book was 'most essential'. [45]

Mrs Earle was one of the very few who dared to criticize her friend, albeit mildly. The illustrations to the new books, she felt, were 'commonplace', 'evidently not taken by herself' and without 'the individual charm so noticeable in the earlier books'. [46] Ellen Willmott and G. F. Wilson had provided some of the photographs for the lily guide, William Robinson, *Country Life* and the late Sir Frank Crisp for *Wall and Water Gardens*. But apart from the fact that walls and rock gardens, especially bare ones, look less enticing than other horticultural subjects, it is difficult to understand why Mrs Earle so sweepingly condemns. Techniques in photography were developing fast, *Country Life* had a high reputation for quality printing, and from about this time, it has been noticed that the quality of paper and general appearance of Gertrude's prints improved. It could be that she was making use of *Country Life*'s facilities, providing glass plate negatives for her photographs while they did the processing. From this time, too, Gertrude took batches of photographs on a single subject. With four books to her name and publishers clamouring for more, the call for illustrations made it worth exploiting fully each opportunity.

'Many a garden has to be made on a hillside more or less steep.' [47] The first sentence of *Wall and Water Gardens* sets a sternly practical tone for a book more obviously didactic than her first two. Later on, when her imagination wanders through closely planted stream gardens, 'boggy pools and oozy places', [48] the lyricism returns. Garden hardware is discussed as thoroughly as the planting, and dry stone walls, sturdy and enduring, had a rather special appeal. In a letter to Dr Rowe of Margate, who worked at the Natural History Museum, she owned, 'I have done with my own hands many hundreds of yards of drywalling

& planting.'[49] The whole question of the relationship between vegetation and architecture, something Gertrude had begun to explore in Algerian gardens twenty-five years before, was, she wrote, 'a very large one'.[50] Even in the smallest detail – ivy-leaved toadflax in the chinks of steps, erinus with its back pressed to the wall in 'soldier-like . . . uprightness',[51] or a stone bridge invaded by creepers – architect and gardener 'must have *some* knowledge of each other's business'.[52] The power of Gertrude's books is in alerting readers to 'quicken the inventive faculty',[53] use no tight rules, but look, deliberate and then experiment. Gardening's perpetual challenge was one of its chief attractions. Each scrap of ground or water surface, every six inches of soil, provided opportunity. No wall was so hot or so cold that had not a plant waiting for such conditions. Bedding plants and straight lines were worth considering along with hardy plants, drifts and curves. Art and good taste would guide the quest for harmony, unity and beauty.

Taking on *The Garden* as joint editor had been a strategic move. Among gardeners Gertrude Jekyll was becoming a household name, and perhaps one of the most exciting aspects of the new books was their simultaneous publication in America, the first of her *Country Life* series to be co-published by Charles Scribner's Sons of New York. With contacts simultaneously at *The Garden* and at *Country Life* she was in a prime position to expand her journalistic repertoire. She had visited places like Avray Tipping's water garden at Mounton in Monmouthshire, a rocky limestone gorge with sheer cliffs and steep tree-clad hangers that showed him to be a true disciple of nature. She knew William Robinson's Gravetye lily pond from its beginnings. In *Wall and Water Gardens*, Italian Renaissance gardens are invoked as examples of near-perfect harmony between architecture and plant life. When she turns, however, to water margins sprouting great tussocks of coarse sedges, 'luscious tufts of Marsh marigolds',[54] water forget-me-not, osmunda and lady fern, there is a nostalgia that finds her in her imagination roaming the old garden at Bramley House.

CHAPTER NINETEEN

1901–2

Gertrude left her contemporaries in no doubt that she was an exceedingly forceful woman. Virtually everyone in the gardening world knew her, and while some were intimidated, her strength was in wielding influence without making enemies. One of Lutyens's colleagues referred to her as 'essentially sane and level-minded';[1] someone else remarked on her 'great poise'.[2] This was part of the trick, it gave people confidence. But in her extraordinary ability to manipulate, her tools were tact and diplomacy. Her relations with William Robinson were a prime example.

Robinson was a brilliant editor. The impact of *The Garden* was recognized even by someone like Canon Ellacombe who admitted, 'I care little for it myself.'[3] But communication between the two men worsened until the friendly clergyman finally gave up 'trying to get his twist right'.[4] Sooner or later Robinson's proverbial tetchiness alienated almost everyone he dealt with; H. J. Elwes, traveller and gardener, George Maw, an authority on the crocus, Reginald Blomfield – the list is endless. With Sir Joseph Hooker, he persistently battled about Latin plant names, and Sussex neighbours were up in arms about access through his land. Gertrude was conspicuous in maintaining a long peaceful friendship. She helped others and they would assist her: the rules of collaboration are timeless. Three gardening books by E. T. Cook were released in the first years of the new century, each with some of her illustrations, and his *Gardening for Beginners* contained the first of several prefaces she wrote for fellow authors.

Perhaps the greatest palpable testimony to collaboration in the new century was the Chance commission at Orchards. During its three-year gestation, in a workshop set aside for him at Munstead Wood, Lutyens 'used up yards of tracing paper. It's very nice for me,' Gertrude said, 'as I have a passion, though an ignorant one, for matters concerning domestic architecture that almost equals my interest in plants and trees.'[5] There was something generous to the point of diffidence about the way she played down her role in his career. Lutyens was one of the few who understood Gertrude's complexities; with him she could be her intimidating or eccentric self and yet be known to be considerate, amusing and affectionate. The liberating influence was crucial to her. She was indebted to him, gave credit to him, and displayed him by diminishing her part in their business relationship. Doing so, she expected to increase his stature. Her loyalty to him was complete.

Harold Falkner had become an exceptional architect, and it was his contention that 'Miss Jekyll had ... a knowledge of the very finest building practices which she transferred to Lutyens, and that "sense of material" made him different from all other architects of his time.'[6] Lutyens designed Orchards when his Jekyllian tutelage was at its height. Visits to 'Bumpstead' were only partly social, 'I must go to Bumps',[7] 'I then did gardens with her [Bumps]',[8] 'I have had a good talk with Woozledown about all manners of things but have done no work with her she being ill.'[9] Almost until the end of her life, every plan was submitted to her for comment, and however busy she was, she would be available. There is a telling story related to Betty Massingham by Oliver Hill, an architect for whom Gertrude also devised planting schemes. Hill was present when she was inspecting some of Lutyens's plans and remembered that the house design was large and perfectly good, but the final touch was an outside lift to transport luggage upstairs. To this frivolity Gertrude, reliable and commonsensical, remonstrated smartly, 'Don't be a fool, Ned, don't be a fool!'[10]

There is no doubt that Lutyens's fresh young vision made a magnificent and original response to what he learned, but Gertrude had the same confidence with buildings that she had with gardens and her teaching was solidly behind him. Parallels between Munstead Wood and Orchards make it plausible that her ideas remained prominent. The homage Gertrude paid to 'the fine taste of the designer' and 'his intimate knowledge of the best traditions of the country'[11] must have warmed her to Lutyens, but posterity has a duty to realize her own part in the conception of his Surrey houses. Roderick Gradidge, writing about Lutyens, seems to have come closest to the truth: 'Without her [Gertrude] we would probably never have had houses of the quality of Orchards, Tigbourne Court, Deanery Garden at Sonning or Little Thakeham – the great masterpieces of Lutyens's early career and the crowning pinnacle of the hundred years of the English Vernacular Revival.'[12] It is a credit to her powers of persuasion that, despite mounting evidence to the contrary, successive chroniclers have accepted her version of events.

Friendship with the Chances, the closeness of their dwellings and the fact that Gertrude was responsible for the commission involved her at every stage. The clients had been by no means passive. Gertrude admired Julia Chance's artistic receptiveness, and to do the younger woman justice, she had realized instantly, the first time she saw Munstead Wood, incomplete and beladdered, that it was something like her dream house. Lutyens's brief had been to design another, a bit larger, a bit grander, and naturally conditioned by its site (twenty-three acres against fifteen), but in the same tradition of Surrey pictur-esque. The result was what Christopher Hussey calls a 'symphony of local materials, conducted by an artist, for artists'.[13] Since harmony was one of Gertrude's most frequently stressed principles, the musical simile was apt. In a venture Jane Brown, author of a book about the partnership, refers to as one of its 'greatest triumphs',[14] there is a form, progression and rhythm that make a musical parallel. 'Look out for Country Life on Friday Orchards will be in it,'[15] Lutyens wrote on 28 August 1901. The previous year Gertrude had penned an anonymous article on Crooksbury; Orchards was the appropriate subject of her first signed full-length article in *Country Life*.

The house rises at the edge of a sandstone plateau, with woodland growing close to the walls on three sides and long views spreading eastwards to the pretty Thorncombe valley, Leith Hill and Dorking. Fittingly, Gertrude begins her article with a sense of place: West Surrey, the sandy soil, a valley-fold running up to a well-wooded plateau, virgin oak trees and native bracken, 'All this has been carefully preserved.'[16] Like Munstead Wood, Orchards is approached by a short drive off the highway and once again, land and building were considered from the start an integral unit. For here was no exiled exotic, but 'a house that sits at home upon its ground and could not be other than the right house of the countryside'.[17] Here is the woodland garden with its varying lights at different seasons, a scene of natural kinship with the changing English climate. Orchards has form, drama, and above all, movement. As in the great eighteenth-century landscapes, one is drawn irresistibly forward to the gradual unfolding of internal and external delights.

Around the house, spaces contract and expand in a dynamic sequence. Gertrude notes the courtyard entered beneath a solid timbered archway, quiet, sparsely planted and without a 'confined feeling'.[18] Along its west side, a wide-arched, monastic cloister leads to an immediate greeting of untamed nature. A grassy glade and one or two paths were cleared for the free play of light and air, otherwise nothing altered the forest character of oak wood. Very gradually, using her stock in trade for woodland margins on light soils – crabs, amelanchiers, gorse, broom and rambling roses – Gertrude merged wood into more formal areas. Terraces, narrow on the west, wider on the south, are sweetened with lavender and climbing roses, drawing the visitor towards the extreme south-eastern corner, and here, at the grand climax, the landscape invites the eye over yew hedges to a magnificent view encompassing half the county of Surrey. 'The scheme of gardening has been kept very simple,'[19] Gertrude wrote. Like most of her simplicity, it results from sophistication. At the crucial, south-eastern angle, the house provides a narrow outdoor loggia, 'a delightful place for summer breakfasting, and as an all-day resort in warm weather'.[20] Breakfast was to be partaken with a restful medley of greens rippling into the distance.

The loggia terrace offered both the long rural view and access via Lutyens's characteristic semi-circular steps to the most secretive and intricate part of the garden. What Lawrence Weaver calls a 'miniature pleasaunce',[21] the sunk or 'Dutch' garden is bounded on the north by the kitchen garden wall to make an enclosure half dwelling, half nature, the sky as roof and plants for furniture. With its fine herring-bone network of brick and stone paving and a water fountain issuing from a lion-head spout made by Julia Chance into a tiled basin, the Dutch garden is really an outdoor room. Curved stone seats repeat the line of circular beds filled with white roses, lavender and golden yew. This garden within a garden, delicate and secluded, was Gertrude's inner sanctuary. Sustaining the musical analogy would make it a small self-contained melody or perhaps an interlude. The climax has been absorbed though its echoes reverberate through the final movement.

Below Dutch garden and lawn, a yew-banked walk leads north to Lutyens's gateway, alternately tiled and stone-decorated like the rays of a setting sun. The arch and its wrought-iron gate create a vista between flower borders that cross the kitchen garden, past a rose-trellised dipping well to another archway. Gertrude constantly used arches for framing landscape, bringing the foreground in sharp focus, allowing the distance to make mystery. At Munstead Wood she had created a similar picture, through a laburnum arch, along borders of Michaelmas daisies to the kitchen garden. It is worth reflecting upon the influence of the long galleries at Wargrave Manor, with their well-proportioned arches separating a series of tiny picture-filled enclosures. Stored in her mind was an endless visual repertoire of absorbed pictures.

At the heart of Orchards was the kitchen garden, where flowers and vegetables portrayed richly yielding domesticity, abundance and productiveness – the practical and symbolical attributes of an orchard site. Bisecting herbaceous borders camouflaged fruit and vegetables, giving an immediate impression of a flower-filled enclosure. At another level, the mixture of flowers, herbs and vegetables was intended to recall the monastic tradition, and a raised path along the outer edge of the walled garden was reminiscent of 'mounts' from Tudor times. Conscious earthiness belied evident luxury. Orchards was a house for wealthy Edwardians, yet it is not overpowering. It has, moreover, what the landscape architect Sylvia Crowe described as so essential to a garden, 'the power of survival into another age'.[22] Its present owners are gradually restoring some of Gertrude's planting. But even without it, 'the ground form, the disposition of mass and void, the relationship of the garden to the house and countryside, the composition of one part with another, and . . . the architectural features remain and are sufficient to preserve the entity'.[23] Like Munstead Wood, it has elegance that is never paraded, a sense of proportion in all its parts and with man. For the woman who taught her architect to build not just houses but homes, it was above all, a place 'that has the true home feeling'.[24]

Where there was talent and mutual interest great things might be accomplished. Lutyens and Edward Hudson of *Country Life* were a strange mixture, but Gertrude's efforts in bringing them together had already paid dividends. Both were largely self-educated, vulnerable, inarticulate and in some ways childlike. Hudson was godfather to Ursula, Lutyens's second daughter, and the young Lutyenses saw a generous, easy-going, good-natured man who fooled with them in the nursery. There was another side to him, clumsy, opinionated and cantankerous. Emily never really liked him, and either way he was an oddball. Lutyens addressed him as 'Huddy', but though he was generally known in his practice as 'Lut-lut', throughout thirty-six years of friendship Hudson stuck to a deferential 'Lutyens'. Hudson worshipped beautiful things. His life was spent in search of them, for himself or his beloved *Country Life*. 'And when he had found some exquisite piece of furniture or china and brought it home, he would touch it lovingly and sit gazing at it benignly, and it would become almost a living inmate of the house in Queen Anne's Gate.'[25] For all his middle-class background and lack of snobbishness, he liked good architecture old and new and fancied the setting of a country squire. Deanery Garden in Sonning was the first creation of an exuberant Jekyll/Lutyens/ Hudson triumvirate.

During Lutyens's preliminary site inspection, on 25 July 1901, Gertrude came in the morning and stayed for lunch and tea. 'Bumps appreciative & kind & admired Sonning.'[26] Tooley suggests that one of the plans in the Reef Point Collection showing lawn, steps and water rill may be hers. At all events, the garden is clearly another unique blend of collaborative inspiration. The plot was an old orchard in the centre of the village, and being entirely hedged and walled, had none of Orchards' potential in the wider landscape. Apart from a glimpse of the parish church spire, it turns in upon itself. Yet the conception does seem 'with intensified discipline and subtlety',[27] to have grown out of the previous work. Little was changed in the character of the ancient orchard, so Lutyens's sophisticated, asymmetrical building backing a public road is enchantingly revealed through a skein of branches and leaves. Garden inter-penetrates house through arches, loggias, great ranges of leaded glass and an exquisitely manicured open courtyard, its minute water rill echoed in a larger one, central to a broad, colour-filled braid of flowers across the front of the house. In the springtime pale daffodils and groups of primroses stud long grass below newly leafing apple, plum and pear. Marian Thompson, a landscape architect who restored the Jekyll planting at Deanery Garden in the 1980s, explained how she discovered a preliminary plan for part of the site leading to the inner courtyard. It was this working meditation on white lilies, drifts of lavender, rosemary, and pink Japanese anemones, irreverently scribbled, crossed and lettered, which brought home to her Gertrude's tough working synthesis.

Cook remained an editor of *The Garden* for twelve years in all, afterwards emigrating to Canada where he took up landscape gardening. Gertrude's editorial period was relatively short. After little more than two years she let it be known that her eyesight made the job increasingly taxing, and shortly after she left. It is impossible to say how much her eyes were responsible for the decision. On top of all the other things she did, trips to London, office work and keeping deadlines must have been incredibly taxing. There was, moreover, increasing tension between image and reality, her public life and private needs. But something must be said about the 'blindness' that affected every part of her working and imaginative life, variously a handicap, convenient shield from social interruptions, excuse from tasks she found uncongenial and part of her unique artistic quality. Before she was sixty she was describing herself as 'oldish and half blind',[28] giving the impression of being an invalid at a time she was in capital health. Physically she was very tough; only once does one hear of a prolonged attack of colitis necessitating a resident nurse. She had a natural focus of only two inches but she used bad eyesight to suggest infirmity, especially when she wished to excuse herself from social engagements. For someone consciously contriving her image, it was convenient to be something of an invalid if it ensured her privileges. 'I wish I could come to see you some day at Camberley but on account of my wretched eyes, which get overdone by the exertion of trying to see in any new place, I have to give up all going away and content myself with the quietest of home life,'[29] she wrote to a client. She could not tolerate interruptions, especially trivial ones. Her ability to progress in the direction she must demanded a certain ruthlessness; she could not afford to be perpetually on demand.

The Garden was the great forum for English gardening and Gertrude's term on it had given her the opportunity to meet those best versed in every speciality. Her next book, *Roses for English Gardens*, was proof that she had indeed cultivated her colleagues. Miss Willmott added 'a number of excellent photographs',[30] reliable E. T. Cook had offered 'frequent advice and assistance',[31] Edward Mawley dealt with the section on cultivation and Edward Woodall had written a chapter on garden roses from the Riviera, where he spent the winter months. A photograph of Mawley in the *Gardeners' Chronicle*[32] shows a dark-suited elegant man with even features, beard, boater, spotted neckerchief and watch chain, standing against a sea of dahlias. He had been educated by his father as an architect. Paternal influence was strong, and not until his father died did he lay a garden round a newly-built Croydon house, become obsessed with roses and relinquish his first career. It was only a couple of years before he joined the horticultural élite by earning his Victoria Medal of Horticulture, known as the VMH. In the meantime he began a thirty-seven-year stint as secretary of the National Rose Society.

When Gertrude was *The Garden* editor she had written to Ellen Willmott that she was translating Henri Correvon, the veteran botanist's, German description of Warley for the paper. Miss Willmott was forty-four, another forceful, single woman, living alone. In fact she lived in considerable style at Warley Place in Essex, where she had been gardening for twenty years. Up to 100 gardeners in boaters and green silk ties tended rambling naturalistic scenery full of rare and precious plants, a haven of which George Wilson wrote, 'It seems to me that your garden is the happiest combination of alpine, herbaceous and florist flowers, I have ever seen.'[33] Miss Willmott had a second garden on the edge of Lake Bourget in the Rhône Valley and was well known to nurserymen. From Correvon, whose garden above Geneva had made him celebrated among alpine gardeners, she bought thousands of plants and acquired a young gardener. The plants that she and her garden gave their name to are a measure of her success. Gertrude was to refer to her as 'the greatest living of women-gardeners'.[34] Gertrude was not a sycophant but she knew the value of sincere commendation. Accomplishment was something that interested her, and, perfectly aware of Miss Willmott's talent, she had made careful, friendly overtures. Besides, after herself, Miss Willmott did deserve the accolade. Quick tongues and abundant energy made them in some ways alike: they painted, sang, made excellent craftwork and studied photography. Their personalities, however, could scarcely have been more different. Gertrude's unprepossessing exterior belied self-esteem; she was stable and disciplined to the hilt. Beautiful, eccentric Miss Willmott was, by turn, proud, nervous, prickly, overbearing and wilful. Diplomacy was not her strong point, though she was to call Gertrude 'a sensitive and great personality'[35] in whom resided 'all the qualities I most admire'.[36]

Mrs Earle was, on the whole, diplomatic, and her reaction to Gertrude's rose book was generally favourable. As if it was a guiding principle not to assent to entire admiration, she owned once again that she was 'much disappointed with the illustrations'.[37] Others may have considered the photographs in the new book a fair guide to the resourcefulness of its author's vision. Roses festoon arches and pillars, hang in ropes from mushroom-headed standards, smother the ground, clothe swinging ropes, slither against brick walls, climb balconies and wriggle their way into trees. But Mrs Earle could afford to indulge harmless private envies, for she was the most supportive friend. Both she and Barbara Bodichon had seen women's education as a keystone to the future. Madame Bodichon had left behind her the reputation of a pioneer feminist and educational innovator. Theresa Earle continued to campaign. With patience and perseverance, she alleged, every girl could do something, and once a woman had made up her mind to earn her living 'no concentration of study for the one particular occupation she has in view can be too thorough or too severe'.[38] Swanley Horticultural College had opened its doors to girls in 1891, demand for places far exceeded supply, and eleven years later Viscountess Wolseley, daughter of Gertrude's old friend, founded the Glynde School for Lady Gardeners. Its three patrons were Gertrude, Mrs Earle and William Robinson.

If Frances Garnet Wolseley's reputation is now relatively obscure, she was in her day a dynamic figure, well known in horticultural circles, the author of seven garden books. Another of Gertrude's bossy, adventurous women friends, Frances had been a surprise to her mother, being almost the son the Field Marshal never had. A well-developed sense of order and a love of riding and of the countryside were her most pronounced attributes. What she referred to as the 'aimless, humdrum existence of many women of wealthy classes'[39] did not entice her in the least, and only reluctantly could she be cajoled into society. It was while she and her mother were staying with friends at Glynde Place on the Sussex Downs that the idea for her school was conceived, and not far from Glyndebourne, on the side of Mount Caburn, her first recruits helped to hack away at high chalk banks, making a sheltered retreat on a bare, windswept cornfield. In recognition of the unpropitious soil, she called her new house 'Ragged Lands'.

It was not Viscountess Wolseley but Miss Willmott through whom Gertrude designed her first garden on foreign soil in 1902, a single herbaceous border with the Munstead Wood colour sequence for Sir Henry Bellingham at his grand villa at Tresserve in the French Alps. The place, Audrey le Lievre tells us, was 'of a peculiar and entrancing stillness and beauty'.[40] Miss Willmott lived at the nearby Château. The other object of Gertrude's French visit was a twenty-three-day slimming cure at Brides-les-Bains. 'Very little to eat. Raging hunger till 14th day, by 16th less hungry and thirsty.'[41] Lutyens protested at losing 'an ounce of her bulb',[42] but at the end of August she was twenty-five pounds lighter. To Gertrude in later life her weight was a persistent battle. It made her behave in public with inept and artificial self-consciousness. Geoffrey Taylor supplies the intriguing intelligence [43] that no man, especially a young one, was permitted to follow her through narrow gaps in her garden. For all her forthrightness and self-knowledge, there was a side to her that did not want to be made to feel peculiar.

Sensibly, Gertrude seduced herself through the diet with the lure of three weeks at Chalet de Sonzier, the place where repression, awkwardness and sense of duty were abandoned, where she felt free to struggle from restricting inhibitions into the warmth of social conviviality. Correvon was also staying there and she was quick to cultivate him. The meeting ensured his visit to Munstead two years later. In Dijon on her return, she stopped to bewail the fact that the old Cloche had been replaced by a smart modern one. The complaint was 'characteristic'.[44] In the new century she was to rate change automatically with decadence. But this was her last trip abroad.

CHAPTER TWENTY

1903–4

At the heart of all Gertrude's books lies the potency of her response to her surroundings. Sometimes her cadence is as measured as that of Richard Jeffries, the nature writer whose prose she occasionally calls to mind. Like him at his best, say in *Wild Life in a Southern County*, she could assume a kind of biblical grace. But had she the imagination to transform things beyond their reality? Fitting in everything she wanted to do was an enormous challenge and writing was always, she said, hard work. A novel was not something to be undertaken lightly, but she tried, and that was like her. *The Death of Iron* was based on the idea of a world suddenly deprived of the metal and all its products, a subject sufficiently appropriate almost to amount to wish-fulfilment. Francis Jekyll read the story and thought it deserved to be published, though he doubted that this was Gertrude's intention. She had appropriate contacts, there would have been no reason for withholding the manuscript unless she was dissatisfied with it. But it has disappeared, giving her nephew the last word on the subject.

It is evident that Gertrude drove herself hard. 'She says she is badly in need of a holiday,'[1] Lutyens wrote to Emily on 27 August. A week later, Gertrude was installed for ten days at Priory Farm, between Seaview and St Helens on the Isle of Wight. She had an ability to throw herself zestfully into new activities; one feels her walking, probing, letting her capacity to respond to her environment spring to life again. The sketchbook for this trip finds her already preoccupied with another big project. Drawings of architectural and agricultural eccentricities now in the Godalming Museum include 'detail of ventilation holes in barn wall', 'gate catches', 'Old Chapel in Rickyard? Surely it is a Dovecot', 'A silly gate made of nonsense tools'.[2] On Saturday 12 September she bought two pairs of sandshoes for five shillings. On Sunday she went to church and put two shillings in the collection. Both expenses were carefully computed.

Old West Surrey, Some Notes and Memories was drawn from long
vigilance. Since childhood Gertrude had been intrigued by the ways of
villagers, their homes and contents. She had climbed into bedrooms,
bacon lofts and granaries, whittling out secrets, investigating details of
clothes, speech, manners and local products with a critical, discerning
eye. She knew, for example, that heath brooms were secured with two
bonds, birch brooms with three. All her life she had gathered samples
of craftsmanship that appealed to her. Little was wasted or forgotten.
After living for the best part of half a century in West Surrey, she dips
with authority into her mind on topics such as gates and fireplaces,
furniture, candlesticks, samplers, patchwork and coconuts carved by
merchant sailors. The book did not appear until 1904 but Gertrude's
material dates back thirty years, gleaning thereby from an earlier
period than the wave of nostalgic writings which emerged at the turn
of the century. Jeffries had discovered, 'in some degree with the tillers
of the soil, old manners and customs linger, and there seems an echo of
the past in the breadth of their pronunciation'.[3] Gertrude's contribution
to oral history alone was significant. One seven-verse folk song she
transcribed was unique to the Godalming area. Shortly afterwards
George Sturt, writing under his 'Bourne' pseudonym, found in almost
the same region that no folk songs or folk culture were left.

The trouble with the rural idyll is its idealization; in elevating the
1870s Gertrude was to some extent seeing what she wanted or was
conditioned to see. She was not alone in this. Birket Foster and his
disciple Helen Allingham's paintings of pretty cottages with honeysuckle round the door and lichen-encrusted brickwork were likely, in
reality, to be hovels fit only for pigs. Agricultural surveys show that
Surrey farmers were slower than their Kent and Sussex neighbours to
adopt new techniques, and mid-century was a time of widespread
indigence. In fact Surrey was one of the most backward counties in
England, one explanation being that soils which proved so good for
building were very infertile. In villages around Godalming, wages for
male labourers varied from 8s to 10s a week in the 1870s. Women
received only 8d a day.[4] Labouring families often had six or seven
children, insanitary conditions caused typhoid, infant mortality was
high and illiteracy ran to 50 per cent of the population. Throughout
the nineteenth century the most obvious characteristic of life for
agricultural workers and their families was deep-seated poverty.

Within the overall pattern there were smaller fluctuations, but by the mid-seventies depression had set in. Farmers faced foreign competition, labourers left the land and local newspapers carried advertisements suggesting emigration to the colonies. Women were hard put to find work at all. By 1904, Gertrude noted, they were no longer being employed to glean. Living conditions improved in the last thirty years of the century but the ancient social order of the countryside, with roots running back to prehistory, was giving place to a new urban society of machinery and mass production. Rural trades declined. The purchasing power in the villages fell, manufactured goods were brought in from the towns, and the local blacksmith, miller and tailor disappeared. As historians report, 'the rich variety of rural occupations that had characterized most villages in the early nineteenth century had rapidly diminished, never to reappear'.[5]

Gertrude echoed the famous words Morris delivered at the town hall in Birmingham, 'Have nothing in your houses that you do not know to be useful, or believe to be beautiful.'[6] She urged people to collect old things before it was too late, and when her interests throw special light on a subject, she was remarkably discerning. The patchwork quilt, for instance, 'interesting, not only for the taste and judgement shown in the pattern and arrangement of colours, but for the designs of the prints themselves'.[7] Like Morris, she loathed bric-à-brac, 'cheap things painfully jarring and out of place',[8] 'articles got up with veneer and varnish'[9] and furniture that was 'shoddy'[10] and 'pretentious'.[11] Pretentious was a word that held especial horror for her. Even such hallowed pieces of English ground as graveyards were, thanks to the 'love of meretricious display',[12] she said, invaded by pattern-book artefacts and artificial wreaths. There was plenty about which to complain, and if *Old West Surrey* manages to give a relentlessly one-sided picture of happy England going to the dogs, there was more to her endeavour than simply recording a passing social life. In her heart, she felt that by lauding old, functional artefacts and berating incongruous replacements, she might revive the spirit of the good old days.

She saw that a sense of community founded on craft would disappear with the craftsmen. What she did not have was Ruskin's optimism about a working man's creativity, and she writes about working people in a deeply if unconsciously patronizing way. So exaggerated is her class-consciousness, indeed, that it is worth considering how she perceived social status. Upper classes had big houses in the country, ideals of nobility and service and a hostility to change that she herself displayed. Working classes, intellectually inferior and further handicapped by a lack of education, were born to serve their superiors. In her mind there was no reason why the cottager's bonnet, dusted after each Sunday church-going, should not 'last a life-time', why a 'good old body'[13] should not tie his baggage in a clean (and picturesque) cotton handkerchief, or the 'limited vocabulary' of the 'cheery old country voice'[14] should change so long as it had 'charm'.[15] What she did begrudge was that 'every sort of folly [was] committed by these poor people in this insane striving to be what they think is "fashionable"'.[16]

George Bourne's *Bettesworth Book*, published in 1920, may have romanticized what Louis Stevenson called 'the eternal life of man, spent under sun and rain and in rude physical effort'[17] but Bourne respected the working man for himself. To fit Gertrude's scheme of what was right and proper, the working classes had to be not only picturesque but humble. Even the illustrations in *Old West Surrey* portray village people whose slight inclination of the head suggests resigned deference. There are references to lives cruelly burdened by overwork, labour lasting daily from 6 a.m. until 9 p.m., hardship and crippling rheumatism. The cottager and his family were not necessarily unhappy, yet their lifestyle was harsh and often deprived. Gertrude approved pride and guts, but repeatedly scorned the working man's attempts to escape from or better his lot. In the 'love of cheerfulness'[18] she claimed to find among the undernourished and overworked, it is tempting to ask whether she was being nostalgic for a childhood vision.

It was easier to make firm judgements about things than about people. Gertrude realized that the artefacts she had collected, many of them plucked from imminent destruction, were of educational value and was keen to give them a useful, permanent home. Three years after her book appeared, when Surrey Archaeological Society opened a museum in Guildford, she presented it with a large part of the raw material of *Old West Surrey*. Mole trap, bridle, spinning wheel and sheep bells are just a few of the objects held today in the borough museum in Quarry Street. Some fine examples of Wealden ironwork have since been loaned to a timbered cottage south of Godalming once painted by Helen Allingham and now owned by the National Trust. Oakhurst Cottage is a pretty, skeletal waif of a dwelling, tucked away behind Hambledon cricket green. Until the mid-1980s it was inhabited, and since then it has been furnished as the family home of a farm labourer might have looked a century before. The association with Gertrude Jekyll is completely appropriate. From just such a place would she have acquired the great iron pot suspended over a hearth on an adjustable hanger, the huge black kettle and iron fire dogs now on display. Jeffries wrote that old-fashioned cottages were practically built around the chimney; palpable recognition that the hearth and its equipment were the centre of cottage life.

One puzzling entry in *Old West Surrey* concerns the 'round' or smock frock, a garment whose disappearance Gertrude deplored. Designs varied from one county or region to another, and it is clear from the text that she knew some had wide embroidered panels over the chest, while others had small smocked or embroidered panels. Both she describes being worn in Surrey, but apart from her premise, Mary Alexander of the Guildford Museum said, they have evidence only of the second type. Gertrude is generally difficult to fault on facts, and she was a needlewoman. Unfortunately, the illustrations simply confuse the issue. The smock worn by an 'old labourer'[19] has no visible smocking, the stitching is difficult to see on the man in 'the white smock-frock'[20] and a rear illustration of the same garment appears to be clumsily criss-crossed on top of the photograph with a pen.

Gertrude's writings were destined to help establish the Edwardian cult of the picturesque country cottage set in a mêlée of woods and flowers, and ironically, like idealized cottage paintings, *Old West Surrey* attracted the wrong sort of people. By the 1900s the railway had created a demand for commuter houses and there were streams of pilgrims seeking the idyll of rural countryside, starry-eyed visitors who saw the village community as an ideal society and flocked after its country cottages. Instead of reviving old crafts, artificial ones were provided to cater for them. The idealization continues today. Reproductions of Birket Foster's and Helen Allingham's contrived scenes of wistful charm and contentment adorn millions of greeting cards of thatched cottages with hollyhocks beside the door. A trend George Bourne saw in embryo has, at least in Surrey, completed its course. 'The old life is being swiftly obliterated. The valley is passing out of the hands of its former inhabitants. They are being crowded into corners, and are becoming as aliens in their own homes; they are receding before newcomers with new ideas, and, greatest change of all, they are yielding to the dominion of new ideas themselves.'[21]

It is difficult to know precisely when Helen Allingham met Gertrude. On at least two occasions, in 1900 and again in 1902, she journeyed from Hampstead to paint Munstead Wood for a collection called *Happy England*. Born Helen Paterson, daughter of a doctor and niece to Laura Herford, the first woman to be admitted to the Royal Academy, Helen had been taught at art school by Frederick Walker, whom Gertrude had met in Algiers. Afterwards, she became the first woman staff member of a revolutionary art magazine known as the *Graphic*. Thomas Hardy fell in love with her while she was producing plates for a serialized version of *Far from the Madding Crowd* in the *Cornhill* magazine, but during the course of the commission she met and married the Irish-born poet, William Allingham. In the late 1880s they had moved to Witley, south-west of Munstead, where she had lived near her mentor, Myles Birket Foster. Despite having a depressive husband, three children, and campaigning ardently on behalf of William Morris's Society for the Protection of Ancient Buildings, she had produced 1,000 drawings and watercolours by 1903. It was a quarter-century since Morris had set up his society and Gertrude, too, endorsed his concern. It was a duty, she felt, 'to retain them [cottages] untouched, to preserve them from decay or demolition . . . I feel sure that in another hundred years this will be known more widely and felt more strongly even than now.'[22]

Plants had been Gertrude's first connection with James Britten, Keeper of the Botany Department at the British Museum. Britten had written for Robinson's various magazines and she had contacted him for assistance on nomenclature. But *Old West Surrey*, with its philological content, was another mutual interest. Gradually she got to know this diabolically gruff and gifted man, a staunch Roman Catholic and author of *Old Country and Farming Words*, published in 1880 for the English Dialect Society; 'a little, elderly, snuffy botanist', Logan Pearsall Smith said of his friend, and 'If you had a special interest, you were apt to find that he knew more about it than you did, and he didn't in the least mind making you aware of his superior knowledge.'[23] Britten could be 'an irascible, fault-finding little man', a cat beside whom Miss Jekyll appeared a 'good-natured dog'.[24] Since Gertrude was addicted to pussies and could not bear canines, Pearsall Smith's description of her was scarcely apt. But it is a measure of her respect for Britten that she allowed him to criticize not only her garden but her accuracy in correspondence. 'Did I really write Campa. pusilla! I still have to send your nephew some Mich. Daisies.'[25] She grew fond of the museum keeper, who was invited on several occasions to Munstead Wood.

It was Britten who introduced his fellow bachelor, a clever and urbane middle-aged American with a taste for painstaking prose. Logan Pearsall Smith was Bertrand Russell's brother-in-law, a belletrist and an author for the Hogarth Press. He hovered on the outer edges of Bloomsbury and vied with the English at the game of being a gentleman, trying so hard that one might have guessed the person behind the carapace was a good deal more morose than the public one. Gertrude's concern with language is evident in a letter she wrote to a fellow botanist: 'what a blessing it is that scientific people . . . can now write in a natural way & not in the stilted language of 50 years ago. I wonder who made the great discovery that this was possible – I suspect Huxley.'[26] But she could be a real pedant on the subject: 'It should be remembered that a Rose garden can never be called gorgeous; the term is quite unfitting,'[27] and a battle of wits found her in her element. Intellectual badinage was a sophisticated game with its own rules and rituals. Performance was what counted; friendship was not emotional, talk defined attitudes but divulged nothing private. It was the sort of communication encouraged within the Jekyll family circle and indulged during her most carefree encounters at Chalet de Sonzier.

As Gertrude gained new friends she lost old ones. The Dean of Rochester's death, she wrote in *Country Life*, deprived them of a high churchman whose outlook had been broad, generous and catholic. The source of his power, she felt, had been in qualities 'essentially English'[28] – 'high courage, valiant maintenance of truth and justice', and 'that sweetest of human kindness'.[29] Reynolds Hole had loved a good horse, all country things and was soon wakened to the beauty of flowers. As such he was one of the first to combat the 'evil influence'[30] of the bedding system.

She had never seen the Dean's Rochester garden but the following April, hard at work on the text for a volume of reproductions by George Samuel Elgood, she needed to know what it was like. Instead of travelling down, however, she wrote to Mrs Hammond of Aldershot for 'some rough description of the garden & its surroundings & general conditions – especially as seen from the point of view of the picture . . . the most roughly scribbled plan would help me much – any notes of soil, difficulties if any, such as smoke, invading cats . . . it does not matter how shortly it is put down – I should use my own words'.[31]

Her quest for assistance was backed by her usual plea of incapacity: 'journeys are to me now impossible'.[32] There was an element of play-acting in Gertrude's excuses and this time her duplicity is revealed by her personal expense book. The following month, on 16 May 1904, she left Munstead for thirteen days, doubtless equipped with the huge Gladstone bag and gig umbrella with a turned wooden handle that are today in the Godalming Museum. A rail fare of 6s 6d followed by a 'fly'[33] costing 3s took her to Trebarwith, in the north of Cornwall, where she stayed with a Mrs Trevillin. From there she visited Tintagel by pony-cart. It was thirteen years since Barbara Bodichon had died; perhaps these were places they had once seen together.

In September she wrote to prevent Mrs Hammond coming to Munstead Wood, and the length of explanation, in a correspondent usually concise, suggests that she felt a certain need to justify herself. She was 'deep in preparation' for 'heavy work . . . already proving more than enough for my time and strength'.[34] In the circumstances a garden visitor, with 'the extra strain on my unfortunate eyes'[35] brought on headaches that might lose her the whole of the following day. 'And I am getting on sixty-two next November!'[36] From about this time, she constantly used her age as a pretext. But her need to avoid social encounters is admitted fairly honestly. 'Having to talk, & hearing much of voices about me is unfortunately the thing that tires me most.'[37] As she explained even more forthrightly to another prospective visitor, 'Nothing, I am sorry to say, tires me so much as my dear fellow creatures.'[38] What she could not easily acknowledge was that for someone almost indefatigable and remorselessly commit-ted, work had to go on.

The new book, *Some English Gardens*, is handsome, oversized and profusely illustrated – one can see Gertrude's insistence on quality – a volume designed to flatter those who lived in elegant homes and to intrigue a curious public. She had chosen to work with the most conventional of artists. Elgood depicts some thirty gardens, mostly formal and Italianate, to each of which Gertrude adds a short account of aspect, climate, history, design, and occasional remarks about plants. Although the format precludes real depth, the book makes a valuable historical record. 'Green walls with their own proper enrichment of ball and spire, bracket and buttress,'[39] reflects her increasing attraction to the architectural, yet her rational component doubted whether the flowerless Italianate was 'in itself the kind of gardening best suited for

England'.[40] George Elgood was a knowledgeable gardener and successful watercolourist raised to fashionable eminence by the vogue for pretty Victorian pictures. He had married a rich wife, lost his heart to Italian Renaissance gardens and become for the grand Italianate pastiche what Helen Allingham was for country cottages, one of the very few able to make a living solely from garden scenes. Characteristic of his paintings are strongly sculpted hedges in subtly dappled green, lichen-encrusted steps, statuary, balustrades and flowers so carefully painted they can often be identified, everything suffused by his famous luminous blue haze. Few would call them great art, but today his paintings are enjoying a second popularity. It is surprising that Gertrude's strong sense of rightness did not disapprove of his period figures adorning the lawns of nineteenth-century restorations. Perhaps it was tactful to accept the idiosyncrasies of an opinionated perfectionist who became increasingly irascible with age. Elgood's photograph shows a monocled and bearded visage which could not easily have turned to humour.

CHAPTER TWENTY-ONE

1905–7

By no means was Gertrude restricting herself to writing. Each year she fulfilled commissions for garden plans, took photographs, entertained visitors a good deal more often than she cared to, and always the garden took first priority. During winter evenings half-finished crafts were patiently resumed. 'Japanned clock top. Made ornamental lid to tea chest. Embroidery of best bed cover, begun three years ago.'[1] Quite early in life she had developed a taste for domestic routine; tidy, varied, everything fitting in. Overall, the design of her days was changing. Apart from annual holidays when the house was being spring-cleaned, she was increasingly reluctant to stray from home. She resented the confusions of cities, no longer needed London as a stimulus and was totally engaged at Munstead. Strangely enough, insularity seemed almost to enhance the singularity of her vision.

In Bramley village there was a narrow plot of land left by the demolition of some Jacobean half-timbered cottages. When Gertrude inspected what had become known as the 'sordid half-acre',[2] it had been derelict for some years; a dumping ground, among docks and nettles, for tin cans chucked from the lane. From half-way down the plot, however, she could see the wooded grounds of Bramley House with the hills of her young primrose-picking forays and hear the 'soothing sound'[3] of the old watermill. It felt restful and countrified. Here she would build a house for sale on the open market, 'not only worthy of the pretty site but . . . also the best small house in the whole neighbourhood'.[4] Lutyens, of course, would be her architect. Financially, she made what he referred to as 'a very unfair bargain [to herself] with her builder. It is naughty of her.'[5] Money was of secondary importance to working together, perhaps rekindling some of the magic of building Munstead Wood. Reinforcing Gertrude's ties with the past was Colonel Ricardo's request for her to work at Bramley House. Nothing, one feels, would have delighted her more than the prospect of enhancing the surroundings which had inspired her gardening life. There are plans to fortify the shrubbery around the stream and add a formal garden. But the late Lord Hamilton was pretty sure the octagonal verbena garden she proposed was never realized. The story of Millmead is told in the first chapter of a book on which Gertrude collaborated with Lawrence Weaver in 1912; the building still stands, a testimony both to the partnership and to the poetry of her childhood.

Often she had opined that size had little to do with merit. 'It is the size of his [the owner's] heart and brain and goodwill that will make his garden either delightful or dull, as the case may be.'[6] The new plot was small in comparison with the gardens she usually planned, more than five times as long as it was wide and bore an awkward diagonal tilt. By dividing it crosswise into three main units on different levels and subdividing these, she achieved the variety and individuality of a much larger area. The house was built between two existing cottages on the unit nearest the lane, set back slightly, in a quietly planted forecourt approached through wrought-iron gates. The court narrows into an oak-beamed, vine-covered pergola of ship's timbers, restfully tunnelling the vision before a 'riot of bright blossom'[7] at the other end. The long garden on the south was filled with a medley of cottage plants, phlox, iris, saxifrages, pinks and aubrietas, hellebores, pansies, tiarella and day-lilies, snapdragons, lavender and catmint, lushly planted, held within a strong linear pattern by rough York stone paths and paired junipers. To stress the potential for variety on a small site, Gertrude included countless architectural features; a rose garden with a sundial centrepiece, a dipping well, dry stone walls threaded with alpines and a summer house. The tool shed beneath its plum tree resembles a miniature Surrey brick and timber cottage, its tiled roofs stuccoed with stonecrops. A photograph she took looking towards the house shows a cottage setting, the epitome of prettiness, every chink burgeoning with flowers.

The project caused an unexpected litigation. 'The excitement is that the By Law people have told us to pull down the Summer House & she is going to fight them,'[8] Lutyens cheerfully related. For Gertrude, controversy over one of the boundaries made a terse diary entry, 'Put up paling, Stapley raged.'[9] Stapley was the unfortunate neighbour against whom, notes she gathered in her defence suggest, she argued with steely precision. On 4 November 1905, when the case came before the Guildford magistrates, one feels her totally prepared. In confrontation she was very controlled. Pearsall Smith had realized Miss Jekyll enjoyed 'a scrimmage now and then'.[10] Lutyens was on hand as witness. Naturally, she won the case.

Millmead was the real victor, a place that struck Harold Falkner 'all of a heap'.[11] 'I have never seen anything before, nor since as perfectly developed, so exquisite in every detail, so much in so small a space.'[12] Falkner had visited long after the place was built and written up. The account in *Gardens for Small Country Houses*, he considered, was 'worthy and painstaking', but 'as nothing to the effect'[13] of the real thing. 'In colour, texture, form, background, setting, smell and associa- tion . . . it was perfect. It was to me the work of a fairy or wizard, and I had found it right under my own nose within a few hundred yards of the house in which I was born, but till then absolutely unknown to me . . . I have seen many of the great gardens in this country and I have never had the least inclination to alter this opinion.'[14] A stand of alders beyond the garden now clouds the view that was a shrine to the old Bramley house, and one of Millmead's past owners made off with the York stone paving; despite which, it has borne the test of time.

Planning gardens and writing books was taking precedence over journalism. But Gertrude's name carried weight and she could, with minimum effort, adapt material from one medium to another. During the summer of 1905 she was able to extend her readership beyond the usual country life and horticultural sphere. Sandwiched between 'The Woman of the World – Which is worse – to be too serious or too frivolous?'[15] and advertisements for hotels in Buxton and Sidmouth, three of her pieces appeared in successive editions of *The World – A Journal for Men and Women*. Later on she tapped the even larger readership of the *Daily Mail*, where 'What can be done with half an acre?' made a two-thirds page spread illustrated by three garden plans. Gertrude was at her most dogmatic. 'There are hundreds – one may almost venture to say thousands – of gardens, not only near London, but throughout the length of the land, that are as bad as this . . .'[16] – a hypothetical model. Shade from a deplored wellingtonia rendered it gloomy, the summerhouse was 'dank', the pool 'a slimy puddle', and paths 'wriggled' for 'lack of design'.[17]

The Jekylls continued to supply Lutyens with clients. Mark Fenwick, a noted amateur gardener who had visited Gertrude at Munstead, commissioned Abbotswood, Stow-on-the-Wold. But work passed both ways. Out of roughly 400 gardens or parts of gardens that Gertrude planned, over 100 were done with Lutyens and they tended to be the biggest, most illustrious jobs. Folly Farm at Sulhamstead comes into this period. The most sensational enlargement was not built for another six years, but to Lutyens's first, 'Dutch', extension to the existing cottage, Gertrude laid out a long rhododendron walk running north and south and old-fashioned borders of plants like aquilegia and poppy in box-edged beds divided by brick herringbone-patterned paths. At Marsh Court, near Stockbridge, where she subsequently planted the garden, Lutyens had recently completed an odd and in some ways remarkable Tudor-style building. Hussey had reservations: 'We are never very far from humbug and pretence when we lose touch of native character, native scenery, and native material.' [18] Lutyens was imaginative and witty; by turn, romantic, flamboyant and severe. But there was always the danger he might go to extremes. To Hussey's list of steadying influences, one might add 'native Bumps'.

Professional letters Gertrude received from her architect are an insight to the creative balance of their shared vision. On New Place in Botley, Hampshire, for instance, Lutyens writes, 'Toute suite, This is the only plan of the ground I have Will you let me have it back Ist enough? I have pencilled in the idea about the house . . . Finish of terrace? Steps? Summerhouse? or parapet? Then big herbaceous borders – grass paths right and left . . . gooseberries sort of fruit garden gradually into wild & away.' [19] By comparing a groundplan sketch which accompanied this letter with the final plan, one sees how a fluid, Jekyllian vista through formal areas towards a viewpoint combines with Lutyenesque geometry of axial walks. At Barton St Mary, a job in hand for Mr Munro Miller, there were similar shorthand messages between the two. 'There are slopes right & left getting deeper towards the house (alas) I want pollard limes? or ilex? walnuts say. Speak! ho!! horacle!!! for the Miller presseth.' [20] Always referring to Gertrude as 'Toute suite', Lutyens commiserates, explains, heeds, argues and refines. 'Why did you so previously scold. I told you that Mrs Miller would probably not come & that there would be no question of lunch. I agree to the Rhodos. The Rectangular shrub clumps leave far too small a margin of grass I think – wouldn't nuts do? or better couldn't you do the veronica traversi with dolly Perkins behind it – in front of yew hedge.' [21] To such masterpieces of informative precision, one wishes only for Gertrude's replies.

Lutyens was completing various commissions, starting his first London building – an office for *Country Life*, and restoring his first castle, Lindisfarne on Holy Island. Hudson had exchanged Deanery Garden for something a good deal more exotic. The derelict shell rising from sheer crags off the coast of Northumberland was 'a real castle . . . out of which he would have to turn if the country went to war!'[22] Lutyens enthused. May 1906 saw Gertrude making her way there with Lutyens and a convalescent raven he called Black Jack. Changing trains in London, she bought 3s worth of peppermint bull's-eyes, her old favourites, presumably to share on the journey. When they reached the coast the tide was high so they crossed to the island by boat, and great was the architect's delight at the sight of Hudson's manservant struggling to carry his ample friend into a tiny craft. The bird, 'an awful anxiety',[23] was housed in a temporary cage, drank a lot of water and ate bread and milk. 'She – or is it he? – mischievously upsets all its basins and plates and makes a fearful mess but she seems all right, and I have got two croaks out of her. Her beak makes a noise like castanets when she, he or it eats and drinks.'[24]

Bumps received as much attention as the bird and was more obviously receptive. 'I am sure she wont mind no drawing room & she is bound to go to bed early,'[25] Lutyens ruminated solicitously. In the event she was 'not too tired', 'charmed', 'appreciative',[26] and went off exploring by herself. The next day there was singing and guitar playing, 'Bumps improvising a second – the Provost fiddling – Hudson reading a heavy mail. Bumps has just been singing a French song with great success.'[27] Gertrude was still on Holy Island when news was brought to her of Hercules Brabazon's death. Immediately she wrote to his sister: 'When old age comes, with its weakness and weariness, perhaps one ought not to wish life to be prolonged; but in the case of so good a friend of many years one cannot help clinging to the mere fact of life. Nobody has helped me more than Mr Brabazon to understand and enjoy the beauty of colour and of many matters concerning the fine arts and I am always most truly thankful to have been able to count him among my friends.' There had been a strange freedom about this man who had sought neither publicity nor conventional approval in life or art. Among friends, however, recognition had been important. A photograph Gertrude took of him in the company of her nieces, Leonard Borwick and Susan Muir Mackenzie, is inscribed by the artist's niece with the words, 'HBB a father to us all'. It was not long before Georgy Duff Gordon died, another to leave a large hole in Gertrude's memories.

After returning from Lindisfarne, Gertrude attended the opening of King Edward VII Sanatorium in Midhurst, Sussex, the tuberculosis hospital where she was involved in a grand therapeutic venture. Sir Ernest Cassel, millionaire banker and a friend of the King, had donated funds; H. Percy Adams and his assistant, Charles Holden, had won a competition with their design. The project was strongly influenced by Arts and Crafts philosophy. Holden in particular was inspired by William Morris and traditional vernacular. Five hundred feet above the Rother valley, on what Gertrude called 'a beautiful piece of forest land',[28] he designed a series of linked buildings with interlocking courts. Gertrude's concern with the 'soul-satisfying' qualities of a garden made her ideal for the job. Her seven knot-like formal gardens edged with rosemary were filled with scented flowers and herbs. The gardens alone were a collaborative enterprise. During the course of the commission, she appealed to Sir William Thistleton-Dyer, Kew's current director, for a gardener to plant 1,200 square yards of rock wall for twenty-six shillings a week, and Viscountess Wolseley's lady gardeners established the remaining flowers and shrubs. The King, who took a special interest in the project, is said to have congratulated Gertrude on its success. She, meanwhile, was busy on her next book.

It was an exciting time for flower arrangers. In 1894 George Leslie had written to his friend Mr Marks about the Eastern approach, 'with a sort of religious, artistic and scientific spirit, which is entirely unknown to European nations'.[29] He had discovered a paper by Josiah Conder of Japan's Asiatic Society, explaining the abstruse symbolism behind an age-old Buddhist tradition. Not long afterwards Conder published a book. Suddenly, Japanese flower arrangement assumed a cult in the West. Alert to the advantages of the new style and anxious to impart what she had gleaned of its philosophy, Mrs Earle added a long appendix on the subject to her first *Pot-pourri*.

Gertrude's *Flower Decoration in the House* is one of the pioneering works in the field yet it is not, Betty Massingham allows, her most important work. It makes reasoned lessons in textural contrast, the effect of repetition and the importance of a dominant, background flower. Treating flower arrangement much, as Gertrude says, like 'a branch of gardening',[30] she applies her usual emphasis on unity and harmony. But most of the text concerns suitable material, and it reads like a collation of the monthly articles that were indeed its source. It was shortsighted of Gertrude to ignore the craze for Japanese arrangement. It was not as if she had failed to recognize the subtlety of a genre but only, in her estimation, was a thing worth doing if it was done well. 'Sticking flowers and branches upright in shallow vessels'[31] because it was fashionable gave such absurd results, she had complained in *House and Garden*, that she did not imagine the Japanese could ever seriously compete with the 'loose and free ways of using our familiar garden flowers'.[32] Sarcastically, she added, 'Happily, we can pick a bunch of Primroses in the wood and put it in water without having to consider whether we have done it in such a way as to suggest a ship coming home or a matrimonial engagement in contemplation.'[33] There is truth in her scepticism, but she underrated the lure of a style that has influenced European flower-arranging throughout the twentieth century. Her chapter on cut flowers in *Home and Garden* contains more wisdom than the whole of the subsequent book, which never went into more than one edition. It is difficult to escape the conclusion that she was trying to cram in too much.

Lutyens's respect for Herbert was of much the same order as his respect for Gertrude. The previous summer he had joined the Herbert Jekylls and two young bachelors on a yachting party to the Baltic financed by a rich American Theosophist. 'I have bought yachting clothes,' Lutyens wrote. 'The little Jekylls are such darlings – so tame & Herbert is quite appreciative of my frivol!'[34] Aggie read aloud on deck at night to the gentle sway of the *Miranda* in deepening light, and not for five days did Lutyens's working conscience begin to fret. Knowing brother and sister in their home environments gave Lutyens a filial awareness of Bumps's needs. When she was working to her limit, there were days, Francis Jekyll tells, when even friends were turned from the door. More and more she was isolating herself and just occasionally, Lutyens recognized, she felt the disadvantage. He did not want her to be lonely. While understanding perfectly the strain she found sociability, he did his utmost to make her feel included.

It must have been his suggestion that Gertrude should join Emily and the children on the south coast. At Rustington house guests included Arthur Chapman, a very early client and brother-in-law to Frank Mangles, Mrs Webbe – Aunt Pussey as the young called her – who talked a great deal (Lutyens thought too much) about women's

Lutyens as a sailor, August 1906.

rights, and Lady Pembroke, whom Ned would have liked to know 'for Wilton's sake'.[35] 'Quite a party of suffragettes.'[36] Bumps travelled, he warned Emily in advance, with a great deal of paraphernalia, drawing boards, writing materials and holdalls full of stationery, and 'she wants to be fairly comfy ... Make her feel she may go to bed when she likes and don't let her feel "out" of it.'[37] Lutyens knew that Gertrude no longer responded easily to unknown situations. Until the last minute his advice continued to arrive. 'Don't forget Bumps likes to go to bed early & then spend time in her room each day doing things. This means a table or something. If there is no table she will delight in inventing a substitute ask her if she would like a carpenter to wait on her.'[38] Agnes motored down with Gertrude laden as Ned had foreseen, with 'delicious funny odd luggage'.[39] She insisted on unpacking before drinking beer with Emily, and then wandered on the beach. The next day Ned sent his love and more concern, 'don't let the children tire her'.[40]

For someone persecuted by noise, children were anathema. Even dogs' barking exasperated Gertrude. One does not know her reaction to her brother's Aberdeen terrier, Jockey, let alone to Polly, his fearsome parrot. But children were messy, lawless and time-wasting, everything she most disliked. In later life, Francis Jekyll reckoned his aunt mellowed. Hitherto 'it must be confessed, she had kept the young somewhat at arm's length'.[41] Mary, the youngest Lutyens, has dim recollections of Bumps, whom she probably met at Folly Farm in the summer of 1916. Her reaction is that of a forthright seven-year-old: 'For a child she had nothing going for her, she was very ugly, very dowdy. I probably thought of her as an old frump, if I saw her coming I'd have turned and run.'[42] Physically, Bumps's image was registered by her powerful spectacles. 'They were particularly noticeable. She didn't remove them for social occasions like other people. She wore them all the time.'[43] Mary's brother, Robert, made no bones about 'dreaded "Aunt Bumps"'.[44]

Herbert's grandchildren reinforce the impression of 'a threatening deity, whose wrath was very much to be feared, only to be conciliated by noiselessness and careful observance of garden paths'.[45] It was a state of affairs Gertrude did little to discourage. Pamela's second son, David McKenna, born in 1911, knew 'Aunt Gertrude', as he respectfully called her, from the age of about five. When he and his brother Michael were staying at Munstead House, she was essentially part of the setting. Frequent errands to Munstead Wood caused the boys a spasm of awe. First they had to climb a bank and reach behind a fence-like barrier for the secret key. Once opened, the gate led them through the copse, and sometimes as they approached the house they would spy her in the garden. She would be wearing a long, darkish dress covered by a blue baize apron with a pocket full of tools and a utilitarian straw hat. When she moved, it was like a bell tent. Her face was impassive, her voice low, her speech economical. She spoke rather distinctly, a calm and slightly frightening disciplinarian, conveying in every directive a persuasive desire that standards be met and order be maintained. 'We were well briefed,' he said. 'Aunt Gertrude was someone who did not like noise, or children who talked too much. Here was someone of obvious authority, with whom one didn't take liberties. The whole relationship was very purposeful, we took things round in a basket and if there was something to go back we'd take it. I can hear her showing us how to open parcels, saying, "Don't cut the string. Untie the knots. Untie the knots."'[46]

David McKenna, future chairman of British Rail's Western Region, was twenty-one when his aunt died. He knew that she had a local reputation for gardening and dabbled in handicrafts, but feels to his chagrin that she was so much part of the pattern that he never readjusted his early impressions and sought a more reflective adult relationship. Above all she remained 'someone with whom one was circumspect'.[47] Children might have opened, but never did, the rich hoard of her mind that kept her buoyant. Rather to the contrary, they brought out her instinct for self-preservation. Children and noise were things that brought her closest to losing her elaborately maintained control. They tended to upset the tension between repose and restlessness that she continually juggled with.

CHAPTER TWENTY-TWO
1907–8

Since Gertrude Jekyll generally avoided children, one might justifiably inquire what prompted her to write a book for them. One answer is that Lutyens asked her, so that his own tribe might be encouraged to garden, another concerns the emotional significance she invested in her own childhood. At sixty-four she owned, 'I can still – when no one is looking – climb over a five-barred gate or jump a ditch.'[1] Well did she remember the time when she thought 'the world really belonged to . . . children'.[2] Ruskin had written, 'The whole difference between the man of genius and other men . . . is that the first remains in great part a child, seeing with the large eyes of children, in perpetual wonder.'[3] Childhood was the source of an enduring optimism and Gertrude wrote for the child in herself. 'I shall so love the child book & will recommend it all round everywhere,'[4] Lutyens promised.

Alicia Amherst, now the Hon. Mrs Evelyn Cecil, was the author of a classic book on English garden history as well as what appears to be the first work devoted solely to gardening for children. It was called *Children's Gardens* and appeared in 1902. 'You may wonder, children, why I trouble you with ugly-sounding Latin names?'[5] Unfortunately she does, giving the impression that she is really addressing adults. Gertrude's *Children and Gardens* neither prates nor sentimentalizes. Like all her writing it has some moral and considerable educational content, but the first is subtly understressed, the second disguised. She speaks with a directness that wipes away her years. It is a tribute to her grittiness and humour that a book which might easily have been indulgent never is. She knew what makes a child tick because she remembered.

Mystery is the first beguiling ingredient. Trim lawns and flower beds harbour a secret world bristling with life. Bats hang in wall cracks, freakish organic forms sprout from good brown soil. Sometimes plants aped people, like the absurd bare-necked delphinium which tried to pretend it was a rose. Purposefulness is another trait: observance is 'one of the ways of being happy',[6] botany is an amusing game, sowing seeds is productive, boiling a kettle and planning a play-house are part of making homes, which was something Gertrude had never stopped doing. Much of the material is drawn from Munstead Wood, where stalactites grew beneath the stone arch of a mushroom house and what the gardener called 'a tortoise-shell'[7] suddenly and unaccountably nosed its way across the lawn. None of her neighbours possessed a tortoise! How did it get there? There are lots of stories about animals, the 'huffy'[8] hedgehog, martins that puncture the sand-pit with holes, and cats, of course, get a high profile. The frontispiece shows a tabby squatting on a gatepost, ingenious diagrams give cats in plan, section and elevation, and the final chapter incorporates Munstead's feline contingent in trugs, on baskets, sniffing catmint, and rolling about in pure abandonment.

One of the photographs is captioned 'a German Princess'. The author consorts with her readers: 'She has brought out her work to the old play-house, and is trying to think herself a child again.'[9] Ellen Willmott took the picture of Elizabeth von Arnim, whose first book, *Elizabeth and Her German Garden*, had been published anonymously in September 1898. It contained few tips for the gardener, but archness, sentimentality, and the secret of its author's identity sold twenty-one editions in the next nine months and put the literary world in a tizzy. Who had written this tantalizing work? How did a German girl compose such idiomatic English? The Countess von Arnim visited Munstead Wood in 1909, but long before that Ellen Willmott had visited the German garden on a storm-swept Pomeranian plain, and Mrs Beauchamp, the princess's mother, was a friend of the Leslies, so Gertrude probaby knew that her Princess was an authoress.

As usual, Gertrude herself had taken almost all the illustrations for *Children and Gardens*, and mostly they depict children. Lush-haired Barbie and Robert Lutyens build sand-houses and sort seed-packets; Jean and Anne Gibson, daughters of artistic friends whom David McKenna vaguely remembers, wash clothes, knit, prick out seeds, water and dabble their toes in Gertrude's tank. Herbert's children, 'Bar and Pam'[10] Jekyll, grace the edge of the same tank with sylph-like forms. An unidentified Christopher poses with his brother in the sandpit and Dorothea, the Chances' adopted daughter, looking the archetypal Victorian Miss Muffet, gathers fir-cones and plays with her kitten. The fetching sun-bonnet she is wearing is in the Tradescant Garden History Museum at Lambeth Church. All the children look clean, well-dressed and a trifle self-conscious. Gertrude only tolerated 'good girls'; maybe that is why they appear so compliant. It is not only the clothes they wear but their attitudes that date the book beyond its comparatively timeless text.

With studied reticence, Gertrude had chosen the first page of her first book to disclaim literary ability. But someone who took so much care over writing, tossed her epigrams about with evident enjoyment and earned the reputation of being something of a philologist was unlikely to think too ill of her own efforts. Critics have argued, mostly in her favour, 'She wrote as a poet',[11] 'near akin to poetry',[12] 'At first glance her writing may seem over-stuffed with words',[13] 'often Herculean prose'.[14] Their estimates are to some extent commensurate with her style. Because her writing was a perfect metaphor of her self, the glow of conviction illumines it, but Gertrude called up different parts of herself at different times. *Children and Gardens* is uniformly simple, the phrases short and keenly sprung, *Old West Surrey* is dry as a catalogue and slightly abrupt, not inapt for its material. *Lilies for English Gardens* is in plain working language and *Flower Decoration* somehow lacks any sparkle. *Wood and Garden* and *Home and Garden* contain strikingly melodic passages, in parts of the first her language glistens and pulsates with life, yet overall they are hard run by her next book. *Colour in the Flower Garden* is almost as lyrical, its every word chosen for effect and phrasing, her pedagogism kept well at bay. Fun or formidable, she was a very conscious stylist who constructed her sentences and paragraphs with precise attention. Her pace is definite, her verbs are thrusting, her focus certain and her books create memorable images, not static, but still, like paintings. Because she stressed the labour of writing, the manuscript of *Old West Surrey* in Guildford Library is a surprise. The text is hardly altered, just a word here and there. The illustrations are cut out and stuck or pinned to the appropriate page, the precise position in the text indicated with blue chalk lines.

Colour in the Flower Garden has been described as 'probably her best-known book' and 'undoubtedly one of the most influential gardening books of the twentieth century',[15] though one might argue that if it were really as well known as her first two, this seminal work would have dispelled a few of the false conceptions about her ideas. Often enough she had written about colour. The new publication was based on the interest of fifty years and the mature synthesis of at least twenty-five. What immediately impresses is the message that colour is a means, not an end; one ingredient, albeit a vital one in a ceaseless endeavour 'to use the plants to the best of one's means and intelligence so as to form pictures of living beauty'.[16] No colour is of the smallest consequence on its own, but two make an immediate statement, the whole concept requiring infinite discretion. Like the mature garden it describes, the book strives for deceptive simplicity. Eighty-five of Gertrude's photographs illustrate the text. Hugh Baillie-Scott, an architect for whom she devised planting plans, risked a rebuff by raising a pertinent point. 'It seems almost a pity in these days of cheaper colour reproduction you should not have some illustration in colour as your flower arrangements depend so much on colour schemes.'[17] Gertrude could have used colour photography. Her books would have cost more, but she must have reckoned that half-tone served her purpose.

The biggest disadvantage to the reader of *Colour in the Flower Garden* is that although several planting schemes are used as illustrations, there is no comprehensive garden plan. Without one, it is difficult to realize the sequence of movements that make the whole, missing thereby the unity that was integral to all of Gertrude's gardening. Every path, bed and view at Munstead Wood made an immediate picture but also bore signs relating it to adjacent areas, leading the eye forward into the greater scheme. Like the garden it describes, the book is subtly cross-referenced, one part linked to another as it rises towards three climactic chapters on the main hardy flower border. As if they were flowers and drifts of flowers, words and phrases are placed to give their fullest value. Beginnings and endings, emphasized but not abrupt, simulate the exits and entrances of carefully modulated garden walks. From March to September, chronological chapters invite the reader where colour is concentrated. Spring flowers are gradually orchestrated into a medley of early bulbs, followed by the multiplying riches of the June garden. Later, the fiery splendour of the main flower border cools into the tawny browns of fruits and soft, misty hues of wintry landscape. The disadvantage of organizing the text in annual sequence is that it gives the impression that Munstead Wood was divided into closed compartments, each reserved for a peak season and empty the rest of the year. This was quite false. Gertrude perceived the entire garden as a place of rhythmic rise and fall. 'The thing that

matters is that, in its season, the border shall be kept full and beautiful.'[18] Months before the main border was at its height, scattered
'incidents'[19] would occur. Even special seasonal gardens were maintained in flower for three months, and no part, she insisted, should
ever be unattractive.

The enormous main border, 200 feet long and fourteen feet wide,
was a spectrum of Turneresque beauty. Behind it, the wall was clothed
by shrubs which took their place in the colour scheme. Nearest the
house the border contained pale contrasting blues and the palest
yellows, set in a haze of grey and glaucous foliage. Stronger, harmoniz-
ing flame colours blazed at the centre, 'but as it is in good harmonies,
it is never garish'.[20] The sequence then ebbed away inversely, from
deep to pale yellow, white to the palest pink and at the far end, purples
and lilacs instead of pure blue. The tour was minutely programmed.
From a definite position on a wide space of grass, the whole glorious
rainbow could be seen, cool at either end, embracing its brilliant
centre. From the path beside the border, the sequence unfolded in a
series of compelling pictures.

The perfection Gertrude aimed for was not easy. She never felt
other people sufficiently realized the pains she took to achieve her ends
and sometimes this made her cross. 'Good gardening means patience
and dogged determination. There must be many failures and losses,
but by always pushing on there will also be the reward of success.'[21]
Artistic receptivity was part of the secret, plant knowledge another
part, but there was also the endless persevering craft. Neatly juggling
coincidences and contrivances, overplanting and pulling down plants
such as clematis, gypsophila and everlasting pea, clipping lower or
removing old stems, tucking in bedding, 'dropping in'[22] reserve pots,
tying and invisibly supporting: every conceivable trick was used to
extend the flowering season and ensure the vital balance of composition. Beauty, she had learned from Chevreul, is the product of good
order. It comes, she is saying, from doing everything well, from
planning space, heights, texture, and colour rhythms to the last detail.

Popular opinion associates Gertrude Jekyll with pale colours, and she
did indeed cherish delicacy. One of the most poignant passages in her
book describes the foliage of *Clematis recta* caught between another
overhanging purple clematis, soft grey *Cineraria maritima* and santolina.
'The leaves are much deeper in tone than these and have a leaden sort
of blueness, whilst the colouring, both of the parts in light and even

more of the mysterious shadows, is in the highest degree satisfactory and makes me long for the appreciative presence of the rare few friends who are artists both on canvas and in their gardens.'[23] In the book that holds perhaps the quintessence of her wisdom, most of all she longs for her old friend, Hercules Brabazon. But while she extolled subtlety, it is essential to understand the context. From strong, unabashed colour she received an almost seductive pleasure. In high summer the hardy border sported blood-red hollyhocks, 'deep scarlet' dahlias, and 'brilliant dwarf scarlet' salvia. Where a 'gorgeous mass'[24] of helenium, nasturtium and coreopsis threatened to become overwhelming, the barest discipline was achieved with gypsophila, whose cloudy mass of 'pretty mist-like bloom'[25] just sufficiently subdued. The effect would not be unlike a Turner sunset.

Perhaps the most ingenious twist resides in the fact that a book about colour begins with scarcely any colour at all. It is March, 'there is but little wind' and 'the sun has gained much power'.[26] Pared sentences set the scene. What Gertrude describes from her pitch in a 'nook of sheltered woodland'[27] is the rich darkness of holly and fading rust of nearly flattened bracken sliced by clean shadows of silver birch. Not until three-quarters of the way through the second page does she introduce a twinkle of purple with *Daphne mezereon*, the tawny red of Lent hellebore and the nodding mauve dog-tooth violet. The tints, she admits, are 'a little sad'.[28] 'But it is a perfect picture.'[29] So far from rushing in with a vigorous medley, colour is introduced with restraint and sophistication.

Gertrude seems to have been one of the first to write about gardening in restricted colours. Victorian writers had anticipated the idea. In 1871, Shirley Hibberd wrote of bedding, 'It is well indeed in every scheme to allow one colour with its related shades to predominate, and to employ others as relief agents.'[30] Twelve years later, William Wildsmith, contributing to Robinson's *English Flower Garden*, approved a planting of marigold, chrysanthemum and nasturtium, 'all shades of yellow, orange, and brown' being 'a fine lesson in temperance'.[31] Like many of the gardens Gertrude planned, Munstead Wood had an area of grey foliage she continued to experiment with for another decade. In 1907 she occasionally heard of a garden for blue or for white flowers, but for their implementation, she declared a little tendentiously, she had neither means nor room. From hearsay she even doubted whether she would approve of others' efforts. Perfectionist she might be, but never a slave to rules. If a blue garden hungered for white lilies or the palest lemon yellow, as far as she was concerned there should be no 'fetters foolishly self-imposed'.[32] With dogmatism equal to that of the purists she was upbraiding, she argued, 'Surely the business of the blue garden is to be beautiful as well as to be blue. My own idea is that it should be beautiful first, and then just as blue as may be consistent with its best possible beauty.'[33] Four years later Lady Vere Galway of Serlby Hall in Bawtry offered *The Garden* a long list of plants for a blue garden with 'A little mauve mingled in'.[34] Gertrude disliked blue and purple flowers in juxtaposition, although she was proud of a pink and purple garden she designed for a client in 1921. But the restricted colour gardens in gold and green and scarlet that she suggested caught the imagination of her readers, laying the basis of a great many attempts at colour gardening.

In her sixties, Gertrude was entering the most dedicated period of her life. She never lost a disarming youthful enthusiasm for the project in hand and believed passionately in her work, but she was perpetually a little weary from the pace. When Jacques Blumenthal died in the spring of 1908, his loss meant a great gap in her life. Six times she had stayed at the Chalet. Its mountains, blue lake, clear light, and setting suns were etched in her mind, with memories of pears ripening to a fine perfection plucked for breakfast on the plant-screened veranda, painting expeditions and the camaraderie that made it her supreme alternative sanctuary; the only place in her middle years where her 'inviolable frontier which none might cross'[35] could be relaxed. Jacques Blumenthal's will was that of a sociable and caring person. Among legacies to a great many people, he left £500 to Gertrude, the same to his godson, the elder of Albert Zumbach's children, and an annuity paid annually towards the father and his wife's retirement. For ten days Gertrude took herself to a hotel on the Dorset coast. On her own, by the sea, the irrepressible youngster in her spent four shillings on boat trips. Each time she returned, the soothing routines of country, copse, garden and workshop seemed especially alluring.

What she would gladly have avoided at Munstead Wood were the invaders, not always subtle, knowledgeable or even very courteous. England is a nation of gardeners, and it was flattering to have so many fans, but they made serious inroads upon her time. There were daily schedules to keep, things to be done of which the visitors appeared to have no notion. She was far too impatient not to resent demands upon her time and energy. In her last book, the short plea for peace and privacy that accompanied *Home and Garden* had been repeated. 'I am growing old and tired, and suffer from very bad and painful sight. My garden is my workshop, my private study and place of rest. For the sake of health and reasonable enjoyment of life it is necessary to keep it quite private, and to refuse the many applications of those who offer it visits. My oldest friends can now only be admitted.'[36] Would readers spare her the task of writing long letters of excuse and explanation on top of an already substantial correspondence?

Bad cases of 'visititis' provoked Gertrude to profound irritation. For 'gush' she had 'wholesome contempt',[37] consoled only by 'the mental substitution of an expletive recently restored to the vocabularies of the genteel from its long Victorian banishment'.[38] The arrantly dismissive faction, 'I only want a lot of common things like that',[39] roused equal antipathy, while those innocently unaware of her pains, the 'anything will grow for you'[40] brigade, received 'a laboured smile'.[41] A fair proportion of her visitors were quite unable to understand the amount of labour she bestowed upon her garden. To a correspondent from the South coast she once wrote, 'You say Margate is not Godalming. I often wish Godalming were Margate or anything but itself – I have no soil – only a limey sand 200 ft deep – When I make a flower border the sand is carted away & I put in any compost I can get together. It is all work.'[42] Acknowledging her frustrations in another private letter, she explained that she had tried limiting the hours to one day, but making exceptions seemed to give people 'a kind of right of entrance, or they take it to be so, and they will come at their own convenience . . . from America, or Ireland, or wherever it may be, and have only a certain day . . . You can have no idea what I have suffered (actually in health) from the pertinacity of Americans and Germans and of journalists.'[43]

In fact she was as anxious to accommodate a truly discriminating caller as she was to avoid a frivolous one. 'If you will come some afternoon, in August, I shall welcome the visit of what I see by your letter, is a true sympathiser.'[44] Other letters confirm the point. To Mrs Furze, who confused *Uvularia grandiflora* with streptocarpus, she wrote hoping her visit might be repeated, while Dr Rowe of the British Museum, who had written to congratulate her on *Colour in the Flower Garden*, received the warmest welcome: 'I shall be very glad if I can help you in any way & at any time. That deterrent paragraph in my preface was an effort to stop the visits of the merely idle & curious & the many Americans & other foreigners.'[45] The receptive and appreciative were as rewarding as those deceived by her naturalism. Making their way along a turf path into the shrubberies, where andromeda, skimmia and alpenrose had grown into solid masses, visitors might find rocky ridges of local sandstone. 'And when my friends say, "But then, what a chance you had with that shelf of rock coming naturally out of the ground," I feel the glowing warmth of an inward smile and think that perhaps the stones have not been badly placed.'[46]

Gertrude excelled as a strategist and the visiting policy at Munstead Wood was a source of amusement to her family. Teaching was her natural instinct. She drew people into her floral empire and once they were part of it they paid homage to her because she was queen. Her reluctance to allow newcomers to tour the garden on their own was understandable; they might miss what was best. But Harold Falkner, summoned by postcard on a certain day at a certain time every month, was a visitor for the best part of twenty years. Local amateur and cabinet minister, he remarked, were equally likely to be there, but invariably alone. All received the same personalized treatment. Falkner was sufficiently idiosyncratic to appreciate Gertrude; he supported the Society for the Protection of Ancient Buildings, and had worked in London with Sir Reginald Blomfield but loathed bureaucracy. Herbert Cowley, editor of *Gardening Illustrated* and later of *The Garden*, was met at Godalming station by a pony and trap to spend the night either at Munstead Wood or at Munstead House. Yet so elusive were his visits that he became known as 'the mystery man'.[47] It was as if Gertrude feared the Munstead experience might be perverted or in some way diminished through interaction. She very much wanted the garden seen in her way. However she rationalized her odd manoeuvres, they were a subtle means of maintaining control.

Sometimes her impatience was ill-concealed. Pearsall Smith tells the tale of an undergraduate visitor he brought along who made unfortunate suggestions about altering the colour of flowers. A snubbing silence ensued. He had failed the test. So, by association, had Pearsall Smith. Falkner introduced newcomers on one or two occasions, with varying results, but Oliver Hill, persuaded to introduce Mrs Barnes-Brand, alias Amy Brandon Thomas, had surprising success. Mrs Brand, as Gertrude referred to her, was the daughter of Brandon Thomas, who wrote a hit play of the twenties, *Charley's Aunt* – a pretty young actress who had made her first stage appearance at the Theatre Royal in 1907. Neither she nor her husband had much knowledge of gardening. It was her sparkly but carefully deferential attitude to horticultural wisdom and her genuine desire to learn that won over Gertrude. Questions on one side, explanations on the other, were soon extended with cakes and tea.

Correspondence was always easier to conduct on Gertrude's terms; if it was time-consuming, she still found writing less tiring than meeting people. To the naïve and horticulturally inexperienced she owed 'many a humorous twinkle and quiet chuckle'. 'Could you spare me some of those lovely flowers I saw in your garden last time I came; I think you called them Peacocks?' Some hard thinking ensued before a parcel of *Narcissus pallidus praecox* was dispatched with an informative postscript. On another occasion, when Gertrude wrote to inquire the aspect of a flower border she was to plan, she received the baffling reply: 'Most of the day it faces south-east, but due north all the morning.'[48]

In nine years Gertrude had written ten books. Her energy had always been phenomenal but the sheer organization involved in producing one after the other, illustrations as well as the script, must have made considerable demands on an oldish, stoutish lady. She had incredible stamina. An unspecified operation on her nose had taken place but it cannot have been serious because the following day Lutyens visited her, 'plastered up & painted pink . . . She was so glad to SEE me & enjoyed herself in bed.'[49] She would not stop writing; four books were still to come, but not at the same pace, and journalism, which had dwindled to a single annual article, would leap to more than fifty in a year. A 1930s *Dictionary of Concise Universal Biography* refers to Gertrude solely as an English writer, born in London, who became editor of *The Garden*. While the entry belittles her total achievement, it is clear that her writings are a major part of it. It was being less of an author that made her more of a gardener.

PART FIVE

GARDENER

CHAPTER TWENTY-THREE

1908

Gertrude's earliest memories engaged the minute beauty of flowers and the tangled magic of shrubs and trees. More surprising perhaps in one so young was her appreciation of such abstract concepts as mass, space, light and shade. She was never seduced by the trivial; this was a great strength and Ruskin entered her consciousness never to fade. Alert scrutiny reinforced her sense of place; truth, unity and beauty became her endless quest. South Kensington nourished a passion for the great masters of art, and impressed upon her the basic precepts of design. European travel was enormously stimulating. In Corfu, Rhodes, Turkey and Greece she drew and gathered plants; in Italy she visited the sites of some of the greatest Renaissance gardens; in Algeria, in her thirtieth year, she was making detailed notes on garden landscape. Instinctively she approved country traditions. A craftsman's respect for the proper way of doing things brought her in line with the Arts and Crafts Movement, and henceforth work spilled into leisure in an entire way of life. It was as if all her actions as an artist integrated and flowed freely into gardening.

At Wargrave she stocked her garden with plants from cottage plots, a process of accumulation and assessment that would never end. At Munstead House intensive trials laid the foundation for her entire garden repertoire. By 1882, before the site for her famous home was even purchased, Gertrude was describing herself by implication as a 'propounder of principles',[1] for whom 'practice must come first and plenty of it, with much care and labour, and that only as a result of practice, well digested and assimilated'.[2] A year later, not yet forty, she had written her classic chapter on colour in Robinson's *The English Flower Garden*. In one of her own books, she wrote, 'Sense of beauty is the gift of God, for which those who have received it in good measure can never be thankful enough.'[3] Where receptivity was concerned, she saw herself a recipient of God's grace. The first part of the twentieth

century brought eclectic styles, good and bad, with a tendency to the
bourgeois ostentation she so deplored. Fine art was not a tenet of the
Morris-type workers, who preferred to think of themselves as practical
craftsmen. But Gertrude, nurtured on Ruskin, Turner and Chevreul's
colour theories, visualized her garden as a canvas for perfect harmonies.
She, 'an artist of no mean capacity',⁴ equipped to 'paint the landscape
with living things',⁵ would reassert the status of gardening as a fine art.
Although she described herself publicly as an 'artist-gardener', 'vigorous
landscape gardening'⁶ was what she acknowledged to Brabazon in
1889. Forthwith she would consolidate all her looking and learning in
garden design. There was no set formula; she created half-wild gardens,
Italian gardens, water gardens like Vann in Hambledon, three miles
south of Munstead Wood, for the architect W. D. Caroe, and a vast
south-facing rock garden for a house with a Lutyens extension, Pasture
Wood, renamed Beatrice Webb House, for Frederick Mirrielees, chairman of the Union Castle Line, at Holmbury St Mary.

She put a certain price on her time. Falkner marked that however
comfortably off Gertrude appeared to the world, she liked commissions
from large estates because she made more money on them; instinctively
businesslike, she made profit where she could. Income was generated
from seeds; polyanthus were bought by Carters among other merchants, lamb's lettuce and a large annual pink poppy by Vilmorin of
Paris, and daffodils and lily of the valley were grown in large beds for
sale as cut flowers to Godalming florists. One of her gardeners, Frank
Young, attributed their success to soaking the young shoots with dilute
manure from the pigsty. Plants were being supplied increasingly for
gardens Gertrude had planned, and there was one occasion when Sir
John Jarvis of Hascombe Court sought an immediate display for his
son's birthday celebrations. A show was produced by uprooting plants
in full flower, transporting them 'up to the Court'⁷ by lorry and
watering them in. But her fees were always modest, Mrs McCreery of
Stowell Hill realized immediately. '£10.10.0 seems very little for all
the help you have given us.'⁸ It was to art she deferred, not Mammon.

Gertrude's nature craved a certain isolation and, resourcefully, she
built her refuge round her. The paradox is that much as she needed
public appreciation to enact her mission, Munstead Wood simultaneously drew the attention she most wished to exclude. Harold Falkner,
who knew the place as well as anyone, recollected the first time he
located its elusive front entrance, 'through an arched opening in a wall

in a stone-lined corridor, with a view of the pantry or larder on the left which generally raised in the uninitiated some doubt as to whether it was the front or the back door'.[9] For Gertrude, an obsessive controller of her environment, the hidden entry had a deeply symbolic relevance. Everything was always dead quiet – even the bell was inaudible on the outside; a silence from which she slid, from garden or workroom, to usher in the guest. Gardening, she was never weary: 'There is nothing of the nature of a relaxation from other work or duty that fills the mind so wholesomely or happily.'[10] 'For a garden's main purpose is that it should be a private place of quiet reward for labour and effort – a place of repose to eye and mind.'[11] Work gave her life a necessary framework and stability: in her domain she created a rarefied atmosphere which was only hers and was never forgotten. It has to be said that visitors varied in their perception of Munstead Wood, and young Harriet Keen from the Brighton Road, scampering, a few years later, between yew hedges on her way to functions at 'the big (Munstead) House', felt Gertrude's seclusion was that of a magician locked in a tower. One accepts the immediacy of the child's emotion; for it was the creation of someone whose peace was endangered by the yelp of a child or a dog. Like its owner, the garden felt reserved. In private life as in work, restraint and control were Gertrude's constant guardians.

At Munstead Wood the importance of integration between house, garden and countryside cannot be over-stressed. The house was built with its south nestling into the woods. Behind, to north and west, lay formally patterned traditional features – nut walk, pergola, the famous hardy border backed by a high sandstone wall and enclosures with seasonal themes. Edward Cook remarked how each window of the house was placed to reveal an appropriate view. From the hall, a little lawn fringed with birches and rhododendrons was 'Absolutely restful';[12] from the upstairs gallery 'a path ran like a river between two long banks of Michaelmas daisies',[13] tumbling purple, lilac, palest lavender and white, making a floral spectacle that Helen Allingham recreated in paint. In the early part of the year, walks could be made along the accessible nut walk, carpeted on one side with Lenten hellebores, on the other with early violets and ferns. When spring arrived one stepped a little further into the spring garden or the primrose garden. By early summer, when the turf was dry under-foot, one made for The Hut, south-west of the house, shrouded by woodland, and used for expanding crafts. Here Gertrude planted the cottage-flower mixture that reappears frequently in her gardening commissions; rosemary, peonies, roses, and other June flowers.

Falkner thought that Gertrude to some extent switched allegiance from naturalism to formalism. 'In her first books she seemed to harp on naturalism in gardens in direct opposition [to Sir Reginald Blomfield] but gradually she and E.L. came to our way of thinking.'[14] He is right only that she chose to emphasize naturalism at the start of her writing career, and even this must be set against her careful appreciation of formality in the *Edinburgh Review*. Everything, she reiterated, had a right place, little was intrinsically wrong though it could easily be wrongly placed. Munstead House had possessed a tiny parterre in pride of place beneath her special wing, and Munstead Wood had its quota of bedding. Rose Standish Nichols noted elements of both naturalistic and conventional gardens there. 'The arrangement is very simple, and largely depends for its beauty upon various delightful colour schemes. It is seldom that both wild and cultivated flowers have been grouped more successfully.'[15] In all she did Gertrude claimed Nature her ally. But as she said, 'like everything else in good gardening it must be done just right'.[16]

Lutyens had little doubt about basic Jekyllian rules but he still returned to Gertrude for consultation. In April 1908 he had been asked by the Architectural Association to reply to an opening speech by Thomas Mawson, author of *The Art and Craft of Garden Making*, a professional rival of whose work he and Gertrude disapproved. As the day approached he grew nervous: 'Tomorrow I go to Bumps to improve my Mawson speech I dread it now right well,'[17] and the following day, 'I must see Bumps about Mawson's gardening paper & today is the only day.'[18] The speech received Gertrude's close attention. Discussing the deceptive perception of 'straight' lines, Lutyens mentioned the curve or trajectory of the Parthenon, a point she had remarked upon in her diary of her Greek island trip in 1863. In other parts, the very wording sounds suspiciously like Gertrude. 'A garden scheme should have a backbone, a central idea beautifully phrased . . . When a design begins to appear as merely a collection of features then I think it is time to look to discover in which direction our India rubber has bounced,'[19] and elsewhere, 'The true adornment of a garden lies surely in its flowers & plants[.] No artist has so wide a palette as the garden designer, no artist has more need of both discretion & reserve.'[20] The speech was well received. Afterwards Lutyens celebrated with a 'happy afternoon with Bumps',[21] moving on to Munstead House for a walk with Herbert before dinner. There was new excitement. The engagement of Herbert Jekyll's daughter Pamela to Reginald McKenna the year he was appointed First Lord of the Admiralty provoked a 'giggly evening'.[22] Lutyens played a duet with the bride-to-be amid 'great discussion on when wedding was to be & how'.[23] 'Aggie wants it at the Admiralty!!'[24]

At Munstead Wood, on 14 May, intermittent rain made the ground exactly right for Gertrude to plant out 'those blessed tall Snapdragons – I have had them 6 feet high,'[25] she told a gardening friend. As summer mellowed into autumn, red hot pokers sprang to attention in the main border and gypsophila, half covered by trailing nasturtiums, turned from a web of silvery grey to brown. Gertrude was a creature of built-in rhythms, and thanks partly to Florence Hayter, housekeeper cum 'personal maid',[26] domestic affairs ran smoothly. Gertrude's knack of getting people to do things for her extended to domestic staff. Miss Hayter had arrived in the spring of 1906, and stayed at Munstead Wood until the end of Gertrude's life. Everything suggests a mutually rewarding relationship. Accompanying Gertrude to the long stretch of Dorset heath and moor between Studland and Poole, the maid kept a watchful eye while her mistress made sorties along a fern-fringed path, 'Watery Lane',[27] and struck across the sands, 'to Wreck'.[28] Two weeks later they were home for the wedding of the youngest niece.

At the lower end of her garden, Gertrude had built a triangular tower with a clear northward view. The 'Thunder House' made a neat finish to a bare-looking piece of wall and a look-out for watching storms. It was from there, one may be sure, with rain falling like knives on the roof, she watched lightning crack and heard thunder roar across the valley of smooth fields and little woods during a late summer storm. The occasion has obvious ties with an episode Lady Duff Gordon had witnessed many years before, staying with the Jekylls in Bramley. 'Rain and a thunder storm that continued a long time. Mr Jekyll was so much interested in it that he sat under the arcade until 9 o'clock at night without coming in.'[29] Like her father, Gertrude was intrigued by the brute force of the elements. Often she had taken her camera to document a storm's aftermath. Nature, disruptive and violent, was part of the comprehensive scheme of things.

It was four years since Lutyens had received his commission at Hestercombe, a garden which represents in Hussey's estimation the peak of his Jekyll collaboration. 'A very bad house architecturally but the gardens might be lovely,'[30] Lutyens wrote of the gaunt place north of Taunton with a wide view overlooking Taunton Dene. 'Such a typical self-satisfied comfortable English sporting-squire of a house . . . I shouldn't be surprised to be presented to porter and oysters between meals.'[31] The client, the Hon. E. W. Portman, 'spends his money on eating, hospitals and cattle breeding and is, to boot, a real good sort . . . When Lord Portman dies they will roll in gold.'[32] Gertrude had accompanied Lutyens to the site and been excited by it. A hasty note she had made at the time read, 'Amphitheatre of big trees . . . [this was the Bowling Green, lying in a picturesque valley behind the house] The levels merge into ground falling to south. Big trees on the grass slope; sun comes through in vivid patches making the place wonderful big and quiet.'[33] Everything suggested dramatic scale, for what Hussey called 'his [Lutyens's] first application of her [Gertrude's] genius to classical garden design on a grand scale . . . with the brilliant handling of the varying levels'.[34] Three terraces rising above a stage-like lower 'plat' or parterre, produced 'a lucid and an intricate horticultural drama'.[35] Money being little object and Ned as prodigal with his clients' wealth as Gertrude was prudent, no expense was spared. Thousands of tons of rubble and rough pink local stone were trundled in by horse and cart, Ham stone for finer surfaces and mill stones from France to implant – as at Munstead Wood – at focal points. Stonework was used to balustrade the terraces against the hill, to line ribbon-like water-rills, and to build an ornate classical orangery at an unconventional angle to the main garden.

Whether Gertrude played her usual active role in the general plan is not of course documented. But contemporary accounts of her collaborations with Lutyens failed to acknowledge her in any capacity whatsoever. Not only are her planting plans for Hestercombe extant, but one of her notebooks registers, 'Plans sent to Mr Cook Dec 1 1904', and 'Written to Mr Hubbard March 25 to say which plants cannot supply.'[36] Since the beginning of her career in garden design she had offered and invariably provided her clients with plants at very cheap rates. So cheap in fact as to make it unlikely that profit from Munstead Wood's nursery garden was her sole incentive. 'My prices should not be quoted to your nursery,' she once wrote to a client, 'or they may assume a grievance against me for "underselling the trade".[37] It is conceivable that she thought a bargain would encourage people to accept her designs, though she sometimes failed to mention the plant side of the business until a transaction was already secure. This leaves the likelihood that she thought her plants were superior. As designer and provider of materials, she had that much more control over her commissions. She was a one-man band and the perfectionist in her prevailed.

The immediate impression at Hestercombe is of very un-Jekyllian openness, of blending blue and grey foliage with pale blue, pink, white and pale yellow flowers; even the stonework is finely embroidered, an integral part of a vast tapestry. Indeed the daisy-like *Erigeron mucronatus* flowers so freely, it is almost a symbol of the garden. Strongly contrasted and textured foliage, tufts of miscanthus, and frills of the inevitable bergenia enhance the pattern concept of the great plat which peaks during June, with delphiniums, roses, and peonies. At this time rose and dianthus, lavender and catmint, waft an unbelievable medley of scents. Separating the garden from the agricultural scene beyond it is a huge pergola. On one side lies the formal, plant-spun plat, on the other, lazy cows saunter into misty pasture across the dale, the two divided by alternately round and square flower-twined pergola pillars. After Bill Mount and Somerset Fire Brigade's laudable restoration in the early 1970s, Hestercombe received more attention than any other Jekyll garden. Most people echo Hussey's applause; it is 'unsurpassed in Lutyens's garden repertory'.[38] Interpenetration of art and nature, contrived in a rare and perfect way, achieves simultaneously serenity, grandeur, and incredible finesse. But not everyone feels the same about this unique and unhomely setting; a garden which virtually ignores the house, of which Harold Nicolson wrote disapprovingly, 'Under the influence of Miss Jekyll, [Lutyens] brought his architecture tumbling down into the garden, and we find the unfortunate masonry of Hestercombe.'[39]

Hestercombe was not completed until 1908, by the end of which Gertrude had advised on about 150 gardens. In roughly a third she collaborated with an architect, usually Lutyens. Several of her architects were associated with the Arts and Crafts Movement, including Charles Voysey and M. H. Baillie-Scott. Voysey had met Ruskin and shared his faith in the Gothic ideal, moralizing sympathetically, 'To be true to your material, true to your conditions, true to your highest instincts, is the surest and only way to true art,'[40] and Baillie-Scott wrote Gertrude deferential letters. One imagines that each taught her something, yet she generally worked on a single garden or at most two properties with each of them. Robert Lorimer's simple shapes and plain surfaces were said to 'have the clarity of a winter landscape'.[41] But news got back to Lutyens that the difference between 'working with Nedi & Lorimer was as between quicksilver & suet'.[42] Perhaps that was the problem; no one quite compared with Lutyens.

Charles Newton was the architect employed by Charles Holme, founder and editor of an upmarket art magazine called *The Studio*, to extend his Jacobean farmhouse. The Manor House, Upton Grey, metamorphosed to a large Edwardian country house, needed a garden to match. Holme knew George Elgood, who had already provided Gertrude with several commissions since they had worked together; he also knew Gertrude at least by reputation. The previous winter, the first of three special garden numbers put out by *The Studio* had included a rambling introductory essay by Holme that suggested a thorough knowledge of her works, so thorough that on occasion its editor virtually copies her text. If he failed to learn from her clarity, he was impressed by her expertise.

The Manor House lies in a valley of red roofs and flowering elder half-way between Alton and Basingstoke. Upton Grey was a pleasant drive from Munstead and Gertrude still visited gardens that were relatively close. But she had begun to work on remoter sites without actually seeing them. This is unusual enough for a visual art to bear some explanation; a prospective inquirer was enlightened, 'I do designs & alterations of gardens now by plan & description ... I find no difficulty in working like this. A proper plan done by a surveyor ... is a necessity whether a place is seen or not. Photographs are a help.'[43] Relevant material was sent to Munstead Wood, and making constant reference to geology maps, she worked on such 'genius of the place' as she, with long experience, could absorb. One slightly perplexing result of the new method is that subsequent garden owners have not known whether that emotionally vital personal touch, the visit, was ever made. The uncertainty is also a token of Gertrude's success. The Manor House lies on the ridge of a hill, next to the parish church and screened from the road by trees fringing undulating ground. On the further, eastern side of the building, grass sloping down to a tennis court opens to long agricultural views broken by sycamores. Wallis and Smith, Architects & Surveyors, produced a careful plan of the existing garden for a mysterious Mr Best, who may have been the head gardener. Presumably the tennis court was Holme's instigation, because Gertrude loathed them. But leaving it where it was, she emphasized three terraces with dry walls of local sandstone. The whole garden is barely four acres but there were obvious resemblances between its east side and the main vista at Hestercombe.

Jekyll restorations tend to be made in gardens where Gertrude worked with Lutyens. The Manor House, restored by its owners during the 1980s under the auspices of Hampshire Garden Trust, is therefore unusual, and a painstaking tribute to its designer. The drive-way curves round a totally Jekyllian wilderness of turf paths cut through long grass. There are glades of crabs, young walnuts, white broom, a light-dappled pond and a smattering of mature trees. West and south-west of the house, enclosed by the road and church, idealized countryside edges right up to the forecourt. But one passes through the hall of the building to confront a garden that is formal, humanized and essentially Edwardian. As at Hestercombe, though incorporating the house, the hillside setting is used to perfection.

The wilderness is always alive. In April one sees through wrought-iron gates an airy picture of amelanchiers and pale daffodils, a fragile wispiness enhanced by shadows and long leaves, *Filipendula venusta*, *Cytisus albus*, tree lupins and bamboos. Greys and reds in the church are echoed in red-leaved *Prunus persica* and silvery *Laburnum vulgare*, cowslips and buttercups scatter long grass, three buff and speckled ducks turn circles on the pond behind groups of bold yellow narcissus. In June the colours are still pale, with the exception of 'Kitchener of Khartoum', an early-flowering, heavy-headed, deep velvety red rose, representing, one feels, the small but prominent red glow Turner so often introduces in his paintings. Architectural giant hogweed was another Jekyll favourite, and two rows of red hot pokers lead up to the pond. They sound an intrusion but look only slightly stagy. Fringing the pond itself, yellow *Iris pseudacorus* is the sole strong colour, like a brimstone butterfly against blue *Campanula latifolia* and mauve *Geranium macrorrhizum* on the far bank.

To look down on the east garden from a top storey window is to see it as Gertrude, at her drawing board, first played with space and density. All her plans are colour-washed and colour-coded. This one is shaded in crayon, red for buildings, ochre paths, green on mown grass and a prussian-blue pen for evergreens. Three terraces move down from the house; the top one, traversed by a pergola of ten stout posts, is linked in two rows by heavy oiled rope. Here jasmine, aristolochia, Virginia creeper and five choice roses intertwine. The second terrace is highly patterned, the third planned and maintained as a grass tennis court. Gertrude is sometimes criticized for repeating the same plant repertoire in her garden designs. It was not that she was unaware of a vast range of species, but the point tends to be made by horticulturists, unaware that designers usually limit the variety of their plant material because the total picture has constantly to be maintained. Favourite roses, for example, she would employ over and again. She liked them to be scented, crimped and puckered, and she adored the apple-blossom mixture of pink and white. The five she used, two of each, at Manor House, Upton Grey, had been well tried. Her beloved 'Garland', with pale narrow leaves and flattish heads of up to thirty flowers held vertically along the ropes; 'Dundee Rambler', the archetypal bridal rose, another smallish white with pink neatly rolled buds; 'Blush Rambler', a medium pink, heavily bossed with stamens, and 'Jersey Beauty', a handsome single cream. 'Grüss an Teplitz', a spicy crimson, replaces 'La Reine Olga', which is now extremely difficult to obtain.

On either side of the top terrace, vertical borders make a cottage-garden medley of poppies and lupins, hollyhocks, maize and delphiniums. Pale yellow snapdragons, always referred to by Gertrude as 'snaps', and pale blue tradescantia near the house give way to deeper-coloured helenium and a succession of flame colours, *Lychnis chalcedonica*, tritoma and Oriental poppies, before fading into whites and mid-blues. 'Use warm colours (reds and yellows) in harmonies, and cold ones (blues and their allies) in contrasts.'[44] It is, of course, her well-known Munstead Wood colour sequence. Like Hestercombe, the garden reaches a climax at the end of June and largely dies down during winter.

In the central terrace, four symmetrical beds surrounding a centre-piece are repeated on either side. Different types of small bedding roses, and enormous pink peonies – *officinale* and 'Sarah Bernhardt' – are interplanted with *Lilium longiflorum*, caressing the eye with a symphony of pink (roses and peonies), grey (mostly *Stachys lanata*), white (valerian) and soft blue (lavender and campanula). Looking up from the tennis lawn towards the house one sees banks of red and white valerian, and white dotted *Rosa pimpinellifolia* flouncing like layers of a petticoat beneath the long, half-tiled house with its oak-beamed heart.

By the spring of 1911, Charles Holme could meditate upon simulated wildness from one side of his home, delight in a profusion of abundance on the other. The last garden issue of *The Studio* suggests that he had learned the ultimate lesson, 'that subservience to a fashion is destructive of true artistic understanding'.[45] With the editor among the initiated, Gertrude had loyal support.

On 8 August 1909 Lutyens complained to his wife, 'At Munstead with Bumps 1/2 my other half with Aggie.'[1] 'Came back to tea with Bumps who was very well – for her – but oh her life now breakfast at 9

> sausages
> iced bun
> eggs
> coffee

Beef tea at 11!!
Lunch at 1 – Beef suet pudding
> beer & stuffed tomatoes
To bed 1.30 – 3.30 coffee
Tea 4.30
dinner 7.30
& it was 86.5 in the shade.'[2]

Concentration on Gertrude's diet distorts the primary object of her self-imposed regime – to squeeze every minute from the day. Another schedule presented by Francis Jekyll clarifies the fact that meals punctuated four one-and-a-half-hour working periods sustained by rest and leisure. Earlier in the year there had been a national outbreak of influenza. Gertrude did not escape and all her activities temporarily ceased. Gradually, with Florence Hayter's solicitations and vigilance from Munstead House, she slipped back to the routine that was both demanding and rewarding. Visits to Munstead Wood were made by, among others, H. Avray Tipping, author of *English Homes*, *The Garden of Today* and a regular contributor to *Country Life*, and by Countess von Arnim.

The Countess no longer possessed her German garden. After a series of bad farming years, the von Arnims' beautiful but remote Nassenheide had gone on the market and she had taken the opportunity of buying a modest house in England. Leaving the Count behind, she took the girls to rural Devon. It was not a success. There were few congenial neighbours and two elder daughters promptly caught the 'flu. While Nassenheide remained unsold, moreover, Elizabeth felt bound to work. She at least had a motive. Increasingly fatigued but intrinsically tough, she made her way to Munstead.

Another visitor was 'ever-welcome'[3] Ellen Willmott, whose volume of photographs, *Warley Garden in Spring and Summer*, had recently been published by Quaritch. Gertrude gave both author and book a warm appreciation in *Country Life*, the first for 'rare intelligence, consummate knowledge and extraordinary personal energy',[4] the second because it stood, in her opinion, 'alone in beauty and interest'.[5] Miss Willmott had a true professional's grasp of the technicalities of photography. Something more recondite, however, was in incubation. For years she had been gathering material for *The Genus Rosa*, a mammoth undertaking that required a good deal of genetic understanding. Temperamental Ellen Willmott's biggest problem was co-operating with other people. But in 1912, despite constant upheavals, the first part of the work emerged, with delicate paintings by Alfred Parsons. When the last quarter was out, Gertrude praised it roundly in the *Quarterly Review*. It had taken, she wrote, more than twenty years' research, 'meeting with untold difficulty and obstruction from the conflicting evidence of former writers, but labouring on single-handed, with utter patience and determination'.[6] Miss Willmott had conquered. Whether the author had been 'completely' single-handed, or 'utterly' patient, seems less important than the strength of Gertrude's support.

Lutyens had been working on another island castle. Gertrude was to plant both rugged Lindisfarne and rocky Lambay in the soft grey Irish Sea. Everything about Lambay fed the architect's fancy. To prepare Bumps he wrote, 'Lambay is an island! about 8 miles NW of Howth & you can only get there by a fishing boat about 1000 or 1100 acres. I saw no shells but then I didn't look. Masses of sea birds – & seals – they breed in a cave there. except on the east the coast is all rock cliff – There is very little frost but fearsome winds – The only sandy place, the harbour, a diminutive storm broken shelter – only possible in certain winds & when the tide allows a passage into it. I had to land on the other side of the island the lee side – & then in a lumpy sea get into a boat but sea-wind – slippery rocks[.]

'The old castle is a rum little place & rather Scotch in character . . .

The house stands in a wind blown wood of sycamores & ashes . . . It is
proposed to build a wall to enclose the wood house – gardens & farm
buildings & then inside gardens to be planted & garden walls built.'[7]

A Tudor fort wheeling with gulls and guillemots was an appropriate
domicile for the Hon. Cecil Baring, the banker, and his new American
wife. Baring had stolen her from his partner and was ostracized, at any
rate to begin with, by society. Lutyens developed the fort 'with utmost
romance of colour and texture',[8] and the couple lived in spartan
simplicity with two tough little daughters, sundry rheas, Japanese
cranes and a Dutch bull. They read Homer in Greek, drank buttermilk,
and Mrs Baring filled holes in the islanders' teeth. Shelter, the first
essential, was provided by a wide shale wall with a grass walk along its
top. Gertrude clothed the ramparts with *Cotoneaster horizontalis*, escallo-
nia, buckthorn and fuchsia, and planned walled gardens with a pergola
of harled piers from an old farmhouse. Garden features inside a
geometrically regular framework were said to merge 'in every direction
into the silver stems of the enclosing and enclosed wood, which
generates a feeling of sheltered secrecy'.[9] Very Jekyllian, and her
plantings thrived.

On a train journey to Newcastle, Lutyens was again writing to
Lady Emily. At Munstead Wood he had shown Gertrude a horticultural snippet in the *West Surrey Times*. A gardener was exhibiting at a
flower show, '"peas in purple pods, a vanity little seen now" & we
giggled & Bumps has sent me the enclose pome.

> Oh for a pea in a purple pod;
> For this I labour and turn the sod;
> and trench it deep for many a rod;
> and carry manure in a bricklayer's hod;
> All for a pea in a purple pod!'[10]

There was something decisive in Gertrude's nature, so that there
could be little dullness or drudgery in her daily round. But as she aged
she grew more reliant on communication with Munstead House. The
bond between brother and sister had endured. After Herbert retired in
1911, they met frequently; towards the end of their lives, almost daily.
Isobel Durrant, formerly Isobel Robinson, second housemaid at Munstead House, remarked on the lack of effusion that distinguished a
relationship based on shared proclivities and shared experience. Neither
could afford to have too many demands made upon them. Herbert's

restraint was beautifully discerned by Lutyens, writing to Emily on the occasion of their silver wedding, 'Nice to have squeezed an almost affectionate letter from Sr Herbert.'[11] Separated physically by the Bramley road, each home had its careful, time-conscious routine, each understood the other's code, and there was endless traffic in *pot pourri* and lavender bags between the two. What David McKenna referred to as the 'creature comforts'[12] of Munstead House were much wider than those of Munstead Wood. Sir Herbert and Lady Jekyll lived according to the conventions of their class and position, with plenty of servants, lunch with notabilities, tea parties, picnics and visits to friends. They were firm upholders of the Church of England and their ratio between work and play was a little more even.

Gertrude had great faith in her brother's opinion, but because she was work-centred and child-intolerant, it is difficult to know how much she, who never acknowledged the birthday of niece or nephew, cared for his family. One would guess that she was profoundly, if fairly passively, involved. She was, of course, present at Barbara's marriage to the Hon. Francis McLaren MP. One of the ushers was Mr Asquith, brother of the Prime Minister. On the last day of January 1910, Pamela produced Gertrude's first great-nephew, Michael McKenna. Within six months the new mother was finding in her son a true Jekyll awareness in his surroundings. 'M. woke and smiled one of his rare magic smiles. He loves looking at trees and clouds and things that move above him. He develops quickly now.'[13] Each generation was encouraged to discover the natural wonders that Gertrude and her younger brothers had absorbed with such intensity. Boats and seascape were also sewn into Gertrude's childhood memories. Once annually, she sought well-being and renewal from the light, scenery and the bracing freedoms of the sea. During May she spent two uncluttered weeks in a boarding house at Bembridge on the Isle of Wight. Returning with coastal gleanings, she would round up Munstead's busy days with more shell pictures.

Artist and critic Roger Fry was such a substantial figure in Bloomsbury and the arts that his Jekyll association has almost been forgotten. But of twelve plans Gertrude was producing during the year, one was for Durbins, his house on a chalk ridge in South Guildford, and Fry's daughter remembered vividly Gertrude's visits there. Fry moved from London to another house in Fort Road, hoping that the surroundings would be salubrious for his mentally unstable and ailing wife. Despite Helen's deterioration, he decided to build his ideal home just below the first one. Durbins still exists, a severe, Italianate house with long windows and a mansard roof, referred to by Pevsner as a 'hard-headed amateur design'.[14] Denys Sutton, editor of Fry's letters, writes of its sun-filled garden falling away to the south, 'it was planned down to the smallest details by that artist of gardens and gardening Miss Jekyll. It was built at four descending terraced levels flanked by two large and long buttressed projections faced with dry walls of rough Bargate stone in the interstices of which were planted aubrietias and alyssums and other rock plants, which were a glorious show in spring. Monthly roses and lavender crowned the buttresses and a square pond with water lilies mirrored the house in the third terrace. There was plenty of room for fruit and vegetables and grand herbaceous borders, where Fry's favourite oriental poppies, blue anchusa and artichokes grow in profusion.'[15]

In November, Fry organized an exhibition at the Grafton Galleries showing work by Manet, Cézanne, Gauguin, Van Gogh and Matisse. Public reaction was predictable; he was pilloried as a dangerous anarchist set to destroy the decency of art. Nonetheless, his nine years in Guildford saw the initiation of the celebrated Arts and Crafts Omega Workshops. Despite his reputation as a champion of the moderns and his affair with Vanessa Bell, the bespectacled critic and painter was a traditionalist of Quaker background. No correspondence with Gertrude seems to have survived and the bottom of her garden with the pond has been cut off, but dry stone walls containing a covered seat remain.

With clients, Gertrude was professional to the last degree, attentive, informative, and adroit. Mrs Terence Turner, wife of a local doctor, extricated forty garden notebooks from the 1948 sale of the contents of Munstead Wood, and these invaluable aids to understanding Gertrude's exemplary, business-like methodology are now in the Godalming Museum. The title of a property is usually followed by appropriate names and addresses, of surveyor, the nearest railway station and the gardener. At Barton St Mary in East Grinstead, a job begun in 1906, primary notification reads 'Any instructions write to gr (talkative man) send for if need.'[16] When plans had been approved by a client, Gertrude transferred the names and numbers of plants from them into 4 × 6 inch notebooks, the source of plant material being thus indicated:

a single ink line – plants to be ordered from Jackmans
a single green – small shrubs from Munstead Wood
A double ink – lilies from Wallace & elsewhere
A red chalk – plants from Munstead Wood in spring[17]

To anyone familiar with the hasty writing on Gertrude's plans, the notebooks are surprisingly stylish. The hand is bold, clear and, even towards the end of her life, indubitably that of an artist. On the left, the number of the plan, written in red crayon, is followed by a letter identifying each bed. Once plants had been ordered they were invoiced and the page deleted, again in red. No method could be infallible. Tracings of the planting plans were sent out accompanied by plants for certain sections with detailed cultural instructions, but in a letter of apology, sent to a client in 1929 who received the wrong plants, Gertrude wrote that 'Such an unlucky mishap has only happened to me once before in all the 30 years that I have been sending away plants.'[18] Precision was a mania; if she had the hands of a craftsman and imagination of an artist, her mind had the order of a scientist.

Clients came in variety, and those like Lord Ruthven of Newlandburn in Midlothian knew precisely what they wanted. 'Something . . . like your beautiful alley of Michaelmas daisies. I dislike plants that don't *smell* . . . I must also at once make a herbaceous border as people are sending me tons of plants.'[19] His garden, however, was never realized. Far more difficult to accommodate was inveterate waverer Sir George Sitwell of Renishaw Hall, an enormous ancient ancestral home aggressively gabled and battlemented. Sir George himself had tinkered with the formal parts of his great gardens. Then Lutyens was approached: 'Sir George wants to build a little water palace (one room) on the lake, which would be a delightful thing to do.'[20] The previous year Sir George had published *On the Making of Gardens*, and 'never', his elder son announced, 'was a book more pondered upon at every stage'.[21] The result was predictably verbose. Sir George had an intimate knowledge of Italian gardens but he saw them in chiaroscuro. According to his elder son, Sir Osbert, 'Such flowers as might be permitted, had, like all else in good taste, to be unobtrusive, not to call attention to themselves by hue or scent, but to form vague pointillist masses of colour that could never detract from the view.'[22] To complicate the matter, Lady Ida consistently demanded colour and scent. Sir George had probably read Gertrude's works before seeking her assistance. In fact his call for 'taste', abhorrence for 'Horticulturists' blossoms' and emphasis on the atmospheric contribution of rugged creeper-clung trees finds him spiritually in tune with her.

Renishaw's Long Alley had two rows of alternately rectangular and circular beds edged in clipped box. It was overlooked by the ballroom, a position Gertrude played off with a dashing pageant of bedding – waves of maize enclosing primrose and orange marigolds in the rectangles, swirls of various marigolds gyrating like spinning tops in the round beds. They lasted only a year. Perhaps the sparkling dashes and baubles offended Sir George's sensitivity to glare. Tooley suggests that the annuals may have prepared the way for herbaceous perennials,[23] but Gertrude was not called on for these and Reresby Sitwell noted, 'it is no longer known what she actually contributed'.[24] What is known is that large numbers of plants were sent by rail from Surrey. Osbert, at least, approved the 'particular richness'[25] of beds, some in blue, orange and lemon, others in 'French eighteenth-century blues and pinks'.[26] In 1912, when the bedded colour scheme was again altered, white dahlias, yellow cannas and 240 stachys were sent from Munstead for the round beds.

Gertrude's system of segregating visitors was relaxed when James Britten was invited specifically to meet a fellow plantsman. 'I will do my best about the weather,' Gertrude wrote cordially, 'although some of my efforts in that direction have, of late, not met with success . . . Remember, you are coming to a cottage with the very simplest ways – no evening clothes are allowed . . . only your barest necessaries in a small bag. Will you look out for my roan cob at Godalming at 5.28 . . .'[27] Helen Allingham was another visitor that summer, and so was Edward Augustus, generally remembered by his horticultural readers as E. A. Bowles, though his colleagues at the Royal Horticultural Society, where he served for more than fifty years, referred to him affectionately as 'Bowley' and gruff fellow plant-hunter Reginald Farrer called him 'Uncle G'. 'It would be difficult to imagine anything more delightful, floriculturally speaking,' opined a reporter in the *Gardener's Magazine* in 1910, 'than to spend an hour or so with Mr Bowles.'[28] Twice that year Gertrude had visited his home, Myddelton House in Enfield, North London, and Bowles had recently returned from an expedition to the Maritime Alps when he arrived in Surrey.

Slowly the Women's Movement was gaining ground. Brougham Villiers' *Case for Women's Suffrage* and Lady McLaren's *Women's*

Charter of Rights and Liberties came out in 1909, followed by *The ABC of Votes for Women* in 1910. Literature on the women's struggle was just one sign of growing momentum, and throughout the country suffragette branches were being set up. Gertrude might not have involved herself with the more extreme manifestations of feminist pioneers, but she was engaged by association when Emily Lutyens, sick with fright, steeled herself to give a five-minute public speech before Emmeline Pankhurst at one of the rallies. Asquith was as unrelenting an opponent as Gladstone had been before him; tirades of graffiti and stone-throwing were countered by imprisonment and the forcible feeding of those on hunger strikes. Lady Constance Lytton, Emily's elder sister and Mrs Earle's niece, exposed the iniquitous treatment of working-class suffragettes by throwing stones and parading under a false name. Without the protection offered to aristocratic and middle-class suffragettes, she was not given a medical examination and was forcibly fed though she suffered from chronic valvular heart disease. The Lytton case caused a scandal. Its victim, permanently invalided, is remembered by Mary Lutyens doing exquisite Japanese flower arrangements with her left hand because her right was paralysed, lying in bed in purple velvet with her medals pinned to her chest.

In 1886 George Watts, on the brink of seventy, had married Mary Fraser Tytler, an aspiring artist thirty years younger. Gertrude attended a meeting convened by Mrs Watts at Compton Picture Gallery, and Francis Jekyll assumes it was in solidarity with the Movement. But Mary Watts was not an obvious proponent of women's suffrage. There was no doubt about her capabilities. She had built a dream house for her husband's old age, laid out shrubberies and started up the Compton Potters' Art Guild. Even before he died, she was busy turning him into a national monument, designing and masterminding the construction of the astonishing hillside chapel that celebrates his memory. In 1904, when Watts did die, she was not yet sixty and enormously energetic. Big garden pots were produced in the pottery alongside art nouveau cherubs. In the true spirit of the Home Arts and Industries, she believed 'neither man nor woman can do better than try to make a *delightful* village industry – beautiful things beautifully made, by people in beautiful country'.[29] Gertrude was to praise the subdued tones of Compton Pottery, which survived until the mid-fifties. According to Watts's biographer, Mary was 'much loved; but she was also much feared'.[30] The small woman with piercing eyes, who dressed after her husband's death in perpetual widow's black, was referred to more than once as 'a tartar'.[31] Uncurtseying children and adults with untidy gardens were apt to receive her reproof. Any loyalty to women's rights she might have felt would have been divided. Velázquez's *Venus* in the National Gallery had been slashed by suffragettes. Watts's nudes might well be at risk, and the Godalming Division of the Surrey Police was called in 'to frustrate what we have every reason to think would have been a serious attempt to do mischief to our Collection'.[32]

At any one time, Gertrude could dip into the various alternative worlds of her garden commissions. It was five years since she had crossed the sands to Holy Island. Hudson had wanted a boggy area between the castle and rising ground on the north to be a water garden, which 'might attract a few birds',[33] and the old walled garden to be a croquet lawn or a tennis court. But Lutyens's schemes had proved so exorbitant that Hudson changed his mind. Besides the rock itself, only the tiny walled garden would be planted. Lutyens tried playing tricks with perspective to make its 72 × 67 feet appear larger than it was, but his conjuring did not work. Gertrude envisaged a jewel of abundance blooming all summer, one side with roses among vegetables and espalier fruit trees, another with gladioli, hollyhocks, fuchsias, Japanese anemones, mallows and sunflowers. For the centre, she planned further cottage garden mixtures in island beds. On 9 March 1911, half a bushel of Sutton's seed potatoes were dispatched for Lindisfarne, with peas and seeds of spinach, dwarf beans, parsley, carrots, cabbage, cauliflower, lettuce, beet and onions. Barrs Nurseries supplied most of the plants; 'I can sow mint, thyme, sage, sorrel, chives, savory,'[34] Gertrude wrote in her notebook.

For someone with Gertrude's devotion to scholarship, contact with Cambridge women's colleges was appropriate. In the seventies she had advised on Girton's interior decoration, through friendship with Madame Bodichon. It was Newnham's turn to seek advice. Mrs Eleanor Sidgwick, the principal, had died. Would Gertrude design a memorial garden? Before the end of the year the committee reported that 'the plan designed by Miss Jekyll which included the erection of two summerhouses was submitted and examined and the majority of the committee recommended acceptance'.[35] The garden was formal and Italianate, a path between two summerhouses being flanked by evergreen hedges clipped into a succession of bays. In the centre of each stood an Irish yew. Existing planting would be thickened behind the summerhouses and either side of the new hedge, and free-growing roses would bloom among the trees. An estimate for the whole job, two summerhouses, plant material, seats and paving came to £642, of which £60 was labour and £50 a fee. Sadly, Gertrude's ideas were not adopted, possibly because plans were afoot for other alterations in the grounds. Several years later, a single summerhouse was erected with a terrace, seat and inscription by Eric Gill.

Gertrude was always prepared to do what she could for her siblings, and Walter, sharing her intellectual discipline and urge to create, had been close to her until life had begun to separate him from the rest of the family. After writing a guide to the botanic garden in Kingston, he had collected and translated Jamaican songs and stories from natives of the Port Royal Mountains behind his home. *Jamaican Song and Story* was, he averred, a tribute to his love for the country 'and its dusky inhabitants, with their winning ways and their many good qualities, among which is to be reckoned that supreme virtue, *Cheerfulness*'.[36] Since then his translation of Schopenhauer had gone to press; perhaps to celebrate, Herbert and Aggie took a holiday in Jamaica with the 'delightful and gifted brother . . . who led a philosopher's life of plain living and high thinking at the foot of the Blue Mountains'.[37] In fact Sir Herbert and Aggie stayed with friends, the Swettenhams, spending only a day with Walter, and that was probably a strain. Walter refused to accept the rules which govern society. After parting with most of his money, he lived a life of modified Buddhism, 'truly a religion of peace and goodwill to men, a religion of love and self-sacrifice'.[38] Egalitarian altruism caused what Herbert called, on his brother's death, a 'drift apart'.[39]

At Munstead Wood a scorching summer brought a host of visitors. Obligingly, Gertrude's favourite 'Garland' rose was 'literally smothered with large clusters of fawn-coloured buds opening nearly white'.[40] A 'melancholy cook'[41] was replaced, and Gertrude rounded off the season with a week at Looe in Cornwall. On her way back she visited the Exeter nursery of Peter Veitch, third in a line of famous nursery-men, and uncle to James, who had branched out so successfully in Chelsea. In 1870 the prized Veitch Memorial Medal had been instituted. It was an accolade she subsequently gained.

On 2 January the 'Garland' rose was throbbing with blood-coloured hips, though armfuls of it had been cut for Christmas decoration. Gertrude's shrewd eye for quality was constantly on the alert, reassessing old favourites and searching for good new garden plants. *Pychnostachys dawei*, she wrote in *The Garden*, was a 'wonderful'[1] labiate from Uganda donated to her by Mrs Alfred Russel Wallace. Three feet high and blue as the March sky, it was an ideal candidate for a blue garden.

There was an enormous number of plants to choose from. In 1804, when the Horticultural Society was formed, a number of exotic species was available, but the British climate accommodates vegetation from regions as diverse as Australia, the Americas and Tibet. It was becoming apparent to botanists and gardeners that there was an almost endless supply of trees, flowers, fruits and vegetables that would thrive in our gardens if they could be safely introduced. Ten years before Gertrude was born, Dr Ward had devised an almost airtight fern case that was to have far-reaching implications for horticultural transportation. Britain already had a foothold in Japan, North America and China, but enterprises such as Kew, the great pioneering nurseries like Veitch and the Royal Horticultural Society itself began sending out a new breed of plant-hunter, the scientific and systematic botanist. This was the era of intrepid British collectors like E. H. Wilson, George Forrest, Reginald Farrer and Frank Kingdon-Ward. Augustine Henry, a doctor serving in the Chinese Imperial Maritime Customs Service, alone sent back some 15,000 dried specimens between 1881 and 1900, including more than fifty new species. By 1912 Wilson's *Lilium regale* was recognized as a separate species; the year before, after enormous difficulties, the first handkerchief tree, *Davidia involucrata*, waved its strange white bracts on English soil. Perhaps it was not a plant that would have interested Gertrude.

From friends, botanists, nurseries and botanic gardens, however, streams of specimens arrived at Munstead Wood. A Jekyll recommendation was considered a fastidious and reliable guide. Gertrude's thoroughness and her tireless efforts to publicize her findings were turning a small corner of Surrey into a centre of national repute. There could scarcely be more potent evidence of the power of her pen than her incoming mail. 'You make me blush – in fact I have been blushing hard ever since I had your letter . . . at all the delightful things you say about my books,'² she replied to Mrs F. King of Alma, Michigan, a founding member and one of four vice-presidents of the Garden Club of America. 'But seriously, it is a great happiness and a rich reward of effort and long years of work, to find such sympathy and appreciation, and I am truly glad to know that you are writing and giving addresses on ways of gardening that I know would be after my own heart.'³

To make beautiful gardens was Gertrude's discriminating aim, and someone who shared her views therefore deserved encouragement. 'I am so glad you are taking up the colour question and trying to show what you mean by colour words.'⁴ The following year, sending by way of compliment a 'pretty little secateur',⁵ Mrs King asked if Gertrude would write a short foreword to a forthcoming book. *The Flower Garden Day by Day* duly emerged with an encouraging recommendation: 'The author's practical knowledge, keen insight, and splendid enthusiasm, her years of labor on her own land and her constant example combine to make her one of the most fitted to . . . instruct.'⁶ The secateurs were 'Almost too dainty for my big working hands', Gertrude wrote forthrightly, she would consider them 'a Sunday tool'.⁷ Interchange continued. Mrs King had sent a book on American gardens and Gertrude commented on the Italian influence, especially at Drumthwacket in New Jersey; 'some genuine Italian feeling',⁸ she felt, had been produced. 'I think the true Italian character is only suitable or completely possible in a corresponding climate such as that of California and others of the Southern States.'⁹

Much of 1912 was occupied with garden plans, among them a memorial to Jack Phillips, the young radio operator from Godalming who continued to relay messages from the sinking *Titanic*. On 15 April he went down with so many others. 'No one can forget . . . the terrible story . . . of the ocean liner Titanic,'¹⁰ wrote Gertrude with deliberation in *Gardening Illustrated*. 'The great steamship, one of the largest of the modern liners, outward bound on her maiden voyage and going half slow in slightly foggy weather, struck a submerged mass of floating ice and foundered within half-an-hour in mid-Atlantic. Hundreds were drowned for there was nothing like enough boat accommodation for the great numbers of the passengers and crew.'[11] In the emotional aftermath, the population of Godalming was unanimous, Phillips must be commemorated on home ground. But quite how the matter should be realized, the *Minutes and Reports of the Godalming Corporation* suggest, raised tiresome debate. Landowner Mr Nash felt that proposals to use his land endangered his privacy and the Council was unable to agree on anything. At length both site (the third proposed) and the type of memorial (the second) were approved. Local architect and founder of the West Surrey Society, Thackeray Turner, would be the designer, and Phillips's memorial would occupy a serene piece of ground north of the town centre, between the church and River Wey. Nothing remains of Gertrude's planting in a quadrangular arched court. Laurustinus, bay trees and *Bergenia cordifolia* disappeared; a central, octagonal tank of waterlilies was replaced by a vandal-proof bed of dwarf conifers, and one side of the cloister, by a wooden pergola supporting wisterias. But when summer draws inhabitants to the bowling green, arched views over the watermeadows make it a very pleasant spot; Surrey Gardens Trust is hoping to restore the Jekyll scheme.

Another commission from the same period is Burgh House in Hampstead's Well Walk, now the Hampstead Museum, where advice was called in by antiquarian polymath Dr G. C. Williamson. Of large numbers of plants sent from Munstead Wood little remains, but the terrace has its Jekyll signature in two fine millstones. In a memoir replete with name-dropping, Williamson refers to himself as the author of 100 books, and someone who had 'been where few others have penetrated'.[12] He edited a dictionary of artists, collected portrait miniatures and drew portraits, gathering in the process a vast circle of acquaintances. Among them was Baroness Burdett-Coutts, who might have been responsible for introducing Gertrude. As usual, Gertrude sought full details of the job by correspondence and one of the items sent her was an old family Christmas card showing engraved views of the house. A rough plan of the flower beds in the forecourt is appended with various inquiries: 'this pencil marking, is it a privet or other hedge?'[13] and against two shaded lumps, 'rock beds which shape & how high middle or top above ground level?'[14]

Burgh House and the Phillips Memorial were relatively minor

assignments; Louisa Wakeman-Newport's Sandbourne near Bewdley in Worcestershire was on a very different scale. Here within a familiar heathland framework, birch and pine fringed the stage for what was to be an astounding nine-terraced 'Italian' garden. It was fifteen years since Gertrude had written her piece about formal gardens for the *Edinburgh Review* and the woodland notes that underpinned her first book. Symbolically they had remained the dual sources of her inspiration, one classical and cognitive, the other artistic and imaginative. Collaborating with Elgood had given a fillip to her study of Italian gardens, and two articles she wrote in *Country Life* towards the end of 1911 suggest an increasing emphasis on formality – stairways, 'always beautiful in garden design',[15] flagged terraces, handsome gate-piers, and massed flowers seen against long hedges of clipped yew. The Italian parterre set in a geometry of box borders had been a feature of great elegance, she argued cogently, but in Britain it was debased by floating the beds in areas of gravel 'quite out of proportion with the design'.[16] The fact that a sales catalogue described Sandbourne as an 'old-world terraced garden'[17] eighteen years after its birth could reflect Gertrude's tendency to look backwards.

The Wakeman-Newports had already invited her advice on one home when they acquired a gracious, brick Georgian house overlooking the Severn valley. The new garden would occupy a bare sloping four-acre field running down towards the Stourport Road, a site Gertrude described bluntly as being 'without any distinctive feature whatever'.[18] Each terrace was delineated and separated by broad yew hedging to form a garden of seasonal beauty, one for roses, another for June flowers – irises and lupins, filled out with rounded drifts of geranium and golden privet. Lutyens was responsible for a sundial on the paved area near the house, otherwise all the hardware, tanks and rills on every terrace, pergola and summerhouse were designed by Gertrude between 1911 and 1913. The soil was a light sandy loam on which a host of plants refused to thrive. '*Do badly* clem montana, hollyhock, lilies, Gentian, Rhodo . . .'[19] Gertrude wrote in a notebook. 'Roses wanted.' 'They have no Paris daisy.'[20] Mrs Wakeman-Newport, a knowledgeable plantswoman, managed what Tooley refers to as a 'remarkable garden'[21] until her death in 1930. Since then various terraces have been cut up for building.

Gertrude was approaching her seventieth year. It was four years since her last book and time for a reaffirmation of her creed. This time she joined forces with Lawrence Weaver, architectural editor of *Country Life*. *Gardens for Small Country Houses* was partly a record of her own design commissions and partly a pattern book of garden features. Seldom had she allied herself more completely with the 'small band of people who by word and deed have shown the right way',[22] by inference Inigo Triggs, Thomas Mawson and other hard-core formalists including Lutyens. All was solid, dependable and high quality; the Edwardian plutocrat could have his earthly paradise provided he could afford the labour to keep his hedges shorn and his carefully considered colour schemes manicured. Illustrations in the new book concentrate on semi-circular steps, framed views, stone walls – 'precious gardening ground',[23] suave Lutyenesque water gardens, wide green walks – 'the most precious possession of the place',[24] stocky pergolas, lofty gateways, feasts of roses and simple, functional-looking sheltered seats, 'a comfort to the eye'.[25]

At Millmead Gertrude had used a sundial, a feature she considered the most appropriate garden ornament in Britain. The only sculptured ornament she had at Munstead Wood was a lion mask waterspout made by George Leslie, inside the tank, and the sculpture illustrated in the new book is largely Italian reproduction. Degas was currently working on bronze figures that might have given an altogether new focus to a Jekyll setting; old formats, however, were reassuring. By 1927 the enormously influential book had gone into six editions, at home and abroad. Robert Lorimer, reviewing it for the RIBA journal, found Miss Jekyll's planting plans of 'extraordinary value',[26] and Christopher Hussey reckoned that 'The English conception of a good-looking house set in a gracious garden among fine trees, which he [Lutyens] so variously realized with the help of Miss Jekyll, raised the standard of domestic design throughout the world.'[27] Praise from such quarters makes it difficult to criticize Inigo Triggs's patent wall panels – yards of moulded brick masonry and parapets of curved tiles that might err towards pretentiousness – or to suggest that the general image of *Gardens for Small Country Houses* might be for its time a little complacent.

Bulgaria, Serbia, Montenegro and Greece had attacked Turkey in order to seize her possessions, and Sir Edward Grey, the British Foreign Secretary, reckoned that 'we were sitting on a powder magazine'.[28] Political turmoil in Eastern Europe was reflected in intellectual restlessness that erupted in modernism after the First World War.

Artists and writers like James Joyce were trying to dispense with old formats in an effort to free themselves and develop an artistic conscience for their time. But old clients were asking Gertrude for more of the same garden formula. She designed three gardens for Victoria Fisher Rowe, three eventually for Edward Hudson and three for Kate Leslie, George Leslie's rich niece, from whom he had bought land in Sussex and built himself a house. Whether or not Gertrude visited the site, a Jekyll garden was something in which they had confidence.

For old friends Gertrude had a deep kind of affection, and if they were gardeners they were likely to have kept in touch. Lady Wolseley's School for Lady Gardeners had gone from strength to strength. Demand for the finished product was so keen that students were often assured positions before they had completed the course. Lady Wolseley had written her first book, *Gardening for Women*, and when a bronze medal was won for the college exhibit at the 1913 Chelsea Flower Show, she was made Citizen and Gardener of London for her services to horticulture. Twelve years after founding her establishment she was able to write, 'the craft is now an established and a coveted one for ladies'.[29]

Apprenticeship generally lasted for two years, during which students learned about the art and science of vegetable, fruit and flower production, the principles of running a commercial business and the history of garden design. The atmosphere was one of pioneering enthusiasm, indeed the 'Captain',[30] sitting in her 'cabin',[31] medals earned for hard work, and the aspiration to impart 'obedience, orderliness and much worldly wisdom'[32] must have conveyed the spirit of the British forces. Recent recruits were likened to Kitchener's bedraggled new army; soon, however, they would acquire the upright, military swing that marked their sister students. Discipline was rigorous – Lady Wolseley could not tolerate untidiness in any form and she abhorred bad manners. Photographs of her students show between fifteen and twenty teenage girls posing with spades and Sussex trugs, potting up seedlings and wheeling vegetable trolleys. They are always impeccably clad, in shortish khaki skirts, white shirts, firmly knotted sailor-striped red, white and blue ties, brown boots, leggings and soft-rimmed felt hats bound with tricoloured twisted corn. During work the uniform was covered by a canvas apron with pockets for gardening indispensables. One day, when they were being entertained at Munstead Wood, an off-duty detective, mistaking them for suffragettes, called in to demand an explanation.

The rounded life required periodic holidays, pacts between nature and Gertrude's self, the great moieties of earthly existence, that were also secretive, furtive forays into the past. Old age never tempted her to the five-star hotel she could well afford. Almost indifferent to comfort and knowing what suited her best, she squeezed into a modest boarding house where the landlady cooked for her. For two years in succession she took her spring-cleaning exeat at Bosham where, as a *Country Life* article appearing shortly after the 1912 trip tells, Gertrude stood among the salt marshes fringing Chichester Harbour, contemplating: 'Those who study colour for garden use often find admirable examples in wild places.'³³ The tide was half-way in, so that lines of water and pale, muddy shore were separated by short blue-green seaweedy growth. On a narrow strip of thrift-covered marsh, various zones lay 'in long level drifts in a perfectly eye-satisfying colour-harmony'. 'The colour of the Thrift was in itself especially beautiful', and close inspection 'to see how Nature painted this miracle'³⁴ revealed infinite colour gradations.

Munstead Wood never failed to bring fresh enchantment. Leonie Blumenthal was entertained for the last time. Thereafter the hitherto hospitable 'Madame' withdrew into seclusion at Cheyne Walk, from which no one could persuade her to emerge. She died fourteen years later, leaving her old friend the £500 legacy M. Blumenthal had set aside. Gertrude's sister-in-law, Edward's wife, Theresa, also died and her unmarried sister moved in to keep Higham Bury in Teutonic trim. Gertrude bowed her head and carried on doing the things which gave her life purpose, burying herself in what might have seemed a punishing routine for a woman of seventy. Pearsall Smith, knowing her critical eye, once asked whether the garden brought her pleasure. 'Very much'³⁵ was her affirmative. Sometimes she caught it unawares and it seemed 'all right'.³⁶ On 4 August two patches of *Ipomoea* 'Heavenly Blue' splashed a south-west facing wall with thirty-three and thirty-eight open blooms. 'The sight of this comparatively large expanse of this most perfect blue was a thing to remember with thankfulness for the gift of such astounding beauty.'³⁷

Year by year Gertrude was establishing her name. In 1905 Lutyens had surveyed a house in Hungary's Zemplen belonging to Princess Stephanie, daughter of Leopold II of Belgium, and her second husband, the Hungarian Count Lonyay. It is not clear whether he carried out the work, but he altered another property for them at Orosvar, bringing in Gertrude to swirl mown paths through an orchard of long grass and lay out kitchen gardens. There were signs that she was beginning to gain recognition on the Continent. In 1907 *Wood and Garden* had been translated by G. von Sanden as *Wald und Garten*, and mounting international tension in the spring of 1914 did not prevent a Belgian association known as Le Nouveau Jardin Pittoresque from approaching her about translations of her books. Unfortunately, war intervened. She had even sent advice to Cecil Rhodes, diamond king and empire builder, on his garden at Groote Schuur in South Africa. In North America, however, her influence was second only to that in England. Her books had been appearing there since 1901 and were promoted, among others, by Helena Rutherford Ely, Louise Beebe Wilder and Mrs Francis King. Mrs King referred to her mentor somewhat gushingly as her 'own adored preceptress'.[38] American publicity might attract some irritating visitors, but it was among those who had actually seen Munstead Wood that her most die-hard and genuine fans were numbered. Grace and Glendinning Groesbeck, her first trans-Atlantic clients, are more than likely to have met her there.

Glendinning is included nominally in the correspondence but it was Grace, the wealthy daughter of a respected physician and a founding member of the Cincinnati Garden Club, who took the initiative in inviting plans. The commission was for their estate in Perintown, Ohio, fifty acres of steep slope rising 150 feet above a river valley. The problems involved were enormous – woodland uncleared, the soil thin and the slopes unstable. Numerous scaled and contoured plans show Gertrude struggling with the landform of dramatic scenery, and twenty-four of them, sent out in October of 1914, give alternative options for a rather grand affair incorporating a swimming pool, pergola, tennis lawn and central lily pond spread before the house in horizontal terraces. Rough, brambly grass led down to the river, and kitchen gardens on one side were screened by berberis and 'trees of wild character'.[39] Uncertainties over siting the house seem to have been resolved in Gertrude's favour: 'Mr Groesbeck and I have come to the conclusion that your idea of the position for the house is best and will ask you to go ahead with your original plan of placing it at the head of the main valley . . . we have perfect confidence in whatever you decide is best.'[40] Francis Jekyll suggests that his aunt's planting was insufficiently hardy, a failure to which he attributes a ten-year gap before she designed her next American garden. Apart from the taxing site, there were liabilities in undertaking work in an unfamiliar climate where many of the plants Gertrude normally used would not survive, and solving problems took mail two ocean voyages. But her nephew was making false assumptions. Two American researchers, Susan Schnare and Rudy Favretti, discovered that, due possibly to unstable slopes, her plans were never realized. For a house closely resembling Munstead Wood, someone else, possibly Grace Groesbeck herself, made a garden.

Meanwhile war clouds might be gathering over Europe, and Gertrude, being a Jekyll, was not indifferent. Every day, after lunch, she set aside time to read the newspapers. But she had also in mind a strange fungus growing among pine trees in the copse. Each year for eighteen years it had appeared. One can see her standing stoutly among the trees, her acute, ordered mind pressing towards the problem. The first impression, duly captured by photograph, was of a large, bright bath sponge. Invited by its look and smell to sample its culinary potential, she found it harmless but unexceptional. Failing to identify it in her books, she penned a note to *The Garden*. Inquiries led her to E. W. Swanton, for whom, on 20 November, she prised out a thirteen-inch fruiting body with a six-inch stem, blackish and swollen into a rank-smelling mycelium. Like an inquisitor she prodded the mystery: 'A curious thing about this fungus is its long duration, for whereas most large fungi of the softer kinds have an existence of a few days only, this one had remained for seven weeks and possibly more, in an apparently perfect condition.'[41] The ball of mycelium was replaced in the ground. Then, as if writing intensified the experience, she told the story of 'Sparassis crispa', the cauliflower or brain fungus, in *Country Life*.

The article was reprinted many times. Gertrude's exposure in *Country Life* was at its peak, and frequently *The Garden* ran duplicate pieces. Her journalism generated authority and recognition. For the National Trust, founded before the turn of the century and incorporated by an act of Parliament in 1907, she was an ideal candidate. The Trust was trying to raise funds to buy and preserve ninety-two acres of wild heath north-east of Hambledon in memory of founding member Octavia Hill. Hydon Ball, so called because its crest was at one time naked and spherical, was only two miles from her home. Few can have known it better or loved it more dearly. In winter, its pine trees were 'a marvel of delicate and complicated tinting', the hollies 'their deepest and glossiest . . . loaded with scarlet fruit', the junipers 'a wonder of their soft grey-green'.[42] Wild forest land was becoming rarer, she appealed to her readers; from Hindhead, Hascombe and other hills there were glorious views across the Weald to the South Downs, but the view from Hydon, nearly 600 feet above sea-level, was unsurpassed. It is impossible to say how much money was raised by Gertrude's plea, but £1,600 of the £4,750 purchase price was raised locally. No sooner was the land bought than she was asked to plant appropriately and plan its pathways.

The last recorded date in her photo albums for many years was 14 August 1914. It was the day on which war was declared. Lutyens spent a weekend at Munstead House with the McKennas. 'War is of course ever in our minds . . . the one subject intermixed with petty gossip & a good deal of cookery I saw Bumps, she is in the Hut.'[43] A week later she was 'making wonderful shirts and kitbags'.[44] Nothing could stop Gertrude making, looking, learning, gardening and writing; plant trials would continue and some gardens were designed, but like everything else, they were pursued in a different spirit in the next few years.

It was impossible to escape the war. In the words of Agnes Jekyll, living close to Gertrude and increasingly a figure upon whom she would depend, 'Then the crash came, and one can remember little but a hideous confusion throughout the next five dark anxious years.'[1] Ever a pragmatist, on 14 January 1915 Gertrude bought from Lady Chance thirty-one Rhode Island Red pullets. The following day their quarters were erected. Henceforth, her notes on poultry-keeping accumulate. 'Sunflower heads given whole, Rats dislike chloride of lime, Fish bones boiled with a little vinegar make a jelly to mix with mash. Main meal two hours before sunset.'[2] Thorncombe Park, the Bramley home of the Fisher-Rowes, became a military hospital and a large consumer of eggs. According to Larner's History of Godalming, children collecting and delivering them sometimes wrote their names with messages on the shells. Sometimes they received replies. Gertrude kept a daily account of what her poultry produced until December 1927, without missing a day.

With a quarter of Godalming's adult males in the forces, resourcefulness was called upon from those left behind. Women might not have a vote, and political issues were temporarily shelved, but throughout the country they were tucking up their skirts and working on the land, surprising their men and even themselves by the vigour of their contribution. Munstead Wood reduced its garden staff, a zeppelin might pass over Busbridge, targeting Guildford, as one did on 13 October 1915; but Gertrude's articles continued to appear. Quick to exploit the crusading spirit, Ladies' Field featured a series on women's careers: medicine, librarianship, and bacteriology, followed in the August number by Gertrude Jekyll on landscape gardening. Scarcely could the climate have been more sympathetic. Designing gardens was 'the highest branch of horticultural practice',[3] she wrote; it was not a career to be undertaken lightly. Familiarity with the fine arts, a keen perception of natural beauty, 'absolute fitness' and 'no ordinary mental capacity'[4] were its taxing requisites, together with something she had always encouraged in herself, a 'constant habit of searching and untiring observation'.[5] The following spring she was recommending gardening to women in *Country Life*. The painstaking care, watchfulness and sympathy that plants required were, she reckoned, particularly feminine attributes. Those who had been 'tenderly guarded'[6] from manual labour – by which she meant pampered – might discover a bracing new world of health and fresh air.

It was a perfect opportunity to boost the educational activities of Lady Wolseley, whose second book, *In a College Garden*, praised the strong governmental backing women's work received in Canada. 'It is not from Canadian women alone, however, that we can learn, for their men can teach us even more. They have fully grasped the fact that the best work is always done when men and women share discussions and decisions, and Englishmen are only slowly awakening to this.'[7]

'Sharing discussions' was what Gertrude had been doing with Lutyens for a good many years, and now that his name was made, Lutyens took every opportunity to involve her. At Marsh Court in Stockbridge, 'Mr and Mrs Johnson would much rather that you should do the planting. The gardener is very pleased with your method of making planting plans as he knows exactly where to put the plants; he says that Cheal's plans are much too vague ... Epps also says that your plants are better than anyone else's.'[8] Lutyens had been engaged with Castle Drogo, built from scratch in a magnificent situation high above a river in Drewsteignton, Devon, for the fabulously rich Mr Drew. As usual he made earnest recommendations on Gertrude's behalf: 'I should suggest to you that Mr Veitch and Myers should lay their scheme before Miss Jekyll who is a great designer, an Artist, old and experienced in the way of plants and a lover of the wilderness & moorland.'[9] Her involvement seems to have been minimal – she did the drive – but Lutyens continued to promote her services. Three days after commending her to Drew, on 16 October 1915, he scribbled her a line: 'Alas I have no time to come to you again this year tear drops etc.'[10]

January 1916 brought mild weather and early snowdrops. In heavy boots, brimmed hat, and for seventy-three, surprisingly energetic, Gertrude organized parties collecting sphagnum moss for surgical use at the front. Twice a week throughout spring and summer she conducted parties of Boy Scouts on Hydon Heath, laying the meandering track she had designed up the east side of the hill. There they cleared undergrowth, built rustic seats, and planted clumps of the gaultheria that has now become such a pest. Lady Peel, formerly Rosemary Readhead from Hambledon, recounts that local people always spoke of the red flannel petticoat Gertrude was said to wear when the weather was chilly.

Agnes's supremely organizing sister, Lady Horner, chose this spring to inform Mr Kendrick, Keeper of Textiles at the Victoria and Albert Museum, that Miss Jekyll was prepared to donate a very beautiful old quilt, noting, 'She has lots of things put away.'[11] Kendrick visited Munstead Wood and sorted through its collections, retaining a bundle of Algerian, Oriental and European clothing and some Italian embroideries. 'It is a great satisfaction,' Gertrude wrote, 'to know that so many of the items I had to offer are acceptable.'[12] In midsummer two copies of monks' frocks joined them, one being the garment that her gardener had worn for his photograph beside the giant cardiocrinums. An inventory of the first assignment notes that every single item was 'worn', 'repaired', 'stained', 'discoloured' or 'slightly damaged'. They had been collected for their intrinsic social or artistic value, and Gertrude was assured that 'the embroideries . . . have been a source of unfailing usefulness to classes working here'.[13] Until 1924 she was adding to the museum stock. The Franciscan frock is on permanent loan to the Norwich Museum and seventy articles remain in London. The collection includes a coat of coarse dark brown wool, patchworked in bright primary colours with tasselled cords hanging from the centres of stylized flowers, the traditional jacket of an Algerian butcher.

Garden routines were by no means abandoned. Canadian soldiers camped at Witley might be Munstead Wood's most frequent visitors, but blooms fading on Gertrude's 'Munstead' bunch primroses in the first days of May anticipated a time-honoured ceremonial. From each of Gertrude's homes, Berkshire to Bramley, Summerpool House to Munstead House and then Munstead Wood, like a trail of clotted cream, the primroses had followed. When they were ready to divide and replant, Gertrude wrote, 'the plants then seem willing . . . some almost falling apart in one's hands, and the new roots may be seen just beginning to form at the base of the crown'.[14] Since the early seventies she had marked the best when they were in flower and transferred them to a reserve path. Ripe seed was gathered, first for stock, then for sale, and laid in the drying room before being stored in an insect-proof shed. Later on, it was sown in cold frames. The bulk of the plants, being 'relieved of the crowded mass of flower stem', and, therefore, 'the exhausting effort of forming seed'[15] were replanted every second year in ground manured from the pigsty. Patience and diligence had been rewarded; from about 1890 the strain had steadily improved. Some of the flowers were well over two inches in diameter and more than fifteen inches high, though selection, Gertrude hastened to add, had not been for size. Some were 'flat and distinctly five-petaled to the eye',[16] others 'so heavily frilled or fluted at the outer edge that they look like double flowers'.[17] They varied so much in detail that her attempt to classify them had failed, but Frank Young, one of her gardeners, recalled six broad types: three whites, seven-eye, nineteen-eye and pheasant-eye, and three yellows, a primrose, canary, and one almost orange called 'Sultan'.[18] She claimed that a red was 'weeded out',[19] but Young recalled it growing behind the wheelbarrow shed. In earlier years 75 per cent were discarded, later, only the odd plant. As the seed went into trade, the purity of the strain was 'jealously guarded'.[20] Other flowers she bred and selected include Lent hellebores, *Nigella* 'Miss Jekyll', aquilegia, double pink poppies and white foxgloves.

Sometimes Gertrude visited William Robinson's Gravetye, a journey with attractions said to be multiplied by the presence of a public house called the 'Tabby Cat'. Very occasionally she was coaxed from Munstead Wood for a night. Lutyens had made two big, 'brilliantly effective'[21] enlargements to Folly Farm. It was one of his favourite houses, and during the summer of 1916 Mrs Zachery Merton lent it to his family for the holidays complete with servants. William Nicholson, friend and painter, was working on murals for the dining room and Gertrude had several parts of the garden to furnish. After work she would take off her hob-nailed boots to play the pianola. Lutyens had various reasons for feeling frustrated – money, problems over the Viceroy's house in New Delhi, estrangement from his wife and wartime paralysis in the profession – but his daughter Mary remembered games of crazy croquet and the happiest summer of her childhood. Young children, alive to the earth's beauty, sometimes seem protected from adult tension.

The following spring, seven-year-old Michael McKenna, a receptive child spending the Easter exeat with his maternal grandparents, found

Munstead House 'just Paradise . . . I have seen my first willow-wren. And oh he was singing so beautifully. I could not mistake that falling scale. The notes started in Heaven and came to comfort earth.

'I heard the chiff-chaff, and saw blue and great tits practising gymnastics on the oak tree by the rock garden.

'If I had my own way I would stay here for as long as I could. I would go round the garden watching my beloved ones and resting myself. I would kiss the daffodils that were drooping, and make them well again, like I did in the evening yesterday.' [22]

Sir Herbert was known decorously as 'Grandfather'; Aggie, 'Grandma', was the archetypal caring grandmother. Lady Peel remembered that she was very fat, with chins rolling down her chest. Michael's brother, David McKenna, recollects fabulous cooking that became the subject of a book called *Kitchen Essays*, and her involvement in the lives of those around her. At breakfast she would say, 'Now what shall we do today?' to which the younger generation rejoined, 'Granny's got the pic-nic look.' [23] Another view of the Jekylls, less intimate but no less keen or relevant, comes from Mrs Mills, born Harriet Keen in 1907, who lived for sixty-eight years in Brighton Road where a small community provided school, choir and a fair complement of staff at 'the big houses' [24] – the Munstead complex. Harriet is recalled by a contemporary as a good-looking 'ring-leaderish sort of girl' [25] known among friends as Sweetie. She attended Busbridge village school from 1914 to 1921, like her friends she was invited to pass through the grounds of Munstead Wood to celebrations at Munstead House, and inevitably she came across the Jekylls. 'They were the big family. They had the say in village affairs. At the school there was the headmaster Mr Send until he went into the army, then Miss Helen Grant [who] was going to teach us good manners. We were vulgar village school children. But every year Mr and Mrs Jekyll would give a Christmas tree to the school and every one of us had an orange and a sixpence. That was all the world to us then.' [26]

Frank Young, born in 1907 at 177 Brighton Road, remembered how each family kept a pig, which they took turns to kill and share. Many of the men worked at the Bargate stone quarries while their wives participated in cottage industries, knitting cricket sweaters for boys at Charterhouse and making epaulettes from horse hair for the military at Aldershot. Most of the girls, including Harriet Mills, belonged to the Girls' Friendly Society, which met in the parish room at the back of the Boys and Men's Institute. 'Lady Jekyll would read classical books like Dickens – she was a very good reader, and we'd be sewing or knitting for the soldiers in the first war.' Mrs Mills's recollections of Gertrude and Munstead Wood are equally clear: 'There were big hedges and you couldn't see over. I never saw her in the garden. She made me think of someone shut up in a castle. She liked to keep herself to herself.' Until the first war, village life had a rigid social structure; working people were deferential and village children curt-seyed to 'the best' or the 'big' people. Often Harriet passed Gertrude in the lanes, either alone or with her brother and sister-in-law. Gertrude would be wearing a dark blue cotton scarf fixed at the nape of her neck. 'You didn't look at her. It was known she didn't like it. She seemed a bit standoffish, but she was a very clever person. Perhaps she didn't have time for ordinary people.' The image of Gertrude as abrupt, time-pressed and inaccessible is repeated by others who met her in the shops and streets of Godalming. She once wrote in a letter to William Nicholson, artist of her famous portrait, 'I am so desperately shy about anything to do with personal exposure.'[27] Her remark needs to be questioned. She had a strong self-assertive nature, and her writing is a form of self-display. What she remained intensely shy of, as Mrs Mills acutely observed, was physical exposure. Gertrude was always a little ashamed of her appearance. It is almost as if her quest for beauty was an escape from the stout unyielding body that imprisoned her.

There was no way of evading the awful grimness of the war. Casualties among officers included Lt-Col. Lawrence Fisher-Rowe from Thornecombe, Ian Graham Hogg, one of Agnes's nephews, mortally wounded at Compiègne, and Barbara Jekyll's husband, the Hon. Francis August McLaren, second Lieutenant and MP for Spalding, killed in an aeroplane accident while flying at Montrose. He was about a mile out at sea in fine weather, on the penultimate day of August, flying at considerable height, when his plane was seen to descend rapidly, right itself, then, from ninety feet above the water, suddenly dive straight into the sea. McLaren was moved unconscious from his machine by the crews of two motor fishing boats. Three days later, when the funeral took place at Busbridge church, Gertrude was among the mourners. The Archdeacon of Surrey officiated, the Canadians from Witley furnished the Guard of Honour and firing party and the church overflowed. William Young, a Brighton Road youngster who became the verger at the church, remembers vividly the half-day break from school, boys and girls lining the road, waving flags, and what for a schoolboy gave the occasion an indelible impact, a gun-carriage rolling past in the procession. Gertrude had a need to be needed. In a tactical move on her brother's part, Barbara, his elder daughter, stayed with her aunt, learning from her to embroider and paint flower pictures.

For Lutyens, pervasive war gloom compounded marital frustration. He did not cease loving Emily, nor did she withdraw sympathy and support; but his workaholism had left her a great deal to her own resources, there were emotional lacunae he could not fill, and she had been for many years infatuated with Krishnamurti, a young man the Theosophists were cultivating to be their Messiah. An immediate remedy for Lutyens was Lady Sackville, the mother of Vita Sackville-West, whose husband had recently taken a mistress. She was a trifle plump, seductive, opulent, equable, and lavish with time and gifts. Lutyens called her his 'bit of blue sky in the background when everything was black and stormy at home';[28] the following year she drove to Munstead Wood. 'Bumps very *epris* with Lady S. They were funny together. There is to be an exchange of foie gras and pot pourris.'[29] Accompanied by her mother and Lutyens, twenty-five-year-old Vita visited Munstead Wood in August. From evidence in her notebooks, she was not greatly influenced by Gertrude's ideas, although the primroses beneath the nut trees at Sissinghurst are generally reckoned to have been inspired by the trip.

In June Lutyens was one of three men selected by the War Graves Commission to advise on British military cemeteries in France. Touring the sites, he was moved by 'Grave yards haphazard from the needs of much to do and little time for thought'.[30] Fellow architect Herbert Baker wanted crosses erected over the graves of Christians; Lutyens did 'not want to put worldly value over our dead'.[31] All victims, he felt, should be honoured alike with simple, uniform headstones. Bitter controversy ensued and Gertrude, turned to for support, wrote at length, endorsing his conception. Bumps, he told Emily, agreed with him. In the end, Lutyens prevailed and Gertrude was asked for planting schemes. War took its toll on everyone. Lutyens saw 'Bumps' in August and was 'rather shocked at her appearance so aged I thought but was fussed at a party – so I let everything go – & promised to go to her on Monday . . . She is worried about her affairs – & says she must give up Munstead – she is so keen about the work in France.'[32] As Lutyens realized, Gertrude's involvement in the war effort was a tremendous moral boost. Only two of seven commissions, Hersin and Warlincourt, are mentioned in her existing notebooks but complete planting plans for five sites are in the Reef Point Collection. Common trees of the field, cottage flowers and wildings were the symbols with which she chose to remember the English dead. One day in December, 1,800 clones of white thrift were lifted from Munstead's sandy soil, packed and dispatched to the offices of the Commission for transit across the Channel.

Gertrude's sense of direction was as tunnelled as the yews that lined the pathway to The Hut. Falkner perceived that she combined 'the energy of the ant, the perseverance of the spider, the unwavering pursuit of an idea, undeterred by a thousand failures and uninfluenced by any outward tendency she did not choose to notice'.[33] Old issues were, with the authority of years and reputation, brought out, dusted and reasserted. She had to protect what she had won, and the public, it seems, never tired of the same message. In 1917 she wrote forty-two items for the press, in 1918 sixty. Resourcefulness could be made to be part of her larger crusade for beauty, unity and rightness. If rhubarb leaves were blanched before cooking, she suggested in *The Garden*, 'it could be the saving of a large quantity of useful greenstuff'.[34] In *Country Life* she enjoined readers to try parsnips, swede, Jerusalem artichokes, salsify or turnip in order to prolong the supply of potatoes for working folk. She herself was growing potatoes in the nursery beds and the main flower border, cleared except for some yuccas and a few other permanents. Artistic sensibility was appeased with a border of marigolds, behind which strong, healthy haulm promised well. An experiment she made with dried plums failed lamentably, she acknowledged. Insufficient attention during a crucial fortnight had resulted in a furious fuzz of mould. But green tomatoes had endless possibilities, and bolted lettuce stems boiled with ginger she could recommend to simulate crystallized sweets. Other foods seemed irreplaceable. 'Very difficult to get meat. No margarine,'[35] her diary regrets that winter. Still being resourceful, she described in one of her writings a wooden rake which had lost a tooth. 'No wonder for the grain of the wood ran diagonally across.'[36] The old countrymen made teeth from blackthorn; having none at hand, she substituted with tough ash. To her there was beauty in a simple, functional implement. It was her careful observation of the rake's construction that allowed her to probe the problem.

In the last year of the war Ned Lutyens and Agnes Jekyll were publicly honoured. Lutyens received a knighthood. Emily wished 'somehow you [he] could have refused it';[37] Lutyens, however, was delighted. So was Agnes. Throughout the war she had worked tirelessly for the Order of St John, and for over ten years she was Chairman of the Visiting Committee of the Borstal Institution for girls at Aylesbury. Now, to her consummate gratification, she became a Dame. Writing to former gardener Frank Young many years later, she handwrote 'Dame of British Empire' below the printed heading on her letter. Gertrude's most recent work was rewarded by the appearance of what amounted to a more detailed version of the second part of her previous book. *Garden Ornament* was an elegantly finished, almost 9-lb folio volume of illustrations to which she wrote notes on each section and a four-page historical preface. Earlier she had decried the 'mass of half useless machine-made articles, for the most part covered with so-called ornament of the most vulgar character'.[38] There was so much to choose from that many would 'easily go astray'.[39] Here was the moneyed man's guide to good taste.

The chief credential, in her estimation, was what she referred to as rightness or relevance. How relevant to the present was a Tudor maze or a gilt birdcage? What about a Japanese garden – a subject she had already broached in her book with Elgood? Notes to a short section on Japanese gardens show a refined appreciation of the subtleties, symbolism and charm of Oriental gardening, where 'imagination inspired by suggestion, answers frequent appeals'.[40] Yet she counselled wariness in appropriating foreign styles. 'Surely it is unwise, when we are already provided with ample means of horticultural expression of our own . . . to attempt any kind of reproduction of these far-eastern pleasure grounds whose whole source of impulse and whose tradition and sentiment differs so greatly from our own.'[41] Elgood's frontispiece of a yew tunnel at Worcestershire's Cleeve Prior is a perfect evocation of the English nineteenth-century Italian garden. Architects receive the accolade for reintroducing formality, especially those who looked back to the Classical ideal. 'We have always to remember that it is to Italy that we have to look for examples of the highest development of ornamental features in connexion with garden design.'[42] But every style, she allowed, had its dangers, and 'Except in rare cases there is no need to keep rigidly to any one style: it is, in fact, almost impossible actually to define a style for whether a garden is called Italian, French,

Dutch or English, each one of these merges into and overlaps the other, for they all have features in common that vary only in detail or treatment.'[43] Overall she paid allegiance to the Arts and Crafts philosophy that good craftsmanship should supersede style.

Shortly before the armistice, Gertrude was receiving preliminary communications from Mrs Nathaniel Davidson of Borlases in Twyford, Berkshire, whose quietly assured, humorous letters are perfect examples of a successful working relationship. 'Yes, dear Miss Jekyll, I quite understand what you mean and *of course* you are right – There is a "boggle" at A ... How exciting it will be when your plan is completed – Thank you so much for your lecture on pergolas which I have read & inwardly digested – Yours affectionately.'[44] It is a pity that Borlases was never realized.

The war ended in November 1918. Soon after, Gertrude was writing of 'indications that the coming year will see a kind of re-birth of gardening'.[45] She had great faith in garden or woodland work for calming the frayed nerves of ex-servicemen. In 'the steady rearing of new beauty ... there is nothing of the nature of a relaxation from other work or duty that fills the mind so wholesomely or happily as gardening ... As his hands harden so his thoughts will sweeten.'[46]

'The War,' Gertrude owned to Mrs King in America, 'brought me an altered life, added to which I have been ill; though, I am thankful to say, now bettering . . .' The cost of labour was 'ruinous', she was seventy-five, 'as good as half blind', with 'very little strength all round'; thankful only to be single, since there was but herself to consider. Ear troubles followed by illness throughout the spring made her uncharacteristically morbid. 'What happens to an old lady does not really matter.' If need be, she would face the end 'quite cheerfully'. More typical was the acknowledgement that she was sublimating her feelings: 'I am afraid this is rather a growl, but as Bacon says, to tell them to a friend "doubleth joys and cutteth griefs in halves." ' [1]

In May she was recuperating for a fortnight with Robert Leslie's daughter, Kate, at Charmouth. Jane Austen had once called its marshy little river valley running down to the beach 'the happiest spot for watching the flow of the tide',[2] and wear on Gertrude's camp stool, necessitating its repair before the close of the trip, suggests that watching, and, of course, assimilating, were pastimes in which she had indulged. Miss Leslie drove a car, which was convenient, and even more important, she was, according to Francis Jekyll, one of the few whose society his aunt could tolerate at any length. Kate had grown up without formal schooling among a clutch of brothers, and all had spent weeks at a time sailing round the coast of Devon and Cornwall in their father's boats. The elder boys left home to become midshipmen, while she moved to Lindfield, exercising her artistic talent, on George Leslie's testimony, with exquisite flower arrangements. Gertrude had known Kate for many years, corresponding with her familiarly as 'My dear Katie'.[3] In 1902 she had planned her Sussex garden and subsequently she assisted with two others to small houses Miss Leslie had built. One of them, Littlecot, was let regularly to Mrs Louis Beauchamp, the mother of Elizabeth von Arnim.

On holiday the pair went shopping and did at least some of the cooking. One day they motored to Bridford where, Gertrude noted frugally, they spent 10d on cake. Another time they treated themselves to lobster. Two days were spent painting names on boats and one afternoon they watched an ancient ceremony, blessing the crops and the sea. The rest was beneficial; in June, Gertrude was sufficiently her old self to visit gardens near her home, an exercise facilitated by the use of Herbert's car. Harriet Mills remembered the garage owner, Mr Champion, being the first in the village to own an automobile, a Rolls in which he transported the 'best people' to and from dinner parties. When Herbert procured a car, it was placed at Gertrude's somewhat unenthusiastic disposal.

Gertrude made no secret of her loyalty to the past. She might devise an ingenious step-barrow by replacing the back legs of a step-ladder with wheeled ones and adding handles, but she was unable to accept modern gadgets and attempts to provide her with a few practical luxuries met stern resistance. The war had revealed technology's Frankenstein aspect, then Rutherford split the atom and physicists warned of the possibility of destroying mankind. Meanwhile Gertrude had selected certain ways, and her commitment to them was complete. As Pearsall Smith explained, 'her plain old, aristocratic face was firmly set against all new fashions and innovations . . . if they were ever forced upon her attention an immense Disapproval would be the expression which would settle on her features.'⁴ Machines and modernity were her hatreds; she accepted neither secretary nor typewriter despite the fact that they might have eased the strain of using her eyes. Only after much persuasion would she install a telephone.

To glimpse Munstead life through the eyes of its youngest member is a privilege given to us by one of Herbert's grandchildren. David McKenna, now, with his brother, Michael, making the transition from preparatory school to Eton, stayed often with his grandparents at weekends. He remembers how the church party from Munstead House would walk back through the garden of Munstead Wood, paying their respects to Aunt Gertrude who no longer joined them in church. Inside her house the boys withdrew to a side-table with a glass of home-made raspberry vinegar topped with water, taking little interest in the adult conversation. Herbert, who read the lesson in church, found his own way home and disappeared until everyone was seated for dinner at a quarter to two. In company he was a perfect host, polite

and attentive; once dinner was over he retired to his study. None
questioned his privilege; McKenna understood what Agnes Jekyll was
to explain: 'Friends indeed have meant much to me and to all of us,
and my life would indeed be very poor without them – perhaps
Herbert only half shares this my passion, and O Beato Solitudine is his
often unanswered ejaculation! But he is very kind and indulgent to my
weakness for human interests!'[5] Agnes was the perfect complement to
her husband.

Gertrude was 'rather extra busy'[6] in September, she wrote to Mrs
Readhead of Great House, Hambledon. It was not until three years
later that Gertrude designed plans for her neighbour, but they had
known one another since the new family moved to a dignified Queen
Anne house in 1911. Mrs Readhead, a great gardener, was presently
building a wall; an undertaking on which Gertrude offered the gardener
careful written instructions: 'Perhaps it would be as well if I came &
saw him about this when he has got the wall begun . . .'[7] After the
war she no longer drove her dog-cart. But provided she was transported, she would make herself available 'the first afternoon that
would suit'.[8] The extra busyness was explained by her entries in *Black's
Gardening Dictionary*, published in 1920, where two of her contributions
were 'Old-Fashioned Flowers' and 'Garden Design on Old-Fashioned
Lines'. Elsewhere she was fighting old battles with familiar pugnacious-
ness. A piece in *The Garden* in January paraphrased the editorial leader,
'False Ideals', which had caused such comment twenty years before.
Outsize modern begonias took first rebuff, and show chrysanthemums
the next. 'Every good quality that the plant might possess',[9] she felt,
had been sacrificed for a single bloom. 'Let anyone take the pot . . .
and see what an ungainly and uninteresting object it is!'[10] Another old
irritant cropped up; could a reader explain, she demanded, why blue
flowers were described as 'amethystine'? It was 'certainly no compliment to a blue flower' and sounded like 'a slip-slop or boggle of
terms'.[11] Had a botanist absent-mindedly mixed amethyst and sap-
phire? If simply ignorant or careless, why was the error not corrected?
Gertrude was not afraid to express an opinion.

A return to carpentry was a good sign of her replenished energy.
Lutyens's work at New Delhi, suspended during the war, had recommenced. Later Gertrude provided plans for herbaceous planting in a
formal pattern to vast horizontal water gardens at the Viceroy's House,
but a model was the first step, for which she supplied some trees. 'Sent

Delhi model trees,'[12] methodical jottings inform, '2 of each three sizes shaped and painted tho the small ones he left with me 32 hours work – paid turner 6/- Received three guineas.'[13] There was also a dining-room corner cupboard, 'going on three weeks',[14] and about twenty landscape commissions commencing during the year. They included several for terraced or semi-detached London houses, one for Sir Lawrence Weaver, and a house near Kew Gardens where Teddy, her eldest brother, had moved from Bedfordshire at the age of eighty-one. The Avenue is a pretty blossom-filled road of late Victorian buildings; number 61, on a corner plot, is detached and larger than most, but it has been divided into flats and of Gertrude's garden no trace remains. Jekylls participated in life as vigorously as they were able until the end. Teddy enjoyed but one season of his new garden before he died.

London was filling with traffic, and Gertrude was giving more thought to the small gardens people needed to retire to. In a *Country Life* article she dwells on the patch not 'really large enough to be called a garden, for it is often nothing but a kind of well, or narrow rectangular space with buildings on every side'.[15] Stone pots of lilies and hostas or permanent plantings of iris sound wholesome enough, but the illustration of a wall terraced with balustraded steps, adorned with Italianate sculpture and a wall fountain by Lady Feodora Gleichen, looks frankly decadent. Lady Feodora, the unmarried daughter of a German aristocrat, was a painter, sculptor and etcher who had achieved royal patronage. Among other works, she had completed a lifesize group with the Queen for Victoria Hospital in Canada, a memorial of King Edward VII at Windsor and a fountain in Hyde Park. But her sculpture was far too grand for a small terraced house. Perhaps Gertrude's mistake lay in choosing to collaborate with an old lady four months from her death.

It was almost thirty years since Barbara Bodichon had died. For the first time in history, women of all classes sat beside men for examinations at British universities, progress in which she had played a significant part. From Girton College, Cambridge, where Gertrude had once helped with interior decorations, Barbara, Lady Stephen, mistress, relative of Miss Bodichon, and Mary Lumsden, a member of council and a governor, had descended upon Munstead Wood in search of garden plans, and it sounds as if Miss Lumsden, a great proponent of gardening for women, was paying for them. Annual college minutes reveal that Gertrude's proposals for the Cloister Court were adopted with modifications, although others for the formal garden were not passed. Over the next two years Gertrude sent tracings of revised plans to 'Miss Swindale, gardener'[16] and in 1924 one for Emily Davies Court. The last one was particularly appropriate, since Miss Davies had been, through Barbara Bodichon, Gertrude's first link with the college.

The project that rounded the year, however, was Lutyens persuading Gertrude to sit to William Nicholson, the man who combined Whistlerian colour harmonies, Japanese prints, reverence for Manet and Velázquez, and a rather old-fashioned love of rich black pigment in an art wholly traditional and utterly his own. At first Gertrude had been horrified by the thought of sitting. For someone deeply insecure about the way she looked, being painted was a brave gesture. Even when she conceded to the idea in general, she did not want to sacrifice daylight working hours, or to sit when she needed to rest, or to allow *Country Life* to reproduce the painting, maintaining, 'the gallery is quite enough'.[17] Nicholson handled the situation brilliantly. From the start he felt it was 'a great event'[18] and she was 'exactly the person'[19] he would enjoy painting. One by one he settled the problems. He would paint her after work, mostly by lamplight, and sitting in the armchair she always used in front of the fire. It 'wasn't an easy job', he admitted later to Agnes, 'because she thought herself unpaintable'.[20] That Gertrude was appeased is evident from her correspondence. Brass screws escaped from an oil lamp Nicholson brought with him and were duly returned with a book about Whistler, on whom their conversation must have touched. 'The letters were so familiar to me that I must have had them before but the 10 o'clock was new and beautiful.'[21]

Lutyens remarked to Emily that he hoped Gertrude's painted image had changed 'from the Bumps that wishes to scold and correct (ME) . . . to the sort engaging a problem or a joke'.[22] Finding 'lovable . . . character'[23] in his sitter, Nicholson had indeed softened her likeness and what he referred to as 'serene charm'[24] became the prominent mood of Gertrude's portrait. Dignity and simplicity make it a wonderful embodiment of Jekyllian ethos; Gertrude's floppy jowls and portly figure offset by the penetrating intelligence just discernible behind tiny spectacles. Hunched slightly forward, her small, well-formed hands with round wrists join lightly, finger-tips pressed together below her breast. Once her fears had been allayed, Gertrude even yielded to *Country Life*: 'Mr Hudson writes so kindly & plaintively about the portrait . . . that I feel obliged to relent.'[25] To wide acclaim it was exhibited at the National Portrait Society's exhibition at the Grafton Gallery, and on Saturday, 29 January 1921, it was published in *Country Life*. Delighted with 'what Ned calls "peonies" of praise',[26] Gertrude professed herself 'glad and proud'[27] to be a 'humble, passive auxiliary'.[28] Writing to Mrs King three years later, she was gratified 'to know that you like to have it [the photograph] but wish it could have represented a more beautiful object – still in spite of the subject, it has some fine qualities as a picture'.[29] To avoid wasting the day, and inspired perhaps by Van Gogh's peasant boots, Nicholson painted the famous Jekyll ex-army boots in which she trudged about her garden. The following year, Lutyens donated the portrait to the Tate, which transferred it in 1947 to the National Portrait Gallery. Lady Emily gave the painting of the boots to the Tate in 1944.

Gertrude began 1921 like its predecessor, with sickness abating in the spring, 'A little ailing . . . but meanwhile carving and gilding and frames for old needlework.'[30] By the summer she was producing articles at a formidable rate, though a letter to Mrs Nellie Allen of New York is guarded about the prospect of a social encounter. Mrs Allen was a member of the Garden Club of America setting up practice as landscape architect, and anxious to visit Munstead Wood. Without prohibiting the visit, Gertrude made a great deal of her by then perfectly restored health. 'I am very slowly recovering from a long illness and am still very weak and my Dr specially warns me against any cause of fatigue – Added to this I am in my 78th year' – since her birthday was in November, it paid to count in time rather than age – '& have very bad & painful sight. So you see you must not expect much of me.'[31] Gertrude was very explicit about the limits her constitution would allow; a talk indoors on Friday after 3.30, when she could rest beforehand, and she could not see more than one visitor in a day. Having set the terms, she declined absolutely to accept a fee for receiving her visitor.

She had striven and it was reassuring to be deferred to, to be made to feel somebody in old age. Regularly she attended meetings of the Hydon National Trust Committee in Godalming, and plant expeditions involved her from time to time. Like rural landscape, rural life continued to disappear, making it all the more imperative to take stock of what remained. She was starting an extensive revision of *Old West Surrey*, drafting plans for National Trust land at Ide Hill near

Sevenoaks, and at Upper Iford House in Dunsfold, Sussex, for Lady
Cynthia Mosley, first wife of the Labour MP Sir Oswald, who later
married Diana Mitford. Then there were meetings to discuss a war
memorial Lutyens had agreed to design in the churchyard at Busbridge.
Local councils are apt to bicker. After the war, moreover, there were
changes in attitude towards the class system of which Gertrude remained blissfully unaware. Nowhere was the undercurrent from those
who refused to kow-tow to the wealthier, more prominent elements
in their society stronger than the local council. She did not always get
her way, and when her opinions on the choice of site and its design
were overruled she resigned from the committee. Some measure of
appeasement seems to have been adopted, since the following summer
found her in charge of laying the foundations for Lutyens's beautiful
cross.

Professor Christopher Tunnard, writing in the late thirties, compared
Gertrude's life with that of her contemporary, Monet. 'Both had an
almost primitive love of the soil, a passion for gathering from Nature
the nourishment to sustain burning convictions and long-cherished
beliefs. Both preferred an existence withdrawn from civilization, surrounded by familiar, daily-renewed contacts with the lesser inanimate
things. Both suffered from failing eyesight, and both achieved greatness
through work and love of the tools and methods they employed.'[32]
The 'fundamental difference' in their achievements, Tunnard believed,
stemmed from the fact that Monet's garden was as great as some of his
paintings, whereas Gertrude's painting was inferior to her planting.
Had her brush equalled in stature her planter's hand, 'the problem of
light and colour which she constantly disregarded might have been
recognized and solved'.[33] The second part of his argument asks to be
questioned. What was the problem which remained unsolved? Ruskin's
exposition of Turner underpinned Gertrude's unstinting quest to understand colour and light, and Ruskin's treatment of light actually antici-
pates the theories of the Impressionists, for whom she retained a
profound respect. Of course Ruskin's once radical views on representa-
tion had lost their following by the time of the Whistler affair, and
between the wars his reputation slumped to its lowest. The very
passion of his concerns led to exaggerations easy to ridicule; he is long-
winded to the point of exhaustion, and to those who saw modern art
as liberation from subject matter, he was anathema. Tunnard believed
that Gertrude was 'the most outstanding planter since the eighteenth

century',[34] and calls her 'the first horticultural Impressionist',[35] which rather contradicts his thesis about light and colour, but his greatest failure is not to appreciate the three-dimensional aspect of her design in the landscape.

The following year, 1922, was the *annus mirabilis* of modernism – the year of Joyce's *Ulysses* and Eliot's *The Waste Land*. If Gertrude rejected the significant manifestations of the post-war era, few in their late seventies are able to enjoy contemporary literature, music and sculpture. To a friend who endeavoured to interest her with a photograph of a modern masterpiece, she owned, 'It says nothing to me except that it is ugly and bizarre.'[36] Generously, she tries to do the artist justice; 'I feel that he believes in it himself & so far has one's respect . . . No wonder it is much visited & much talked of – it would be, being very large & very odd – but this is nothing to prove any merit . . . I so much dislike things that strike me as ugly, that if I was in London and had a shilling to spare (which I neither am nor have) I should not go to see it.'[37] There was a flurry in the family when Barbara McLaren took as her second husband a man with an outstanding war record; Bernard, later First Baron Freyberg, was thirty-three, had served in the Dardanelles and had received a Victoria Cross for bravery. Sir James Barrie, who claimed that the conception of Peter Pan took place while he was staying at Munstead House, was best man. For Gertrude there was horticultural recognition in the shape of a Veitch Memorial Gold Medal.

Despite her poor eyesight, Francis Jekyll tells, his aunt read fast, widely and attentively, up to 100 books a year until she died; modern literature, fiction, travel and biography besides old favourites such as Dickens and Austen. On occasion she would contact an author to compliment or exchange information. In January, for instance, researching *Old English Country Life*, she wrote to C. H. B. Quennell, joint author with his wife of *Life in the Old Stone Age*, a long, appreciative letter, bringing up themes that especially interested her, adding information, and even – a mark of ultimate respect – inviting the authors to see her garden in the fullness of summer. Quennell was an architect and member of the RIBA Council, author of books such as *Norwich Cathedral* and *Modern Suburban Houses*. After marrying Marjorie, a painter and curator in the Geffrye Museum, he joined forces with her to produce an invaluable series of social history. 'You must be a happy couple – working together like that,' Gertrude wrote, with something between congratulation and envy. 'I take it that the admirable figure drawings are Mrs Quennell's.'[38]

That year she took no holiday. Tree-cutting at Christ's Hospital near Horsham and inspecting gardens at places like Major Chichester's Enton Hall were the furthest she strayed from home. Four times in all Gertrude visited Enton in Witley, twice that year and twice the following one, when beds for azaleas were being dug to her plans. Concentration on small gardens meant that clients who approached her were no longer exclusively rich. Admittedly Captain Greenhill of Fishers in Sussex felt 'rather as if I had asked Sir Joshua Reynolds to help me paint my stable doors!!'[39] But every commission was a challenge; Fishers was a far cry from her traditional labour-intensive commissions, yet all were taken on in a spirit of learning. Lady Peel felt that it had been 'an honour'[40] that Gertrude supplied plans for her parents, but Gertrude does not appear to have turned down offers for work. Ten years before, Greenhill had built a farmhouse in the old Sussex style, in the middle of a grass field. Being a farmer and its sole gardener, he wanted surroundings with low maintenance. Work could commence in the winter when his cattle were all under cover. Shelter being the first imperative, Gertrude planted great avenues of Austrian pine interplanted with larch, and inside these she planned shrubberies around the house.

War had segregated the generations. While the young set Charlestoned with frenetic energy, looking to the future for hope, worth and beauty, the elders, numbed by their dead, sought tranquillity from life's impossible battles. Still the memorials rose. Winchester College memorial garden is one of thirteen commissions Gertrude worked on in 1923, when two tracings were sent to the college for a twenty-guinea fee and two more followed. The plans show four flowery borders in patriotic pink, white and blue; vinca, plumbago, *Iris stylosa*, nepeta, white thrift, white roses and bergenia in a south-facing bed, in front of which four cruciform paths meet centrally at a hexagonally-based plinth. The picture is seen through a beautiful wrought-iron gate in Herbert Baker's simple square walls. At Munstead Wood, the summer brought an illustrious trio from the musical sphere who had moved to Woking: Sir Henry and Lady Wood, he the conductor who gave his name to the Promenade concerts, and Dame Ethel Smyth, composer, writer and suffragette, who conducted her own song, *March of the Women*, from Holloway Prison with a toothbrush after being imprisoned for throwing stones at a cabinet minister's window. In September, Gertrude took a three-day break at a hotel in her favourite part of the coast, Hayling Island, in Chichester harbour. The following month she endured a wet week in a friend's cottage near Bognor.

Lutyens had designed his dream house, a doll's house for Queen Mary, perfect, exquisite and complete with furnishings: linen, glass, china, books, pictures, curtains, chandeliers, motor cars, and a delightful array of domestic miniatures. Various celebrities participated, and Gertrude created a model garden, an art in constructional ingenuity since 'not only flowers and plants on walls and in borders, but also tall trees over two feet high, iron gates and sundry architectural features'[41] had to be contained in a drawer that measured eleven inches deep, she wrote in her contribution to a book about the endeavour. A green velvet lawn was accompanied by a minute mowing machine, beds were planted in blue and purple iris with a standard rose at each angle and a filling of summer flowers, edged in special, factory-made box hedging. Italian terracotta pots held agapanthus, square wooden tubs, hydrangeas and rhododendrons. Tree trunks were fashioned from solid metal, a branching effect being obtained by copying real twigs of dwarf growth from Dartmoor, with every leaf bent to shape by hand. Finishing touches comprised snails, a thrush's nest, birds and butterflies.

Gertrude's eightieth year was celebrated, though not without hesitation on her part, by the installation of a radio. Someone who had spent sixty years sustaining the vitality of her first twenty could not be expected to rethink her way into a twentieth century obsessed with innovation. But during the long winter evenings she found it a blessing.

CHAPTER TWENTY-EIGHT

1924–7

One of the pains of growing old is the death of friends. Kate Leslie, who managed with tact and gentleness not to put Gertrude on her guard, and James Britten, the temperamental botanist, were next to go. Both had been single, capable and acute, both had in their ways embraced life. Meanwhile Gertrude's writing and gardening had accustomed her to the solitary organization of the day's hours, routine and accomplishment, the soothing twin observances of Munstead Wood with which no visitor was allowed to interfere. Sunday was spent in bed. Otherwise, from 8 a.m. when Florence Hayter summoned her mistress until bed-time at eleven, the day was broken into manageable portions, study and gardening alternating with meals, an afternoon nap, newspapers, and after-dinner relaxation – a comfortable read or 'listen-in'.[1] Gardens continued to be planned and articles to be written. The need to say what she had to say would not die, nor even fade.

Mothering Sunday was the subject of her first writing to reach the public in 1924. Gertrude was fascinated by old customs with their traditional, social and religious connotations. In Hampshire's Chilbolton, she informed readers of the Busbridge parish magazine, there were ancient moulds, heart-shaped and circular, still in use for preparing special Mothering Sunday cakes. During the year she wrote one or two articles for *Country Life* and a long preface to a book by George E. Tilney called *Colour Planning of the Garden*. Most of her output, however, was channelled into *Garden Illustrated*, where her old friend Herbert Cowley presided. A positive relationship with one's editor was essential for someone with strong objections to having her prose altered, and Cowley's riposte, 'I would rather have clipped the wings of an archangel',[2] was a worthy credential. He was not free from reprimand, his knuckles, he owned, were 'rapped on occasion, but for all that I worshipped her'.[3] It was Cowley who took the grandmotherly photograph of Gertrude with a walking stick, in her eightieth year.

Potatoes were once more restricted to kitchen gardens, and the great hardy border flickered and glowed before bursting into colourful seasonal flames. On 8 April she found time to fumigate and send to the Victoria and Albert Museum her last offering, a felt hat bought in Ravenna around 1875, 'as ordinary wear of the labouring class. It has been badly moth-eaten while in my careless possession but has been in the oven and is now free.'[4] Shell pictures varied winter evenings; a craft she taught Herbert's butler, Richard Howes, a robust Yorkshire-man blessed with a keen humour whose death in 1950 was marked with a *Times* obituary. In it Lady Freyberg wrote: 'He had a deep regard for my aunt, Miss Gertrude Jekyll, who helped him to develop his natural gift for flower decoration and for handcrafts, and the charming pictures made of sea shells, which at first he used to copy faithfully, from her own.'[5] The one that occupied Gertrude on this occasion was a floral conception dominated by 'ormers' – the bivalve with mother-of-pearl insides that is sometimes used as an ash-tray. Her arrangement was in pink, coral, silver and pale brown, and the picture, now at the Godalming Museum, is backed with oak from seats surplus to Bramley church after its enlargement in 1848. Gertrude wrote these details on the back of the picture because the power of association added an extra dimension. According to her nephew, she had an outlet in North America for selling them.

Country Life had suggested a revision of *Old West Surrey* to meet a wider audience; her most absorbing project on hand was undoubtedly adapting the script to what became *Old English Household Life*. The new book shares with its predecessor a concern with the disappearing craftsman and his simple, functional, often beautiful products, but it is quite different in its emphasis, skipping through centuries from Tudor times and across the broad face of England, incorporating quantities of material from writers like Cobbett, Gilbert White, and J. B. Pyne, author of the three volume *Microcosm*. *Old English Household Life* is less personal and therefore less opinionated than its predecessor; neverthe-less, Gertrude comes through fairly strongly. She loved her country. 'Is there any North European land that can show the traveller so much charm and beauty on country roads as our dear England, or any such diversity of beauty?'[6] But she could not accept clattering machines in hitherto quiet fields or motor cars and petrol stations that made the countryside 'offensive and unsightly'.[7] How seldom, she asks, rejecting the modern industrial world in a grand wholesale manner, 'except in the wilder south-west, does one now see a ridden horse?'[8] Pessimistically, she thought there was hardly any exception to the trend; everything that had been acceptable if not 'actually beautiful'[9] was being rendered ugly. In lamenting the loss of 'charming friendliness'[10] that belonged to people centred in their homes, she was applauding parochialism at a time when 'being content with the place to which it had pleased God to call you' had gone for good in Britain.

Gertrude's England was full-blooded and John Bullish. The Fitzhardinges of Berkeley Castle were delighted that she 'knew how to feel a fat beast'.[11] There was croquet, beer, and, naturally, the thrills of the chase. As a child she had had a passion for horses. When she was a young woman she had hunted throughout the county, and February 1925 brought an occasion so memorable that she promptly recorded it – a foxhunt that began and ended a quarter mile from Busbridge parish church. 'Ever since last September we had known that a fox had made a home in a strong growth of an American undershrub named Gaultheria shallon.'[12] The detail is unmistakable. 'Perhaps in all our district there is no other close mass of vegetation that offers such snug and safe harbourage to a wild animal.'[13] The villain was often seen or otherwise accounted for; rabbits and pheasants disappeared, holes were scratched in the lawn, and large ones excavated in the vegetable garden where kitchen refuse had been buried. Duly summoned, the Chiddingfold hounds arrived to pursue the prey. With consideration for lawn and garden ground, they entered Munstead Wood on foot, Gertrude guided them to the thicket, and the fox bolted. Its fate was sealed: hemmed in by gardeners and horses, the villain fell almost immediately to the jaws of the hounds.

Gertrude did not, she once explained dryly to Amy Barnes-Brand, go to tea parties, which gave her more time than other people. The moot point was whether she ever wanted to socialize more than she did. For if she badly wanted to do something, little would stop her. Tuned, as ever, to the natural world, she scratched on a gardeners' calendar on 10 April 1925, 'Cuckoo at 4.45 am.'[14] Nor was she completely averse to tea parties. A month later she posted a memorandum to Viscountess Wolseley to say that the lady gardeners were expected – for tea! Garden design commissions for the year numbered about fifteen, no small achievement for an eighty-two-year-old. If some were relatively small, one was in the USA, and another, Gledstone Hall in Yorkshire, was as large a project as any she had accomplished in her younger days.

She was engaged in extensive correspondence with a number of clients. Either they had read her books – 'One of the chief joys of winter is that we can read & reread your books in the evenings – I know them almost by heart!'[15] – or they had been enchanted by Munstead Wood: 'I often think of you & your house & garden with such joy.'[16] Requests for her presence were continually made and refused: 'I am old now & never leave home though I am still working at my desk & bench . . . & have done this for the last few years with satisfaction to my clients . . . I have now four plans going on in this way, one near New York [at Greenwich, Connecticut], another in France [the Jardin des Sports at Versailles], and two nearer home.'[17] Suggestions have been made that Gertrude was less good, in old age, at adapting to the needs of a site, that at Gledstone, for instance, she underestimated the severity of the Yorkshire climate.[18] There is one occasion on which her mathematics erred: 'I think you have miscalculated the measurements a little,'[19] wrote Mr Henry Barratt of Widford in Haslemere. At the same time she was often complimented for being able to evaluate a situation so astutely from the information she was sent: 'You are quite right,'[20] agreed Mrs McCreery from Stowell Hill in Templecombe, Somerset, 'the whole place is overplanted at present . . . a garden made from a field makes one long for shade & shelter.'[21]

At the age of seventy-one Edward Hudson had become engaged to Ellen Woolrich, an editor of *Homes and Gardens*. It was through his fiancée that Mr and Mrs Stanley Resor of New York had the pleasure of meeting Gertrude. 'Mr Resor and I consider our afternoon with you the happiest time that we experienced in the seven weeks we were abroad.'[22] They must also have liked what they saw at Munstead House and Munstead Wood, because on returning to America they asked her to design a garden for a new summer place, Cotswold Cottage, in Greenwich, Connecticut. Unlike the plan for the Groesbecks in Ohio, it was mostly wild. 'No grass' being specified, Gertrude concentrated on linking the garden and its surroundings with spring-blooming shrubs and ground cover, vinca, cotoneaster and trailing Virginia creeper. Explanatory letters made their way to the USA: 'I have put China roses (the Common Pink or Monthly Rose) in front of windows. It is delightful to see these pretty things in one's foreground when looking out.'[23]

All Gertrude's American gardens have disappeared but the third and last, much smaller than the others and of cottage garden heritage, has been restored. The Old Glebe House in Woodbury, Connecticut, was a 'lovely old house'[24] dating in parts back to 1690. Towards the end of the nineteenth century three priests of the episcopal diocese bought it for the bishop of the state, and in 1925 it was opened to the public complete with a society to promote its interests. Miss Annie Burr Jennings, founding member of the Seabury Society, was a gardener and a do-gooder of the highest recommendations. She had made the Munstead Wood tour, 'that delightful afternoon and tea with you'.[25] The outcome was an 'old-fashioned'[26] garden at Glebe House, with deep borders of hollyhock drifting into delphiniums, columbine, lavender and iris.

At Gledstone the client was Mr Amos Nelson, later Sir Amos, grown rich on the Skipton and Nelson cotton mills. His 'little palace'[27] was set in the dip of a spur of Yorkshire Moors, approached through 'magnificent'[28] gates by a long drive (still there) laid out by Gertrude. The lines of the building were carried forward into the garden, with parterres below the principal rooms, a long central sunk tank flanked by grass walks, and herbaceous borders taking their cues from loggias and casement windows. The entire unit is highly architectural, Lutyens at his boldest and most inspired. But a Lutyens home was considered almost incomplete without its Jekyll garden. Gledstone entailed twenty-four different planting plans and was, according to *Country Life*, equal to any of the collaborations. Hussey says, 'It is the conception of the English country house, as an art form, raised to its highest pitch, and thus ministering to the spirit rather than to the body.'[29]

The secret of success lay in Lutyens's masterminding. Samples of house wall and columns, soil from various depths and a roll of thick white tracing paper were sent to Munstead Wood on his instructions. Short of actually visiting, no trouble was spared in acquainting Gertrude with the site. With Herbert Thomas at Lutyens's office maintaining contacts and Sir Amos's employee, Mr Bond, endowed with a first class certificate from the Royal Horticultural Society, efficiency prevailed throughout. Merging the formal garden into agricultural and wooded landscape was of first importance. The carriage approach was to have been through an orchard of long grass and top fruit, but the orchard never materialized. Yet Gledstone was considered comparable to Hestercombe. Narrow rectangular tanks or rills extending from the front of his houses had long been a Lutyens feature, and as at Marsh Court, Gertrude's planting softened the fine sunken garden with groups of white, pale yellow, crimson, pink and scarlet water lilies, moving from the house in this sequence. The only hitch seems to have been getting Gertrude's pay cheque past Mr Bond. 'Nothing yet from Sir Amos Nelson but the near prospect of £105 warms the cockles of the depleted exchequer!'[30]

Another current job was at Combend Manor, in sublimely undulating countryside outside Gloucester. The garden lies on sloping land south and east of an enlarged farmhouse, where formal areas give way to a series of ponds and an arboretum with a fabulous opening view of Elkstone Valley. The ground was very poor and Asa Lingard, engrossed with shooting parties, communicated through his architect, Sidney Barnsley. Of six plans, not all were realized. Gertrude's proposal for a pergola was turned down and her plans for a nut walk and curved paths above the largest pond were not carried out. Close to the pond she was 'greatly in favour of keeping the planting rather quiet',[31] she wrote in true Jekyllian spirit, 'with mostly plants and shrubs of beautiful foliage, avoiding anything like the common mixture of Lilac laburnum Ribes. This plan would make the planting interesting at every point & would give the place the feeling of refined wild gardening.'[32] Herbaceous borders extending north and south along a grey stone wall with a pretty central dovecot arch were restored in the early 1980s. The colour scheme is similar to that of her own main hardy flower border, though, surprisingly enough, roughly half the plants were used as annuals – antirrhinums of course, African and French marigolds, hollyhocks and dahlias.

It is not obvious how Lingard heard of Gertrude, but it was reading two of her 'beautiful'[33] books that prompted Lady Madge Llewelyn of The Court, St Fagan's, to approach her prior to laying out as a pleasure ground a small portion of field adjoining her front lawn. Eight children between four and sixteen precluded her, she warned, from sparing the time a garden demanded. She was sorry Gertrude could not see the place. But to Gertrude's offer to play hostess, Lady Llewelyn answered huffily, 'I too am a very busy woman ... so the chances are somewhat remote.'[34] Shortage of time did not prevent her writing, and conciseness was not a strong point. An enormous correspondence from The Court accumulated, at least twenty-one letters from the client in addition to long, detailed instructions and almost as many letters from Mr Hibbert, her stolid gardener: 'I am afraid Hibbert in his letters to you does not convey exactly what it is we

want to know.'³⁵ Hibbert found Gertrude's plans extremely difficult
to decipher and her Ladyship, while anxious to involve her – 'after all I
should not have consulted you if I were not in such great doubt &
difficulty as to what was the best plan'³⁶ – often failed to accept her
advice. Throughout more than two years Gertrude remained courteous,
helpful and adamant.

The first problem was a tennis court she naturally hoped to tuck
away somewhere inconspicuous. 'The nets and poles and white mark-
ings necessary for the game are so unsightly that the designer must
insist on their being kept out of sight.'³⁷ Lady Llewelyn felt the
position she suggested was too public and overhung by leaf-falling
trees. Even when the site had been decided upon, there was endless
trouble excavating, getting the ground level around the courts and
making steps into them. 'How would you protect children from
falling over low wall onto steps below?'³⁸ Every job, large or small,
was put to arbitration. Her Ladyship wanted to pave round a chestnut
tree. Gertrude explained the disadvantages: '. . . the pollen bloom that
falls first followed by the buzzies & then the leaves, are swept up?'³⁹
All the time she was guiding, coercing, cajoling. 'In general I do not
care for variegated leaved shrubs,' 'I have beautiful Peonies . . . easily
better planted than could be got elsewhere.'⁴⁰ But two steps forward
were followed by one back. Were 100 stachys marked on the plans for
one or four rose beds, Hibbert wanted to know? Her Ladyship
preferred the newer sort of roses. The heart of the chestnut tree was
now going rotten. What did the oracle suggest? Once again, Lady
Llewelyn had her own preferences: '. . . personally, I find white rhododendron somewhat dull.'⁴¹ Gradually Gertrude made headway, and
the last two months of 1926 saw peonies, asters and other plants
arriving in quantities from Munstead Wood. But the last letter from St
Fagan's requested an alternative to laurels, 'as her Ladyship does not
like common laurels at all'.⁴²

Compared with The Court, the Wells's job at Ickwell House in
Biggleswade, 'a little old house . . . gentle & dignified'⁴³ progressed
smoothly. Nevertheless, the battle of attrition over its sequoias was a
prime example of Gertrude's powers of persuasion. Seeing two welling-
tonias out of scale and character with the ground, Gertrude naturally
wanted them removed. The reaction was horrified: 'They are enormous
things and probably quite misplaced but we have got to like them . . .
one is a great big thing we couldn't cut down!'⁴⁴ Relentlessly Gertrude

returned to the case: 'you must forgive me . . . but I should not feel that I was a faithful garden adviser unless I did so . . . I feel that it is just these trees that give the garden the confined look [May Wells's sister had complained of its feeling cramped]. Sir Edwin Lutyens was here a few days ago & saw the plan. I daresay you know his fame as a garden designer as well as architect. He said at once that those two trees spoil all hope of good garden effect.'[45] This, one feels, was a turning point; Mrs Wells consulted her husband. On 22 August 1926, after three uncomfortable weeks, she accepted Gertrude's advice. A month later she wrote, 'The trees are down & the garden looks much brighter.'[46]

It had been an appropriate year for Mrs King's dedication in *Chronicles of the Garden* to Miss Jekyll, 'who, more than any other has made the planting of gardens in the English-speaking countries one of the Fine Arts'. Thanking her for a gift of some trilliums, Gertrude wrote graciously, 'though I shall be 83 towards the end of this month, I still hope for a year or two more of life for the enjoyment of your dear gift and all the other beautiful growing things. My love & thanks go out to you with both hands, Yrs affec.'[47]

The Jekyll family expected to make claims on each other's expertise. Reginald McKenna had had an estimable career. As First Lord of the Admiralty he expanded the fleet just before the First World War, a move opposed by Lloyd George and Winston Churchill but one which paid dividends. At the height of the war, as Chancellor of the Exchequer, he levied what he is best remembered for, McKenna's surtax of 40 per cent. After the war he left politics and became Chairman of Midland Bank. In July 1926 Gertrude designed some rose beds and planting round a sunken garden at Mells Park, his fourteen-bedroomed Lutyens manor in Somerset. Herbert had designed the extension for his daughter and family; Pamela, the Jekyll, was gardener of her family.

In this year Gertrude lost her friend, Helen Allingham. Like Gertrude, she had been a disciple of Ruskin and an indefatigable campaigner for his ideals. Gertrude finished painting a sign-board for the White Horse Inn at Hascombe, which local residents remember hanging there in their youth, and began the first of ten articles in *The Garden*. 'The Joy of making a New Garden' was publicized as 'a series of the greatest assistance to the ever-increasing band of suburban gardeners'.[48] Gertrude was an iconoclast turned grumpy conservative, but with all her resistance to the mechanical ethos of the twenties, she understood the needs of the average *Garden* reader. Each article took up a definite case, real or imaginary – the old-world patch round a thatched cottage, a garden on the Hampshire coast, a plot in mid-Sussex with a partly disabled owner. The houses illustrated were modest, their gardens roughly fifty feet wide and three times as long.

CHAPTER TWENTY-NINE

1926–9

How many gardeners were employed at Munstead Wood? Unsubstantiated guesses begin with a careful 'seven'[1] rising through 'about a dozen'[2] and 'seventeen'[3] to 'twenty men'.[4] When Thomas Frank Young became an under-gardener there in 1926, Zumbach was supervising four. It is possible there had been a larger, pre-war workforce, yet Young's memories, twice collected, contain no reference to such an earlier team. Lutyens wrote in retrospect of 'the eleven essential gardeners',[5] but extra staff were on occasion borrowed from Munstead House and he may have added them to the count. This would at least tally with Lord Freyberg's surmise, 'It is unlikely that these numbers were exceeded even before the First World War.'[6] The exaggerations, however, bear interesting scrutiny. It is hard to escape the inference that hordes of gardeners have been invented in an attempt to denigrate Gertrude's work. She was capable of achieving what she did only because she had so much help.

Young was eighteen when he moved in to replace 'Stacey', who left after a row with Zumbach. Like Harriet Mills and William Young – though not related to the latter – he was born in Brighton Road and educated at the Busbridge village school. He was a bookish boy who wanted to be an engineer, but suitable education being denied him, he returned to the school for evening classes in 'gardening science'[7] when he was eighteen. Before joining Gertrude's staff he had worked for a year and a half at Munstead House. At Munstead Wood he joined Arthur Berry from Hascombe in the pleasure gardens; Bill Boxall and Freddie Hawkes, another Brighton Road recruit, grew vegetables, and Jarot, the groom, looked after the pony which performed as grass-cutter and method of transport. Only he and Zumbach could read and write. Gardening hours were maintained as rigorously as Gertrude's own. At 10 a.m. Zumbach paid his respects at the house to receive instructions: routine work, hoeing or trimming, was arranged directly with his men, but tasks such as mixing pot-pourri entailed singling out one or two of them to assist Gertrude. After lunch she generally appeared in person, even as an old lady, to take stock of events. Young reckoned that Zumbach was paid £4 a week, the under-gardeners 25 shillings (£1.25) rising to 35s (£1.75) for a working day that began at 7 a.m. and finished at 5 p.m., with a Christmas bonus of five shillings and a warm pullover.

Apart from the youngest, gardeners referred to one another by surname, and house and garden staff, among themselves, called Gertrude 'Gertie Jekyll'. Despotism tends to move down the ranks, and Zumbach, remembered as stocky, dark, taciturn and bow-legged, was doubtless as autocratic with his men as Gertrude was with him. To David McKenna he was 'formidable', and not as nice as the gardener at Munstead House – 'Ern' Shurlock, who allowed him to sit on the grass-cutting pony. But arthritic Zumbach was replaced by Arthur Gibbins the year after Young arrived, and Hawkes and Boxall, dying before Gertrude, were succeeded by Arthur's son, William Berry, and an old man from Busbridge called Bailey. Reference to 'my drunken gardener',[8] 'What a relief it must be to you to have got rid of . . . a man like that',[9] suggest that incidents sometimes required sensitive handling, but Gertrude had mellowed and Young spoke with affection of an employer with whom they worked as a team and knew where they stood. Generally, he reckoned, she was fair, and when they were ill she was solicitous. Zumbach and his wife had been receiving a yearly annuity towards retirement since his first employer, Jacques Blumenthal, died. When Zumbach retired, Gertrude found the ageing couple a boarding house on the coast. On Alfred's death, Mrs Zumbach lived with her daughter, Molly, a respected and capable head teacher at Seale School, near Farnham.

Although she paid lip service to propriety, it did not stop Gertrude from scaling ladders. To her gardeners' amusement, she would climb up in voluminous clothes; the wind blew them out and the gardener holding the ladder dutifully turned his back to her. Loyalties and traditions developed. As the longest-serving gardener, Hawkes was sent to Munstead House on Sir Herbert's birthday, 22 November, clutching a bunch of violets, 'with the good wishes of the gardeners at the "Wood"'.[10] He was received by Sir Herbert, with a glass of brandy that Gertrude reckoned did the old man good. Their employer's sense of humour was definitely appreciated. Young remembered Gertrude appearing in the orchard one afternoon as they were going home. They were allowed fallen fruit but none was on the ground, so she suggested, while she turned away, that they shook an apple tree. Frank shook and nothing happened, whereupon Gertrude rocked it hard and walked off saying, 'Make the most of it, I shan't shake so hard next time.'[11]

It was during the autumn of 1926 that Amy Barnes-Brand of Woodhouse Copse, Holmbury St Mary, began to develop under Gertrude's direction the grounds of her thatch-roofed house designed by Oliver Hill with a lake and streams. So anxious was she to learn, so naturally swift to compliment: 'It is awful to know so little'[12] ... 'I read hard all the time to try & learn. I was too shy to tell you all your books have meant to me, & how wonderful it was to meet you, & to be going to have a tiny garden designed by you.'[13] Amy, with her professional woman's confidence, knew just how her new teacher should be treated. It was partly her recognition of Gertrude's expertise and partly her own striving for perfection that made her such a rewarding pupil. The success of the relationship also lay in mutual recognition that each party had a rich life of her own. Amy Brand did not often mention her professional engagements, but she had been rehearsing Shaw's *Back to Methuselah*, a revival at the Court Theatre which 'unfortunately . . . kept me from the garden'.[14]

Gertrude's initial plan was four guineas, and 'If you have no reserve of plants & would like me to supply them or partly, I can do it a good deal to your advantage as to price and strength compared with the usual resources!'[15] Several years later, she was offering 330 London pride for 14 shillings, 'which . . . is a fraction less than a half penny a plant'.[16] Endless directions accompanied plans and plants for Mrs Brand; invoices and money were exchanged and pieces of tarragon sent from Munstead Wood '(for love) for you to pot & keep in a kitchen window for the winter'.[17] 'Please do not hesitate about asking for advice or help.'[18] Road carriage was better than rail transport: 'I know the expense of the van would be a good lot but I am careful of my clients' interests in these matters & strongly urge it . . . The rosemarys are such beautiful bushes and to send them by carrier they would have to be crushed into several packages.'[19] There followed a plan for the driver to find the way. If correspondence between the two women builds a picture of Amy as being as winsome as she appears in her theatrical photograph, the image was dispelled by Joe Mitchenson, who met her in 1945–6 when he was 'Bob Chesney' in *Charley's Aunt* at the Grand Theatre in Croydon and she was an arthritic fifty-five. His memory is of 'A very tough lady. Not kind about the performance which was being played contemporary for the first time.' [20] With Gertrude, however, she had a touching relationship.

About six direct miles separate Munstead Wood from Woodhouse Copse, in its lush valley created by a tributary of the Tillingbourne. Amy Brand was a special customer, and invitations to Munstead Wood to see the azaleas were extended to 'any afternoon', [21] 'and I hope you will come again whenever you should be inclined and bring any friends'. [22] Gertrude does not seem to have been to Woodhouse Copse but she was totally involved in the project, for which she continued to send plans until the spring of 1929. One of forty instructive letters comments on some sort of upheaval that occurred in the Brand family during the second year of the garden's reshaping; for a while it looked as if Amy would have to leave her home and Gertrude was quick to commiserate. She even offered to alert a neighbour who might be interested in buying it. But fortune changed, an event celebrated by Mrs Brand with a rough drawing for a peony and iris border. The sketch was inadequate, Gertrude wrote: 'I know you said it was not to scale but it is so very vague that it is impossible to work to, and there is no compass work to show the aspect. Could you . . . give me a little more light on it all . . . If I have plenty of measures [and] figures I can put it into scale.' [23] Diplomacy prevailed; the next plan was 'capital', [24] and instructions continued to flow in. Raw manure should not actually touch the roots of plants, 'the best thing for a windbreak in the boggy soil next to the Cypress . . . would be Bambusa Metake . . .' [25] 'Please always ask questions.' [26]

The best report of Gertrude's progress in her eighty-fourth, amazingly hard-working year is her correspondence with Amy Brand; 'my . . . troubles are only what I must expect at my now great age and my troublesome sight. I do not actually see as I write, only a hazy grey line, but I think the letters carefully and hope it is legible. My doctor orders me perfect quiet, a difficult thing to one who is still mixed up in so many interests. I cannot now do whole garden plans though I am glad to do flower borders.' [27] The effort of using her eyes may have been considerable, though the letter itself, and the neat, detailed plans she was still able to produce, suggest that she was able to see better than she claimed. The 'perfect quiet' ordered by her doctor was what she needed to devote every ounce of her strength to working. The day she wrote to Mrs Brand, on 27 August 1927, a 1,750-word article based on her early reminiscences appeared in *Gardening Illustrated*. It had been read in London before the Garden Club.

Among other rewards the revised edition of *Garden Ornament* appeared, co-authored with the young architectural historian Christopher Hussey. He was only nineteen, but fast revealing the qualities which were to make him editor of *Country Life* and author, among several classic publications, of an authoritative biography of Edwin Lutyens. Perhaps Hussey's youthful vision inspired Gertrude to reassess some of her ideas about ornament; at any rate, the new introduction maintains a new slant. 'Sympathetic modern design, imaginative, of good workmanship and making skilful use of local materials, is in every case better than the reproduction of an ancient example, how admirable soever.'[28]

The newest garden ornament at Munstead Wood was celebrated in a different article. Gertrude was slightly apologetic about the yew cat, since her garden, she owned, was unsuited for topiary. Nor had it been intended. 'But some Yews at the end of a clump of shrubs grew into a form that suggested some kind of bold sculptural treatment',[29] and naturally enough, a cat developed. It grew in the shrubbery by the hidden garden and Frank Young clipped the face while standing on a plank balanced between wheeled steps while Gertrude supervised.

In her eighty-fourth year she was invited to be the president of the newly founded Garden Club with its headquarters in Mayfair. Travelling to London was out of the question, but she must have been flattered. Avray Tipping had given a lecture to its members on her life and work.

All Gertrude's senses were finely tuned. She once told her nephew she could identify a tree from the sound of the wind in its foliage, and since the days when the smell of dandelions in Berkeley Square first made a heady impact upon her, the scent of leaves and flowers had been almost a life study. She was always eager to extend primary experience, and must have been alerted by something Dr Frank Anthony Hampton had written about natural perfumes before corresponding with him. Initial contact concerned a horse smell in tobacco plants during the daytime, theories on the cause of opening and closing in flowers, and a lemon scent lurking behind the resinous smell of *Fraxinella* (ash). Hampton was a physician who wrote gardening books under the name of 'Jason Hill', and his letters, continuing over eighteen months, suggest that he was much in tune with Gertrude's inquiring spirit. In reply he asked whether she had noticed a pleasant, coconut smell in rue before the typical cat smell, or that *Thymus azoricus* suggested tangerines?

Gertrude wrote to Dr Hampton at least six times the following year; long letters, 'full of interest', 'very valuable',[30] and perfectly legible, enclosing numerous materials under discussion. Though it bothered him to be the reason for so much labour, Hampton found time amid a busy domestic and professional life – the birth of his third child and a heavy patient load – to reply with articles, specimens of essential oil, results of his distillations and replies to numerous esoteric inquiries. Did the scent of *Calycanthus floridus* contain a suggestion of old wine bottles or of Russian leather? Real Russian leather was unprocurable because it had been made in monasteries disbanded during the revolution. Did carnations lose their scent when growing by the sea? It was interesting, he recognized, that she could detect London in the north-easterly wind at Godalming. Just after Christmas he was thanking her for crab apple jelly and pecan nuts, hitherto untasted; sending in return some nigella seeds, used in Albania for scattering on cakes and biscuits as the British use poppy seeds.

For one who shared vicariously in the garden at Woodhouse Copse, accounts from Amy Brand were a permanent source of pleasure. 'The drive really looks quite thrilling, at any rate to me as I planted it all myself . . . I am growing plants from seeds when I can.'[31] Deciding on London pride, a Jekyll favourite, for edging to her kitchen garden, she ordered 330 plants from Munstead Wood. After Holmbury St Mary with its waters, flowery borders and tall trees, the garden round Margaret Stuart Illitch's smallholding in Belgrade sounds a very different world. Snow prevented measuring the ground and Mrs Illitch doubted whether she could find a local surveyor to satisfy Gertrude's specifications. There was a glorious view from a bow window, but the whole place was fenced with nine rows of barbed wire, the black soil was so sticky it clammed to their feet, and after June the sun was scorching. Despite obvious disadvantages, Mrs Illitch wrote optimistically, 'No one in Servia appears to have a pretty garden & I want mine to be an inspiration.'[32] Provision was to be made for a cow house, a sty for two pigs, a potting shed, garage, stable and summerhouse, most of which the family expected to erect themselves, and a clover lawn would provide fowl with mowings. Gertrude dismissed a demand for crazy paving since the client herself felt the stones might sink in the mud, and forwarded a detailed plan.

The youthful ebullience Gertrude had begun to channel into industriousness during adolescence had become a deeply inculcated way of life. Life and work were one; as long as she remained able, she was going to maintain the pace. A gardeners' calendar, retained by Frank Young after her death, shows a year beginning as many before it must have done. On the first day in January, garden seeds were ordered and fruit trees pruned; three days later, seakale was prepared for forcing, *Hydrangea paniculata* pruned, and a reminder made to sow primrose and gladiolus seeds. On 15 April Gertrude saw her first *Ipomoea* 'Heavenly Blue'. More than forty times in 1928 she submitted articles, some of them very brief, mostly to Mr Cowley at *Gardening Illustrated*. Admittedly she had written sixty-six the previous year, but garden plans were up to ten, at least two of which were sizeable and significant projects. In the summer she planned the first of two areas for Viscount Ridley and Lutyens's daughter, Ursula, at Blagdon in Northumberland; in October she worked on a third property for Edward Hudson. Needless to say Lutyens was the architect.

Two massive white stone bulls guard the entrance to the Ridleys' eighteenth-century home. Blagdon is near Newcastle, on a coalfield yet surprisingly rural. Winter is especially dour, and Lady Ridley's first concern was for plantings to brighten the scene. Using photographs and a map prepared by Lord Ridley's agent, Gertrude set out to contrive a bosky, semi-wild quarry garden, with a rubble core that 'should look as if it was a sort of moraine of debris and pieces of rock fallen from the cliff to be planted with gentians . . . saxifrages . . . alpine campanulas . . . and so on'.[33] Guided by her old principles, simplicity and unity, she proposed damming a stream into a pond and thickened existing plantings, eliminating superfluities. 'The Wellingtonia of course must go.'[34] Many of the shrubs and trees were her stock in trade for wild gardens. At Upton Grey she had also used laburnums and amelanchiers, set off by a screen of hollies, *Rubus parviflorus*, *Prunus cerasifera* 'Pissardii', and the unlikely giant hogweed, a riparian scourge Gertrude unwittingly spread.

Lady Ridley confessed to disappointment with Bumps's plan, 'I . . . long for father to come and to discuss it with him. It is difficult for her so far away,' she conceded, 'but she seems to want to plant too many hollies – rather dull things, and I do want colour in it so badly at all times of the year.'[35] But Gertrude's effects had been intentional. 'The great thing here is not to have too many things seen at the same time – to compose one quiet picture and then pass on to another.'[36] Two seats were Lutyens's sole contribution. Near them Gertrude naturalized choice spring flowers, acanthus, hellebores and Solomon's seal beside mown paths. Perhaps it was Lutyens who urged his daughter to maintain her faith in Gertrude. The following year she planned a herbaceous garden inside a yew walk between house and walled kitchen garden. It was based on eight linked hexagonal beds, 200 feet longer than Munstead, an enormous scale, but planted broadly on Munstead's colour scheme. Subsequent additions to the garden by Lutyens have survived, but of Gertrude's plantings in the quarry garden, or her elaborate herbaceous beds, there is little trace.

Old friends were as supportive to Gertrude as she was to them. Hudson had bought Plumpton Place, a derelict moated manor beneath the Sussex Downs, and Lutyens extended it, building two weather-boarded lodges with prominent brick chimneys on the far side of an oaken footbridge and renovating a humble mill cottage so comfortably that Hudson chose to occupy it instead of his manor. A survey of moat and mill ponds was sent to Gertrude with a request for a full set of plans: 'I need not point out to Miss Jekyll the advisability of good reflections in the water.'[37] The planting around the mill house was to be reminiscent of The Deanery. 'The tumbling roses at Sonning . . . were very beautiful & I think this effect might be aimed at.'[38] It was trust in her that prompted clients to return to Gertrude, and whether or not he realized it, Hudson was preaching to the teacher almost in her own words: 'I want to keep the planting quite simple throughout the place. I want it to look . . . as though it had always been there for hundreds of years. I don't want what I call the "swagger" sort of garden-ing.'[39]

In August there was an SOS from Lutyens: 'I must find time to come to you for a conversational etude.'[40] Gertrude was busy as ever communicating her message. 'Changes of Fashion in Gardening', ap-pearing in a national monthly paper, *The Nineteenth Century and After*, was a summary of garden history during the past seventy years, from 'circles and stars and crescents, sprinkled about without any sense of design or cohesion',[41] horizontally tricoloured ribbon borders and roses 'grown as standards in little rings in the grass',[42] to present 'harmonies and concords'.[43] Since the period was that of her own participation, many of the people involved had been personal friends: William Robinson, the Rev. Wolley Dod and Canon Ellacombe, Peter Barr, who brought narcissi from Spain and Portugal, G. F. Wilson, collector of lilies, Lord Penzance, who worked on sweetbriars, and Dean Hole on roses. In Gertrude's eyes, fashion would always be suspect. The pergola that she had favoured was in danger of being employed without proper consideration. 'Its purpose is to be a covered way leading distinctly from one part of the garden to something definite at the end.'[44] Even the practice of planting between pavings, an essentially Jekyllian feature, could be abused. Trade, she realized, had played its part in the horticultural revolution. The amount of material for garden use was now 'almost bewildering in its abundance'[45] but like everything else, new plants should be used with caution. None of the old clarity or precision was lost; Gertrude's writing was as punchy and clear-headed as ever.

Frederick Eden had died in 1916 and Carry, returning to England four years later, took a house near the Brompton Oratory in Alexandra Square. Mrs Durrant remembered her as a little like Gertrude, by which she meant 'strongly artistic'. David McKenna retained the image of a frail old woman's wavery hand over a cup of tea, white hair, pendant diamond earrings and a velvet choker. In December, aged ninety-one, she too died, and Agnes remarked in an appreciation that Caroline had been 'only partially emancipated' by her marriage. Jekylls were falling like leaves; two months later, on 17 February, Walter died amid his beloved Blue Mountains. A stone plaque erected in his memory in the parish church at Lucea read, 'Musician, gardener, philosopher, teacher and writer, he lived 34 years in this island of his adoption where he gave himself to the service of others . . .' Millicent von Maltzahn, Teddy's daughter, was his sole heir. Herbert rushed out to Jamaica to claim material for his family history. From time to time he had corresponded, exhorting Walter to be prudent in parting with his possessions. Now producing a photograph of them together as young men in Venice, Herbert remarked that his brother's appearance altered a great deal in later years. Letters he wrote express incomprehension that they who had once been so close should have virtually ceased to communicate. In Herbert's eyes, Walter's idealism must have seemed baffling. Long before, the youngest Jekyll had given up playing the game. 'I was never Noah in the ark, but one of the perishing children outside . . . I was the rich man – when I grew up – who lifted up his eyes in torment, for did I not belong to that well-to-do class of which it was said, How hardly shall a rich men enter into the kingdom of heaven.'[46]

However irreplaceable old friends and family were, Gertrude was capable of forging new, meaningful attachments. This was the year seven-year-old Christopher Lloyd of Great Dixter, son of Nathaniel Lloyd, whose *Garden Craftsmanship in Yew and Box* Gertrude held in high esteem, was taken by his mother to Munstead Wood. It would have been in May, for Gertrude was splitting polyanthus at the time. Lloyd, a youngster with a precocious horticultural interest, remembers being impressed by her '& she must have been a little by me because she put her hand on my head & blessed me, saying that I would grow up to be a great gardener'.[47] Gertrude was not involved with planning or planting at Dixter, but she had put her faith in a winner. Something that Gertrude's books have in common with Christopher Lloyd's is an extra dimension missing from ordinary gardening books.

The following spring Gertrude explained to Mrs Brand that pressure of 'work out of doors in an interregnum of gardeners'[48] had delayed sending out a plan for hill and streamside gardens by several months. One of the notebooks records that she conducted a huge stocktaking in the autumn, possibly as Zumbach left.

CHAPTER THIRTY

1929–32

Different images of Gertrude in her final years must be brought together. Russell Page, a garden designer much influenced by her, catches the resoluteness of 'a dumpy figure in a heavy gardener's apron, her vitality shining from a face half concealed by two pairs of spectacles and a battered and yellowed straw hat'.[1] This is somebody still extracting meaning from her days. Graham Stuart Thomas thought she had remained remarkably like William Nicholson's portrait – the poised visage that could also be very direct, practical, amusing, and sharp. Logan Pearsall Smith described her face as 'some ancient, incredibly aristocratic'[2] denizen of the jungle, gazing gravely out from tangled river reeds, which rather contradicts Barbara Sotheby's likeness. Mrs Sotheby, from neighbouring Littleton, drew the portrait illustrated in Francis Jekyll's *Memoir* in time for an exhibition she held with the Royal Society of Portrait Painters in 1930. Gertrude chose a similar pose to the one she struck in Nicholson's painting nine years before, but her expression is more like a benevolent matron than Queen Victoria. Perhaps Mrs Sotheby endeavoured to flatter her sitter.

There is no sign that Gertrude was dependent upon the public, but recognition was evidence that her mission had been achieved. The dedication to her of an issue of the *Botanical Magazine* was therefore a highlight of her eighty-sixth year. With it appeared a supplementary volume bearing short biographies of all her predecessors. She had not made time for good works, so friends and visitors arriving the day she opened the garden for charity was another kind of reward. Being something of a national celebrity did not give her automatic rights in local affairs; the water committee's report in the annual minutes of the Godalming Corporation informs that an application for a charge on her garden meter to be discontinued was quashed 'as a matter of principle'.[3] So was Lady Jekyll's request to be allowed free use of a key to Munstead Tower.

Lutyens's drawing, 'Lifting his halo, God walks with Bumps in her
garden', 16 January 1932.

Nor was Gertrude among those invited to the inaugural meeting of
the body which became the Institute of Landscape Architects, although
their object – to harmonize the works of nature with works of man –
had been her expressed goal. A grand old galleon was sailing more
slowly, her flags flying but in hazardous seas. For several months one
misfortune seemed to follow another. Exceptional gales toppled,
among other trees, some of Munstead Wood's cherished, shallow-
rooting silver birch, a loss Gertrude's nephew referred to as 'almost . . .
personal'.[4] There were floods everywhere on lower ground, though
the flood in her greenhouse was due, she wrote, 'not . . . to Jupiter
Pluvius, but rather to Bufo vulgaris . . . a fine fat toad sitting on the
ball-cock!'[5] Then she caught pneumonia, which raged from mid-
January well into the following spring. By April, 'slowly recovering',[6]
with 'next to no strength',[7] and 'very shaky about doing sums',[8] she
felt bound to ask clients to check her bills.

The last four years of Gertrude's life were held together by continued
attempts to live the rounded existence she had perfected, with its
integrated pattern of work and leisure. She was again corresponding

with Dr Hampton, returning samples of distilled plant oils with notes – an apple scent in civet was 'quite obvious to me now that you point it out',[9] and enclosing twigs of mistletoe to support a conjecture that the pollen flowers bore scent lacking in those which had been fertilized, an observation Hampton thought worthy of communicating to E. A. Bowles. In 1929 she began five garden commissions. Mr Warner of Marylands, not far from her in Hurtwood, was sorry to hear of her indisposition, waiting anxiously throughout March and into April for plants which did not appear. Gertrude's reply finally arrived in a very uncertain hand, professional commitment was asserted; all but andromedas, which it was then too late to plant, would come the following day. Edward Hudson of *Country Life* had married Ellen Woolrich at the age of seventy-five. To Gertrude he had sent a Christmas photograph of Plumpton inscribed, 'from one who has been honoured by your friendship & kindness for so many years'.[10] A note on progress followed. When some new gates were up there would be another set of photographs.

The constant sketching Gertrude had cultivated was in the spirit of Ruskin's 'strong instinct in me which I cannot analyse to draw and describe the things I love – not for reputation, nor for the good of others, nor for my own advantage, but a sort of instinct like that for eating and drinking'.[11] During her last years, conscious of leaving her life as tidily as she had led it, she made a comprehensive, cross-referenced index to all her sketchbooks: 'Aldborough narcissi, Algiers – fireplace, studio 6, summerhouse, Allium, Amsterdam museum.'[12] Topics range from Lake Geneva to patchwork quilts, the pavements in St Mark's Square, sails, the fireplace at Scalands, plants growing on the Simplon Pass and Snowdenham Mill pond. The list remains even if most of the sketchbooks have disappeared.

But she was entering a decade of Modernism in the arts, resenting, sometimes angrily, the ugliness and noise of modern life, inveighing against customs that seemed to her without charm, purpose or sincerity. 'Forgive us our Christmases as we forgive them that Christmas against us,'[13] she exclaimed a trifle sourly, refusing to join in the fashion for exchanging gifts and cards. If she felt inclined she would send a card, as she did to Amy Barnes-Brand in 1927 – a pressed frond of adiantum stuck on a small blank card with a handwritten greeting, wrapped in pale blue tissue paper – what she objected to was being a slave to commerce, and, predictably, she objected to cheap, ill-made toys.

'Young children have not much natural sense of beauty, but there is nothing that is more easily cultivated ... it is almost sinful to give a child anything that is unsightly or debasing.'[14] The teddy bear just about escaped her invective, being 'harmless, fairly soft, unbreakable and companionable',[15] but fashion was a permanent bone of contention, even fashion in clothes, in which she took sufficient interest to have kept records pasted in a scrap book since 1895. On a page devoted to hats she wrote acidly, 'You cannot invent a new hat, you can only invent absurdities.'[16] Until 1931 she was adding and commenting.

A few garden visitors managed to penetrate Munstead Wood, leaving records that help to fill in the last years. It was 6 September 1931 when Graham Stuart Thomas bicycled from his home in Woking. In the foreword to the 1983 edition of Gertrude's book on *Colour Schemes*, he explains how the curator of Cambridge University Botanic Garden, Mr Preston, realizing a profound interest in his former student, had begged special permission: 'I was welcomed, bidden to go round the garden, pick a piece of anything I wished to talk about, and come back and have some tea with her.'[17] If Munstead Wood had suffered neglect in Gertrude's increasing age, to Stuart Thomas 'it did not seem so'.[18] She had, after all, been perfecting it for more than thirty years, and 'there were no half-measures with Miss Jekyll'.[19] With the formal areas near the house he professed himself 'spellbound';[20] borders were 'overflowing with flowers'.[21] 'There were the yuccas and clumpy evergreens acting as foils ... My notebook records *Aster corymbosus* (*A. divaricatus*) among other things; groups of the exquisite *Lilium krameri* (*L. japonicum*), which I had grown at Cambridge; Delphinium 'Blue Fairy'; Michaelmas Daisies showing early flowers; and dahlias of all colours found their right places in the schemes.'[22]

One hears only sketchily about the ageing lives at Munstead House and Munstead Wood in these last years, and Gertrude's correspondence with Mrs Brand after a two-year gap emphasizes the feeling that trials were encroaching upon pleasures. On 29 March 1932, 'with my eighty-eight years & worn out heart',[23] she was 'a very poor creature'.[24] She was pleased to hear from her friend, however, had entered her order and promised to send plants at the appropriate time. A whole sentence duplicated and an extremely unsteady hand betrayed waning strength: 'Just now the Dr is coming every day.'[25] For a fortnight she had been inside; another week was ordered in anticipation of getting out when the days warmed up. She did not easily give in; with endurance that is a clue to moral courage, the old tenacity reasserts itself; 'I have a splendid lot of good hardy plants in bigger plants & at lower prices than the nurseries.'[26] It was the last letter Mrs Brand received from her.

In May Gertrude was carried downstairs by her gardeners into a wheelchair, a gift from Lutyens, to see the primroses bloom. Much as she disliked enforced dependence, she relished the clues that carried her back to childhood. She may even have captured something of the sublime rapture the sight once moved her to: 'It must have been at about seven years of age that I first learnt to know and love a primrose copse . . . more than half a century has passed, and yet each spring, when I wander into the primrose wood, and see the pale yellow blooms, and smell their sweetest of sweet scents, and feel the warm spring air throbbing with the quickening pulse of new life, and hear the glad notes of the birds and the burden of the bees, and see again the same delicate young growths piercing the mossy woodland carpet; when I see and feel and hear all this, for a moment I am seven years old again and wandering in the fragrant wood hand-in-hand with the dear God who made it.'[27] Like Ruskin, she was committed to the idea of nature as an absolute, overriding force in human destiny.

There were a few whom Gertrude still enjoyed seeing. Events of garden interest inspired brief notes to Herbert Cowley, who wrote after her death, 'a day never passes but what I am reminded of her'.[28] Another welcomed in these last years was Burne-Jones's son-in-law, Dr J. W. Mackail, an academic, one-time Oxford Professor of Poetry, and prolific author, notably of a biography of William Morris. Mackail was the father of the novelist Angela Thirkell, whose photograph as a chunky barefooted youngster Gertrude had taken more than thirty years before.

Logan Pearsall Smith had maintained correspondence since he left Haslemere, befriending in the interval Robert Bridges, Poet Laureate, and joining his committee of the Society for Pure English. Pamphlets he wrote for the society had been duplicated for Gertrude, and twice during her last year he was to visit. The first time he was conducted across the road from Munstead House via the gate in the fence, where the key hung, as always, on a nail hidden from view. It was all as before; the hushed mood of intense stillness, the path leading through the copse, making as secluded and mysterious a garden as the secret one in Frances Hodgson Burnett's celebrated children's tale. Pearsall Smith was amazed to find his hostess sitting in her accustomed chair; 'her eyes still twinkled behind her heavy glasses, the sound of her deep chuckle . . . as rich as ever'.[29] There was no reason why she should discuss plants or gardens with him, indeed, 'a veil of fatigue, of boredom with all the garden chatter of the world, seemed to dim her face'[30] if he raised the subject. Words were what they shared, and time had not altered the rules of verbal repartee: 'Miss Jekyll was as ready as ever for a scrap . . . it was impossible, or almost impossible, when she held a view strongly, to make her give way an inch.'[31]

A contest that specially appealed to Pearsall Smith is worth repeating, because competitive wit was one of Gertrude's most beguiling tools of friendship and the argument anticipated Nancy Mitford's 'U' and 'non-U' debate. This time it concerned the distinction between 'ride' and 'drive'.

'But, Miss Jekyll, if you go on a bus, don't you take a "ride" on it?'

'But I never go on a bus!' she triumphed.

'But if you were given a lift by a farmer on the road?'

'I should call it a lift; a lift, certainly, not a "ride".'

'But suppose, Miss Jekyll, that you wanted to go home from a hayfield on a loaded haycart? Wouldn't you ask if you could have a "ride" on the cart? Wouldn't you have to say "ride" – not "drive"?'

Miss Jekyll looked disconcerted. 'Well,' she said at last, 'no, I shouldn't call it a "drive". No, certainly not a "drive".'

'Would you ask for a lift, then?'

'No, I shouldn't call it a "lift".'

'Now, Miss Jekyll,' her adversary insisted, imagining he had almost cornered his goal. 'Now, honestly, what would you ask for?'

Miss Jekyll seemed almost to sweat blood at this question. 'I should ask, I should ask if you will insist on knowing, – I suppose I should ask for a "ride" on the haycart. But,' she added, with what was almost a wicked wink from behind her spectacles, 'but then, you know, I should be speaking to quite uneducated people.'

This wasn't fair; she knew it wasn't fair; and her wink betrayed her.[32]

It would be a mistake to think that age had altered Gertrude's humorously critical outlook, the strong ingrained attitudes towards culture or her ferocious snobbery. On Pearsall Smith's final visit, Gertrude had prepared a list of 'quality' or 'armigerous' words and expressions; ones, that is, particular to the class with which she identified. When these had been discussed, and before taking his leave, the inquirer requested advice on word usage for a 'non-armigerous person'[33] like himself. Her reply, after assorted snorts, struggles, almost-winks and chuckles, was that he should stick to the ways of his class.

Despite constant fatigue, Gertrude was by no means idle. In her last year she read 100 books, wrote a short essay on trees and began work on a new posthumously published edition of *Wall and Water Gardens*. All summer she presided over the garden from her chair, cogitating, 'And as the quick years pass and the body grows old around the still young heart, and the day of death grows ever nearer; with each new spring-tide the sweet flowers come forth and bloom afresh; and with their coming – with the ever-renewing of their gracious gift and still more precious promise – the thought of Death becomes like that of a gentle and kindly bearer of tidings, who brings the inevitable message, and bids the one for whom it is destined receive it manfully and be of good hope and cheerfulness, and remember that the Sender of Death is the Giver of the greater new Life, no less than of the sweet spring flowers, that bloom and die and live again as a never-ending parable of Life and Death and Immortality.'[34]

For someone innately independent, old age was full of frustration. 'I feel that I do not deserve the great goodness and kind helpfulness of my own [servants],' she wrote to Miss Willmott, 'it is a kind of make-up for my present almost entire loss of strength. I am keenly feeling the loss of power for doing all the little things about the garden that want doing directly you notice them, and that, though really of some importance, it would seem silly to call a man to do; and I fret at being hauled about in wheeled chairs instead of the leisurely solitary prowls of close intimacy with the growing things . . .'[35] After Avray Tipping, Miss Willmott had given a second lecture on Gertrude at the Garden Club. Gertrude had seen the script and said it had given her more pleasure than anything else written about her.

Ellen Willmott was feeling ill, but a strong presentiment that she must travel to Munstead Wood took her down that summer. Eleven thousand roses were being gathered for pot-pourri, a four-day operation, Gertrude noted with a sensibility that saw all progress in terms of time and labour. There were seeds to be collected from the giant erythronium and the new blue *Meconopsis baileyi*. That life was completing its circle, she was acutely aware. Childhood was often on her mind, and stimulated by daily visits from her brother, she was writing her final publications, recollections of old Bramley for the parish magazine. In her mind, once again, she could smell Mr Snelling's apples, climb the primitive step-ladder into the Bowbricks' bedroom and watch Lord Grantley's old yellow chariot being pulled through the village by a pair of greys. 'Throughout her life,' Francis Jekyll wrote, 'she had, almost instinctively, met the advances of others with a barrier which experience warned them not to overstep.'[36] But Herbert had shared her gifts, her work ethic and her need to be alone. She was fortunate, in an old age which might otherwise have been isolated, to have the warmth and thoughtfulness of Munstead House. 'No item of domestic news was too trivial, no swing of her pendulum between strength and weakness too minute, [not] to be recounted to a sympathetic ear ... every day she had problems to set him on her daily affairs.'[37] This daily companionship of her brother's family was reinforced by '. . . countless little services'.[38]

Gertrude showed every sign of surviving another winter when Herbert died quite suddenly on 29 September. His *Times* obituary mentioned that 'one of his sisters is Miss Gertrude Jekyll, the famous gardener and artist'. The funeral was held at Busbridge church; Lutyens told Emily, 'It was very well done and the music exceptionally good. Crimson damask covered the coffin flanked by Italian candlesticks, very Munsteady, but dignified with his stars and orders displayed thereon. The lesson Aggie chose remarkably befitting. It was all horribly moving.'[39] Afterwards he saw 'Bumps, self-possessed and herself – very feeble. She was in her bedroom with a delicious duck blue felt cap on her head.'[40] Her hands, he noticed, had shrunk and shook slightly, she looked brown-complexioned, otherwise well but very old.

Gertrude was delighted with her wheelchair, which, she said, made 'the whole difference'[41] to her. Bernard Freyberg, Barbara's soldier husband, was asking her 'endless questions',[42] waiting 'in delight for her deliberate answers',[43] but the gap would not be filled. For over thirty years she and Herbert had lived side by side, and she missed him terribly. Miss Willmott recognized, 'It was Sir Herbert's death which must have hastened her death for her last letter to me was very pathetic.'[44] For two months Gertrude lingered, passing her eighty-ninth birthday into her ninetieth year, enjoying an illustrated book on Manet, but profoundly shocked. 'The leaves are all down by the last

Lutyens's drawing of Gertrude Jekyll in bed, 4 October 1932.

week of November, and woodland assumes its winter aspect.'[45] She died when plant life was quiescent, and the forest had assumed its winter mood, when the hollies shone brightly against the yew, and stripling birches gleamed from the wood-walks. On 8 December, a Thursday night, fearless, she spoke her last words, 'Peace, perfect peace in Jesus Christ,'[46] and collapsed in the arms of Florence Hayter. It was a careful performance; after all, she was an 'old, erudite, accomplished and famous expert; the world had acknowledged her pre-eminence, and applauded her achievement'.[47]

It was like Gertrude to be represented at her funeral not only in spirit but in tangible and self-created images. The printed order of service contained an extract from *Wood and Garden*, the coffin was covered with a linen pall designed for her by Herbert, and walking immediately behind it, as the cortège proceeded from church to grave, stepped Florence Hayter, carrying on a cushion the Royal Horticultural Society's Victoria Medal of Honour, the Veitch Memorial Medal and the American Horticultural Society's gold medal. Ellen Willmott, still recovering from her indisposition, took a train from Warley, and William Robinson, aged ninety-four, travelled thirty miles on wintry roads to see Gertrude lowered to rest by her gardeners, a few feet from Herbert, in a grave lined with travellers' joy and yellow chrysanthemums.

Epilogue

Gertrude was buried in a mossy corner beneath a yew tree on the east side of Busbridge church. Three tomb slabs to Miss Gertrude, Agnes, Lady Jekyll and Sir Herbert Jekyll guard the open end of the plot, and behind them stands Lutyens's monument to the family that meant so much to him. Pevsner describes the broken stone wall surmounted by a simple oval urn as 'oddly like Soane translated into the blunt obtuse forms of the 1930s'.[1] Its curved crosswise bars are reminiscent of a hand-operated washing mangle, and local opinion is less complimentary.

Inscriptions on the monument remember 'Herbert and Gertrude Jekyll, long time dwellers in their homes at Munstead who passed to their rest in the Autumn of 1932. Their joy was in the work of their hands. Their memorial is the beauty which lives after them. Also of Agnes Jekyll whose spirit ever dwelt in loving kindness.' On Gertrude's personal stone the words stand singly, one beneath the other, Artist, Gardener, Craftswoman. The order might imply, as Betty Massingham suggests, that the second and third qualifications depend on the first, and this would be as Gertrude would have liked herself to be remembered. But she once admitted, 'I have been more or less a gardener all my life,'[2] and like Ruskin, her love of nature preceded her love of art.

Six weeks before she died Gertrude revised her will, leaving Mary Irons, her cook, and Florence Hayter, her personal maid, £100 and their bedroom furniture. Mary Platt, houseparlourmaid, received £25, and Arthur Gibbins, the head gardener, £50. All the rest of her property and £20,091 went to Agnes, 'widow of my brother Herbert',[3] sole executor and trustee. Agnes died two years before the Second World War, when Munstead House became a day nursery. When the war ended, Barbara Freyberg moved in with her husband, subsequently Lord Freyberg.

Barbara's brother, Francis (Timmy) Jekyll, did not inherit Munstead

Wood until after Agnes' death. Timmy was fifty when his aunt died. As Herbert's only son, author of the much quoted *Memoir* and manager of Gertrude's nursery for some years, he is part of the jigsaw of her life and reputation. This must be said because a cloud of something between irritation and bewilderment has settled on the memory of the least-mentioned Jekyll. It was not always so. At Eton Timmy won a Foundation Scholarship, received the Newcastle prize, was conscientious, dutiful and, in the words of his classics tutor, was 'in many ways a brilliant scholar, sparing himself no pains where his interest was aroused, and full of enthusiasm'.[4] Macnaughton could think of no one among his pupils, past or present, whom he would more gladly recommend for a post at the British Museum. At Balliol College, where Timmy was an exhibitioner, the record continued bright, his Greats tutor was happy to put down a disappointing second class degree to his 'taste for specialization',[5] after all, he was 'one of the most interesting men of his standing in the college'.[6] Yet the praise that took the new recruit to the British Museum Department of Printed Books was not sustained. Eight years later he left his post, 'a man of undoubted ability'[7] but 'Mr Jekyll finds the regulations of the museum very irksome.'[8] Timmy's first and rapturous love had been music. Herbert had built an organ room at Munstead House, but there was tension between the two over priorities. Barbara Jekyll was to be, like her parents, decorated for public service. It is evident that the strongest members of the family were its women.

For six months nothing at Munstead Wood was touched. It was thick with her presence; a veritable gingerbread house of graded shells, coral and beads, gathered and sorted in a tangible replica of their coordinator's well-stocked mind. Her clothes hung in her bedroom cupboard, her boots, soil-encrusted, stood by the back door, and Francis Jekyll wrote, 'Cupboard doors swung open to reveal the accumulations of seventy acquisitive years.'[9] The part of her that had answered only to excellence was encapsulated in Pigot, tutelar deity and guardian of the workshop 'by whose eyes she was wont to swear, on the completion of each task, that it was well and truly accomplished'.[10] When Gertrude died, Timmy had been without structured work for eighteen years. In his aunt's biography lay the perfect project for the gifted, wayward son. Installed in The Hut, with free access to all Gertrude's papers, he began writing, the summer after her death, the *Memoir* that is now such an important source. 'My son,' Agnes wrote, 'is deep in research with a view to his Memoir of Miss Jekyll & we learn much about her before the days . . . when I came into the life of the Jekylls here.'[11] Lutyens's verdict, after reading 'some 5 or 6 chapters'[12] was 'quite good but "deadish" somehow'.[13] The *Observer* review was mildly favourable: 'It was right and proper, it was necessary, that the life of such an Englishwoman should be put on record.'[14]

Timmy planned two more books from his Aunt Gertrude's material, but after playing his part in her future, he made no apparent moves to safeguard her archives. Gertrude's collection of papers was donated to a RHS Red Cross Sale in September 1940, a transaction in which garden historian and horticulturist Dr William Stearn assisted with misgivings. The garden plans and accompanying correspondence were acquired for Beatrix Farrand, the designer of Dumbarton Oaks, who made her purchase from a London dealer for 'a moderate sum'.[15] In October 1956 garden plans and six photograph albums, part of the Reef Point Collection, were moved from Maine to the University of California.

Following the sale of Munstead Wood in 1947, the bulk of Gertrude's belongings was dispersed on the first two days of September 1948 at a sale run by Alfred Savill & Sons, an act of insouciance that has contributed to the problems of researchers ever since. Room after room was stripped of its contents. Alongside a Jacobean chest of drawers and a bedstead designed by Lutyens went a huge collection of furniture, books and music, Barbara Bodichon's paintings, Gertrude's pianola, eleven photograph albums and her camera. To what became a huge social occasion, people flocked from surrounding villages to purchase as mementoes some of the objects that have since found their way into museums.

'We miss Miss Jekyll here very continually,'[16] Agnes had written to the American landscape architect Mrs Nellie Allen, the first spring after Gertrude's death. 'She had so impressed her individuality on her surroundings . . . that I find it very difficult not to turn to her in all the daily happenings, & to feel that her earthy eyes will not look on the flowers which she loved so well, & which are coming out with quite unusual charm in this exceptionally lovely Spring.'[17] But the rate at which nature reclaims gardens is legendary. In the summer of 1933, according to Lutyens's third daughter, Elisabeth, who 'adored'[18] staying there, Munstead Wood was still 'wonderful'.[19] But Mary Lutyens, who was there the following season, thought it had lost its contours and 'felt neglected'.[20] Tó their father's tutored eye it was 'sad to see the garden collapsed . . . but it can't be helped No Bumps.'[21] Only one gardener remained. It is not obvious what Gertrude wished for the future of Munstead Wood. Falkner had introduced the secretary of the Royal Horticultural Society, who had tried to discuss the subject, but each time it was tentatively raised, she spoke of something else. Two months before her death Lutyens had commented, 'Timmy arrived and is proving not too tactful. He has already proposed the alterations he intends to make in the garden.'[22] Today the land has been split: Hut, Stables and gardener's cottage are separate residences and a new house has been built on the old kitchen garden site. The garden that was Gertrude's joy, inspiration and greatest work of art sleeps peacefully; the framework remains, trees and shrubs, stonework, pergola and walls; a visitor versed in her works can almost clothe it with appropriate pictures.

Timmy ran the nursery garden in a desultory fashion. In August 1937 he informed loyal Mrs Brand, 'As you are an old & faithful customer of ours, I should like to supply you with what you ask for as far as possible.'[23] A copy of the latest edition of the Munstead Wood catalogue was enclosed with a caution that many items on it were no longer available. No hellebores were on offer, though he hoped for some the following year, and primrose seed was all dispersed to the trade. There were young seedling alstroemerias, a few choice lilies in pots and a good quantity of evergreens. Mrs Brand was welcome at any time to visit the gardener, Mr Stove. The Rev. Stanley Dedman, a librarian in Godalming, and Joan Charman, a young girl working in the library, remember the elderly Timmy Jekyll as a quiet, self-contained, rather dour man who made evening visits to borrow books and sometimes fell asleep in one of the chairs. Mrs Charman says she felt sorry for him, being 'well dressed' and 'living in a place called The Hut'.[24]

Gertrude lives in her books, gardens, photographs and the plants she helped to breed and select, 'Munstead' lavender, *Lupinus polyphyllus* 'Munstead Bounty', and the Munstead primulas, yet Nicholson's *Still Life* of her gardening boots has struck a special chord with the public in the last, ecologically conscious decades of the twentieth century. For the old boots, repaired and unequally sized, are invested with so much of her character that they seem to have a life of their own. Timmy

Jekyll sent them to Mrs Allen, 'because I consider you, among all American Visitors loved her most'.[25] This, it transpired, was the first episode in a restless odyssey.

It was Mrs Allen's intention to donate the boots to the Garden Club of America, but the occasion for such a gift never arrived. Year after year they were kept wrapped in a metal box until the spring of 1956, when their recipient, then aged eighty-seven, returned them to England with a request to the Tate Gallery that they be shown near the Nicholson portrait. The Tate replied courteously, thanking her for the generous gift and explaining that it had no facilities for exhibiting such objects; nor did the National Portrait Gallery, for the Tate had taken the trouble to inquire. Perhaps Miss Allen would like an inquiry lodged with the Royal Horticultural Society, who then possessed the boot portrait? During endless communications, the boots became something of a liability. The RHS suggested Haslemere Museum: 'Please forgive my troubling you about this but it is a rather difficult and unusual problem.'[26] The search, however, was nearing its end. The Haslemere Museum passed the message to the Guildford Museum, who wrote, on 24 July, 'Dear Mrs Allen, I have just received through the mediation of Miss Mary Chamot of the Tate Gallery the famous "Boots" once worn by Miss Gertrude Jekyll. We are most pleased to have them.'[27]

Nicholson's paintings have become separated, the portrait in the National Portrait Gallery, the boots in the Tate. E. V. Lucas felt that 'the one is the complement of the other',[28] that 'Mr Nicholson, with nice insight, perceived that both extremes were needed'.[29] Mary Lutyens likewise suggested that the boot painting ought really to be hung in the National Portrait Gallery 'as a predella to the portrait'.[30]

Gertrude's obituary described her as 'a great gardener, second only, if indeed she was second, to her friend William Robinson'.[31] But the fact that her name is coupled with William Robinson, grand promoter of freer, more natural gardening, may have helped to distort her real achievement. Five years after death, a compilation of her short writings was made by her nephew and Geoffrey Taylor. An introductory essay to *A Gardener's Testament* helps to complete the picture of someone used to having the last say about things, including herself.

REFERENCES

Foreword

1. Jane Brown, *Gardens of a Golden Afternoon*, Allen Lane, 1982, p. 99.
2. H. Avray Tipping, *English Gardens*, Country Life, 1925, p. 239.
3. Russell Page, *The Education of a Gardener*, Collins, 1962, p. 94.
4. Michael and Rosanna Tooley (eds), *Gertrude Jekyll: Artist, Gardener, Craftsman*, Michaelmas Books, 1984, p. 11.
5. Anthea Callen, *Angel in the Studio*, Astragal Books, 1979.
6. Roderick Gradidge, *Edwin Lutyens: Architect Laureate*, Allen & Unwin, 1981, p. 26.
7. *The Garden*, 81: 121.
8. Gertrude Jekyll, *A Gardener's Testament*, Country Life, 1937, p. 80.
9. Christopher Hussey, *The Life of Sir Edwin Lutyens*, Country Life, 1953, p. 23.
10. J. Morton, *Journal of the Royal Horticultural Society*, 92: 270.

PART ONE: BEGINNINGS

Chapter 1: 1843–8

1. Gertrude Jekyll, *Children and Gardens*, Country Life, 1908, p. 4.
2. Gertrude Jekyll, *Wood and Garden*, Longmans Green, 1899, p. 2.
3. Gertrude Jekyll, *Children and Gardens*, p. 4.
4. ibid.
5. ibid.
6. ibid., p. 5.
7. Logan Pearsall Smith, *Reperusals and Recollections*, Constable, 1936, p. 60.
8. Francis Jekyll, *Gertrude Jekyll: A Memoir*, Cape, 1934, p. 198.
9. Logan Pearsall Smith, *Reperusals and Recollections*, p. 60.

10. *Dictionary of National Biography*, London, 1892, p. 289.
11. Lady Duff Gordon, journals, 6 October 1843.
12. Somerset House, Edward Jekyll's will.
13. Lady Duff Gordon, journals, 27 February 1854.
14. Gertrude Jekyll, *Home and Garden*, Longmans Green, 1900, pp. 112–13.
15. ibid., p. 108.
16. ibid., p. 112.
17. *The Times*, 10 December 1932, p. 12.
18. Lady Duff Gordon, journals, 27 February 1854.
19. ibid., 20 November 1874.
20. ibid., 24 February 1874.
21. ibid.
22. ibid., 2 August 1857.
23. ibid., 29 April 1859.
24. ibid.
25. ibid., 22 June 1873.
26. Geoffrey Taylor, *The Victorian Flower Garden*, Skeffington, 1952, p. 161.
27. John Ruskin, *Works* (ed. E. T. Cook and Alexander Wedderburn), London, 1903–9, Vol. 18, p. 122.

Chapter 2: 1848–60

1. Gertrude Jekyll, *Gardens for Small Country Houses* (with Lawrence Weaver), Country Life, 1912, p. 1.
2. Gertrude Jekyll, *Home and Garden*, Longmans Green, 1900, p. 224.
3. Gertrude Jekyll, *A Gardener's Testament*, Country Life, 1937, p. 321.
4. Priscilla Metcalf, *James Knowles: Victorian Editor and Architect*, Clarendon, 1980, p. 20.
5. Jane Brown, *Gardens of a Golden Afternoon*, Allen Lane, 1982, p. 19.
6. Priscilla Metcalf, *James Knowles: Victorian Editor and Architect*, p. 21.
7. Reef Point Collection, Drawer 11, File 40, item 2.
8. Gertrude Jekyll, *A Gardener's Testament*, p. 10.
9. Francis Jekyll, *Gertrude Jekyll: A Memoir*, Cape, 1934, p. 28.
10. Gertrude Jekyll, 'The Changes of Fashion in Gardening', *The Nineteenth Century and After*, 104: 195.
11. Gertrude Jekyll, *Children and Gardens*, Country Life, 1908, p. 51.

12. Gertrude Jekyll, *Wood and Garden*, Longmans Green, 1899, p. 100.

13. Gertrude Jekyll, *A Gardener's Testament*, p. 11.

14. Gertrude Jekyll, *Home and Garden*, p. 110.

15. Gertrude Jekyll, *Old West Surrey*, Longmans Green, 1904, p. 310.

16. Photographs from the Reef Point Collection, Guildford Library, Box 1.

17. Gertrude Jekyll, 'Recollections of Old Bramley', Bramley parish magazine, October 1932.

18. Gertrude Jekyll, *Home and Garden*, p. 109.

19. Penelope Fitzgerald, *Edward Burne-Jones*, Michael Joseph, 1975, p. 55.

Chapter 3: 1848–60

1. Lady Duff Gordon, journals, 12 September 1854.

2. ibid., 8 April 1854.

3. ibid., 1 January 1847.

4. Wilfred Blunt, *England's Michelangelo*, Hamish Hamilton, 1975, p. 41.

5. ibid.

6. Lady Duff Gordon, journals, 12 February 1849.

7. ibid., 15 November 1873.

8. ibid., 22 August 1865.

9. ibid., 4 April 1854.

10. ibid., 31 December 1857.

11. Sir Andrew Duff Gordon, verbal, 1989.

12. Lady Duff Gordon, journals, 9 August 1866.

13. Francis Jekyll, *Gertrude Jekyll: A Memoir*, Cape, 1934, p. 35.

14. Lady Duff Gordon, journals, 13 March 1855.

15. ibid., 1 December 1855.

16. Gertrude Jekyll, 'Recollections of Old Bramley', Bramley parish magazine, September 1932.

17. Gertrude Jekyll, *Children and Gardens*, Country Life, 1908, p. 67.

18. ibid., p. 65.

19. Lord Hamilton of Dalzell, correspondence, 6 January 1990.

20. Gertrude Jekyll, *Children and Gardens*, p. 68.

21. RIBA, Lutyens Family Papers, LuE/6/9/7(iii).

22. ibid., LuE/6/9/12(iv).

23. Gertrude Jekyll, *Old West Surrey*, Longmans Green, 1904, p. 306.

24. Francis Jekyll, *Gertrude Jekyll: A Memoir*, p. 33.

25. RHS, Gertrude Jekyll to Mrs Furze, 14 July 1905.

26. Francis Jekyll, *Gertrude Jekyll: A Memoir*, p. 34.

27. ibid.

28. ibid.

29. Gertrude Jekyll, *Home and Garden*, Longmans Green, 1900, p. 112.

30. *The Times*, 10 December 1932, p. 12.

31. Francis Jekyll, *Gertrude Jekyll: A Memoir*, p. 120.

32. Gertrude Jekyll, *A Gardener's Testament*, Country Life, 1937, p. 342.

33. Gertrude Jekyll, *Wall, Water and Woodland Gardens*, Antique Collectors' Club, 1986, p. 366.

34. *The Times*, 10 December 1932, p. 12.

35. ibid.

36. Gertrude Jekyll, *Wood and Garden*, Longmans Green, 1899, p. 101.

Chapter 4: 1861–2

1. David Barrie (ed.), *Modern Painters – John Ruskin*, Deutsch, 1987, p. 51.

2. ibid., p. xvii.

3. Francis Jekyll, *Gertrude Jekyll: A Memoir*, Cape, 1934, p. 38.

4. E. P. Thompson, *William Morris: Romantic to Revolutionary*, Merlin, 1977, p. 95.

5. Richard Thames, *William Morris*, Shire Publications, 1979, p. 15.

6. Anthea Callen, *Angel in the Studio*, Astragal Books, 1979, p. 29.

7. Mrs C. W. Earle, *Pot-pourri from a Surrey Garden*, 21st edn, London, 1900, p. 307.

8. ibid., pp. 311–12.

9. Clive Ashwin, 'Art Education and Policies 1768–1915', *Social Res. Higher Ed.*, October 1975, p. 46.

10. ibid., p. 49.

11. Stuart Macdonald, *The History and Philosophy of Art Education*, University of London, 1970, p. 195.

12. Christopher Frayling, *The Royal College of Art*, Century, 1987, p. 41.

13. Clive Ashwin, 'Art Education and Policies 1768–1915', p. 44.

14. Mrs Oliphant, *Miss Marjoribanks*, Virago, 1988, p. 138.

15. Christopher Frayling, *The Royal College of Art*, p. 48.

16. Stuart Macdonald, *The History and Philosophy of Art Education*, p. 235.

17. Christopher Frayling, *The Royal College of Art*, p. 38.

18. Stuart Macdonald, *The History and Philosophy of Art Education*, p. 50.

19. ibid., p. 249.

20. Nikolaus Pevsner, *Academies of Art*, Cambridge University Press, 1940, p. 231.

21. David Barrie (ed.), *Modern Painters – John Ruskin*, p. 33.

22. M.-E. Chevreul, *Principles of Harmony and Contrast of Colours*, London, 1854, p. 17.

23. David Barrie (ed.), *Modern Painters – John Ruskin*, p. xxxvii.

24. *The Garden*, 22: 177.

25. Fiona MacCarthy, *Eric Gill*, Faber, 1989, p. 274.

Chapter 5: 1863

1. Lady Duff Gordon, journals, 31 December 1857.

2. ibid., 4 August 1863.

3. William James, *The Order of Release*, Murray, 1948, p. 30.

4. ibid., p. 33.

5. Sheila Birkenhead, *Illustrious Friends*, Hamish Hamilton, 1965, p. 126.

6. William James, *The Order of Release*, p. 110.

7. Sheila Birkenhead, *Illustrious Friends*, p. 103.

8. ibid., p. 128.

9. Francis Jekyll, *Gertrude Jekyll: A Memoir*, Cape, 1934, p. 40.

10. Gertrude Jekyll, *Wood and Garden*, Longmans Green, 1899, p. 4.

11. David Barrie (ed.), *Modern Painters – John Ruskin*, Deutsch, 1987, p. xliii.

12. Francis Jekyll, *Gertrude Jekyll: A Memoir*, p. 47.

13. Gertrude Jekyll, *Home and Garden*, Longmans Green, 1900, p. 296.

14. ibid., p. 214.

15. Francis Jekyll, *Gertrude Jekyll: A Memoir*, p. 45.

16. ibid., p. 58.

17. ibid., p. 49.

18. ibid., p. 50.

19. ibid., p. 58.

20. ibid., p. 46.

21. ibid., p. 68.

22. ibid., p. 61.

23. ibid., p. 62.

24. ibid., p. 64.

25. David Barrie (ed.), *Modern Painters – John Ruskin*, p. 30.

26. Francis Jekyll, *Gertrude Jekyll: A Memoir*, p. 64.

27. ibid., p. 63.

28. ibid.

29. ibid., p. 64.

30. ibid., p. 66.

31. ibid., p. 71.

32. Gertrude Jekyll, *Wood and Garden*, p. 236.

PART TWO: ARTIST

Chapter 6: 1864–7

1. Lady Duff Gordon, journals, 21 January 1864.

2. ibid., 8 August 1864.

3. ibid., 31 December 1856.

4. ibid., 6 April 1870.

5. ibid., 31 November 1854.

6. Wilfred Blunt, *England's Michelangelo*, Hamish Hamilton, 1975, p. 99.

7. ibid., p. 43.

8. Isobel Durrant, verbal, 1990.

9. Lady Duff Gordon, journals, 18 February 1865.

10. ibid., 1 March 1865.

11. ibid.

12. Francis Jekyll, *Gertrude Jekyll: A Memoir*, Cape, 1934, p. 78.

13 Wilfred Blunt, *England's Michelangelo*, p. 43.

14. Lady Duff Gordon, journals, 19 February 1866.

15. ibid., 23 January 1865.

16. Stuart Macdonald, *The History and Philosophy of Art Education*, University of London, 1970, p. 175.

17 William Gaunt, *Victorian Olympus*, Cardinal, 1988, p. 76.

18. Christopher Wood, *Dictionary of Victorian Painters*, Antique Collectors Club, 1978, p. 161.

19. Francis Jekyll, *Gertrude Jekyll: A Memoir*, p. 78.

314   *Gertrude Jekyll*

20. ibid.
21. Peter Quennell, *John Ruskin: The Portrait of a Prophet*, Collins, 1949, p. 184.
22. ibid., p. 156.
23. Lady Duff Gordon, journals, 8 January 1867.
24. John Ruskin, *Works* (ed. E. T. Cook and Alexander Wedderburn), London, 1903–9, Vol. 13, p. 235.
25. ibid., p. 189.
26. Lady Duff Gordon, journals, 25 October 1866.
27. William Gaunt, *Victorian Olympus*, p. 72.
28. Wilfred Blunt, *England's Michelangelo*, p. 109.
29. Mrs C. W. Earle, *Memoirs and Memories*, Smith, Elder & Co., 1882, p. 242.
30. Wilfred Blunt, *England's Michelangelo*, p. 207.
31. Lady Duff Gordon, journals, 20 June 1867.
32. ibid., 7 August 1867.

Chapter 7: 1868–9

1. Gertrude Jekyll, *A Gardener's Testament*, Country Life, 1937, p. 25.
2. Gertrude Jekyll, *Garden Ornament* (with Christopher Hussey), Country Life, 1918.
3. Gertrude Jekyll, *Home and Garden*, Longmans Green, 1900, p. 113.
4. ibid., p. 114.
5. ibid.
6. Anthea Callen, *Angel in the Studio*, Astragal Books, 1979, p. 26.
7. Lady Duff Gordon, journals, 12 August 1867.
8. Francis Jekyll, *Gertrude Jekyll: A Memoir*, Cape, 1934, p. 82.
9. George Leslie, *Our River*, London, 1888, p. 129.
10. Francis Jekyll, *Gertrude Jekyll: A Memoir*, p. 83.
11. George Leslie, *Our River*, p. 36.
12. ibid.
13. Francis Jekyll, *Gertrude Jekyll: A Memoir*, p. 82.
14. ibid., p. 83.
15. Lady Duff Gordon, journals, 8 August 1864.
16. Harrow School Archives.
17. Lady Duff Gordon, journals, 1 August 1866.
18. Walter Jekyll, *The Bible Untrustworthy*, Watts, 1904, p. 283.
19. ibid.

20. Francis Jekyll, *Gertrude Jekyll: A Memoir*, p. 85.

21. Gertrude Jekyll, *Wall, Water and Woodland Gardening*, Antique Collectors' Club, 1986, p. 255.

22. Gertrude Jekyll, *Children and Gardens*, Country Life, 1908, p. 51.

23. ibid.

24. Lady Duff Gordon, journals, 9 February 1869.

25. Francis Jekyll, *Gertrude Jekyll: A Memoir*, p. 87.

26. E. P. Thompson, *William Morris: Romantic to Revolutionary*, Merlin, 1977, p. 89.

27. Ian Bradley, *William Morris and His World*, Thames & Hudson, 1978, p. 11.

28. E. P. Thompson, *William Morris: Romantic to Revolutionary*, p. 99.

29. Jack Lindsay, *William Morris, His Life and Work*, Constable, 1975, pp. 153–4.

30. ibid.

31. Gertrude Jekyll, 'House Decoration', *National Review*, 24: 523.

32. Lady Duff Gordon, journals, 14 August 1863.

33. George Leslie, *Our River*, p. 35.

34. Michael and Rosanna Tooley (ed.), *Gertrude Jekyll: Artist, Gardener, Craftsman*, Michaelmas Books, 1984, p. 117.

Chapter 8: 1870–71

1. Francis Jekyll, *Gertrude Jekyll: A Memoir*, Cape, 1934, p. 89.

2. ibid.

3. Hester Burton, *Barbara Bodichon*, Murray, 1949, p. 21.

4. ibid., p. 143.

5. Lady Duff Gordon, journals, 7 July 1868.

6. ibid., 28 June 1870.

7. Frederick Eden, *A Garden in Venice*, Country Life, 1903, p. 10.

8. Lady Duff Gordon, journals, 13 December 1866.

9. ibid., 2 August 1867.

10. ibid., 1 April 1870.

11. John Ruskin, *Works* (ed. E. T. Cook and Alexander Wedderburn), London, 1903–9, Vol. 13, p. 249.

12. Gertrude Jekyll, *Home and Garden*, Longmans Green, 1900, p. 16.

13. ibid.

14. ibid., p. 113.

15. Francis Jekyll, *Gertrude Jekyll: A Memoir*, p. 88.

16. Gertrude Jekyll, *Home and Garden*, p. 124.
17. *Wargrave Magazine*, May 1870.
18. ibid., April–May 1870.
19. Gertrude Jekyll, *Children and Gardens*, Country Life, 1908, p. 47.
20. ibid.
21. ibid., pp. 47–8.
22. *Wargrave Magazine*, June 1873.
23. Lady Duff Gordon, journals, 2 May 1874.
24. ibid.
25. ibid.
26. ibid.
27. *Wargrave Magazine*, July 1870.
28. ibid.
29. Lady Duff Gordon, journals, 1 May 1870.
30. Francis Jekyll, *Gertrude Jekyll: A Memoir*, p. 87.
31. ibid.
32. ibid.
33. ibid.
34. ibid.
35. ibid.
36. ibid.
37. ibid.
38. Gertrude Jekyll, *A Gardener's Testament*, Country Life, 1937, p. 78.
39. Francis Jekyll, *Gertrude Jekyll: A Memoir*, p. 88.
40. William Gaunt, *Victorian Olympus*, Cardinal, 1988, p. 71.
41. ibid., p. 144.
42. Christopher Hussey, *The Life of Sir Edwin Lutyens*, Country Life, 1953, p. 7.
43. William Robinson, *The Wild Garden*, 1st edn, 1870, p. 33.
44. ibid., p. 11.
45. George Leslie, *Our River*, London, 1888, p. 35.
46. Francis Jekyll, *Gertrude Jekyll: A Memoir*, p. 46.

Chapter 9: 1872–4

1. *The Times*, 10 December 1932, p. 12.
2. Lutyens Family Papers, LuE/7/8/4(i–).
3. Eileen Barber, verbal, 1989.
4. ibid.

5. C. Lewis Hinde, *Hercules Brabazon Brabazon: his art and life*, George Allen, 1912, p. 56.

6. Francis Jekyll, *Gertrude Jekyll: A Memoir*, Cape, 1934, p. 92.

7. Lady Duff Gordon, journals, 24 December 1872.

8. ibid., 3 June 1873.

9. Hester Burton, *Barbara Bodichon*, Murray, 1949, p. 43.

10. ibid., p. 95.

11. ibid., p. 94.

12. Lutyens Family Papers, LuE/4/9/4(i–).

13. Francis Jekyll, *Gertrude Jekyll: A Memoir*, p. 96.

14. Jehanne Wake, *Princess Louise*, Collins, 1988, p. 133.

15. Eileen Barber correspondence.

16. ibid.

17. Lutyens Family Papers, LuE/3/10/4.

18. Eileen Barber correspondence.

19. Francis Jekyll, *Gertrude Jekyll: A Memoir*, pp. 96–7.

20. Hester Burton, *Barbara Bodichon*, p. 83.

21. Gertrude Jekyll, *Wood and Garden*, Longmans Green, 1899, p. 14.

22. ibid.

23. *The Garden*, 17: 124.

24. ibid.

25. Francis Jekyll, *Gertrude Jekyll: A Memoir*, p. 99.

26. ibid.

27. George Leslie, *Our River*, London, 1888, p. 36.

28. ibid.

Chapter 10: 1874–6

1. Lady Duff Gordon, journals, 11 February 1874.

2. ibid., 12 January 1874.

3. ibid., 6 January 1874.

4. ibid., 28 February 1874.

5. ibid., 26 February 1874.

6. Mark Girouard, *The Victorian Country House*, Yale University Press, 1979, p. 1.

7. Nikolaus Pevsner and Edward Hubbard, *The Buildings of England: Cheshire*, Penguin, 1971, p. 208.

8. Lady Duff Gordon, journals, 29 August 1874.

9. ibid., 26 August 1874.

10. ibid.

11. ibid., 14 July 1874.

12. ibid., 17 August 1874.

13. Francis Jekyll, *Gertrude Jekyll: A Memoir*, Cape, 1934, p. 100.

14. ibid.

15. ibid.

16. Nikolaus Pevsner and Edward Hubbard, *The Buildings of England: Cheshire*, p. 208.

17. Michael and Rosanna Tooley (eds), *Gertrude Jekyll: Artist, Gardener, Craftsman*, Michaelmas Books, 1984, p. 37.

18. Francis Jekyll, *Gertrude Jekyll: A Memoir*, p. 101.

19. ibid.

20. Denys Sutton, *Nocturne: The Art of James McNeill Whistler*, Country Life, 1963, p. 64.

21. ibid., p. 91.

22. J. R. Gretton (ed.), *Gertrude Jekyll: Letters to William Nicholson*, Dereham Books, 1981, p. 9.

23. Gertrude Jekyll, *Colour Schemes for the Flower Garden*, Country Life, 1914, p. 115.

24. George Leslie, *Our River*, London, 1888, p. 35.

25. ibid.

26. Gertrude Jekyll, *Wood and Garden*, Longmans Green, 1899, p. 158.

27. Shirley Hibberd, *The Amateur's Flower Garden*, London, 1878, p. 15.

28. Mea Allan, *William Robinson*, Faber, 1982, p. 115.

29. ibid., p. 111.

30. ibid., p. 115.

31. ibid.

32. ibid.

33. Lady Duff Gordon, journals, 28 March 1874.

34. ibid., 18 January 1875.

35. Edward Jekyll, will.

36. ibid.

37. Francis Jekyll, *Gertrude Jekyll: A Memoir*, p. 102.

38. John Ruskin, *Works* (ed. E. T. Cook and Alexander Wedderburn), London, 1903–9, Vol. 9, p. 38.

39. ibid., Vol. 10, p. 82.

40. George Leslie, *Our River*, p. 36.

41. ibid.
42. ibid.

PART THREE: HOME-MAKER

Chapter 11: 1877–81

1. Gertrude Jekyll, *Home and Garden*, Longmans Green, 1900, p. 233.
2. Robert Lutyens, *Sir Edwin Lutyens, An Appreciation in Perspective*, Country Life, 1942, p. 42.
3. Ian Nairn and Nikolaus Pevsner, *The Buildings of England: Surrey*, Penguin, 1971, p. 377.
4. ibid.
5. Mea Allan, *William Robinson*, Faber, 1982, p. 142.
6. ibid.
7. Francis Jekyll, *Gertrude Jekyll: A Memoir*, Cape, 1934, p. 105.
8. Bodichon Mss. in possession of Anne Moore, n.d.
9. Hester Burton, *Barbara Bodichon*, Murray, 1949, p. 206.
10. Gertrude Jekyll, *Wood and Garden*, Longmans Green, 1899, p. 120.
11. Gertrude Jekyll, *A Gardener's Testament*, Country Life, 1937, p. 58.
12. Bodichon Mss. at Girton College.
13. Francis Jekyll, *Gertrude Jekyll: A Memoir*, p. 105.
14. *The Garden*, 22: 191–3.
15. ibid.
16. Gertrude Jekyll, *Wood and Garden*, p. 156.
17. Miles Hadfield, *Gardening in Britain*, Hutchinson, 1960, p. 373.
18. Geoffrey Taylor, *The Victorian Flower Garden*, Skeffington, 1952, p. 178.
19. Gertrude Jekyll, *A Gardener's Testament*, p. 12.
20. *The Garden*, 57: 17.
21. Gertrude Jekyll, *Wood and Garden*, p. 184.
22. Gertrude Jekyll, *A Gardener's Testament*, pp. 12–13.
23. *The Garden*, 22: 192.
24. Francis Jekyll, *Gertrude Jekyll: A Memoir*, p. 108.
25. ibid.
26. David Barrie (ed.), *Modern Painters – John Ruskin*, Deutsch, 1987, p. 480.
27. William Robinson, *The Wild Garden*, 1st edn, 1870, p. 11.
28. ibid., 2nd edn, 1988, p. 4.
29. *Ampthill & District News*, 12 March 1921.

30. Simon Houfe, 'Gertrude Jekyll and Bedfordshire', *Bedfordshire Magazine*, 19: 218.
31. Bedfordshire Record Office, DV1 C119.
32. ibid.
33. Marion Shepherd, verbal, 1989.
34. David McKenna, verbal, 1989.
35. Frances Horner, *Time Remembered*, Heinemann, 1933, p. 20.
36. Mary Lutyens, *Edwin Lutyens*, Murray, 1980, p. 24.
37. Francis Jekyll, *Gertrude Jekyll: A Memoir*, p. 104.

Chapter 12: 1882–5

1. Mea Allan, *William Robinson*, Faber, 1982, p. 135.
2. *The Garden*, 22: 330.
3. ibid., 177.
4. David Barrie (ed.), *Modern Painters – John Ruskin*, Deutsch, 1987, p. 207.
5. Michael and Rosanna Tooley (eds), *Gertrude Jekyll: Artist, Gardener, Craftsman*, Michaelmas Books, 1984, p. 67.
6. *The Garden*, 22: 177.
7. ibid., 470.
8. ibid., 562.
9. ibid., 177.
10. ibid., 470.
11. ibid.
12. ibid.
13. Gertrude Jekyll, *A Gardener's Testament*, Country Life, 1937, p. 13.
14. Betty Massingham, *Miss Jekyll: Portrait of a Great Gardener*, David & Charles, 1966, p. 56.
15. Francis Jekyll, *Gertrude Jekyll: A Memoir*, Cape, 1934, p. 111.
16. Gertrude Jekyll, *A Gardener's Testament*, p. 12.
17. Agnes Jekyll, *Ne Oublie*, privately printed, n.d., p. ix.
18. Kew Mss., 90: 118.
19. ibid., 66: 501.
20. *Country Life*, 31: 737.
21. William Robinson, *The English Flower Garden*, Murray, 1895, p. v.
22. ibid.
23. Kew Mss., 147: 623.
24. *The Garden*, 25: 248.

25. ibid.
26. National Library of Wales, Ms 20, 139C, p. 159.
27. ibid., pp. 163–4.
28. ibid.
29. ibid., p. 159.
30. Betty Massingham, *Miss Jekyll: Portrait of a Great Gardener*, p. 146.
31. Francis Jekyll, *Gertrude Jekyll: A Memoir*, pp. 112–13.
32. *The Garden*, 27: 141.
33. ibid.
34. ibid., 277.
35. Mea Allan, *William Robinson*, p. 142.
36. Francis Jekyll, *Gertrude Jekyll: A Memoir*, p. 116.
37. Judith B. Tankard and Michael R. Van Valkenburgh, *Gertrude Jekyll: A Vision of Garden and Wood*, Murray, 1988, p. 10.
38. Reef Point Collection, Album 2, photo 310.
39. ibid., photo 376.

Chapter 13: 1886–91

1. Wordsworth, *The Prelude*.
2. *The Garden*, 19: 527.
3. *Country Life*, 31: 737.
4. Herbert Read, *Anarchy and Order*, Faber, 1954, pp. 161–2.
5. Gertrude Jekyll, *Home and Garden*, Longmans Green, 1900, p. 296.
6. Francis Jekyll, *Gertrude Jekyll: A Memoir*, Cape, 1934, p. 117.
7. Gertrude Jekyll, *Edinburgh Review*, 184: 183.
8. Mrs C. W. Earle, *Memoirs and Memories*, Smith, Elder & Co., 1882, p. 207.
9. ibid., p. 208.
10. Francis Jekyll, *Gertrude Jekyll: A Memoir*, p. 117.
11. Gertrude Jekyll, *Children and Gardens*, Country Life, 1908, p. 94.
12. Betty Massingham, *Miss Jekyll: Portrait of a Great Gardener*, David & Charles, 1966, p. 52.
13. Francis Jekyll, *Gertrude Jekyll: A Memoir*, p. 118.
14. Gertrude Jekyll, *Gardens for Small Country Houses*, Country Life, 1912, p. 54.
15. *Garden Illustrated*, 48: 312.
16. ibid.
17. Reef Point Collection, Album 3, photo 710.

18. Francis Jekyll, *Gertrude Jekyll: A Memoir*, p. 4.
19. ibid.
20. ibid.
21. Mary Lutyens, *Edwin Lutyens*, Murray, 1980, p. 15.
22. Francis Jekyll, *Gertrude Jekyll: A Memoir*, p. 7.
23. ibid.
24. Mary Lutyens, *Edwin Lutyens*, p. 24.
25. Gertrude Jekyll, *Wood and Garden*, Longmans Green, 1899, p. 278.
26. Francis Jekyll, *Gertrude Jekyll: A Memoir*, p. 118.
27. Betty Massingham, *Miss Jekyll: Portrait of a Great Gardener*, p. 55.

Chapter 14: 1892–5

1. C. Lewis Hinde, *Hercules Brabazon Brabazon: his art and life*, George Allen, 1912, p. 6.
2. 28 January 1882.
3. J. S. Dearden (ed.), *The Professor: Arthur Severn's Memoir of John Ruskin*, London, 1967, p. 80.
4. Gertrude Jekyll, *Edinburgh Review*, 184: 182.
5. Fine Art Society catalogue, 1974.
6. George Moore, *Modern Painting*, London, 1893, p. 209.
7. Fine Art Society catalogue, 1974.
8. Christopher Hussey, *The Life of Sir Edwin Lutyens*, Country Life, 1953, p. 23.
9. Edwin Lutyens, *The Letters to his wife, Lady Emily*, ed. Clayre Percy and Jane Ridley, Collins, 1985, p. 24.
10. Katherine Everett, *Bricks and Flowers*, Constable, 1949, p. 129.
11. RIBA, Lutyens Family Papers, LuE/9/2/8(i–).
12. Betty Massingham, *Miss Jekyll: Portrait of a Great Gardener*, David & Charles, 1966, p. 145.
13. Christopher Hussey, *The Life of Sir Edwin Lutyens*, p. 6.
14. ibid., p. 24.
15. Francis Jekyll, *Gertrude Jekyll: A Memoir*, Cape, 1934, p. 8.
16. ibid.
17. Christopher Hussey, *The Life of Sir Edwin Lutyens*, p. 25.
18. Francis Jekyll, *Gertrude Jekyll: A Memoir*, p. 8.
19. ibid.
20. Herbert Baker, *Architecture and Personalities*, Country Life, 1944, pp. 15–16.

21. Mea Allan, *William Robinson*, Faber, 1982, p. 142.
22. Francis Jekyll, *Gertrude Jekyll: A Memoir*, p. 101.
23. ibid., p. 121.
24. Gertrude Jekyll, *Home and Garden*, Longmans Green, 1900, p. 289.
25. ibid.
26. ibid.
27. ibid.
28. *The Garden*, 45: 167.
29. Gertrude Jekyll, *National Review*, 24: 519.
30. ibid., 519–20.
31. Betty Massingham, *Miss Jekyll: Portrait of a Great Gardener*, p. 52.

Chapter 15: 1896–7

1. Gertrude Jekyll, *Home and Garden*, Longmans Green, 1900, p. 9.
2. Christopher Hussey, *The Life of Sir Edwin Lutyens*, Country Life, 1953, p. 28.
3. Francis Jekyll, *Gertrude Jekyll: A Memoir*, Cape, 1934, p. 124.
4. Gertrude Jekyll, *Home and Garden*, p. 16.
5. ibid., p. 10.
6. ibid., p. 8.
7. ibid., p. 17.
8. Christopher Hussey, *The Life of Sir Edwin Lutyens*, p. 31.
9. Gertrude Jekyll, *Home and Garden*, p. 18.
10. ibid., pp. 18–19.
11. ibid., pp. 2–3.
12. ibid., p. 3.
13. ibid., p. 2.
14. ibid., p. 14.
15. Mavis Batey in Michael and Rosanna Tooley (eds), *Gertrude Jekyll: Artist, Gardener, Craftsman*, Michaelmas Books, 1984, p. 19.
16. Peter Savage, *Lorimer and the Edinburgh Craft Designers*, Paul Harris, 1980, p. 25.
17. ibid.
18. Gertrude Jekyll, *Home and Garden*, p. 1.
19. Peter Savage, *Lorimer and the Edinburgh Craft Designers*, p. 25.
20. Christopher Hussey, *The Life of Sir Edwin Lutyens*, p. 32.
21. Francis Jekyll, *Gertrude Jekyll: A Memoir*, p. 7.

22. Betty Massingham, *Miss Jekyll: Portrait of a Great Gardener*, David & Charles, 1966, p. 146.

23. Logan Pearsall Smith, *Reperusals and Recollections*, Constable, 1936, p. 51.

24. Gertrude Jekyll, *Home and Garden*, p. 10.

25. ibid., p. 9.

26. ibid., p. 8.

27. Gertrude Jekyll, *Wall, Water and Woodland Gardens*, Antique Collectors' Club, 1986, p. 66.

28. Gertrude Jekyll, *Home and Garden*, p. 8.

29. Edwin Lutyens, *The Letters to his wife, Lady Emily*, ed. Clayre Percy and Jane Ridley, Collins, 1985, p. 43.

30. RIBA, Lutyens Family Papers, LuE/3/2/8.

31. ibid.

32. ibid., LuE/1/1/1.

33. Mary Lutyens, *Edwin Lutyens*, Murray, 1980, p. 31.

34. ibid.

35. Edwin Lutyens, *The Letters to his wife, Lady Emily*, p. 12.

36. Mary Lutyens, *Edwin Lutyens*, p. 31.

37. ibid.

38. RIBA, Lutyens Family Papers, LuE/1/3/3(ii).

39. Edwin Lutyens, *The Letters to his wife, Lady Emily*, p. 19.

40. Christopher Hussey, *The Life of Sir Edwin Lutyens*, p. 40.

41. RIBA, Lutyens Family Papers, LuE/1/3/5(ii–).

42. Edwin Lutyens, *The Letters to his wife, Lady Emily*, p. 43.

43. RIBA, Lutyens Family Papers, LuE/1/3/11(i–).

44. ibid.

45. ibid., LuE/1/4/14(i–).

46. ibid., LuE/1/5/13(ii).

47. ibid., LuE/1/5/17.

48. ibid., LuE/1/6/1(i–).

49. ibid., LuE/1/6/4(ii).

50. ibid., LuE/2/3/10(i–).

51. ibid., LuE/1/6/3(viii).

52. ibid.

53. ibid., LuE assim.

54. ibid., LuE/1/6/3(iv).

55. ibid.

56. Edwin Lutyens, *The Letters to his wife, Lady Emily*, p. 43.

57. RIBA, Lutyens Family Papers, LuE/1/5/15(i–).
58. ibid.
59. ibid.
60. ibid., LuE/1/3/17(i–).
61. ibid., LuE/6/5/20(ii–).
62. ibid., LuE/2/1/4(iv).
63. Francis Jekyll, *Gertrude Jekyll: A Memoir*, p. 161.
64. ibid.
65. RIBA, Lutyens Family Papers, LuE/2/2/10(i–).
66. Christopher Hussey, *The Life of Sir Edwin Lutyens*, p. 74.
67. RIBA, Lutyens Family Papers, LuE/2/2/11(i–).
68. ibid.
69. Edwin Lutyens, *The Letters to his wife, Lady Emily*, p. 49.
70. RIBA, Lutyens Family Papers, LuE/2/3/16(i–).
71. ibid., LuE/2/4/6(vi).
72. ibid., LuE/2/4/1(vi–).
73. ibid., LuE/2/6/6.
74. ibid., LuE/2/6/17(ii–).
75. ibid., LuE/1/6/74(i–).
76. Gertrude Jekyll, *Home and Garden*, p. 294.
77. *Gardeners' Chronicle*, 30 October 1897, p. 310.
78. *Journal of Horticulture*, 28 October 1897, p. 414.
79. ibid.
80. ibid.
81. *Gardeners' Chronicle*, 30 October 1897, pp. 316–17.
82. *The Glory of the Garden*, Sotheby's catalogue, January 1987, p. 157.
83. Peter Savage, *Lorimer and the Edinburgh Craft Designers*, p. 25.
84. Roderick Gradidge, *Edwin Lutyens: Architect Laureate*, Allen & Unwin, 1981, p. 29.

PART FOUR: WRITER

Chapter 16: 1896–7

1. Francis Jekyll, *Gertrude Jekyll: A Memoir*, Cape, 1934, p. 161.
2. ibid., p. 58.
3. Gertrude Jekyll, *Country Life*, 10: 272.
4. Gertrude Jekyll, *Home and Garden*, Longmans Green, 1900, p. 231.

5. ibid., p. 280.

6. Gertrude Jekyll, *Guardian*, 51 (1): 500.

7. ibid.

8. ibid.

9. Gertrude Jekyll, *Wood and Garden*, Longmans Green, 1899, p. 211.

10. Gertrude Jekyll, *Home and Garden*, p. 165.

11. Gertrude Jekyll, *Guardian*, 51 (1): 500.

12. Gertrude Jekyll, *Wood and Garden*, p. 1.

13. Gertrude Jekyll, *Guardian*, 51 (1): 500.

14. Gertrude Jekyll, *Wood and Garden*, p. 2.

15. Gertrude Jekyll, *Guardian*, 51 (2): 610.

16. ibid.

17. ibid. (1): 951.

18. John Ruskin, *Works* (ed. E. T. Cook and Alexander Wedderburn), London, 1903–9, Vol. 10, p. 203.

19. Michael and Rosanna Tooley, *The Gardens of Gertrude Jekyll in Northern England*, Michaelmas Books, 1982, p. 1.

20. ibid.

21. Gertrude Jekyll, *Guardian*, 51 (1): 792.

22. ibid. (2): 1106.

23. ibid.

24. ibid. (2): 1221.

25. ibid. (2): 1317.

26. ibid. (1): 355.

27. ibid.

28. Christopher Hussey, *The Life of Sir Edwin Lutyens*, Country Life, 1953, p. 87.

29. Gertrude Jekyll, *Country Life*, 39: 542.

30. Gertrude Jekyll, *Wood and Garden*, p. 196.

31. Gertrude Jekyll, *Guardian*, 51 (1): 268.

32. ibid.

33. Mrs C. W. Earle, *Memoirs and Memories*, Smith, Elder & Co., 1882, p. 224.

34. Mrs C. W. Earle, *Pot-pourri from a Surrey Garden*, 21st edn, London, 1900, p. 170.

35. Gertrude Jekyll, *Wood and Garden*, p. 273.

36. Mrs C. W. Earle, *Memoirs and Memories*, p. 296.

37. RIBA, Lutyens Family Papers, LuE/4/6/19(i–).

38. ibid., LuE/1/3/16(ii).

39. Mrs C. W. Earle, *Memoirs and Memories*, p. 337.
40. Mrs C. W. Earle, *Pot-pourri from a Surrey Garden*, p. 250.
41. ibid.
42. ibid., p. 251.

Chapter 17: 1898–1900

1. Reynolds Hole, *Our Gardens*, Dent, 1899, p. 234.
2. Betty Massingham, *Miss Jekyll: Portrait of a Great Gardener*, David & Charles, 1966, p. 67.
3. RIBA, Lutyens Family Papers, LuE/3/10/4.
4. Gertrude Jekyll, *Wood and Garden*, Longmans Green, 1899, p. 82.
5. ibid., p. 3.
6. ibid., p. 2.
7. ibid., p. 176.
8. ibid., p. 175.
9. ibid., p. 185.
10. Mea Allan, *The Tradescants*, Michael Joseph, 1964, p. 26.
11. Gertrude Jekyll, *Wood and Garden*, p. 243.
12. ibid., p. 250.
13. ibid., p. 251.
14. ibid., p. 222.
15. ibid., pp. 221–2.
16. ibid., p. 223.
17. ibid., p. 228.
18. ibid.
19. Betty Massingham, *Miss Jekyll: Portrait of a Great Gardener*, p. 165.
20. Gertrude Jekyll, *Home and Garden*, Longmans Green, 1900, p. 216.
21. ibid., p. 219.
22. ibid., p. 220.
23. ibid., p. 223.
24. Gertrude Jekyll, *Wood and Garden*, p. 263.
25. ibid.
26. ibid., p. 266.
27. ibid., p. 272.
28. ibid.
29. ibid., p. 279.
30. Gertrude Jekyll, *Old West Surrey*, Longmans Green, 1904, p. 262.
31. ibid., p. 264.

32. ibid.

33. Harriet Mills, verbal, 1989.

34. Ian Nairn and Nikolaus Pevsner, *The Buildings of England: Surrey*, Penguin, 1971, p. 124.

35. Gertrude Jekyll, *Home and Garden*, p. vii.

36. ibid., p. viii.

37. Logan Pearsall Smith, *Reperusals and Recollections*, Constable, 1936, p. 50.

38. RIBA, Lutyens Family Papers, LuE/17/9/1 (iv).

39. ibid., LuE/1/3/2.

40. ibid., LuE/1/5/16(i–).

41. ibid., LuE/1/5/15(i–).

42. ibid., LuE/3/10/4.

43. ibid., LuE/4/2/9.

44. Gertrude Jekyll, *Home and Garden*, p. 49.

45. ibid.

46. ibid., p. 52.

47. ibid., pp. 52–3.

48. Gertrude Jekyll and George S. Elgood, *Some English Gardens*, Longmans Green, 1904, p. 94.

49. Betty Massingham, *Turn on the Fountains*, Gollancz, 1974, p. 182.

50. ibid.

51. Gertrude Jekyll, *Home and Garden*, p. 295.

52. ibid.

53. ibid., p. 11.

54. Mary Lutyens, *Edwin Lutyens*, Murray, 1980, p. 27.

55. Gertrude Jekyll, *Home and Garden*, p. 120.

56. ibid., pp. 120–21.

57. ibid., p. 116.

58. ibid., p. 117.

59. Francis Jekyll, *Gertrude Jekyll: A Memoir*, Cape, 1934, p. 158.

60. RIBA, Lutyens Family Papers, LuE/1/6/7(i–).

61. Francis Jekyll, *Gertrude Jekyll: A Memoir*, p. 164.

62. Gertrude Jekyll, *Home and Garden*, p. 260.

63. ibid., p. 255.

64. John Nicholls Correspondence, Gertrude Jekyll to Kate Leslie, 13 February 1900.

65. Hilary Spurling, *Secrets of a Woman's Heart*, Hodder & Stoughton, 1984, p. 90.

Chapter 18: 1900–1901

1. John Ruskin, *Works* (ed. E. T. Cook and Alexander Wedderburn), London, 1903–9, Vol. 8, p. xlii.
2. *The Garden*, 57: 37.
3. John D. Sedding, *Garden Craft Old and New*, Kegan Paul, 1895, p. vi.
4. ibid., p. 153.
5. ibid., p. 31.
6. ibid., p. 64.
7. Reginald Blomfield, *The Formal Garden in England*, Macmillan, 1892, p. 2.
8. Gertrude Jekyll, *Edinburgh Review*, 184: 179.
9. Geoffrey Taylor, *The Victorian Flower Garden*, Skeffington, 1952, pp. 84–5.
10. William Robinson, *The English Flower Garden*, Murray, 4th edn, p. 12.
11. ibid., p. 16.
12. Gertrude Jekyll, *Edinburgh Review*, 184: 178–9.
13. Gertrude Jekyll, *Wall, Water and Woodland Gardens*, Antique Collectors' Club, 1986, p. 141.
14. ibid., p. 365.
15. Reef Point Collection, uncat. file.
16. Gertrude Jekyll, *Edinburgh Review*, 184: 178.
17. Gertrude Jekyll, *Wall, Water and Woodland Gardens*, p. 141.
18. ibid.
19. ibid.
20. Thomas Twidell, verbal, 1990.
21. George Leslie, *Riverside Letters*, Macmillan, 1896, p. 168.
22. Hilary Spurling, *Secrets of a Woman's Heart*, Hodder & Stoughton, 1984, p. 90.
23. ibid.
24. *The Times*, 19 September 1936.
25. Hilary Spurling, *Secrets of a Woman's Heart*, p. 90.
26. Michael and Rosanna Tooley (eds), *Gertrude Jekyll: Artist, Gardener, Craftsman*, Michaelmas Books, 1984, p. 114.
27. *The Garden*, 59: 223.
28. *The Times*, 30 September 1932, p. 7.
29. *Who Was Who*, III, p. 709.

30. RIBA, Lutyens Family Papers, LuE/4/5/8 (i–).
31. ibid.
32. Michael and Rosanna Tooley (eds), *Gertrude Jekyll: Artist, Gardener, Craftsman*, p. 113.
33. ibid.
34. Reef Point Collection, Drawer 1, File 17, item 5.
35. ibid., item 1.
36. Edwin Lutyens, *The Letters to his wife, Lady Emily*, ed. Clayre Percy and Jane Ridley, Collins, 1985, p. 86.
37. RIBA, Lutyens Family Papers, LuE/4/5/15.
38. Edwin Lutyens, *The Letters to his wife, Lady Emily*, p. 85.
39. ibid., p. 86.
40. ibid., p. 85.
41. Betty Massingham, *Miss Jekyll: Portrait of a Great Gardener*, David & Charles, 1966, p. 76.
42. RIBA, Lutyens Family Papers, LuE/5/3/10(ii–).
43. ibid.
44. Mrs C. W. Earle, *A Third Pot-pourri*, 1903, p. 245.
45. ibid.
46. ibid., p. 244.
47. Gertrude Jekyll, *Wall, Water and Woodland Gardens*, p. 15.
48. ibid., p. 154.
49. British Museum Additional Mss. 45926.
50. Gertrude Jekyll, *Wall, Water and Woodland Gardens*, p. 120.
51. ibid., p. 18.
52. ibid., p. 120.
53. ibid., p. 134.
54. ibid., p. 284.

Chapter 19: 1901–2

1. Betty Massingham, *Miss Jekyll: Portrait of a Great Gardener*, David & Charles, 1966, p. 92.
2. ibid., p. 146.
3. ibid., p. 80.
4. ibid.
5. Herbert Baker, *Architecture and Personalities*, Country Life, 1944, p. 15.
6. Betty Massingham, *Miss Jekyll: Portrait of a Great Gardener*, p. 93.

7. RIBA, Lutyens Family Papers, LuE/7/5/7(ii).

8. ibid., LuE/4/7/4.

9. ibid., LuE/5/4/13(i).

10. Betty Massingham, *Miss Jekyll: Portrait of a Great Gardener*, p. 93.

11. Gertrude Jekyll, *Country Life*, 10: 272.

12. Roderick Gradidge, *Edwin Lutyens: Architect Laureate*, Allen & Unwin, 1981, p. 27.

13. Christopher Hussey, *The Life of Sir Edwin Lutyens*, Country Life, 1953, p. 86.

14. Jane Brown, *Gardens of a Golden Afternoon*, Allen Lane, 1982, p. 56.

15. RIBA, Lutyens Family Papers, LuE/5/3/22(i).

16. Gertrude Jekyll, *Country Life*, 10: 272.

17. ibid.

18. ibid., 10: 275.

19. ibid.

20. ibid.

21. Lawrence Weaver, *Lutyens Houses and Gardens*, Country Life, 1921, p. 40.

22. Sylvia Crowe, *Garden Design*, Country Life, 1959, p. 63.

23. ibid.

24. Gertrude Jekyll, *Country Life*, 10: 279.

25. *The Times*, 23 September 1936.

26. RIBA, Lutyens Family Papers, LuE/5/1/3(i–).

27. Christopher Hussey, *The Life of Sir Edwin Lutyens*, p. 96.

28. Gertrude Jekyll, *The Garden*, 64: 405.

29. RHS, Gertrude Jekyll to Mrs Furze, 14 July 1905.

30. Gertrude Jekyll, *Roses for English Gardens*, Country Life, 1902, p. 9.

31. ibid.

32. *Gardeners' Chronicle*, 1916, 148–9.

33. Audrey le Lievre, *Miss Willmott of Warley Place*, Faber, 1980, p. 72.

34. Gertrude Jekyll, *Children and Gardens*, Country Life, 1908, p. 13.

35. Betty Massingham, *Miss Jekyll: Portrait of a Great Gardener*, p. 171.

36. ibid.

37. Mrs C. W. Earle, *A Third Pot-pourri*, 1903, p. 246.

38. Mrs C. W. Earle, *Pot-pourri from a Surrey Garden*, 21st edn, London, 1900, p. 332.

39. Sally Festing, 'Viscountess Wolseley and her College for Lady Gardeners', *The Garden*, 106: 404.

40. Audrey le Lievre, *Miss Willmott of Warley Place*, p. 56.

41. Francis Jekyll, *Gertrude Jekyll: A Memoir*, Cape, 1934, p. 141.
42. RIBA, Lutyens Family Papers, LuE/5/6/9(i).
43. Geoffrey Taylor, *The Victorian Flower Garden*, Skeffington, 1952, p. 163.
44. Francis Jekyll, *Gertrude Jekyll: A Memoir*, p. 141.

Chapter 20: 1903–4

1. RIBA, Lutyens Family Papers, LuE/4/6/15(i–).
2. Godalming Museum, Sketchbook Chalet . . . Algiers, B980.18(1).
3. Richard Jeffries, *Wild Life in a Southern County*, London, 1879, p. vii.
4. John Connell, *The End of Tradition, Country Life in Central Surrey*, Routledge, 1978, p. 119.
5. ibid., p. 21.
6. Michael and Rosanna Tooley (eds), *Gertrude Jekyll: Artist, Gardener, Craftsman*, Michaelmas Books, 1984, p. 19.
7. Gertrude Jekyll, *Old English Household Life*, Batsford, 1925, p. 101.
8. Gertrude Jekyll, *Old West Surrey*, Longmans Green, 1904, p. 296.
9. ibid., p. viii.
10. ibid.
11. ibid.
12. ibid., p. 298.
13. ibid., p. 265.
14. ibid., p. 219.
15. ibid.
16. ibid., p. 264.
17. George Bourne, *Bettesworth Book*, Duckworth, 1920, p. xi.
18. Gertrude Jekyll, *Old West Surrey*, p. 243.
19. ibid., p. 219.
20. ibid., p. 258.
21. George Bourne, *Change in the Village*, Duckworth, 1912, p. 17.
22. Gertrude Jekyll, *Old West Surrey*, p. 287.
23. Logan Pearsall Smith, *Reperusals and Recollections*, Constable, 1936, p. 53.
24. ibid., p. 49.
25. Kew Mss, 122: 1969.
26. BM Additional Mss 45926.
27. Gertrude Jekyll, *Roses for English Gardens*, Country Life, 1902, p. 18.

28. Gertrude Jekyll, *Country Life*, 16: 395.
29. ibid.
30. ibid.
31. Godalming Museum, Gertrude Jekyll to Mrs Hammond, 17 April 1904.
32. ibid.
33. Godalming Museum, 920Jek, Notebook 39.
34. Godalming Museum, Gertrude Jekyll to Mrs Hammond, 27 August 1904.
35. ibid.
36. ibid.
37. ibid.
38. Francis Jekyll, *Gertrude Jekyll: A Memoir*, Cape, 1934, p. 186.
39. Gertrude Jekyll, *Some English Gardens*, Longmans Green, 1904, p. 2.
40. ibid., p. 3.

Chapter 21: 1905–7

1. Francis Jekyll, *Gertrude Jekyll: A Memoir*, Cape, 1934, p. 135.
2. Lawrence Weaver, *Lutyens Houses and Gardens*, Country Life, 1921, p. 94.
3. Gertrude Jekyll, *Gardens for Small Country Houses*, Country Life, 1912, p. 1.
4. ibid., p. 3.
5. RIBA, Lutyens Family Papers, LuE/7/8/14(–).
6. Gertrude Jekyll, *Wood and Garden*, Longmans Green, 1899, p. 171.
7. Gertrude Jekyll, *Gardens for Small Country Houses*, p. 3.
8. RIBA, Lutyens Family Papers, LuE/7/9/5.
9. Francis Jekyll, *Gertrude Jekyll: A Memoir*, p. 143.
10. Logan Pearsall Smith, *Reperusals and Recollections*, Constable, 1936, p. 49.
11. Betty Massingham, *Miss Jekyll: Portrait of a Great Gardener*, David & Charles, 1966, p. 101.
12. ibid.
13. ibid.
14. ibid.
15. Gertrude Jekyll, *The World*, 15 August 1905, p. 287.
16. Gertrude Jekyll, *Daily Mail*, 23 April 1907, p. 13.
17. ibid.

18. Christopher Hussey, *The Life of Sir Edwin Lutyens*, Country Life, 1953, p. 98.
19. Reef Point Collection, Drawer 2, File 48.
20. ibid., Drawer 3, File 51.
21. ibid.
22. RIBA, Lutyens Family Papers, LuE/5/2/15.
23. ibid., LuE/8/1/11.
24. ibid.
25. ibid., LuE/8/2/8(i–).
26. ibid., LuE/8/2/11.
27. ibid., LuE/8/2/12(i).
28. Francis Jekyll, *Gertrude Jekyll: A Memoir*, p. 143.
29. George Leslie, *Riverside Letters*, Macmillan, 1896, p. 9.
30. Gertrude Jekyll, *Flower Decoration in the House*, Country Life, 1907, p. v.
31. Gertrude Jekyll, *Home and Garden*, Longmans Green, 1900, p. 142.
32. ibid.
33. ibid.
34. RIBA, Lutyens Family Papers, LuE/8/5/6(i–).
35. ibid., LuE/9/1/10(ii).
36. ibid., LuE/9/1/14(i).
37. ibid.
38. ibid., LuE/9/2/7(i).
39. Edwin Lutyens, *The Letters to his wife, Lady Emily*, ed. Clayre Percy and Jane Ridley, Collins, 1985, p. 141.
40. ibid., p. 142.
41. Francis Jekyll, *Gertrude Jekyll: A Memoir*, p. 156.
42. Mary Lutyens, verbal, 1989.
43. ibid.
44. Robert Lutyens, *Sir Edwin Lutyens, An Appreciation in Perspective*, Country Life, 1942, p. 29.
45. Francis Jekyll, *Gertrude Jekyll: A Memoir*, p. 120.
46. David McKenna, verbal, 1989.
47. ibid.

Chapter 22: 1907–8

1. Gertrude Jekyll, *Children and Gardens*, Country Life, 1908, p. 1.
2. ibid., p. 10.

3. John Ruskin, *Works* (ed. E. T. Cook and Alexander Wedderburn), London, 1903–9, Vol. 11, p. 66.

4. Reef Point Collection, Drawer 3, File 56.

5. Hon. Mrs Evelyn Cecil, *Children's Gardens*, Macmillan, 1902, p. 40.

6. ibid., p. 63.

7. ibid., p. 83.

8. ibid., p. 82.

9. ibid., p. 11.

10. ibid., p. 96.

11. Richard Bisgrove, preface to Gertrude Jekyll, *Colour Schemes for the Flower Garden*, Windward, Frances Lincoln, 1988, p. 9.

12. E. T. Cook, *Country Life*, 8: 730.

13. Richard Bisgrove, preface to Gertrude Jekyll, *Colour Schemes for the Flower Garden*, p. 9.

14. Jane Brown, *Gardens of a Golden Afternoon*, Allen Lane, 1982, p. 156.

15. Richard Bisgrove, preface to Gertrude Jekyll, *Colour Schemes for the Flower Garden*, p. 9.

16. Gertrude Jekyll, *Colour in the Flower Garden*, Country Life, 1908, p. 3.

17. Reef Point Collection, Drawer 3, File 63.

18. Gertrude Jekyll, *Colour in the Flower Garden*, Country Life, 1908, p. 55.

19. ibid., p. 49.

20. ibid., p. 51.

21. ibid., p. 54.

22. ibid., p. 55.

23. ibid., p. 61.

24. ibid.

25. ibid., p. 71.

26. ibid., p. 1.

27. ibid.

28. ibid., p. 2.

29. ibid.

30. Shirley Hibberd, *The Amateur's Flower Garden*, London, 1878, p. 19.

31. William Robinson, *The English Flower Garden*, Murray, 1895, p. 228.

32. Gertrude Jekyll, *Colour in the Flower Garden*, p. 90.

33. ibid.
34. *The Garden*, 76: 8.
35. Francis Jekyll, *Gertrude Jekyll: A Memoir*, Cape, 1934, p. 160.
36. Gertrude Jekyll, *Colour in the Flower Garden*, p. viii.
37. Francis Jekyll, *Gertrude Jekyll: A Memoir*, p. 138.
38. ibid.
39. Gertrude Jekyll, *Wood and Garden*, Longmans Green, 1899, p. 177.
40. ibid., p. 141.
41. ibid.
42. BM (NH) Handwriting collection, Gertrude Jekyll to Dr Rowe, 14 May 1908.
43. Francis Jekyll, *Gertrude Jekyll: A Memoir*, p. 136.
44. ibid., p. 137.
45. BM (NH) Handwriting collection, Gertrude Jekyll to Dr Rowe, 14 May 1908.
46. Gertrude Jekyll, *Colour in the Flower Garden*, p. 19.
47. Betty Massingham, *Miss Jekyll: Portrait of a Great Gardener*, David & Charles, 1966, p. 97.
48. *The Times*, 10 December 1932, p. 12.
49. RIBA, Lutyens Family papers, LuE/9/3/7(i–).

PART FIVE: GARDENER

Chapter 23: 1908

1. Gertrude Jekyll, *The Garden*, 22: 470.
2. ibid.
3. Gertrude Jekyll, *Colour in the Flower Garden*, Country Life, 1908, p. 9.
4. Gertrude Jekyll, *Wood and Garden*, Longmans Green, 1899, p. 212.
5. ibid.
6. Betty Massingham, *Miss Jekyll: Portrait of a Great Gardener*, David & Charles, 1966, p. 52.
7. Martin Wood, 'Gertrude Jekyll Remembered', *Hardy Plant Society Journal*, Spring 1989, p. 11.
8. Reef Point Collection, Drawer 9, File 190, item 6.
9. Betty Massingham, *Miss Jekyll: Portrait of a Great Gardener*, p. 69.
10. Gertrude Jekyll, *Country Life*, 42: 514.

11. ibid., 28: 690.

12. E. T. Cook, *Country Life*, 8: 735.

13. ibid., 732.

14. Betty Massingham, *Miss Jekyll: Portrait of a Great Gardener*, p. 83.

15. Rose Standish Nichols, *English Pleasure Gardens*, Macmillan, 1902, p. 292.

16. Gertrude Jekyll, *Wood and Garden*, p. 210.

17. RIBA, Lutyens Family Papers, LuE/9/6/2(i–).

18. ibid., LuE/9/6/4.

19. ibid., LuE/9/6/6(vii–).

20. ibid.

21. ibid., LuE/9/6/13(i–).

22. ibid.

23. ibid.

24. ibid., LuE/9/6/10.

25. BM (NH) Handwriting Collection, Gertrude Jekyll to Dr Rowe, 14 May 1908.

26. Gertrude Jekyll, will.

27. Francis Jekyll, *Gertrude Jekyll: A Memoir*, Cape, 1934, p. 165.

28. ibid.

29. Lady Duff Gordon, journals, 10 August 1865.

30. RIBA, Lutyens Family Papers, LuE/6/5/1(i–).

31. ibid., LuE/6/8/27(ii–).

32. ibid.

33. Godalming Museum, 920Jek, Notebook 9.

34. Christopher Hussey, *The Life of Sir Edwin Lutyens*, Country Life, 1953, p. 126.

35. ibid.

36. Godalming Museum, 920Jek, Notebook 9.

37. Reef Point Collection, Drawer 9, File 192, item 28.

38. Christopher Hussey, *The Life of Sir Edwin Lutyens*, pp. 125–6.

39. Harold Nicolson, *Friday Mornings*, 1944, p. 213.

40. *Encyclopedia of Architecture*, Batsford, 1985, p. 362.

41. ibid., p. 236.

42. RIBA, Lutyens Family Papers, LuE/4/10/7(i–).

43. Reef Point Collection, Drawer 9, File 190, item 6.

44. Gertrude Jekyll, *Home and Garden*, Longmans Green, 1900, p. 143.

45. *The Studio*, Spring 1911, p. xvii.

Chapter 24: 1909–11

1. RIBA, Lutyens Family Papers, LuE/10/5/7(i).
2. ibid., LuE/10/5/8(ii–).
3. Francis Jekyll, *Gertrude Jekyll: A Memoir*, Cape, 1934, p. 171.
4. Gertrude Jekyll, *Country Life*, 28: 689.
5. ibid.
6. Gertrude Jekyll, *Quarterly Review*, 221: 363.
7. Reef Point Collection, Drawer 3, File 56.
8. Christopher Hussey, *The Life of Sir Edwin Lutyens*, Country Life, 1953, p. 116.
9. ibid.
10. RIBA, Lutyens Family Papers, LuE/10/5/10(iii).
11. ibid., LuE/8/7/2.
12. David McKenna, verbal, 1990.
13. Pamela McKenna, *Michael*, privately printed, 1932, p. 3.
14. Ian Nairn and Nikolaus Pevsner, *The Buildings of England: Surrey*, Penguin, 1971, p. 288.
15. Denys Sutton (ed.), *Letters of Roger Fry*, Vol. ii, Chatto, 1972, p. 31.
16. Godalming Museum, 920Jek, Notebook 36.
17. ibid., Notebook 27.
18. RHS, Barnes-Brand Correspondence, letter 31.
19. Reef Point Collection, Drawer 2, File 45, item 5.
20. Edwin Lutyens, *The Letters to his wife, Lady Emily*, ed. Clayre Percy and Jane Ridley, Collins, 1985, p. 159.
21. George Sitwell, *On the Making of Gardens*, Duckworth, 1951, p. xiii.
22. ibid., p. xv.
23. Michael and Rosanna Tooley, *The Gardens of Gertrude Jekyll in Northern England*, Michaelmas Books, 1982, p. 18.
24. ibid.
25. Osbert Sitwell, *Great Morning*, Macmillan, 1948, p. 60.
26. ibid.
27. Betty Massingham, *Miss Jekyll: Portrait of a Great Gardener*, David & Charles, 1966, p. 131.
28. Mea Allan, *William Robinson*, Faber, 1982, p. 94.
29. Wilfred Blunt, *England's Michelangelo*, Hamish Hamilton, 1975, p. 231.
30. ibid., p. 237.

31. ibid.

32. ibid., p. 236.

33. Michael and Rosanna Tooley, *The Gardens of Gertrude Jekyll in Northern England*, Michaelmas Books, 1982, p. 10.

34. Godalming Museum, 920Jek, Notebook 29.

35. Michael and Rosanna Tooley (eds), *Gertrude Jekyll: Artist, Gardener, Craftsman*, Michaelmas Books, 1984, p. 124.

36. Walter Jekyll, *Jamaican Song and Story*, London Folk-Lore Society, 1904, pref.

37. Agnes Jekyll, *Ne Oublie*, privately printed, n.d., p. xi.

38. Walter Jekyll, *The Bible Untrustworthy*, Watts, 1904, p. 282.

39. Copy of letters obtained by Michael Tooley from the Jamaica Archives, Herbert Jekyll to Mr Cundall, 20 June 1929.

40. Gertrude Jekyll, *The Garden*, 76: 1.

41. Francis Jekyll, *Gertrude Jekyll: A Memoir*, p. 174.

Chapter 25: 1912–14

1. Gertrude Jekyll, *The Garden*, 76: 75.

2. Francis Jekyll, *Gertrude Jekyll: A Memoir*, Cape, 1934, p. 169.

3. ibid.

4. ibid.

5. ibid.

6. Mrs Francis King, *The Well-Considered Garden*, Batsford, 1916, p. ix.

7. Francis Jekyll, *Gertrude Jekyll: A Memoir*, p. 169.

8. ibid.

9. ibid., p. 170.

10. Gertrude Jekyll, *Gardening Illustrated*, 46: 351.

11. ibid.

12. George C. Williamson, *Memoirs in Miniature*, Grayston, 1933, p. 23.

13. Reef Point Collection, Drawer 5, File 101, item 3.

14. ibid.

15. Gertrude Jekyll, *Country Life*, 30: 701.

16. ibid.

17. Michael and Rosanna Tooley (eds), *Gertrude Jekyll: Artist, Gardener, Craftsman*, Michaelmas Books, 1984, p. 76.

18. Gertrude Jekyll, *Country Life*, 36: 290.

19. Godalming Museum, 920Jek, Notebook 8.
20. ibid.
21. Michael and Rosanna Tooley (eds), *Gertrude Jekyll: Artist, Gardener, Craftsman*, p. 76.
22. Gertrude Jekyll, *Gardens for Small Country Houses*, Country Life, 1912, p. 55.
23. ibid., p. 119.
24. ibid., p. 43.
25. ibid., p. 35.
26. Peter Savage, *Lorimer and the Edinburgh Craft Designers*, Paul Harris, 1980, p. 126.
27. Christopher Hussey, *The Life of Sir Edwin Lutyens*, Country Life, 1953, p. 240.
28. Virginia Cowles, *Nineteen Thirteen: the Defiant Swan Song*, Weidenfeld, 1967, p. 37.
29. Frances Wolseley, *In a College Garden*, Murray, 1916, p. 17.
30. ibid., p. 13.
31. ibid., p. 15.
32. ibid., p. 6.
33. Gertrude Jekyll, *Country Life*, 34: 87.
34. ibid.
35. Logan Pearsall Smith, *Reperusals and Recollections*, Constable, 1936, p. 56.
36. ibid.
37. Gertrude Jekyll, *The Garden*, 77: 419.
38. Mrs Francis King, *Chronicles of the Garden*, New York, 1925, pp. 98–9.
39. Reef Point Collection, Drawer 5, File 120.
40. ibid., File 120 and 127.
41. Gertrude Jekyll, *Country Life*, 35: 161.
42. ibid., 229.
43. RIBA, Lutyens Family Papers, Lu14/5/13(i–).
44. Christopher Hussey, *The Life of Sir Edwin Lutyens*, p. 333.

Chapter 26: 1914–18

1. Agnes Jekyll, *Ne Oublie*, privately printed, n.d., pp. xi–xii.
2. Godalming Museum, 920Jek, Notebook 16.
3. Gertrude Jekyll, *Ladies' Field*, 69: 534.
4. ibid.

5. ibid.

6. Gertrude Jekyll, *Country Life*, 39: 541.

7. Frances Wolseley, *In a College Garden*, Murray, 1916, p. xii.

8. Reef Point Collection, Drawer 11, File 44.

9. ibid., Drawer 6, File 128, item 10.

10. ibid., item 11.

11. Victoria and Albert Museum, Dept. Textiles, Frances Horner to Mr Kendrick, 23 May 1916.

12. ibid., Gertrude Jekyll to Mr Kendrick, 14 June 1916.

13. ibid., Mr Kendrick to Gertrude Jekyll, 11 April 1924.

14. Gertrude Jekyll, *Wood and Garden*, Longmans Green, 1899, p. 217.

15. ibid.

16. Gertrude Jekyll, *Country Life*, 53: 569.

17. ibid.

18. Martin Wood, 'Gertrude Jekyll Remembered', *Hardy Plant Society Journal*, p. 10.

19. Gertrude Jekyll, *Country Life*, 53: 568.

20. ibid.

21. Christopher Hussey, *The Life of Sir Edwin Lutyens*, Country Life, 1953, p. 127.

22. Pamela McKenna, *Michael*, privately printed, 1932, p. 18.

23. David McKenna, verbal, 1989.

24. Harriet Mills, verbal, 1989.

25. William Young, verbal, 1990.

26. Harriet Mills, verbal, 1989.

27. J. R. Gretton (ed.), *Gertrude Jekyll: Letters to William Nicholson*, Dereham Books, 1981, p. 7.

28. Mary Lutyens, *Edwin Lutyens*, Murray, 1980, p. 196.

29. RIBA, Lutyens Family Papers, LuE/16/5/16(iii).

30. ibid., LuE/16/4/2(iii–).

31. ibid., LuE/16/5/16(iv).

32. ibid., LuE/16/5/14.

33. Betty Massingham, *Miss Jekyll: Portrait of a Great Gardener*, David & Charles, 1966, p. 140.

34. Gertrude Jekyll, *The Garden*, 81: 197.

35. Francis Jekyll, *Gertrude Jekyll: A Memoir*, Cape, 1934, p. 179.

36. Gertrude Jekyll, *The Garden*, 82: 426.

37. Edwin Lutyens, *The Letters to his wife, Lady Emily*, ed. Clayre Percy and Jane Ridley, Collins, 1985, p. 356.

38. Wilhelm Miller, *The Charm of English Gardens*, Hodder & Stoughton, 1911, preface.
39. ibid.
40. Gertrude Jekyll, *Garden Ornament*, Country Life, 1918, p. 41.
41. ibid.
42. ibid., p. xi.
43. ibid.
44. Reef Point Collection, Drawer 6, File 134, item 14.
45. Gertrude Jekyll, *Country Life*, 42: 512.
46. ibid.

Chapter 27: 1919–23

1. Francis Jekyll, *Gertrude Jekyll: A Memoir*, Cape, 1934, pp. 179–80.
2. Donald Maxwell, *Unknown Dorset*, Bodley Head, 1927, pp. 149–50.
3. John Nicholls Correspondence, Gertrude Jekyll to Kate Leslie, 13 February 1900.
4. Logan Pearsall Smith, *Reperusals and Recollections*, Constable, 1936, p. 60.
5. Agnes Jekyll, *Ne Oublie*, privately printed, n.d., p. xii.
6. Tradescant Trust, Gertrude Jekyll to Mrs Readhead, 6 September 1919.
7. ibid.
8. ibid.
9. Gertrude Jekyll, *The Garden*, 84: 56.
10. ibid.
11. ibid., 86: 418.
12. Godalming Museum, 920Jek Notebook 2.
13. ibid.
14. Francis Jekyll, *Gertrude Jekyll: A Memoir*, p. 187.
15. Gertrude Jekyll, *Country Life*, 50: 458.
16. Godalming Museum, 920Jek Notebook 2.
17. J. R. Gretton (ed.), *Gertrude Jekyll: Letters to William Nicholson*, Dereham Books, 1981, p. 7.
18. Francis Jekyll, *Gertrude Jekyll: A Memoir*, p. 188.
19. ibid.
20. *The Glory of the Garden*, Sotheby's catalogue, p. 157.
21. J. R. Gretton (ed.), *Gertrude Jekyll: Letters to William Nicholson*, p. 7.

22. Edwin Lutyens, *The Letters to his wife, Lady Emily*, ed. Clayre Percy and Jane Ridley, Collins, 1985, p. 381.
23. Francis Jekyll, *Gertrude Jekyll: A Memoir*, p. 189.
24. ibid.
25. J. R. Gretton (ed.), *Gertrude Jekyll: Letters to William Nicholson*, p. 8.
26. ibid., p. 9.
27. ibid.
28. ibid.
29. Francis Jekyll, *Gertrude Jekyll: A Memoir*, p. 188.
30. ibid., p. 189.
31. Guildford Museum, Gertrude Jekyll to Mrs Allen, 22 June 1921.
32. Christopher Tunnard, *Gardens in the Modern Landscape*, Architectural Press, 1948, p. 108.
33. ibid.
34. ibid.
35. ibid., p. 56.
36. Francis Jekyll, *Gertrude Jekyll: A Memoir*, p. 192.
37. ibid.
38. ibid., p. 196.
39. Reef Point Collection, Drawer 8, File 167, item 6.
40. Lady Peel, verbal, 1990.
41. A. C. Benson and Sir Lawrence Weaver (eds), *The Book of the Queen's Dolls House*, Methuen, 1924, p. 153.

Chapter 28: 1924–7

1. Francis Jekyll, *Gertrude Jekyll: A Memoir*, Cape, 1934, p. 195.
2. Betty Massingham, *Miss Jekyll: Portrait of a Great Gardener*, David & Charles, 1966, p. 145.
3. ibid.
4. Victoria and Albert Museum, Gertrude Jekyll to Mr Kendrick, 8 April 1924.
5. *The Times*, 9 March 1950, p. 9.
6. Gertrude Jekyll, *Old English Household Life*, Batsford, 1925, p. 179.
7. ibid.
8. ibid., p. 166.
9. ibid., p. 167.
10. Gertrude Jekyll, *Old English Household Life*, p. 3.

11. Francis Jekyll, *Gertrude Jekyll: A Memoir*, p. 115.
12. Busbridge parish magazine, 23(3) n.p.
13. ibid.
14. In possession of Mrs Kenward.
15. Reef Point Collection, Drawer 9, File 197, item 15.
16. ibid., Drawer 8, File 184, item 29.
17. ibid., Drawer 9, File 190, item 6.
18. Jane Brown, *Gardens of a Golden Afternoon*, Allen Lane, 1982, p. 139.
19. Reef Point Collection, Drawer 9, File 187, item 7.
20. ibid., File 190, item 6.
21. ibid.
22. ibid., File 191.
23. ibid.
24. Susan Schnare and Rudy Favretti, 'Gertrude Jekyll's American Gardens', *Garden History*, 10(2): 161.
25. Reef Point Collection, Drawer 9, File 196.
26. ibid.
27. Christopher Hussey, *The Life of Sir Edwin Lutyens*, Country Life, 1953, p. 471.
28. ibid., p. 472.
29. ibid.
30. Reef Point Collection, Drawer 9, File 195, item 24.
31. ibid., Drawer 8, File 185, item 1.
32. ibid.
33. ibid., Drawer 9, File 192, item 28.
34. ibid.
35. ibid.
36. ibid.
37. Gertrude Jekyll, *Gardening Illustrated*, 46: 216.
38. Reef Point Collection, Drawer 9, File 192, item 28.
39. ibid.
40. ibid.
41. ibid.
42. ibid.
43. ibid., File 200, item 20.
44. ibid.
45. ibid.
46. ibid.
47. ibid., Drawer 10, File 224, item 18.

48. Gertrude Jekyll, *The Garden*, 90: 535.

Chapter 29: 1926–9

1. Richard Bisgrove in Michael and Rosanna Tooley (eds), *Gertrude Jekyll: Artist, Gardener, Craftsman*, Michaelmas Books, 1984, p. 34.
2. Jane Brown, *The English Garden in our Time*, Antique Collectors' Club, 1986, p. 34.
3. Jane Brown, *Gardens of a Golden Afternoon*, Allen Lane, 1982, p. 50.
4. Martin Wood, 'Gertrude Jekyll Remembered', *Hardy Plant Society Journal*, Spring 1989, p. 15.
5. RIBA, Lutyens Family Papers, LuE/20/4/1–11.
6. Freyberg, correspondence in *The Garden*, 113(10): 489.
7. Valerie Kenward, verbal, 1990.
8. RHS, Barnes-Brand Correspondence, letter 26.
9. Reef Point Collection, Drawer 9, File 197, item 15.
10. Martin Wood, 'Gertrude Jekyll Remembered', p. 10.
11. Jane Brown, 'Thomas Frank Young: Memories of Munstead Wood', *The Garden*, 112(4): 162–3.
12. Reef Point Collection, Drawer 10, File 208, item 13.
13. ibid.
14. ibid.
15. RHS, Barnes-Brand Correspondence, letter 1.
16. ibid., letter 22.
17. ibid., letter 7.
18. ibid., letter 6.
19. ibid.
20. Joe Mitchenson, verbal, 1990.
21. RHS, Barnes-Brand Correspondence, letter 23.
22. ibid., letter 38.
23. ibid., letter 15.
24. ibid., letter 20.
25. ibid., letter 29.
26. ibid., letter 22.
27. ibid., letter 12.
28. Gertrude Jekyll, *Garden Ornament* (with Christopher Hussey), 1927.
29. *Gardening Illustrated*, 49: 641.
30. Reef Point Collection, Dr Hampton to Gertrude Jekyll, 18 March 1928.

31. ibid., Drawer 10, File 208, item 13.
32. ibid., File 215.
33. ibid., File 221.
34. ibid.
35. Michael and Rosanna Tooley, *The Gardens of Gertrude Jekyll in Northern England*, Michaelmas Books, 1982, p. 34.
36. Reef Point Collection, Drawer 10, File 221.
37. ibid., File 222, item 9.
38. ibid.
39. ibid.
40. ibid.
41. Gertrude Jekyll, *The Nineteenth Century and After*, 104: 195.
42. ibid.
43. ibid., 198.
44. ibid., 197.
45. ibid., 199.
46. Walter Jekyll, *The Bible Untrustworthy*, Watts, 1904, p. 283.
47. Christopher Lloyd, correspondence with author, 17 June 1990.
48. RHS, Barnes-Brand Correspondence, letter 26.

Chapter 30: 1929–32

1. Russell Page, *The Education of a Gardener*, Collins, 1962, p. 93.
2. Logan Pearsall Smith, *Reperusals and Recollections*, Constable, 1936, p. 64.
3. Godalming Museum, Minutes and Reports of the Godalming Corporation.
4. Francis Jekyll, *Gertrude Jekyll: A Memoir*, Cape, 1934, p. 201.
5. Gertrude Jekyll, *Gardening Illustrated*, 151: 832.
6. RHS, Barnes-Brand Correspondence, letter 36.
7. ibid.
8. ibid.
9. Reef Point Collection, Dr Hampton to Gertrude Jekyll, 19 April 1929.
10. ibid., Drawer 10, File 222, item 9.
11. John Ruskin, *Works* (ed. E. T. Cook and Alexander Wedderburn), London, 1903–9, Vol. 10, p. xxvi.
12. Godalming Museum, 920Jek Notebook 1.
13. Francis Jekyll, *Gertrude Jekyll: A Memoir*, p. 193.

14. ibid., pp. 193–4.
15. ibid., p. 194.
16. ibid., p. 193.
17. Graham Stuart Thomas (ed.), *Colour Schemes for the Flower Garden*, Penguin, 1983, p. v.
18. ibid., p. vi.
19. ibid.
20. ibid.
21. ibid.
22. ibid.
23. RHS, Barnes-Brand Correspondence, letter 37.
24. ibid.
25. ibid.
26. ibid.
27. Gertrude Jekyll, *A Gardener's Testament*, Country Life, 1937, p. 321.
28. Betty Massingham, *Miss Jekyll: Portrait of a Great Gardener*, David & Charles, 1966, p. 67.
29. Logan Pearsall Smith, *Reperusals and Recollections*, p. 57.
30. ibid., p. 62.
31. ibid., p. 57.
32. ibid., pp. 58–9.
33. ibid., p. 64.
34. Gertrude Jekyll, *A Gardener's Testament*, p. 322.
35. Francis Jekyll, *Gertrude Jekyll: A Memoir*, pp. 202–3.
36. ibid., p. 204.
37. ibid.
38. ibid.
39. RIBA, Lutyens Family Papers, LuE/20/4/9(i–).
40. ibid.
41. ibid.
42. ibid.
43. ibid.
44. Betty Massingham, *Miss Jekyll: Portrait of a Great Gardener*, p. 172.
45. Gertrude Jekyll, *Guardian*, 52(1): 99.
46. Francis Jekyll, *Gertrude Jekyll: A Memoir*, p. 206.
47. Logan Pearsall Smith, *Reperusals and Recollections*, p. 60.

Epilogue

1. Ian Nairn and Nikolaus Pevsner, *The Buildings of England: Surrey*, Penguin, 1971, p. 125.
2. Gertrude Jekyll, *Children and Gardens*, Country Life, 1908, p. 1.
3. Gertrude Jekyll's will.
4. British Museum, Central Archives, Original Papers 1914, No. 3253, 6 July 1914.
5. British Museum, Testimonial from H.W.C. Davis of Balliol College, Oxford, 29 October 1905.
6. ibid.
7. British Museum, Central Archives, Original Papers 1914, No. 3253, 6 July 1914.
8. ibid.
9. Francis Jekyll, *Gertrude Jekyll: A Memoir*, Cape, 1934, p. 205.
10. ibid.
11. Guildford Museum, Agnes Jekyll to Mrs Allen, 16 April 1933.
12. RIBA, Lutyens Family Papers, LuE/10/5/10(i).
13. ibid.
14. *Observer*, 19 September 1934.
15. Jane Brown, *Eminent Gardeners*, Viking, 1990, p. 155.
16. Guildford Museum, Agnes Jekyll to Mrs Allen, 16 April 1933.
17. ibid.
18. Elisabeth Lutyens, *A Goldfish Bowl*, Cassell, 1972, p. 70.
19. ibid.
20. Mary Lutyens, *Edwin Lutyens*, Murray, 1980, p. 27.
21. RIBA, Lutyens Family Papers, LuE/20/4/3(iii–).
22. ibid., LuE/20/4/9(i–).
23. RHS, Barnes–Brand Correspondence, letter 38.
24. Joan Charman, verbal, 1990.
25. Guildford Museum, Agnes Jekyll, note.
26. Guildford Museum, The Tate to the Curator, Haslemere Museum, 13 July 1956.
27. Guildford Museum, Miss Dance of Guildford Museum to Mrs Allen, 20 July 1956.
28. E. V. Lucas, *English Leaves*, Methuen, 1933, p. 167.
29. ibid.
30. Mary Lutyens, *Edwin Lutyens*, p. 26.
31. *The Times*, 10 December 1932, p. 12.

SELECT BIBLIOGRAPHY

GERTRUDE JEKYLL'S WORK

Wood and Garden, Longmans Green, 1899.

Home and Garden, Longmans Green, 1900.

Lilies for English Gardens, Country Life, 1901.

Wall and Water Gardens, Country Life, 1901.

Roses for English Gardens (with Edward Mawley), Country Life, 1902.

Old West Surrey, Longmans Green, 1904.

Some English Gardens; After Drawings by George S. Elgood, Longmans Green, 1904.

Flower Decoration in the House, Country Life, 1907.

Colour in the Flower Garden, Country Life, 1908.

Children and Gardens, Country Life, 1908.

Gardens for Small Country Houses (with Lawrence Weaver), Country Life, 1912.

Annuals and Biennials, Country Life, 1916.

Garden Ornament (with Christopher Hussey), Country Life, 1918.

Old English Household Life, Batsford, 1925.

A Gardener's Testament, Country Life, 1937.

ORIGINAL MANUSCRIPTS

Lady Duff Gordon's journals covering Gertrude Jekyll's lifetime, 1845–53, 1869–71, and her daughter, Georgina's, 1845–7, are among the *Harpton Court Papers 2904–21*. Those for 1843, 1844 and 1846 are *NLW MSS 15588–90B*, all at the National Library of Wales in Aberystwyth. Lady Duff Gordon's journals 1854–61, 1863–8 and 1872–5 belong to Sir Andrew Duff Gordon.

Lutyens Family Papers are at the Royal Institute of British Architects Library in Portland Place.

Many letters to Gertrude Jekyll from clients are filed with garden plans in the Reef Point Collection at the College of Environmental

Design's Documents Collection, University of California, Berkeley.

Other correspondence in public collections includes the *Sherborne Bequest* in the Manuscripts Room and Central Archives at the British Museum, manuscripts at Godalming Museum, Guildford Library, Kew, and the Royal Horticultural Society's Lindley Library.

Published Works

Joan Abse, *John Ruskin: The Passionate Moralist*, Quartet, 1980.

Mary Alexander, 'The Surrey Round Frock', *Surrey Archaeological Collections*, Vol. 77, Guildford, 1986.

Mea Allan, *The Tradescants*, Michael Joseph, 1964.

Mea Allan, *William Robinson*, Faber, 1982.

Richard D. Altick, *Victorian People and Ideas*, Dent, 1974.

Alicia Amherst, *A History of Gardening in Britain*, Quaritch, 1895.

Clive Ashwin, 'Art Education and Policies 1768–1915', *Social Res. Higher Ed.*, October 1975.

Herbert Baker, *Architecture and Personalities*, Country Life, 1944.

David Barrie (ed.), *Modern Painters – John Ruskin*, Deutsch, 1987.

Mavis Batey, 'Landscape with Flowers', *Garden History*, 2(2).

Quentin Bell, *A New and Noble school – The PreRaphaelites*, Macdonald, 1982.

A. C. Benson and Sir Lawrence Weaver (eds), *The Book of the Queen's Dolls House*, Methuen, 1924.

Sheila Birkenhead, *Illustrious Friends*, Hamish Hamilton, 1965.

Richard Bisgrove, preface to Gertrude Jekyll, *Colour Schemes for the Flower Garden*, Windward, Frances Lincoln, 1988.

E. C. Black, *Victorian Culture and Society*, Macmillan, 1973.

Reginald Blomfield, *The Formal Garden in England*, Macmillan, 1892.

Wilfred Blunt, *England's Michelangelo*, Hamish Hamilton, 1975.

George Bourne, *Bettesworth Book*, Duckworth, 1920.

George Bourne, *Change in the Village*, Duckworth, 1912.

Ian Bradley, *William Morris and His World*, Thames & Hudson, 1978.

Jane Brown, *Eminent Gardeners*, Viking, 1990.

Jane Brown, *The English Garden in Our Time*, Antique Collectors' Club, 1986.

Jane Brown, *Gardens of a Golden Afternoon*, Allen Lane, 1982.

Jane Brown, 'Thomas Frank Young, Memories of Munstead Wood', *The Garden*, Vol. 112, Part 4 (April 1987), pp. 162–3.

Hester Burton, *Barbara Bodichon*, Murray, 1949.

Jenni Calder, *The Victorian Home*, Batsford, 1977.

Anthea Callen, *Angel in the Studio*, Astragal Books, 1979.

Hon. Mrs Evelyn Cecil, *Children's Gardens*, Macmillan, 1902.

Ronald Chapman, *The Laurel and the Thorn: A Study of G. F. Watts*, Faber, 1945.

M.-E. Chevreul, *Principles of Harmony and Contrast of Colours*, London, 1854.

Andrew Clayton-Payne and Brent Elliott, *Victorian Flower Gardens*, Weidenfeld, 1988.

John Connell, *The End of Tradition, Country Life in Central Surrey*, Routledge, 1978.

E. T. Cook, *Gardening for Beginners*, Country Life, 1901.

E. T. Cook, 'Munstead House and its Mistress', *Country Life*, 8 December 1900.

Virginia Cowles, *Nineteen Thirteen: The Defiant Swan Song*, Weidenfeld, 1967.

Sylvia Crowe, *Garden Design*, Country Life, 1959.

J. S. Dearden (ed.), *The Professor: Arthur Severn's Memoir of John Ruskin*, London, 1967.

Leslie De Charms, *Elizabeth and Her German Garden*, Heinemann, 1958.

Mrs C. W. Earle, *Memoirs and Memories*, Smith, Elder & Co., 1882.

Mrs C. W. Earle, *Pot-pourri from a Surrey Garden*, 21st edn, London, 1900.

Mrs C. W. Earle, *More Pot-pourri*, London, 1899.

Mrs C. W. Earle, *A Third Pot-pourri*, 1903.

Frederick Eden, *A Garden in Venice*, Country Life, 1903.

Brent Elliott, *Victorian Gardens*, Batsford, 1986.

Encyclopedia of Architecture, Batsford, 1985.

Katherine Everett, *Bricks and Flowers*, Constable, 1949.

Peter Faulkner (ed.), *William Morris: The Critical Heritage*, Routledge, 1973.

Penelope Fitzgerald, *Edward Burne-Jones*, Michael Joseph, 1975.

Christopher Frayling, *The Royal College of Art*, Century, 1987.

William Gaunt, *Victorian Olympus*, Cardinal, 1988.

Mark Girouard, *The Victorian Country House*, Yale University Press, 1979.

Roderick Gradidge, *Edwin Lutyens: Architect Laureate*, Allen & Unwin, 1981.

A. Stuart Gray (ed.), *Edwardian Architecture*, Duckworth, 1985.

J. R. Gretton (ed.), *Gertrude Jekyll: Letters to William Nicholson*, Dereham Books, 1981.

Miles Hadfield, *Gardening in Britain*, Hutchinson, 1960.

J. A. Hammerton (ed.), *Concise Universal Biographies*, Educational Book Co. Ltd, n.d.

Shirley Hibberd, *The Amateur's Flower Garden*, London, 1878.

L. Higgin, *Handbook of Embroidery*, London, 1880.

C. Lewis Hinde, *Hercules Brabazon Brabazon: His Art and Life*, George Allen, 1912.

Penelope Hobhouse and Christopher Wood, *Painted Gardens: English Watercolours 1850–1914*, Michael Joseph, 1988.

Reynolds Hole, *A Book about Roses*, London, 1869.

Reynolds Hole, *Our Gardens*, Dent, 1899.

Frances Horner, *Time Remembered*, Heinemann, 1933.

Christopher Hussey, *The Life of Sir Edwin Lutyens*, Country Life, 1953.

William James, *The Order of Release*, Murray, 1948.

Richard Jeffries, *Wild Life in a Southern County*, London, 1879.

Agnes Jekyll, *Ne Oublie*, privately printed, n.d.

Francis Jekyll, *Gertrude Jekyll: A Memoir*, Cape, 1934.

Gertrude Jekyll, 'Gardens and Garden Craft', *Edinburgh Review*, 184, Longmans, July–October 1896.

Walter Jekyll, *The Bible Untrustworthy*, Watts, 1904.

Walter Jekyll, *Jamaican Song and Story*, London Folk-Lore Society, 1904.

Walter Jekyll, *The Wisdom of Schopenhauer*, Watts, 1911.

Mrs Francis King, *Chronicles of the Garden*, New York, 1925.

Mrs Francis King, *The Well-Considered Garden*, Batsford, 1916.

Michael Langford, *The Story of Photography*, Focal Press, 1980.

H. M. Larner, *Busbridge, Godalming, Surrey*, Cambridge, 1947.

Audrey le Lievre, *Miss Willmott of Warley Place*, Faber, 1980.

George Leslie, *Letters to Marco*, Macmillan, 1893.

George Leslie, *Our River*, London, 1888.

George Leslie, *Riverside Letters*, Macmillan, 1896.

Jack Lindsay, *William Morris, his Life and Work*, Constable, 1975.

E. V. Lucas, *English Leaves*, Methuen, 1933.

Edwin Lutyens, *The Letters to his wife, Lady Emily*, ed. Clayre Percy and Jane Ridley, Collins, 1985.

Elisabeth Lutyens, *A Goldfish Bowl*, Cassell, 1972.

Mary Lutyens, *Edwin Lutyens*, Murray, 1980.

Mary Lutyens, *To Be Young*, Hart-Davis, 1959.

Robert Lutyens, *Sir Edwin Lutyens, An Appreciation in Perspective*, Country Life, 1942.

Fiona MacCarthy, *Eric Gill*, Faber, 1989.

Stuart Macdonald, *The History and Philosophy of Art Education*, University of London, 1970.

Pamela McKenna, *Michael*, privately printed, 1932.

Betty Massingham, *Miss Jekyll: Portrait of a Great Gardener*, David & Charles, 1966.

Betty Massingham, *Turn on the Fountains*, Gollancz, 1974.

Donald Maxwell, *Unknown Dorset*, Bodley Head, 1927.

Priscilla Metcalf, *James Knowles: Victorian Editor and Architect*, Clarendon, 1980.

Wilhelm Miller, *The Charm of English Gardens*, Hodder & Stoughton, 1911.

J. Saxon Mills, *Sir Edward Cook: A Biography*, Constable, 1921.

George Moore, *Modern Painting*, London, 1893.

Ian Nairn and Nikolaus Pevsner, *The Buildings of England: Surrey*, Penguin, 1971.

Charles Newton, *Travels and Discoveries in the Levant*, Vol. II, 1865.

Rose Standish Nichols, *English Pleasure Gardens*, Macmillan, 1902.

Harold Nicolson, *Friday Mornings*, 1944.

Mrs Oliphant, *Miss Marjoribanks*, Virago, 1988.

Russell Page, *The Education of a Gardener*, Collins, 1962.

Joan Percy, 'Author by Accident', *The Garden*, 114: 3, March 1989.

Sir Charles Petrie, *The Victorians*, White Lion, 1960.

Nikolaus Pevsner, *Academies of Art*, Cambridge University Press, 1940.

Nikolaus Pevsner and Edward Hubbard, *The Buildings of England: Cheshire*, Penguin, 1971.

Peter Quennell, *John Ruskin: The Portrait of a Prophet*, Collins, 1949.

Marian Ramelson, *The Petticoat Rebellion*, Lawrence & Wishart, 1967.

Herbert Read, *Anarchy and Order*, Faber, 1954.

W. J. Reader, *Victorian England*, Batsford, 1974.

F. M. Redgrave, *Richard Redgrave: A Memoir*, Cassell, 1891.

William Robinson, *The English Flower Garden*, Murray, 1895.

William Robinson, *The Garden Beautiful*, Murray, 1907.

William Robinson, *Garden Design and Architects' Gardens*, Murray, 1892.

William Robinson, *The Wild Garden*, 1st edn, 1870; 2nd edn, 1881; 3rd edn, 1894; republished Century, 1983.

John Ruskin, *Works* (ed. E. T. Cook and Alexander Wedderburn), London, 1903–9.

Peter Savage, *Lorimer and the Edinburgh Craft Designers*, Paul Harris, 1980.

Susan Schnare and Rudy Favretti, 'Gertrude Jekyll's American Gardens', *Jour. Garden History Society*, 10: 2, Autumn 1982.

John D. Sedding, *Garden Craft Old and New*, Kegan Paul, 1895.

George Sitwell, *On the Making of Gardens*, Duckworth, 1951.

Osbert Sitwell, *Great Morning*, Macmillan, 1948.

Logan Pearsall Smith, *Reperusals and Recollections*, Constable, 1936.

Ethel Smyth, *As Time Went On*, Longmans, 1936.

Hilary Spurling, *Secrets of a Woman's Heart*, Hodder & Stoughton, 1984.

Denys Sutton (ed.), *Letters of Roger Fry*, Vol. ii, Chatto, 1972.

Denys Sutton, *Nocturne: The Art of James McNeill Whistler*, Country Life, 1963.

Judith B. Tankard and Michael R. Van Valkenburgh, *Gertrude Jekyll: A Vision of Garden and Wood*, Murray, 1988.

Geoffrey Taylor, *Some Nineteenth Century Gardeners*, Skeffington, 1951.

Geoffrey Taylor, *The Victorian Flower Garden*, Skeffington, 1952.

Richard Thames, *William Morris*, Shire Publications, 1979, p. 15.

E. P. Thompson, *William Morris: Romantic to Revolutionary*, Merlin, 1977.

Ann Thwaite, *Waiting for the Party*, Secker, 1974.

H. Avray Tipping, *English Gardens*, Country Life, 1925.

Michael and Rosanna Tooley, *The Gardens of Gertrude Jekyll in Northern England*, Michaelmas Books, 1982.

Michael and Rosanna Tooley (eds), *Gertrude Jekyll: Artist, Gardener, Craftsman*, Michaelmas Books, 1984.

Christopher Tunnard, *Gardens in the Modern Landscape*, Architectural Press, 1948.

Jehanne Wake, *Princess Louise*, Collins, 1988.

Lawrence Weaver, *Lutyens Houses and Gardens*, Country Life, 1921.

Al Weil, Fine Art Society Catalogue of H. Brabazon exhibition, 1974.

George C. Williamson, *Memoirs in Miniature*, Grayson, 1933.

Frances Wolseley, *Gardening for Women*, London, 1908.

Frances Wolseley, *In a College Garden*, Murray, 1916.
Christopher Wood, *Dictionary of Victorian Painters*, Antique Collectors' Club, 1978.
Martin Wood, *Journal of the Hardy Plant Society*, Spring 1989.

INDEX